Apartment Investing
The Ultimate Guide

Apartment Investing
The Ultimate Guide

THERESA BRADLEY-BANTA

Big Fish Top Dogs Publishing

Cover and book design by: Bradley Banta Design

ISBN 978-0-9859681-2-0

FIRST EDITION

Big Fish Top Dogs Publishing
501 South Cherry Street, Suite 1100
Denver CO 80246
Printed in U.S.A

Dedication

To Richard, always

Contents

Preface

This is my second book on investing in multifamily properties. My first book *Invest in Apartment Buildings: Profit Without the Pitfalls* is an easy read that demonstrates through stories how investing in apartment buildings is not for the faint of heart. It's also where I debunk all the garbage put out there by the so-called gurus. You've probably heard their promises: that it doesn't take money, time or much talent to make a killing investing in apartment buildings.

In this book, you'll learn that investing in multifamily properties is a business and how to treat it as one. To work on, not in, your business. It's a must-read for those starting out and for those who already own a property but know that it could perform better. Read this before you buy a property and especially before you hire a property manager.

I mentor and consult multifamily investors all over the US. There's nothing I love more than looking at new potential apartment acquisitions. And planning for the success of that property. I love this business so much that I've been writing, speaking and mentoring on investing in multifamily real estate since 2007. That writing is the genesis of this book.

Enjoy. You'll learn a ton. Keep it on hand as a daily reference. Want to learn even more? Work with me by contacting me at the email below.

Best wishes!

Theresa Bradley-Banta
theresa@theresabradleybanta.com

Introduction

Have you ever wondered how the operators of big multifamily investment properties think? What they do on a daily basis? How they plan for the future? How they value the properties they acquire and know how much to offer on deals? Landlords with hundreds of units generally practice well-conceived acquisition, improvement and operational strategies. They have a spend now, save later approach. They don't step over a dollar to pick up a dime.

For example, say your property needs new roofing material. Among your choices are a cheap tar and paper overlay or a bright white, reflective material such as Duro-Last®. The Duro-Last® material costs more but in addition to protecting your property, its reflective quality can significantly lower your heating and cooling costs. And this material will last longer than tar and paper. Furthermore, it often comes with a warranty that will transfer to a buyer of your property—making your building easier to sell. An experienced owner-operator is likely to choose the more expensive but longer lasting material.

Big operators employ long-term thinking recognizing the often-high cost of short-term strategies. They also have procedures. And rules. And systems. They complete jobs faster and get paying tenants in units quickly. They embrace sustainability and know about free funding resources. They have strategies to improve NOI through things like branding; upgrading curb appeal; identifying and offering in-demand amenities; increasing revenue through ancillary income such as pet fees or concierge services; and strategic implementation of today's smart apartment technology.

Big landlords know that when they offer white glove customer service and implement strategic capital improvements, they support long-term value-creation. And do you know what? It's not rocket science. You can do it too. This book is an immense, epic compilation of how-to tips, resources and strategies that will add value to your property—no matter how big or small.

Your first pro tip? Don't wait to read this until after you buy your first property. Read it now. What you learn will inform your investment strategies and will help you value prospective acquisitions. You'll make the leap from property manager to asset manager. And you'll need this knowledge in order to successfully manage your property manager.

Chapter One:
Becoming a Real Estate Investor

The important thing is this: To be ready at any moment to
sacrifice what you are for what you could become.
– Charles Du Bos

~

Why Invest in Multifamily Real Estate?

Here's a fun short answer. Years ago, I worked with a woman investor. She would walk into a property she was thinking about buying and gleefully say, "Hmmm. It smells like cat pee!" What she was referring to is the acronym "CATP" as in,

- Cash flow
- Appreciation
- Taxes (benefits)
- Principal paydown (building equity by paying down a mortgage)

Imagine the surprised looks she received from sellers and seller's agents! A shocking thing to say? Perhaps. Memorable? Definitely!

In addition to cash flow, you must calculate all of the ways your investment benefits you to get a clear picture of how your asset will perform. And you'll need to account for each element of CATP when presenting your deal to prospective lenders and partners.

CATP

Besides implying she would probably negotiate the asking price on the property, when my friend made her "CATP" comment she was also noting that a property wasn't necessarily beyond hope. She knew she could fix it up and make a profit. That's one of the great things about investing in real estate. It's a tangible asset.

Real estate historically has been a safe, sound, solid investment. It tends to go up in value, provides cash flow from rental income and offers tax benefits and incentives. And over time equity value increases as your loan is paid down.

Also, with some real estate investments you can force appreciation by making improvements to the property—improvements to management and operations and through upgrades and renovation.

In a nutshell, CATP is what real estate investing is all about. And what a simple way to remember the benefits.

What's It Really Like to Be a Real Estate Investor?

Late-night infomercials depict real estate investors as tanned, smiling, and conducting business by the pool of their mansion. Some investors do have a fleet of expensive cars, a beach house, and an affinity for tanning beds. However, what is not accurately portrayed in this idealized representation is all the hard work, boring work, and failures that are part of being a real estate investor.

Many people are drawn to real estate investing for all of the benefits, but they fail to consider the day-to-day responsibilities that come along with building a profitable real estate portfolio.

Auctions and low-ball offers

A large part of every workday is dedicated to searching for properties. One of the most disheartening realizations every real estate investor will encounter early on is that there are a lot of people out there trying to buy investment properties.

Some people have been investing for decades. Others are novices hoping to find a fast track to financial independence. A steady supply of new investors tends to drive up bids on properties. As a prudent investor, you have to base your offers on the return on investment you can reasonably expect from a property, not on the price the seller is willing to accept. That can mean a lot of offers do not get accepted.

Crawl spaces and contractors

Real estate investors should have passion for what they do, but they absolutely must have knowledge about building repairs and property management. You always need to look at properties with a highly critical eye. That involves visiting properties personally and looking for potential problems. Moisture and foundation issues are common.

You are not going to order a home inspection for every property you consider. You will spend some time visiting properties and negotiating with sellers without reaching an agreement. You will also spend some time viewing properties that are not even worth making an offer on.

When you do find a property that you can't talk yourself out of buying and you reach an agreement on price with the seller, your work is just beginning. You will most likely have several properties at various stages of the process at any given time.

While some of your work can be completed poolside, most of it requires you be on site and on the road. Even the best contractors need you to push them to stay on schedule. Be sure you have a good-quality, hands-free device for your phone!

How to Not Look Like a Tire Kicking Novice Real Estate Investor

Many of my clients who decide to invest in multifamily real estate complain that multifamily brokers won't take them seriously. It's a common dilemma faced by new multifamily real estate investors. Brokers are frequently reluctant to work with new investors and often with good reason.

Brokers often feel that new investors—including those with significant experience in single-family real estate investing—approach multifamily investing with a "tire kicker" mentality.

So, what's a tire kicker?

Tire kickers are potential investors who:

- Are just "feeling out the market"
- Don't have the education or knowledge to make a final decision to buy
- Will never make an offer to buy or will pull out of a contract before the deal closes due to fear and uncertainty

Instead, a broker wants to see that an investor has a clear investment strategy (market, property type, investment period) and a realization that multifamily real estate investing is a *business*.

Also, quite frequently these tire kickers haven't arranged the necessary resources to complete a deal such as having:

- Capital to fund a down payment, closing costs and other acquisition fees.
- Experienced team members who are ready to go the day the deal closes.
- Reserve capital for cash needs.

However, unless you are sourcing multifamily property listings on your own, chances are pretty good that you'll be working with a multifamily broker to find and broker potential acquisitions.

So what do you do if you are new to multifamily investments? How do you avoid coming across as a tire kicking newbie real estate investor? Here are some thoughts to remember for getting the best of your relationship:

Always remember: Your broker works for you

Your attitude goes a long way in establishing the kind of working relationship you can expect to have with your broker.

If you approach a broker with anything short of 100% confidence in your decision to invest, then it's hard to grasp the idea that the commercial broker actually works *for you* and not the other way around. You become a supplicant rather than a leader.

Your confidence comes from your:

- Level of education
- Commitment to purchasing a multifamily property
- Team and mentors
- Clear vision and intention to own multifamily investment real estate
- Ability to lead

A great opening line for approaching a new broker is, "I will be buying an apartment community in your area and I'm looking for the best broker in that submarket." This approach shows that you are committed to doing the deal. You aren't telling the broker, "I'm *thinking* about investing" you are saying straight out, "I will be buying a property."

Don't worry if you haven't completely narrowed down a submarket. Part of your broker's job is to provide guidance, resources and data on their core markets.

Lead your team

Don't approach a potential broker with hat in in hand and an attitude of, "Gosh, I'm not sure of my plan, or really how to go about buying a multifamily property. What do you think my strategy should be?" In the broker's mind that opens the door to: doubts about your qualifications; doubts in your ability to close; and questions about how committed you are to acquiring a property.

If you're not fully committed, and with the necessary resources at hand, why should a broker be committed to working for you?

A broker is well paid (for a lot of hard work)

The services a broker provides during the acquisition process are often priceless. A good broker will provide you with:

- Invaluable market research, rental and sales comps
- Knowledge of *historical* market data (often critical to your decision making)
- Access to off-market listings
- Ideas for successful investment strategies

A broker will also act as your diplomat and intermediary with the seller. In many cases this can eliminate potential problems or misunderstandings during the negotiation process.

Another good thing to keep in mind is that at some point after you own a property, you will most likely be listing the property for sale. A broker who has served you well can be rewarded with the listing. Don't forget, your broker works *for you*.

How do you find a broker?

A great way to find active brokers in your area is to take a quick look at Internet listing services (ILS) like LoopNet.com. In fact, an ILS offers resources for your market and specific asset class such as: data on markets; average price per door; local cap rates; local vacancy rates; and local building construction and style.

Networking with other local and successful multifamily investors is always a good idea and a great source for referrals to multifamily contractors and service providers.

A final word on confidence

Be educated and learn, through your networking and research, to talk the language. Be willing to walk away if the broker is not a good fit for you. Visualize a positive outcome of the meeting before you get there. Perhaps the broker has a listing for you. Or some company- or self-branded market research!

Before you contact a broker it's a good idea to have:

- Your funds or partners lined up
- Clear investment strategies that identify your desired: real estate market(s); property type, style and class; stabilization (turnkey—ready to rent or value add—needs improvements); investment holding periods; and investment goals

- Education in multifamily investments
- Experienced mentors
- Team members who are ready to start the day you close, such as a good, local property management company

You can show respect for a broker's hard-earned knowledge and skills while at the same time demonstrate your own ability to lead your business and close on a deal.

Be Smart About Hot New Trends in Real Estate Investing

By the time you hear about hot new trends in real estate investing there's a good chance you're too late to the party. Warren Buffett summed it up beautifully when he said:

> *"Only when the tide goes out do you discover who's been swimming naked."*

In 2008 and 2009 I told my investing partners multifamily real estate would be the hot real estate investing market in the next years. I was right.

How did I know multifamily was the up-and-coming hot new trend? First, the changing demographics pointed that way. Second, I keep up with industry news, magazines, books and market reports—and I network within the industry.

There are two important messages here:

One: Stay on top of your industry and know that when the media hype begins, chances are the tide is going out.

Two: Investing in real estate is a smart thing to do but you must know your market.

Back in 2007 we saw the condominium conversion craze. Investors were snapping up apartment buildings with the idea of converting rental units to condos. By the time the real estate investing gurus were holding condo conversion boot camps across the country, it was too late in a large number of markets.

The investors who arrived late to the condo conversion game found themselves unable to sell condominium units. Instead, they saw their high-end conversions back on the rental market as apartment rentals. Nicely appointed apartment rentals.

If you're a multifamily investor, or new to the game, I recommend you make keeping up on industry news a daily habit. You'll find a list of resources for staying on top of apartment trends in Chapter Twenty-Three: Pro Tips for Success.

You can also set up a Google Alert (google.com/alerts) for search queries such as "multifamily." You'll receive e-mail updates of the latest relevant Google results (web, news, etc.) based on your specific search query.

Chapter Two:
Getting Started

You can't be that kid standing at the top of the waterslide, overthinking it. You have to go down the chute. – Tina Fey

~

How to Get Started Investing in Apartment Buildings

Are you serious about investing in multifamily real estate? Here's what you do. Right now. Get in your car, or hire a taxi or an Uber or Lyft, and start cruising around town. Picture yourself owning every small multifamily property and large apartment building you see.

When you look at apartment buildings or smaller multifamily properties and imagine yourself as the owner, *amazing* things will start to happen.

Why? Because you'll:

- Set the intention of ownership in your mind, and
- Begin to get a feel for what you'll do as an owner of investment real estate.

You'll start to see how you can turn your dream of property ownership into something that can actually happen. Your dream moves out of the world of fantasy and becomes something you can touch, see and feel.

Picture yourself owning the property

When you see and picture yourself owning a residential investment property, you'll find yourself thinking about the lives you can impact by being a superb landlord. As you drive around various markets, you'll start thinking about things like:

When it snows, who's going to be shoveling those walks? You? A property manager?

How about when it rains? Does the roof leak? Is there proper drainage around the building? Are all of the windows intact? Is the property in a flood prone area?

If it's late at night, notice who's hanging around the neighborhood. Are the residents safe and secure? Does the property have good security lighting?

When I first started looking at properties, I saw myself improving the health and well-being of my residents by providing a clean and safe living environment. I still do. As an owner you are able to make life so much better for the residents.

Look at each multifamily property and picture yourself as the owner. How many units does it have? How many bedrooms are in each unit? What amenities does the property offer? How can you improve on that?

Two hours of intense activity every two weeks is just not going to cut it. Time flies. It's easy to be well-intentioned only to find yourself thinking, "Oh no! I've been completely distracted, and I haven't spent one minute on real estate in the last couple of weeks."

Can you commit to a regular, daily schedule? And stick with it? If the answer is, "Yes!" you will succeed.

Pro tip: You'll find a weekly planning schedule and tips for following your plan in Chapter Three: Goals, Activities & Weekly Schedule.

Determine your area of specialization

Successful real estate investing requires knowledge. There are many different types of real estate investments. Don't kid yourself into thinking that you can master all of them. Your time and capital are both valuable and in limited supply.

Determine the type of investing that best matches your strengths and approach it with focus. Perhaps a turnkey property that will command market rents and is ready to go the day you close would be appropriate for you. Or, you might have the skills or team required to buy a property in need of repair.

Trying to dabble in a bit of everything will prevent you from ever gaining the expertise needed for long-term success in all economic climates.

Know the numbers

There are mathematical formulas for each area of real estate investing that determine whether you should or should not invest in a particular property. Learning the formulas is important because you have to know that the numbers work, and that the property will make money for you before you invest.

You don't get the option of following your gut instinct to make real estate investment decisions. You have to understand the investment formulas for your type of properties, and you must take the time to conduct a proper analysis of any property you seriously consider.

Some of the formulas specific to multifamily investments are:

Debt service coverage (DSCR): a measurement of the cash flow that is available to pay the property's current debt obligations.

Operating expense ratio (OER): the percentage of income used to pay expenses.

Cash on cash return (COCR): the ratio of annual before-tax cash flow to the total amount of cash invested.

Net operating income (NOI): the money remaining after all operating expenses have been paid, excluding debt service and major capital improvements.

Gross rent multiplier (GRM): a screening tool used to determine if a property is in line with similar properties.

We'll cover the investment formulas specific to multifamily investments in Chapter Nine: Deal Analysis.

Develop strategic partners

As a real estate investor, you will need counsel and advice from experts from time to time. These include attorneys, contractors, inspectors, commercial mortgage lenders, commercial property brokers, and property managers.

Your business is valuable to each of them. Develop relationships with these professionals so you can call upon them when needed and have them respond quickly. As they get to know you and understand your objectives, they can help you avoid hidden pitfalls and hard-learned lessons.

Identify the right opportunities

The best baseball players wait for their pitch. The best poker players know that being successful requires folding a lot more hands than they play. You cannot make the market what you want it to be.

Just because you are ready, willing, and able to invest doesn't mean the time is right. It means when the right opportunity does become available, you will recognize it and be in a position to capitalize on it.

One Thing Every Multifamily Real Estate Investor Should Know

I firmly believe that there is one rule above all others that all real estate investors should know and abide by. It seems so simple, but people really struggle with this rule. Here it is:

Rule #1: Don't hear what you want to believe.

I've done it. You've probably done it. We all want to believe the very best about our real estate investments. We want to believe that:

- Our property is in a great market.
- We made a good deal—the price was right.
- The property is bound to appreciate in value. Soon.
- Our renovations won't cost much.
- The property is in great shape.
- We'll have no problem refinancing.

And sometimes we get in a hurry. Unfortunately, this thinking may cost you time, money and even possibly your sanity.

How to protect yourself

Discuss your prospective real estate deal with your multifamily mentor, local property owners and other experienced multifamily investors and "hear" the truth. If they tell you something you don't want to hear or believe, pause, breathe deeply and take it in. In all likelihood the negative things you hear from your mentors about an investment property or market are probably the truth.

It's important that you talk with people who will not gain from your decision to buy a property. You can:

- Hire an experienced multifamily inspector to look at the property you are considering.
- Talk to local commercial property managers about the location.
- Network with multifamily real estate investors in your area.
- Visit with other apartment building owners in the area. Ask them if in hindsight they would have handled things differently before purchasing their property.

You can also be proactive in your real estate investing activities by:

- Working with experienced multifamily and apartment building lenders.
- Studying your market and become well informed of the current and historical market statistics such as: vacancy; rental rates and demand; new multifamily construction; sold and rent comparables; and job and employment growth.
- Saying "No" if a deal or property doesn't meet your investment requirements no matter how excited you are.

Pause before you do the deal and be completely honest with yourself. Ask yourself these questions:

- Does this opportunity meet my investment rules?
- Does it fit with my overall investment strategy?
- Have I taken the time to conduct proper due diligence?

Asking yourself these questions should lead you to the right decision on any investment. It's also extremely helpful to establish your own investment rules that will help guide your decisions. You'll find more on money rules at the end of Chapter Three: Goals, Activities & Weekly Schedule.

Don't Treat Real Estate Investing as a Hobby

It's next to impossible to invest in real estate and expect a solid return if you treat it like a hobby. Yet thousands believe they can create a lucrative sideline business by working only a few hours per week.

Why? Most likely because real estate investing gurus, late night infomercials, and those with a vested interest in promoting real estate as an investment, insist it's a piece of cake—that anyone can do it. Not everyone can. And it's not because they lack talent—it's a result of a lack of dedication, education, time, money and help.

Do you play golf? Are you any good? Exactly! If you said, "Yes," it's because you've worked hard at it. You've probably had some coaching too. And if your answer was "No," well you and I both know you could improve with time, training and dedication, barring physical limitations of course.

How much time does it take to excel at real estate investing?

Should you work half an hour per day? Two hours?

Most people have trouble sticking to a daily plan. They end up cramming those half hours into a single sitting. I've seen it happen hundreds of times. Usually the time spent in a cram session is woefully inadequate because there's no direction—no plan or goals.

Start seeing real estate investing as your other career. A career you work on daily and with tremendous consistency.

Go for it

Set aside 30 to 60 uninterrupted minutes per day and devote that time exclusively to real estate investment research, education, and networking. Plan your time carefully and stick to your schedule.

Make real estate investing a priority amid all of your other obligations. You will succeed. You'll know you've really accomplished something huge the day you close on your first solid investment property. It's like winning your home tournament!

And then your work has just begun.

But I don't have any money!

This is probably the biggest stumbling block in most people's minds.

Do you know how I started in multifamily investing? How I was able to raise hundreds of thousands of dollars for my first deal? It's simple. I found a property that friends and family wanted to invest in.

It's not the money. The trick is in finding a fantastic investment opportunity—one that provides attractive returns to you and your partners. Along with that, you must be able to demonstrate a solid working knowledge of:

- your goals and investment strategies
- the property financials and due diligence requirements
- the local multifamily real estate market
- your operations plan
- your likely investment returns
- your exit strategy

You'll also need a good team with the ability to carry out your investment plans. And don't forget, your lender or bank is also your partner. This level of preparation goes a long way in attracting financing.

So…we're right back where we started with research, education, and networking. How do you find a deal that people will be interested in? You network.

How do you know you've found a good property in a solid rental market? You learn how to research real estate investment markets and how to analyze investment property financials and potential returns.

Are you, at heart, a real estate investor?

The bottom line is your heart has to be in it. It's much easier to become engaged in the process of real estate investing when you have goals.

It also helps to find some pleasure in what you're doing. I love that we provide safe and secure housing for our residents. I also love to play golf, especially when I combine it with real estate investing. (Ask me how sometime!)

What do you want to accomplish? What is your vision? What are your dreams? Are you willing to work long, hard hours to get there? On top of your already busy schedule?

Take action now

Now that you're committed to research, education, and networking let's add action to your list.

Be careful not to spend all of your time in solo endeavors. Don't get stuck in front of your computer. Connect with other like-minded individuals. Network with successful real estate investors. Get out of the house or office.

Start looking at markets to begin to get an idea of where you'd like to invest. Think about what types of properties will meet your specific goals. For instance, are you looking for cash flow? Properties in appreciating markets? Opportunities to add value by renovating and improving operations and management? Do you want to slowly trade up to larger properties? Or would you be happy owning several small multi-units as a retirement plan? And how will you pay for all of this?

Can You Really Invest in Real Estate with No Money Down?

Banks have their own ideas about what constitutes a good investment. They tend to be rather linear in their processes, and they do not look for the big picture or place much value on vision.

To make a loan, the project or real estate investment must meet several specific criteria. For instance, a lender might require that the property has a stabilized occupancy (typically 90%) for 90 days prior to funding. Or they might require that the buyer has prior multifamily investing experience. That is not necessarily a bad thing, but traditional financing does not work for some people and some real estate investments.

The big question for many novice investors is if they can purchase investment property with no money down. The answer to that? Absolutely. Is that the best way to go about purchasing rental properties? Not necessarily.

The main problem with no money down investing

Perhaps the worst thing an investor can do is try to manage rental property when they are under-capitalized. After all, there are times when spending money on repairs and maintenance saves considerable money down the line.

A well-maintained property is much more appealing to potential tenants than an unkempt property. Being in a position to spend money when needed puts you as an investor in a better position for profitability. Investors can take a cash flow positive property to foreclosure within a few months when they do not have the funds to repair or replace a non-functioning HVAC system.

There's a lot of discussion online about the responsibilities of tenants and how landlords can ensure their renters comply with rules and laws, but landlords and property managers also have obligations. These property owner responsibilities include maintaining a safe environment, keeping the property clean, and responding to repair requests promptly. You must be properly funded in order to perform these duties.

Another big legal requirement is the proper keeping of tenants' security deposits. Specific requirements vary by state, but in the eyes of the law, security deposits belong to the tenants unless the landlord has some right to utilize the funds.

Thirty Ways to Invest in Real Estate Without Using Your Own Money

The real estate investing dream

Do you know there are thousands of people who share the real estate investing dream? They just don't have the opportunity or know-how to pursue it.

You however have probably invested time—and money—getting the education to invest wisely. With that education you're able to recognize solid real estate investment opportunities. The very opportunities your friends and family don't know about. And you're in a place to share.

The hardest job of any real estate investor

Discovering a great real estate investment property, in the right market, is the hardest first step for most prospective investors. It's why so many people only dream about investing in real estate.

By finding a great investment property you've solved most interested investor's dilemma. You've earned your weight in gold! In addition to finding great deals, there are absolutely dozens of ways you can contribute without actually writing a check. You can:

- **Contribute capital:** Instead of investing cash why not use your good credit (used to get financing), collateral (assets or property to secure a loan) or self-directed IRA funds to name but a few?
- **Make an entrepreneurial contribution:** What if you find other investors with capital? Or source lender financing? Both are extremely valuable contributions. Or you might be a CPA who will handle the books and taxes or the lawyer who drafts the partnership agreement.
- **Provide labor or specific skill sets:** Do you have contracting or property rehabilitation skills? Experience with property management?

Here's a list of ways to invest in real estate without using your own money — and still bring value to a real estate partnership.

- The top of the list? Finding the real estate investment property!
- Find other investment partners with capital.
- Contribute collateral or credit.

- Create the investment memorandum for prospective investors.
- Prepare the loan application documents and financials.
- Prepare financial analysis of the investment property at acquisition.
- Prepare pro forma operating budgets and projections.
- Research potential investment markets and submarkets to include sold comps (a list of recent property sales); rent comps (a list of competing property rental price points); renter demographics and local competition.
- Provide continuing rental market research during ownership period.
- Strategize on increasing property net operating income (NOI) by increasing income and lowering expenses.
- Plan investment exit strategies like property sale projections; refinance objectives; executing a 1031 Exchange (tax deferred exchange into a like property); or conversion to other use (such as a conversion to condos).
- Handle bookkeeping, accounts payable, and rent collections.
- Lease and pre-lease rental units.
- Create marketing materials for potential renters.
- Form and manage the investment entity.
- Prepare the entity Operating Agreement.
- Renovate and rehab common areas and/or individual rental units.
- Improve the property and address deferred maintenance.
- Evaluate current service providers and vendors (trash removal, property insurance, pest control, landscaping, etc.) and shop for better rates/service.
- Prepare year-end tax reports.
- Broker the real estate transaction (purchase and/or sale).
- Market the property for sale.

- Manage legal issues such as collections and evictions.
- Manage the property.
- Oversee property maintenance.
- Oversee contractors and property inspectors.
- Manage tenant relations and set up policies and rules.

Whew! It's a long list. Do you see how successful real estate investments need time and teamwork? And specific skill sets and talent? All of the services listed above are services the partnership pays for. Somebody's got to do the work. Why not you?

There are literally dozens of ways to invest in real estate without using your own money! Non-monetary contributions that allow you to feel great about your role in the success of the investment. So, are you ready to start making offers on properties?

How to Stop Being Afraid of Making Offers on Apartment Buildings

In the world of multifamily investing, you may make several if not many offers to purchase an apartment building before you actually close on a property. In fact, serious negotiations on the investment property will not begin until after you are in contract.

Often times you will get in contract and a deal will never close. Knowing this, can you see why waiting to find—and make on offer on—that "perfect" apartment building may backfire? Your fear may be stopping you from finding and negotiating a great deal. It might also be stopping you from finding the money to fund a deal.

If you are not actively making offers, you will never acquire a property.

Fear is a natural part of the process

You might have some reasonable sounding excuses (a.k.a. fears) about why you're holding back from making offers, such as:

- You're afraid of having an offer rejected.
- You're focused on learning absolutely everything there is to know about multifamily investing before you "make your move."
- You think you might lose the earnest money if the deal doesn't close.
- You're afraid you might buy an apartment building that was not a good deal to begin with.
- You're not entirely sure how to make an offer and you don't want to risk looking foolish in front of a seller or broker.
- You're not fully funded.

These are natural and real fears. Most beginning investors face them. Even experienced investors can get hung up on concerns like these. I've faced them. And as the deals get larger in size, I continue to feel those little jitters common to taking a huge financial step. You're not alone—being fearful of making a large financial commitment is normal human behavior.

Negotiations start when you are in contract

It is critical that you understand most negotiations begin after you are in contract. Many commercial property contract terms and conditions allow for ongoing negotiations. These negotiation points include:

- Undisclosed maintenance and repair issues uncovered during physical inspections.
- Undisclosed expenses (or inflated income numbers) uncovered in a review of the seller's Year-to-Date financials and current tenant leases.
- Unsatisfactory availability, terms, conditions and costs for a new loan. In other words, you may not be able to find acceptable financing.
- A purchase price that exceeds the property's valuation determined by an appraiser.

Be sure to review all terms and conditions before signing a contract. Working with a good mentor, attorney or commercial broker, especially if you are new to investing, is essential to success.

Pro tip: When you negotiate a great deal, you will attract funds and financing.

Start making offers on apartment buildings

When I work with mentoring students we don't sit around in a classroom. After determining which market my clients want to pursue, they start making offers on active listings meeting their criteria. It's the best way to get out of analysis paralysis and on your way to becoming an apartment building owner.

Don't sit on the sidelines paralyzed by fear. Get a sufficient education through books, mentoring, and seminars and by networking with successful apartment building investors. Put a great support system in place.

Then get going.

Once you are in contract to buy an apartment building your learning curve will skyrocket. You will be amazed at how much—and how fast—you learn when real money is on the table. You will learn how to:

- Analyze an apartment deal by using actual property financials.
- Conduct thorough due diligence and inspections.
- Determine who needs to be on your team.
- Offer a fair purchase price.
- Fine-tune your negotiating skills.
- Attract funds.
- Say "No."

The best learning is in the street.

A last word

Hire an attorney, commercial real estate broker or an experienced multifamily investing mentor before you present a formal contract to buy and sell real estate.

Keep in mind most standard contracts to buy and sell commercial real estate cover the basics however you will want to hire a professional to include your precise concerns and terms in the language of the contract.

For instance, you might want to stipulate that the seller provide documents that are not specifically covered in the contract, or that the seller not execute any new resident leases below a certain dollar amount.

The Pros and Cons of Apartment Building Ownership

Investing in real estate, particularly an apartment building, can be the best decision you've ever made. Stabilized, performing properties make great assets. They can be a wonderful source of income. But it takes hard work, mitigation of risk, and knowledge of what can go wrong to keep your investment profitable.

Owning your own investment property can be your dream come true with stable cash flow and the opportunity to provide affordable housing to good people. The advantages to owning an apartment building investment property are:

It is an asset that produces income while appreciating in value: Given the right market, your apartment building should be increasing in value, while your tenants are paying you monthly rent live there, thus paying down the principal debt. Virtually no other investment opportunities can deliver those kinds of results.

Your rents offer a means of stable and predictable cash flow: You know how much money will be coming in any given month. You can budget and plan for renovations and contingencies. You can also add amenities that create even more positive cash flow like laundry facilities, storage, or parking.

Tax breaks: These two amazing little words can mean a world of difference when it comes time to pay your taxes. You may be able to deduct mortgage interest and real estate taxes on your rental properties, write off standard operating expenses and depreciate the cost of your building over time. This will vary by individual and property type so always include your CPA in tax decisions.

You benefit from economies of scale (having multiple renters in one space): They share walls, a roof, a boiler, landscaping, etc. This saves you a ton of money compared to if you rented out single-family homes. One roof to repair, one yard to landscape… you get the idea.

You are providing a clean, safe, and affordable home for your tenants: With competitive rents and ensuring your building is up to safety and health standards, you are providing the public a service.

Renters aren't going anywhere anytime soon: In the U.S. 43 million households are renters and 37% of renters live in apartments. The majority of renters tend to be millennials who don't want the hassle of dealing with the upkeep of their own home and may be stuck with student debt.

So, if owning an investment property is so great, why doesn't everyone do it? Well, there are drawbacks. It takes money to invest and knowledge in managing not only the property but the tenants as well. This can eat up more hours than a full-time job if you can't afford a property management company and aren't able to attract investors.

Most importantly, by definition, an investment is a risk, and it can pay off, or it can put you into debt. Apartment building ownership is not always as rife with rainbows and sacks of cash as the infomercials would lead you to believe.

It can be difficult to attract and keep good tenants: Renters who pay their rent on time and who stay are the lifeblood of positive cash flow and they are hard to find. You can do your best to mitigate this by adhering to tight screening policies like checking tenant references, verifying income guidelines, and checking criminal and credit reports.

You will have tax implications when you sell: Consult with your CPA about how to minimize your taxes if you sell the property. Long-term capital gains taxes and depreciation recapture hits are never fun. Make sure that a tax professional is making these calculations for you before you sell so you know what to expect.

A decline in the market with no viable exit strategy can be crippling: External factors like a decline in the economy and changes in the local housing market can cause your apartment building investment to fall in the red. If your exit strategy either doesn't exist or will not work, you are stuck with a debt that is no longer producing cash flow.

Government regulations can interfere with profit margins: When the government interferes with housing and creates rules around rent control, building ordinances, or environmental regulations, you might have to make changes that affect your bottom line.

Your property needs to be managed: Advertisement, maintenance, tenant management, landscaping, rent collection… the list could continue on and on, but someone needs to manage your property. If you don't have enough money to hire a professional management company to do this for you, you have to be your own property manager, and this takes time.

An apartment building investment is much less liquid than many other investments: If you need cash fast, it is difficult to just sell it off like a stock. Keep this in mind when investing and diversify your investments when possible.

There is a risk of your property not being resilient: All real estate goes through ups and downs: market highs and losses due to mismanagement or natural disasters. A resilient property will bounce back from the lows.

Just like with any investment, there is risk. Staying informed of your greatest risks and knowing how to overcome them is key in becoming a successful multifamily real estate investor.

Real Estate Investment Decisions That Will Help You Sleep

Real estate is a funny thing. You can buy an investment property that is virtually problem free, or you can buy a property that just seems to present problems at every turn. A problem property will drain you emotionally, physically, mentally, and possibly financially.

You don't want to find yourself asking, "What was I thinking? This property is a dog. It's in the wrong neighborhood, it's costing me money every single month and I'm stuck with it. Wasn't real estate supposed to be a great investment?"

Well-conceived real estate investment decisions will help you:

- Avoid risk
- Meet your investment objectives
- Create and maintain positive returns
- Realize long-term growth

In other words, your "sleep at night" plan. Solid real estate investment decisions can save the day. You might even end up looking like a genius. The following commitments will help you avoid risk.

Expect unexpected operating expenses

There is one thing real estate investors will agree on: unexpected operating expenses will arise. And chances are good you won't even see them coming. For example, unexpected leasing fees, exorbitant pest control expenses, or property damage repair costs can pop up when you least expect them.

An excellent way to prepare for the unexpected is to become intimately familiar with the typical operating expenses of comparable properties in your specific submarket.

Take a look at the financials for three to five comparable properties and compare those against the property you're considering. Does your property have expenses that are out of whack in comparison? If so, why?

Keep your partners happy

Don't make the mistake of thinking about you first, partners second. If a deal is too skinny to satisfy investment partners with a certain degree of surety, don't do the deal.

Know your exit strategies

An investor who is crystal clear about their long-term investment plans and who has well-defined exit strategies will never rely on dumb luck for success. What is your long-term—or short-term—plan for the property? Will you:

- Eventually sell the property?
- Fix it up and flip (sell in a short amount of time) it for a profit?
- Refinance and hold it for cash flow?
- Leave it as a legacy for your heirs?
- Trade it into a new property and defer capital gains taxes with a 1031 exchange?
- Convert it to an entirely new use, for instance a conversion to condominiums?

These are your exit strategies.

Let's say you want to keep the property as rental for now and convert it to a condominium when the condo market improves. Do you see how this decision will inform your renovation decisions? You might do very little renovating today (enough to attract good renters) and then do a high-end renovation (meeting the expectations of a condo buyer) at a later date.

41

Having a plan is the very best way to alleviate the closing jitters. When you have solid investment exit strategies you have a better idea of how you will operate the property today.

Buy on facts, not emotion

Have you ever heard someone say, "Oh! I just fell in love with the property!" When I hear this I tend to think, "Oh no! And how much will that cost you?"

It's true. Love is blind. When your heart leads, critical thought just seems to fly out the window. Do your due diligence. Inspect the property. Use actual, historical operating data (trailing income and expenses) in your analysis.

Invest in the right area

Always do your real estate market research—and don't ignore submarket data. You don't want to be the property owner on the wrong side of the dividing line between a profitable market and a market where properties languish at 100% vacancy.

Make money the day you close on the deal

If you pay too much for a property or you must rely on forces outside of your control—such as your local rental market, market appreciation and the economy—in order to see a profit, then your acquisition strategies are not working.

On the other hand, when you know you've negotiated a solid deal when you can turn around and immediately list your property for a profit or enjoy positive cash flow from day one. When you invest in a rental property that you can immediately sell for a profit, you've made money the day you close. On paper anyway—of course you actually have to sell it to make real money.

The idea is to negotiate a decent price and to not overpay for the property. Don't buy the first property you see—there are plenty of good investment properties available.

This strategy helps you rely less on forces outside of your control such as market appreciation or the economy. A good solid real estate investment is one where you buy at a negotiated price and then create added value through

- smart management
- appropriate upgrades and renovations
- a good team and
- a solid operations plan.

Work "on" your business not "in" it

When you're managing your own property, collecting rents, and unplugging clogged toilets, you are working "in" your business. But if you're looking to make a growing and profitable business of real estate investing, then you've got to start seeing the big picture. That's hard to do when you've got your tool belt on and you're knee-deep in goo.

This is where having a great team is critical. A wise investor delegates property operation to qualified team members and focuses on property acquisition, asset management and long-term business strategies.

Look at real estate investing as a business. Your job is to manage your business assets and to carry out strategies that grow your investment portfolio. You don't want to lose sight of your long-range plans or compromise your ability to consistently carry out your plans.

Hire the right team

Your real estate mentor, commercial broker and property management company are the three most important members of your team. Most of my referrals for prospective team members came from these three key individuals.

The most important thing an experienced real estate investor knows

A super smart investor never believes real estate is a way to get rich quick. You can't. It's a measured process that takes time, energy, education and good planning.

Chapter Three:
Goals, Activities and Weekly Schedule

Be not afraid of growing slowly, be afraid only of standing still – Chinese Proverb

~

How to Create Time for Your Real Estate Investment Business

Like many new investors you might be finding it difficult to carve out time for your real estate investment business—especially if you have a full-time job.

If you were to ask me, "What's the biggest mistake you see new investors make?" I would tell you that 9 out of 10 investors who fail did not devote enough time to their investing endeavor or they mismanaged their time. They didn't give an all-out effort and have an all-in attitude.

If you're a new real estate investor, you've probably faced the same uncertainties. How much time and what activities will guarantee success? Stop for a minute and honestly answer the following three questions:

- Are you informed enough about real estate investing to understand where to network, who to hire, what markets to invest in, when to invest, and what risks you might face?
- Have you decided on a specific real estate investment asset class? (Classes include single-family or multifamily residential, retail, industrial, office, REITs, self-storage, mixed-use and land.)
- Do you have the time and motivation to succeed?

Here are some good habits to get into—starting today.

Always track your time

Keep a daily calendar in order to track the amount of time you spend on your real estate investing business. Plan ahead.

A frenzied two hours per week, in one sitting, will never have the impact that daily activity provides. Small successes can be incredibly powerful. As suggested earlier, put aside 30-60 minutes per day—time that is specifically devoted to education, networking, and research. Consistency is key to your success. Your daily activities should focus on:

Real estate news, mentorship

Read absolutely everything related to your specific asset class and markets. Some of the best magazines covering multifamily market research, rental market research and multifamily data are:

- CIRE Magazine (ccim.com/cire-magazine)
- Multifamily Executive Magazine (multifamilyexecutive.com)

- Multi-Housing News (multi-housingnews.com)
- Apartment Finance Today (housingfinance.com)

Start compiling your own list of similar sites, specific to your asset class, and visit these websites on a regular basis.

Find a mentor. Start associating with other successful real estate investors. It's important to connect with investors who specialize in your asset class of choice. You don't want a retail storefront investor giving you tips on buying and operating an apartment building.

Education around your specific niche investment asset class is key.

Pro tip: As a successful owner of investment real estate it's your job to stay on top of real estate trends, cycles, markets and news. This will become a lifelong habit—especially when you catch the real estate investing 'bug.'

Investment property deal analysis

Until you've run the numbers on dozens of comparable investment properties, your investment plan will succeed (or fail) based on a foundation of guesswork, misguided but well-intended assumptions, and, hopefully, a lot of good luck.

In order to find potential investment properties, you'll be speaking with commercial brokers, realtors, third-party management companies and other investors and service providers within your niche market. Networking is essential to your success.

How much time will you devote to sourcing potential investment properties? And how much time will you spend practicing thorough deal analysis within your niche market? It's critical to think in terms of your daily calendar.

Your specific real estate investment market

A lack of good solid market research is another way in which erroneous assumptions are formed. It's difficult to make accurate assumptions about the future of vacancy rates, expenses, and market rents, for example, without solid market research. These assumptions, however, assist you in making accurate income projections for your investment property.

The same is true for overall market data such as new construction (the amount of new multifamily product on the market), absorption rates (the rate at which new units are successfully rented), market rental concessions (what landlords are willing to give up in order to rent units), and financing trends and loan products. Becoming an expert in this information will lead to your success.

When you make a habit of reading data related to your investment, you'll begin to collect solid information that will lead to successful strategies.

Start some good real estate investing habits today

When you do anything often enough, it becomes a habit. Your 30-60 minutes a day (good quality time vs. poking around on the Internet) will lead to your success.

Supercharge Your Multifamily Investment Business with This Weekly Schedule

Despite the growing opportunities in real estate and increased renter rates, multifamily investing is a crowded industry with stiff competition. Such circumstances may make it seem impossible for you to grow your multifamily investment business.

Fortunately, you can enter and succeed in the real estate market through consistency and action.

A weekly calendar for multifamily investment business success

By integrating the following activities in your weekly schedule, you will be able to focus your efforts, grow your network, and identify the ideal property to feature in your next investment.

Dedicate your Mondays to research

It does not matter whether you have been in business for some time or you are new, you need to understand your market to ascertain the areas with the most attractive potential returns on your investment dollars.

You can begin your week by picking a market or two of your choice then dig deep into the relevant information. Your market research should include data at the submarket level, local market news or trends, position in real estate market cycles, as well as renovation strategies and trends.

Here is how researching will impact your operations:

- It offers a better understanding of your target renter audience and market. This strengthens your business position and keeps you ahead of the competition
- Investing in research minimizes investment risks
- Through research, you get to identify potential opportunities and threats
- You discover your weaknesses and strengths, as well as those of your competitors
- It enables strategic planning
- You can identify emerging trends
- It helps evaluate your business' success
- It helps you determine property valuations

Your multifamily property market research should include:

Submarket data. Look at the sold and rent comps, the average price per door, average cap rates, and average asking rents. Commercial brokers are a great resource for submarket research. Their research can help you pinpoint specific neighborhoods that offer the best return on investment (ROI).

Market news. Staying up to date can help you make smarter investment choices. Current market news may give you insight into potential issues looming in the future, too. For example, many owner-operators of apartment buildings have been forced to find convenient and inexpensive solutions for securely accepting delivery of tenant packages.

Market trends. What amenities are renters looking for? Wood floors? Building-wide Wi-Fi? What is the market like in your target areas? Follow both local and national trends.

Renovation trends and strategies. What are other multifamily property investors doing to bring in their target demographic? This can help you plan for your future properties more effectively.

Real estate cycles. Become familiar with real estate cycles in your target markets. Is the market moving out of recession and into recovery? Or is it moving from expansion and into hypersupply? Understanding these cycles can help you pinpoint the best times to buy and sell. Market cycles and multifamily market research are covered extensively throughout Chapter Five: Market Research.

Network on Tuesday

An investment is not a solo venture, and the success of your multifamily investment business also relies on the way you reach out to knowledgeable industry insiders. You can easily build your multifamily property portfolio when you surround yourself with trusted experts who will answer your questions. This helps avoid any issues that can turn you into a 'lone wolf' investor.

To find investment partners, begin by joining investment clubs, multifamily industry associations, and groups. Attending events and reaching out to your family and friends are also beneficial.

Networking benefits your multifamily business in the following ways:

- You can access great deals and industry education
- If you are new in the field, you can learn to interact
- It can save research time
- It facilitates team building

Investing shouldn't be a solo venture. You'll build your portfolio more effectively when you have a trusted team around you. Industry insiders can answer questions and help you avoid issues that would trip up a "lone wolf" investor. Put your email, social media, and phone to use. Network by:

Joining investment groups and clubs. Connect with other investors who can advise and support you. Sometimes it's just nice to know someone who understands what it's like to be an investor in multifamily property!

Joining industry associations and attend events. This is a great way to build your network quickly and learn a lot in the meantime. The National Apartment Association (naahq.org) is a perfect place to find multifamily industry-specific events.

Reaching out to friends and family. The people you already know are often your best resource for investment information! They might be able to connect you with someone who is doing exactly what you want to do.

Source deals on Wednesday

Networking could be among the most effective ways of finding deals, but you also need to include online searches into your business schedule. Not only does it help you discover new networking opportunities, but it also helps you identify unique investment ideas.

You can connect with brokers in person or online and search the web for property listings. While the latter may not be the ideal way of finding a property, it offers a wealth of information that is helpful to your multifamily investment business, particularly if you are a new investor.

For instance, an online search at an internet listing service (ILS) like LoopNet (loopnet.com) will help you learn more about potential markets and research important data like average cap rates, average price per door and rental rates for local markets. ILS sites are also a great way to find commercial brokers. You'll read more about ILS searches in Chapter Six: Finding Deals.

Conduct deal analysis on Thursday

You will master the art of analyzing multifamily property deals only through practice, practice, and more practice. Therefore, you will benefit much if you dedicate this day in the weekly schedule to analyzing a deal in your particular submarket and asset class. With time, this will earn you more confidence to go out there and make your offer.

When practicing deal analysis for multifamily properties, make sure you:

- Take notes about your observations and questions regarding the property.
- Develop proficiency with your favorite deal analysis spreadsheets.
- Determine what renters want versus what the market is currently offering.

53

- Learn how to do a proforma analysis to project your potential ROI.

You'll find more on deal analysis, including proforma analysis and working with spreadsheets in Chapter Nine: Deal Analysis.

Finish the week by building your investment library on Friday

Smart multifamily investors understand that learning will never stop, and some have portfolios dating back over 20 years yet are still expanding their investment libraries. You can also boost your multifamily investment business operations by establishing your personal library to build and grow your knowledge base.

You should stock it with:

- Educational blog posts, white papers and articles on multifamily real estate
- National and local real estate market research
- Documents and forms used by deal sponsors
- Documents and forms used by landlords
- Updated information on fair housing compliance and local housing requirements

The key benefit of the resource library is that it provides timely, relevant information on the ever-changing market.

Landlords should have rental forms on hand at all times. These include, but are not limited to, lease application forms, lease agreements, lease renewal notices, notices to vacate or pay, eviction notices, and receipts for any payments received. You should download these documents from your state website and know each section and paragraph. Your landlord/tenant attorney can also supply you with documents that comply with state and local rules.

There are many sources for finding free forms, such as your local library, real estate agents, commercial property brokers, and your real estate investment club or professional associations such as the National Association of Realtors. You can also purchase forms online but be very careful of your sources and be certain the forms are in compliance with state law.

Consistency creates a better portfolio

Bear in mind that multifamily investing requires you to be consistent and patient, while also dedicating sufficient time. In the long run, sticking to this effective weekly schedule will significantly boost your bottom line. Whenever you get off track, remember not to be hard on yourself, get back, and keep paddling. Just get back to your established investing schedule and keep growing through networking and research.

It is also helpful if you connect with a mentor or accountability partner in the industry. Not only do they keep you focused, but they also help you avoid any common pitfalls associated with first-time investments.

Investing Habits That Will Boost Your Bottom Line

It's easy to get caught up in the busy pace of today's world, isn't it? Family obligations, work requirements and doing errands fill your life. How do you do all that and develop real estate investing habits that will make your investment dreams come true?

Plan your time

You know the answer, of course. You plan ahead of time. It doesn't have to be much time, just thirty minutes a day ought to do it—if you are consistent. Remember, slow and steady wins the race and is the surest way of developing lifelong real estate investing habits.

Be disciplined. Procrastination will not make you wealthy.

Thirty minutes every day at the same time practicing real estate investing skills will become a habit. Shut the door and take the time to invest in your future. Turn the volume off on your phone and know that emails can wait.

If you spend thirty minutes each day devoted to learning and growing your real estate business momentum will take hold.

Practice the investing habits and skills you need to master

Being a successful real estate investor involves many skills. Break down what you need to know and practice those skills. For example, organize your daily thirty minutes with a different skill set each day of the week as we covered earlier.

- Monday: Research real estate markets, follow market news and trends

- Tuesday: Network through face to face contact, social media or email
- Wednesday: Source deals online and through contacts
- Thursday: Practice deal analysis
- Friday: Build an investment library

Keep yourself accountable

Choose your company wisely. Stop and think about who you want to become. Don't settle. Surround yourself with people who share the same goals and interests you aspire to.

Join your local REIA (Real Estate Investment Association), real estate investing club or apartment association. Spend time with people who encourage your dreams and ambitions. They are out there; go find them.

Good real estate investing habits begin with goals

Before you reach your goals, you have to have goals. Write them down. Create SMART goals by making them specific, measurable, attainable, risky and with a time limit.

You might decide to buy, fix and sell 3 properties in 6 months, or buy 3 single-family rental homes to hold for 10 years. These are very specific goals.

Be old fashioned – get out a piece of paper and a pen. Literally write your goals down. You might have rewrite them a few times, that's a normal part of the process.

Once you are happy with the goals tape them up where you can see them every day. Yes, every day. They will remind you to spend thirty minutes a day, every day, on your real estate business.

Find a mentor

Athletes have coaches and you should have a mentor as well. Real estate is not a game and mistakes can cost money, serious money. Mentors are like lighthouses, shining a light on unseen rocks and potential hazards.

More than practical, mentors can talk you through all of the fears and insecurities you might encounter. They can guide and teach you terrific real estate investing habits and skills such as networking and research. Sometimes we need someone who has been there to navigate the pep talk and the tough love.

Find someone who resonates with you and send them an email about a potential mentorship. You have everything to gain!

How to set business goals you can achieve

The difference between wildly successful people and those who struggle to succeed is that successful people learn how to move forward when they feel "stuck."
They set goals to advance. They're expert at setting business goals that are meaningful and achievable.

You can do the same thing. Here are some ideas to get you thinking and motivated, along with some steps you can take today to start creating change in your life.

Set a goal

Set a simple goal that gets you on your way to your larger goals. What can you accomplish in a short period of time? Small successes can be incredibly powerful. You can:

- Attend a multifamily property showing.
- Have an introductory phone call with a broker who works an investment market of interest.
- Ask a friend if they've ever thought about investing in real estate.

Start hanging out with the right crowd

This task isn't easy. You'll have to make some difficult choices. If you are spending time with people who are negative, who are stuck doing the same stuff day in and day out, who will never make an effort to change their lives and constantly come up with excuses about why they won't change, you are hanging out with the wrong crowd.

Find a mentor in your chosen field. Network with individuals who have already achieved success.

Decide on one business plan and go for it

Have you ever heard of bright shiny objects? Those are those ideas that sound or look really great when you first hear about them. You think to yourself, "Why not jump on the bandwagon? Everyone else is doing it and they claim they are wildly successful."

If you chase the newest and greatest real estate investment idea, all your good plans and careful work go out the window. Stick to your plan. If your plan is to buy a 4-unit investment property, then work doggedly towards that goal.

Shift your energy

When those thoughts of, "I can't do this" pop up, don't be hard on yourself. Acknowledge negative thoughts as limiting beliefs and change your energy. Start thinking in terms of, "Why the heck not? I've got the drive, I can stick with a plan, I have fantastic mentors, and anything is possible!"

Make a list

Write down the goals you want to accomplish. Get a clear picture in your head of where you see yourself in your ideal life.

Let your imagination run wild.

For example, do you want to own a vacation home? Something you can share with your friends and family? Picture your favorite room in your new home… down to the smallest detail. Picture yourself spending time there. What do you do? Where are you? The beach? The mountains?

Poke holes in your limiting beliefs

Once you have your list of goals you want to accomplish, write down the excuses you come up with for why each goal will never be possible.

Are your excuses legitimate? Do you really believe them? Poke as many holes in these limiting beliefs as you can.

Find someone you trust and read your list to them…out loud. Don't hand over your list, read it in a clear, loud voice. This is a good way to hear how ridiculous some of your excuses sound. Give your trusted friend permission to challenge your underlying assumptions. Keep an open mind—don't take the feedback personally.

Take a risk

Taking one tiny step that scares the hell out you is the very best thing you can do even if you think you might fail.

Set an intention about what you want to do. See it clearly. Success begins with a desire to take action. Ask questions about each goal on your list:

- Is your goal realistic? Is it too easy, too hard? (Hard is good.)
- Do you see an area where you might "step it up?" Can you be more aggressive with your goal? Is it challenging enough, and will it be a stretch for you?
- Is there a good life balance? Will the time spent achieving your goal cause you to sacrifice important areas of your life? Is it worth it?
- Is your goal a "no kidding" goal? Are you really committed to achieving this goal?
- What concerns do you have? Do you see areas where you might fall back on old paradigms? Will old preconceived assumptions and expectations about reaching your goal come up? Can you handle it?

- Do you have a "SMART" Goal? Check your goal against the following SMART criteria:

SMART criteria:

Specific: Your goal should be specific, unambiguous and written so that anyone can read it and have a clear picture of what you are going to accomplish.

Measurable: Your goal should be measurable and/or have a final outcome so you can determine if it has been achieved.

Attainable: It must be possible to attain the goal in the time frame stated.

Risky: Your goal should be risky and must be a stretch for you.

Time Limit: Giving a time limit to achieving your goal creates urgency and prevents you from stating open-ended goals.

Carefully weigh the criteria above against each of your goals. It's okay to modify your goals. And once you get started with the implementation of your plan, you'll probably find that minor course corrections are necessary.

How to Create a 10-year Multifamily Investment Plan

You're feeling enthusiastic. You're ready to dive in with your multifamily investment plan. That's great–but don't overestimate the time, ability, and capital that you have to dedicate to the project!

Many real estate investors invest in one property and then quit. Maybe they bought a bad property and they're struggling to recover financially. Perhaps they have goals that are too big–and entirely unrealistic–for that first year of activity, then give up when they fail to reach that arbitrary goal within the first year of operation.

Instead, make sure you create a solid 10-year plan to help you really reach your goals. As Bill Gates famously said,

"Most people overestimate what they can do in one year
and underestimate what they can do in ten years."

What will a 10-year plan accomplish?

With a 10-year multifamily investment plan, you can raise your odds of reaching your goals and sticking with your real estate investments. For example, a 10-year plan may help you:

- Make sure you have enough capital to quit your day job
- Generate the income you need for retirement
- Create a solid legacy through a portfolio of properties
- And so much more!

What are your 10-year goals? How do you plan to accomplish them? With the right strategies, you can go the extra mile and design a solid plan that will ultimately have incredible benefits.

Method #1: Start small

Don't feel as though you have to jump into multifamily real estate investing with both feet. Instead, consider starting with a single-family rental or two, or even flipping a couple of single-family houses to help you build the capital you need for a larger investment.

Then, invest in a small multi-unit: a 2-4 unit, for example. Over time, you can purchase a small apartment complex, then move on to a larger rental property.

By working your way up, with solid goals set for every step of the process, you'll find that you get a better idea of what you can really handle. As you work your way up, you will also build a solid network of individuals who can help you reach your investing goals, from contractors to property managers.

Method #2: Try house hacking

Put your life where your money is. Purchase a small multi-unit property and live in one unit while renting out the other ones. Once you get the hang of that, you might buy a larger rental property; or, you might choose to keep the same size property, depending on your management capability and needs.

There are number of excellent tax and financing incentives to living in the property you're renting out, too. This "house hacking" strategy can transform the way you handle your real estate investments, especially if you're just getting started. There's more on house hacking and other strategies like fix & flip, and short-term rentals in Chapter Twelve: Real Estate Investment Strategies.

Method #3: Start a little bigger

Have you dabbled with real estate investing before, giving you a pretty good idea of how you're going to handle it? Do you have experience in a related field or a mentor to help you get started?

You might choose to dive in with a small apartment building, of around 12-20 units. You'll manage it yourself, learning the ropes and deepening your understanding of the property management process. In about 5 years, plan to make a 1031 exchange into a larger property and hire third-party managers.

This strategy can allow you to get your feet wet and expand your knowledge while developing a wider multifamily investment plan.

Method #4: Dive in with partners

Do you have friends and family who are interested in investing with you–and, therefore, in supporting you along the way? This often means that you can jump in with a bigger deal: a complex with around 20-50 units.

You will find that the team approach is a critical element in this strategy, especially when it comes to property management. In other words, you will need a great team supporting you.

What should your multifamily investment plan include?

With a wide range of methods to choose from, you need a plan to help guide you through the next ten years. Make sure your 10-year multifamily investment plan includes the right elements!

Know what requirements your lender will have of you: Or of your team, if you're borrowing together. You'll need to meet net worth and liquidity requirements, have a certain level of investing experience, and other key elements to make you a solid risk. Include how you will reach each stage of investment, financially speaking, in your 10-year plan.

For a good example of loan requirements view the Freddie Mac multifamily products website and term sheets at mf.freddiemac.com.

Develop an exit strategy: How are you going to capitalize on your investments? Your plan should include whether you want to sell or refinance your properties to fund new purchases, or if you plan to hold solidly producing and stabilized income properties. For example, you might not want to sell a property that produces cash flow, appreciates annually and gives you great tax benefits, all while your residents pay down the mortgage. You also, however, want to have a solid plan for how you will move away from real estate investments that aren't working for you or how you will increase your investment over time.

Have a strategy to work your multifamily investment plan: You'll need to hone your real estate investing skills, create solid relationships, and build value through appreciating assets and principal paydown. And have the right team to help you understand your tax benefits and your cash flow.

Smart renovations and operational know-how can also help improve your investment plan–but you must have a solid plan for developing and using those skills.

How to Set Real Estate Investing Goals

Here's an example of three great goals to get you started:

- Find a broker or real estate agent you would love to work with.
- Ask a successful real estate investor to mentor you.
- Explore 3 or 4 real estate markets to invest in.

Your tasks:

- Network like crazy with your friends, family, business associates, teachers, etc. and get introductions to people who are already successfully investing in real estate.
- Network with real estate agents and commercial multifamily brokers. Who do your friends know and trust?
- Set up at least ten meetings over coffee or lunch with the people you are referred to. Let them know you're just getting started and would like to learn.
- Start exploring the 3 or 4 markets you've identified. Drive around. Or fly to the locations. Picture yourself as the owner. Start networking with locals.
- Look at rental listings for those 3 or 4 markets on Zillow.com to get an idea of market rents, unit style, amenities in demand and also supply and demand. Are landlords offering deals to attract renters?

- Talk to your brokers and mentors about the markets they like. Find out what they think about the markets you're considering.
- Read three real estate investing books.
- Go to at least three property showings.

One last very important step…

Ask yourself this very important question: "Who is going to hold me accountable?"

What Does It Take to Succeed as a Multifamily Investor?

Here are some of the things you'll need. And there's good news! There are people out there who will help you learn this. You'll need:

A plan: Multifamily investing takes time. You are not buying a single-family property with 2 or 3 bedrooms, fixing it up, posting it on Zillow and finding a quick renter. You must plan for income and expenses; annual budget forecasts; renovations and repairs; leasing and marketing; short and long-term financing; tax events; and exit strategies to name some.

Time: You can be successful while holding down a full-time job—but it won't be easy. Get ready to give up your evening television programs and much of your weekends.

Dedication: It will not be enough to give investing a whirl for the next couple of months. You've got to be prepared to spend the next one to three years working hard on finding deals, acquiring a property and then becoming an owner of an apartment building or other smaller multifamily property. You cannot be in a hurry and expect to succeed. That's when big mistakes occur.

Commitment: Like any successful athlete or professional you must be willing to put your trainers on and work hard every day—rain or shine. No excuses.

Money: In order to attract partners (and money) to your deals you must be able to demonstrate superior knowledge about your prospective deal. When I put my first deal together I did so only after learning how to analyze deals from experienced investors. I also hired a mentor to educate me in partnership deal structuring and operating agreements.

Your own money: Most lenders will want to see that you have "skin in the game." This means that you have invested some of your own money. They want to know that you have as much at stake as everyone else. It's also likely that your prospective partners will want to see that you have invested some of your own funds.

Set Goals that Meet Your Own Money Rules for Real Estate Investing

What's a real estate investing money rule? Money rules are non-negotiable rules or guidelines set by you specific to your investment activities and strategies. This is the criteria you apply prior to making all of your real estate investment decisions. Without deviation. Without exception.

Money rules are a personal thing. They are your rules. No two individual's rules will look alike. You will probably continue to tweak them for years to come as your investment strategies change and as you continue to learn from experience. Here are some of my top rules:

Rule #1: Remember, everything is negotiable

When presented with an investment opportunity negotiate terms that work for you rather than accept a deal as presented. Everything is negotiable—especially in real estate investing.

Rule #2: Use your own pro forma numbers in your cash flow or acquisition analysis

In this rule I define pro forma numbers as financial projections based on assumed events or circumstances. Brokers and sellers are famous for using pro forma analysis when presenting a real estate property or business for sale—and for basing the asking price on those projected numbers.

Pro forma numbers will include items such as:

- Market, rather than actual, rent on an apartment unit. For example, pro forma numbers may show higher rents upon completion of proposed renovations.
- Decreased management costs under new management.
- Higher income and lower expenses under new management.
- Utility costs if/when residents pay a portion of utilities.

These are what I call the "grass has been fertilized" numbers—numbers that can quite possibly qualify as wishful thinking. For instance, if renovations do not equal higher rents, your tenants do not end up paying for utilities, and you struggle to get expenses down and income up, then the pro forma numbers become meaningless to your cash needs. And you'll most likely discover that you paid too much for the property.

If you are buying a single-family, multifamily or apartment building property you'll want to use the current financials for the property, not the pro forma financials. Better still, use your own pro forma assumptions based on solid market research and operational know-how.

Pro forma financials and pro forma budgeting are covered in detail in Chapter 9: Deal Analysis.

Rule #3: Know your exit strategies before you make the investment

Your exit strategy is how you plan to capitalize on your investments. For instance, you:

- Renovate and sell a property.
- Refinance a property.
- Convert a property to another use such as: converting rental units to condominiums; tearing down the building and selling or redeveloping the land; or converting space to another use such as retail or office.

It is possible and advisable in most cases to have several exit strategies in place. When planning on how to capitalize on an investment use pro forma financial analysis conservatively and judiciously.

Rule #4: Diversify your portfolio

Establish what type of diversification you desire to have in your portfolio. You might target diversification as follows:

- **Short-term real estate flips:** You buy, renovate and sell the property quickly.
- **Long-term hold rental properties**: You are the landlord of a tenanted property.
- **Single assets in multiple locations:** You might invest in apartment buildings in Denver, Atlanta, and Portland.
- **Multiple assets in a single location:** You own a 4-plex, several single-family properties, a small apartment building and some self-storage facilities in a single market or its suburbs.

Having a strongly diversified portfolio will protect you from short-term fluctuations in each asset class. Establish short-term and long-term plans for your investments to include cash flow, passive income, equity growth and capitalization on your investments (how you get paid or get your money out).

One other important item to consider here is your liquidity needs. You do not want to find yourself in a situation where you badly need funds and they are tied up in a long-term hold.

Rule #5: Decide if you're going to be an active or passive investor

Do you need to feel in control of your investments? How much time do you have for hands on management of your portfolio?

I've been able to find a good balance through experience and have over time decided on what I enjoy doing. When I began investing in real estate I started with single-family properties and found it took too much of my time because of the hands-on management involved. I later moved to multifamily and apartment building properties that supported the hiring of a third-party professional management company.

Changing my investment strategy freed up my time so that I could continue to build businesses, acquire assets and to manage those assets rather than being involved in property management on a daily basis.

Rule #6: Decide what ROI is acceptable to you

What type of return on investment do you require? Are you comfortable with a 7% return? How about 10%? If a deal comes your way that does not satisfy your minimum requirements, don't do the deal.

Rule #7: Don't follow the crowd

Never invest in a property type just because everyone else is doing it.

This rule speaks for itself. It is easy to fall into the trap that if everyone is doing something it must be good. The danger here is that you are unlikely to do your own due diligence if you believe the group or crowd has already done it. And who knows? The "crowd" could be dead wrong.

Remember the handful of investors in my area who are renting out condominium quality residential units as apartment units because they came too late to the condo conversion game? A very expensive mistake you do not want to make.

Rule #8: Verify, verify, and verify some more

Always complete due diligence and inspections of financials, tenant leases, contracts, and physical properties. Obtain everything in writing. Speak to others who have experience in a particular asset class and compare notes. Ask for referrals and follow through by contacting those referred.

Run the numbers and make sure you believe they make sense. If you are not confident in running the numbers get someone on your team to do this for you and have them give you their evaluation of the deal.

Have the proper tools and know how to use them (or a team that does). These tools will include real estate investment analysis and financing spreadsheets, and commercial due diligence checklists.

Resource alert: Download and print your own due diligence checklist at theresabradleybanta.com/book_resources.

Rule #9: Take advantage of tax benefits

Prior to investing you need to clearly know what the tax implications and benefits are both on your investment and your current income. When you invest be aware of the tax implications not only for the current year but also for the following years and for the day you exit your investment.

Use a CPA or tax attorney to assist you in reviewing how your investment returns will impact your tax rate and your regular income.

Rule #10: Ask for the property financials

Create a list of all documents required by you. For example, when looking at a real estate investment ask for the trailing financials (past 12-24 months) in addition to an offering memorandum. Documents such as cash flow statements, balance sheets, profit and loss statements and pro forma analysis will assist you in understanding how an investment will perform.

Rule #11: Don't try to time the market

This is just too hard to pull off. By this I mean don't try to second-guess the timing in a market. Don't try to guess when a real estate market has reached its peak or bottom. By the time you realize a market has moved most of that movement has already taken place.

No matter how tempting, do not forgo diversification to jump into a "hot" asset class with a large portion of your investment dollars.

Rule #12: Don't invest more money than you can lose

Know your worst-case scenarios and determine if you can ride them out. Take *calculated* risks. Be sure you have an emergency fund and the proper funds for maintaining your real estate investments.

Follow your money rules religiously. Always remember, no one knows your investing psychology, goals, priorities, risk and comfort levels more than you do.

Recording your own money rules can be a fun and profitable exercise. Real estate investing rules can help you avoid doing deals you're not 100% sure about.

Chapter Four:
Build Your Team

*I measure my own success as a leader by how well the
people who work for me succeed. – Maria Shi*

~

You Need the Best People on Your Team

Most successful multifamily real estate investors all have a carefully
selected team. They realize the importance of choosing team members with
specialized knowledge and experience. When you have a team of people
working with you toward the common goal of successful real estate
investing, it improves your likelihood of profit.

It takes time to build a team. You start with recommendations from people
you trust and then see how well you get along with each person. You do
not want a team of people who will just do what you say. You want
independent thinkers who are experts at what they do. Here's why.

Diversity of opinions

As they go about their duties, your team members should be mindful of
protecting your interests. That is often accomplished by bringing things to

your attention that you would have missed without them. Each team member views your business from a different perspective. It is up to you to give careful consideration to the council from each one as you make your decisions.

Inspiration for one another

When you build a team of top professionals, there is a higher level of effectiveness and quality throughout every aspect of your business. Consider the thoughts and feelings you have when you enter a property that is meticulously maintained compared to one that allows landscaping and housekeeping to go undone.

People who already take pride in what they do operate at their best among others with a similar work ethic.

Collaboration fosters innovation

When people are working with others, they're comfortable when they think bigger than themselves. Successful people working together often come up with creative ideas related to what they are doing. These innovations help you stay ahead of the competition.

They celebrate your success

Having a large group of people happy for your success gives more meaning to your accomplishments and adds an extra level of enjoyment to the work you do each day.

They enhance the quality of your life

Some of the most miserable people in the world are CEOs of large corporations who can't get a decent night's sleep due to worrying over what one of their mid-level managers might handle poorly. When you build a team of top-quality people, you trust them to know what they are doing and always conduct themselves in a manner that reflects positively on your organization. Money is great, but that peace of mind is of considerable value, too.

Having the right team in place can boost your real estate investment success to new heights, so create a plan and find the right people!

The Best Way to Build Your Multifamily Real Estate Investing Team

Building your multifamily real estate investing team is not as hard as you may think. It's easy for beginning investors to be intimidated by the thought of hiring a great team. Not to worry. You do not have to post ads on Craig's list, conduct interviews and put someone on your payroll. You can build a great team by networking.

The first thing to do is get in action by connecting with people and specialists in the multifamily industry such as:

- Commercial real estate brokers and lenders
- Apartment building managers
- Local title company or real estate attorneys
- Multifamily mentors

You will not build a team by reading books or by poking around online. Here are some tips for finding and hiring your team:

Build your core multifamily investing team first

I built the majority of my multifamily investing team after I was in contract on an apartment building. This might surprise you. Before I was actually in contract, I was busy interviewing commercial property brokers, interviewing apartment building property management companies and touring properties.

Your real estate mentor, commercial broker and property management company are the three most important members of your team. Most of my referrals for all other prospective team members came from these three key individuals. They helped me build a team of commercial contractors, inspectors, leasing agents, on-site managers, and even other investors.

Network only within the multifamily investing industry

My single-family Realtor friends and acquaintances simply did not have a network that included contractors, renovators and other specialists who had experience working on apartment buildings. Some may, but in my experience most don't.

When you think about it, it makes sense doesn't it? In order to include multifamily investors, rehabbers, management companies and contractors within their network a Realtor would have to make a concerted effort to connect with those individuals. Most Realtors generally do not have a need to do so.

Start asking for referrals

After I found several commercial brokers who I liked and thought I could work well with, I began having conversations about who they thought were the very best specialists in town. I also asked for referrals from my property management company and from several multifamily mentors that I work with.

In a very short time, I was referred to excellent companies and individuals such as:

- **Commercial roofing companies:** My broker had three roofing company referrals for me. Each company met me at the property and gave me bids on roof repairs. Then, I used those bids to negotiate a seller credit for roof repairs. After we closed on the property, I hired one of the companies to install a new roofing system—on the seller's dime.
- **Structural engineer and real estate inspection service companies:** Always, always, always inspect your property before you buy it. Again, my broker gave me several referrals. I met each at the property while still in contract and got bids on the inspection costs for the property. Then I hired both a structural engineer and a general apartment building inspector to inspect the property. Again, this was done while in contract.
- **Concrete and asphalt repair specialists:** My mentor had three concrete repair specialist referrals for me. I met all three companies at the property and had them bid on the necessary repairs. I negotiated a seller credit for repairs on these items too. After we closed on the apartment building, I hired one of the three

81

companies to install new sidewalks and asphalt driveways. This team of contractors also helped me turn an ugly and underutilized loading only zone into a courtyard with trees, flowers and stamped concrete.

- **Other specialists:** Through my network I was able to get introductions to repair and installation contractors specializing in areas such as; carpet and tile; wood flooring; boilers; sewer; plumbing; painting; appliances; signage; and lighting and electric. All of these contractors worked out well. Today I think of these specialists as part of my team and I'm able to pass their names along to my consulting and mentoring clients where appropriate—as warm referrals!

- **General multifamily specialists such as:** Commercial title companies, 1031 exchangers and commercial lenders.

It's important to note that all of these contractors had experience in the multifamily real estate industry. Not one of these contractors came from the single-family side of real estate investing. This is important for you to know. It's extremely difficult for single-family specialists to move into the multifamily industry.

Single-family renovators and repair people have a tendency to over-renovate when working on apartment buildings. This can break your budget almost overnight. Also, they typically do not have experience with major apartment building systems such as roofs, elevators, cooling systems and boilers.

It is critical to your success that you know and understand the importance of hiring team members with experience in the multifamily arena.

Should You Hire a Commercial Broker When Buying Apartment Buildings?

Have you ever heard a single-family investor say, "I've saved thousands in commissions by cutting the Realtor out of the transaction!" But is this wise? And does this hold true in the multifamily and apartment building investment world?

With multifamily real estate investments is it really possible or advisable to cut out the "middleman?" Consider that a commercial broker can provide you with:

- a wealth of information about local markets
- warm introductions to vendors and service providers (your team!)
- diplomat services

It's always possible to find that rare property where you deal directly with a buyer or a seller. But it's important to know that networking is one of the very best ways to source potential deals. You must network to:

- find the hidden gems,
- learn the many nuances particular to submarkets, and
- build a great team.

Brokers understand their local apartment markets

A good commercial broker knows the history of the deals being done in their local markets. They know of the apartment building owners who have had success with their investments—and why. They are intimately familiar with:

- Current and historical market vacancies.
- Average rents and historical rents.
- The sizzle that rents units.
- Supply and demand.
- Which markets to avoid.

They're familiar with the popular amenities. They know if renters are looking for units with wood floors or in-unit washers and dryers. A broker will also know how many new apartment units are coming online and whether or not the market can adequately absorb the new construction.

Pro tip: Don't stop with one interview. To fully understand a submarket plan to interview a minimum of 5 commercial real estate brokers who specialize in that market. Then follow-up your market research by interviewing 2 or 3 apartment building property managers who manage properties in that submarket.

Brokers know the service providers and the vendors in the local apartment markets

Networking with local apartment brokers is your golden opportunity to obtain warm introductions to a very specialized class of contractors and vendors—those who work exclusively in the apartment industry.

Always ask for referrals. Again, your broker can provide an invaluable service by referring and recommending the following specialists:

- Apartment building inspectors and structural engineers.
- Property management companies that manage apartment buildings exclusively.
- Lenders who finance the majority of local apartment deals.
- Contractors who handle repairs and maintenance on apartment buildings. This can include roofing; concrete and asphalt; and boilers and other major building mechanicals to name a few.

Pro Tip: It is critical to know that some of your best apartment building deals may come from your personal relationships with these specialists. You must expand your connections in order to source your own deals.

A commercial broker can be an extraordinary diplomat

When you communicate with a buyer or a seller over complex issues such as negotiations, due diligence and property inspections your broker can act as the intermediary. This is especially crucial when you have delicate issues to present to a buyer or a seller. This alone can be the means by which a deal actually reaches the closing table.

Before committing to any brokerage relationship take some time to get to know the local brokers in your target markets. Here are the questions to ask—before you make a decision to hire:

Question #1: What apartment markets do you work in?

Most commercial real estate brokers specialize in specific submarkets. They do not list and market apartment buildings citywide particularly if they work in large metropolitan areas. Ask how long they have specialized in their markets of choice and why they like the markets they work in.

Question #2: What apartment submarkets should I avoid and why?

To be a successful investor you must drill down to specifics on each apartment submarket you invest in. I have seen investors purchase properties in markets that the local property managers refuse to take on. It's that important!

Question #3: What types of apartment buildings are in your favorite markets?

This question is especially important if you are new to a market. Have a discussion with your broker about the various property types in his/her markets. This will enable you to determine what you will need to do in order to be competitive. Be sure to cover:

- **Style:** What types of properties are in the market? This includes building materials and construction; average property age; and unit types such as studio, one-bedroom and two-bedroom units.
- **Condition:** Have most apartment buildings been upgraded? Is it common to find properties that may need significant upgrades and renovations?
- **Class:** Are most properties older class B or C properties? Are the properties new, recently built Class A buildings? What amenities does each class offer?

Question #4: What can you tell me about local apartment inventory?

Ask about the current supply and demand of existing rental units. For instance, is there a shadow rental market such as single-family rental housing that could negatively impact occupancies in apartment buildings?

What is happening on the construction front? A large uptick in inventory could negatively impact your property and add downward pressure on property values.

Question #5: Where is your market in terms of multifamily real estate cycles?

Have a conversation about how the local multifamily market has performed over the past ten, fifteen and twenty years. Most real estate markets go through cycles of recovery, expansion, hypersupply and recession.

What stage is your submarket in today? How will that affect your buying decision and exit strategies? How have the cycles affected your broker's clients? What do they expect to occur over the next 10 years?

Pro tip: An understanding of local market cycles is critical to your investment success. This knowledge helps you accurately place a value on properties you are buying and selling. Market cycles, and how to read them, are explained in detail in Chapter Five: Market Research.

Question #6: Can you tell me about local apartment deals that have closed?

Have a conversation with the broker about the deals they have personally closed and those deals that were closed by their competitors. Who bought or sold those properties? What were the asking prices and the final sales prices? How long was each property on the market?

Question #7: Which of your clients have done really well?

This may be one of the most critical questions you ask before you hire a commercial broker. The answers will definitely help you decide if this is the broker for you. Ask:

- When did your client buy the property?
- When did your client sell the property? Did the broker handle the sale?
- What were their investment strategies and goals, and did they meet them?
- If they have not sold the property how are they doing with leasing, operations and cash flow?

Spend some time on this topic. If your broker has only done one deal...well, then you know. If many deals, then drill down to how well their clients have done with their investments.

This is also a great time to get referrals for the vendors and service providers those clients are using. For example, which companies are they using for property management, leasing, marketing, maintenance, and renovation?

Question #8: Who is financing local apartment deals?

This is fairly self-explanatory. Your broker should be able to put you in touch with lenders who are financing deals that actually close. Ask about the rates and terms that are being offered.

Pro tip: Ask about what types of deals are not closing and why.

Question #9: Can you tell me about the current listings on the market?

This is more than likely the number one conversation your broker will want to have with you. Don't let your conversation begin and end here.

It's natural that any broker you speak with will want to let you know about their listings but notice the question isn't, "Can you tell me about your listings?" You are inquiring about all of the current listings on the market.

Who has listings out there? Are properties selling or are they languishing on the market? What does the broker know about each listing? You may be surprised to find your broker knows a great deal about many of the properties within a submarket.

Question #10: Can you provide the following submarket research?

- **Rent comparables:** This is a study of market rents. What does each type of unit command in rents within a specific submarket? Ask your broker to include concessions in their research. For example, are owners offering free rent, free utilities or reduced deposits in order to rent units?
- **Sold comparables:** This is a list of recent apartment building sales. Be sure you receive all recently sold comps not just hand-picked apartment building sales. If some properties sold below market you want to know about it.
- **Information on current listings:** What does the broker know about each property? It's history? It's location? Who bought the property? Who brokered the deal? How much is the property listed for and is the seller likely to receive that price?
- **Local multifamily market research:** Most brokerage firms offer detailed market and submarket reports. If your broker is part of a large national firm, the firm may also offer nationwide apartment market reports.

Lastly, you will want to know all of the current and historical statistics for use in property analysis such as: local capitalization rates; gross rent multipliers; operating expense ratios; and lender debt service coverage ratios.

How to Approach Multifamily Brokers When You're Just Starting Out

Calling on multifamily brokers for the first time can be an intimidating process. Sweating begins and that eye twitch starts up. Relax. Remember, you are building a team here. A team, and you are the captain of that team. Before you start picking from the lineup here are some tips you need to stay fearless. You can do this!

Know what you want

First of all, you should have some idea of what type of property you're looking for and in which specific markets. This will fuel your confidence. Don't go in blind, looking for an education. Do your research beforehand.

Your first contact with a broker will be much easier on you when you refine your general perimeters. For instance, what size multifamily building are you looking for? Are you looking to start with a small multi-unit property? Or, would you prefer a larger deal?

Where would you like to invest? An urban core? In outlying submarkets? How about rural areas? How much work are you willing (and able) to complete on a building in need of repair? Would a turnkey property be more appropriate for you?

Look for multifamily brokers who know your target market

Brokers are salespeople who market their services. Most can be found online through LoopNet, Find a CCIM (findaccim.com) or through a Google search for multifamily brokers.

In most metropolitan areas you'll find that brokers specialize within niche markets. As you search online, look for brokers who are active in your target markets. It's okay to have several markets or neighborhoods in mind.

During your online research, take a look at each brokers' bio and sales experience. Also look at their active multifamily property listings. What markets do they specialize in? What was their sales volume last year? Have they won industry related awards? What high school did they attend? What kind of dog do they own? Take notes and use this information to break the ice in your first conversation.

You are interviewing them

Now's the time to pick up the phone and make appointments. Don't get stuck on this action step; you have goals and a general idea of what you're looking for. Start there.

If you are unsure of yourself, then use sincere flattery to ease into the meeting. Get to know each other. That's the point of your initial meeting. Be genuine and curious. Here are some sample openers to break the ice:

- "You had an impressive sales record last year."
- "I lived in New Town."

- "I loved your online bio."
- "My cousin went to Evergreen High School."
- "You must know a lot about the market."
- "My aunt owns a Labrador."

Your goal is to find someone you are comfortable working with. Someone to build a long-term relationship with. In a way, your first meeting is like a first date.

Don't be afraid

Remember, brokers are salespeople and they want your business. Even if you are trembling with fear and spill coffee all over their desk you can start again. The broker may not offer you another beverage, but they will gladly accept a commission for brokering the deal. This is part of networking.

Eliminate fear but don't fake bravado. Pretending to be someone you are not is not how to start a relationship. Be your authentic self when approaching multifamily brokers. This is a win-win situation.

Be gracious

Whether or not you select a broker to be on your team is entirely up to you. Either way, each professional you speak with has given you their time, gratis. Send them a thank you note acknowledging that courtesy.

You never know how connections will pan out in the future. Through your networking, you are establishing your reputation, your brand. You cannot go wrong being gracious.

Don't sign anything . . . yet

The brokers you interview may want you to sign an exclusive deal with them. Don't sign anything right out of the gate. You are still in the interview stage.

Your team has yet to be assembled and you should not submit to any pressure tactics. Meet with at least 5 different brokers, in a single market, before agreeing to an exclusive relationship.

Experience will build your confidence. Always remember this is a win-win relationship. Long-term business relationships can be profitable to everyone on your team. Be choosy about who you let join.

Should You Hire a Property Manager or Do It Yourself?

One of the most important decisions you must make as a real estate investor is whether to hire a property manager or handle things yourself. For novice investors with a small number of units, it is possible to manage things themselves. As their business expands, however, they will need to pay for some help.

Property managers and property management companies are extremely helpful, but they do come at a price. For many real estate investors, this is something they cannot afford. Here are a few things to consider as you choose what is right for you and your business.

The duties of a property manager

Regardless of who is in charge, there are some things that must be done in the area of property management. By utilizing technology and properly setting up your rental business, you can streamline many aspects and minimize the required man-hours.

With that in mind, here are the critical tasks that are the responsibility of the property manager:

- Setting the right rental rates for the market
- Collecting and depositing monthly rents
- Marketing and advertising properties
- Interviewing potential tenants
- Dealing with maintenance workers, contractors, landscapers and other vendors
- Ensuring compliance with Fair Housing laws and other regulations

Property management company or resident manager?

Unless you live on-site or very close to all your properties, you will eventually need the services of a property manager or property management company.

For a property management company, you can expect to pay anywhere from 5 to 10 percent of your rent revenue. Most will also charge additional fees for leasing units, maintenance and repairs, renovation services, and legal and court costs.

If your properties are part of an affordable housing program, you must comply with a complicated set of government rules to continue receiving financial assistance from the government. In this situation, it is typically best to rely on the expertise of a property management company that has experience with your particular housing program.

A property manager should maximize the profitability or your investments and your time. Consider how much you will be paying them and how long it would take you to do the job yourself. The more units you have, the more likely it is that a property manager is worth the cost.

Self-Managing? Here Are Some Things You Might Want to Outsource

It is great to love what you do and to want the highest level of quality for every aspect of your real estate investing business. However, it is also important to understand that there are many other people who are passionate about their livelihood and take great pride in performing their services well.

If you really want things done right, you will sometimes use a specialist who has more knowledge and experience in an area than you do. There may also be some duties that you should outsource so you can focus your attention on other tasks. Here are some things you may want to outsource.

Things you are not good at doing

Money is often tight for new investors. It takes time to build a stable, reliable revenue stream that will cover paying someone to do many of the tasks that must be done. That limited budget also has many investors watching how-to videos on YouTube and attempting repairs or upgrades that they have never done before.

It's okay to get your hands dirty but know your limitations. A skilled contractor can complete some tasks better and quicker than you can. Your time is valuable, and the only way you can grow your business is by doing what you do best.

Things that are not an efficient use of your time

Performing and completing mundane tasks such as cleaning, landscaping, and managing necessary paperwork can be very therapeutic. It is also a good way to know your business and your renters. People appreciate a company owner who is down to earth.

However, these everyday tasks can be a sanctuary for procrastinators who are timid about tackling some of the more daunting elements of real estate investing. You will never grow and expand your business if you are spending all of your time self-managing rental property.

Things you will not do without help

For your business to operate at optimal efficiency, you need preventive maintenance. When you are trying to do everything alone, some cost-saving measures will fall by the wayside and go undone.

The decision to manage things yourself can end up costing money. Moreover, when you are so bogged down with other aspects of your business that you overlook new opportunities, you stand to lose even more money. Creativity favors a relaxed mind. You can relax and be confident that your properties are being managed properly, even when others are doing some of the work.

Outsourcing is a smart way to move forward, so do not be afraid to ask for help when you need it.

How to Find a Real Estate Investing Mentor

Most successful real estate investors had a mentor at some point. Mentors play an important role in the life and business of a novice investor. A real estate investing mentor leads by example, listens to you, and provides useful knowledge from personal experience.

That is not to say, however, that a mentor can prevent you from making your own mistakes. Mentors advise and guide you, but it is ultimately your real estate business. You succeed or fail based on your own actions. Nevertheless, a trustworthy mentor will improve your odds of success.

Finding a quality mentor

You want a mentor who is not competing against you but is active in real estate investments. Ultimately, you'll want to learn from a person who is truly passionate about real estate investing.

You can find useful information by networking with other investors in the Real Estate Investment Association (REIA). Look for and network with some of the more successful investors.

There are many people who label themselves real estate gurus and sell mentoring services, so be sure to conduct some thorough research on any program you seriously consider.

Qualifying a mentor

You have already had lots of mentors in your life. Your parents were the first ones. If you excelled at sports or displayed some musical talent, you probably had a coach or teacher who took pride in helping you achieve your potential. The best kind of mentor is someone who has a pre-existing relationship with you and the mentoring grows naturally from that.

Even if you do not have an existing relationship with an expert, you can still find trustworthy mentors. Finding a real estate investing mentor should be approached like hiring any professional: ask them for references and ask other people what they know about them. Any person worthy of being your mentor should have some people who have already received valuable guidance from them.

As a real estate investor, you need a team of trustworthy people you can rely on for honest and objective counsel. Building this team is an ongoing process, and you do not have to be in a rush to form what will be one of your most important relationships.

The Amazing Benefits of Hiring a Multifamily Real Estate Consultant

There is a lot to learn when you are starting out in multifamily housing investing. Some people choose to go at it alone, doing their own research and learning from their mistakes as they go. Others choose to learn from others' experience by hiring a multifamily real estate consultant.

Real estate investment consultants have real-world experience they pass onto clients to help them reach their own investing goals. A consultant can help guide you through the process of becoming an investor for the first time. They can also assist you in making smart financial choices when you've been investing for decades. Their services can help you avoid common pitfalls experienced by solo investors.

Is hiring a multifamily real estate consultant the right choice for you? Make sure you know all the pros and cons of hiring a consultant in the multifamily real estate industry. Understanding the benefits of their services may help you make that final decision.

They are only here to help you succeed

There are a lot of people in the real estate business who have a commission on the line. That doesn't work to your advantage in most situations. When money is at stake, those paid on commission may be unable to give you smart, impartial advice on your own options.

A consultant is different. Because there isn't a big commission on the line, they are working for you and you only. They have no vested interest in anything but your personal success. They only succeed at their job when you succeed at your real estate goals. Because of this, a consultant is a perfect person to help you strategically plan your first or next investment.

Some consultants provide services such as a SWOT analysis of your multifamily portfolio. This service can help you identify the strengths, weaknesses, opportunities, and threats of your current portfolio. Examining these areas with a knowledgeable consultant can help you develop a strategy to take your investments to the next level. This is all done with your best interests in mind, putting you in the strongest possible position for success.

You'll see more on how to conduct a SWOT analysis in Chapter Twenty-Three: Pro Tips for Success.

They shorten the learning curve on investing

Multifamily real estate investing has a long learning curve. It can take you years to fully understand the ins and outs of deal making and market research. It can take many more years to develop the best practices that reduce expenses and increase profits.

A multifamily real estate consultant can help you cut that learning time dramatically. They've been there, done that and can share their knowledge with you. They can help bring you up to speed quickly and address your most immediate concerns. Their knowledge can also help you avoid unnecessary risk, by filling you in on areas that you might not have considered.

They can also help with the practical side of real estate investment. There is a lot of paperwork involved with rental real estate, and it's imperative that it's all done correctly. That includes things like preparing and reviewing documents for partnerships, providing deal analysis, and setting up budget spreadsheets.

A consultant can also assist you in reviewing contracts or writing your investor statement of experience, aka resume, something your lender is likely to require.

They are your go-to source of information, eliminating the need to dig for unreliable documents on the internet. With their help, you don't end up reinventing the wheel on your way to real estate success.

They inspire action towards your goals

Some investors find they couldn't build their portfolio as well without the help of a consultant. Consultants are like your own personal real estate cheerleader. They can inspire confidence in your investment abilities and help drive you towards action and commitment.

The best real estate consultants don't blindly cheer you on, though. They also challenge you. A consultant should be your best champion, but also the person who drives you to take calculated chances for bigger successes.

Investment consultants will ask you to examine your assumptions and biases. Then they will guide you to the right choices based on their own real-world experience. A real estate investment consultant will ask tough questions about prospective multifamily acquisitions. Those tough questions along with your honest answers will help you make choices that move you towards meeting your goals.

Whether you are a first-time investor or an investor with decades of experience under your belt, hiring a multifamily real estate consultant can be a smart move. They can help you identify ways to strengthen your portfolio and increase your profitability. A consultant can take an impartial look at your portfolio and help you decide where to go next.

The Pros and Cons of Hiring a Multifamily Investing Mentor or Consultant

So how do you get started with a consultant or mentor? When it comes to paid multifamily real estate investing education there is no "one size fits all" solution.

Here are your options:

- Home study courses and/or multi-day in-person seminars
- Multifamily mentoring programs
- Professional real estate investment consulting

Let's look at the pros and cons of each.

Home study multifamily real estate investing courses and multi-day seminars

Home study: Apartment investing home study courses usually consist of a workbook with several instructional CDs. There is no interaction between you and the instructor. You read, listen and take notes. The course may well be one you purchase online or at a multi-day seminar.

Live seminars: Multi-day investment seminars are usually more dynamic with time for questions and answers.

Both home study courses and live seminars are geared toward the general real estate investing public.

The pros:

- Gives you a good fundamental education—with a warning. The education is only as good as the source.
- Can raise your excitement level.
- The information is usually easily referenced.
- You receive a well-rounded overview of many of the basic elements of multifamily real estate investing.
- The excitement of other new investors can be contagious.

The cons:

- Home study and in-person seminars are not likely to get you into action.
- Often only the very basics are covered.
- The education is not geared to your specific goals, market, deal or due diligence.
- The platform could be an upsell to a second- or third-tier program without which you've only received a portion of the education necessary to your success.
- Can keep you in analysis paralysis indefinitely.

Once you close on a multifamily property, you own it. After you've signed the contract it's too late to discover that you:

- Paid too much for the property
- Bought a property that experienced investors would not buy
- Don't know how to operate the property

- Do not have the right team, or skills, to make the property profitable

In order to accurately evaluate a deal, first-time multifamily investors must rely on the advice of more experienced investors. When you hire a multifamily investing mentor or consultant you will be certain that you've made a wise investment.

The differences and similarities between multifamily real estate investing mentors and consultants

A good multifamily investing mentor can also act as a paid real estate investing consultant on a fixed fee or hourly basis. For example, you can hire a consultant to help you look at a specific deal.

Your mentor or consultant should have knowledge in managing multifamily properties; market analysis; negotiating the purchase and sale of investment properties; renovating and upgrading rental properties; and financing deals.

Pro tip: Not all mentors are experienced consultants and would prefer that their students or clients enroll in their pre-designed mentoring programs. Most pre-designed mentoring programs will walk you through the elements of finding, acquiring and managing properties.

Multifamily real estate investing mentoring programs

The pros:

- You'll gain education specific to your goals and strategies.
- Gets you off the sidelines and into action.
- You can save tens of thousands of investment dollars through strategic negotiation and deal structuring. Often this will cover the cost of the mentorship program.
- You'll receive warm leads and referrals so you can start building your team.
- You're not a lone ranger. A mentor has a large resource base with expertise in multifamily investing, finance, management, and renovations.
- A mentor can instill confidence and remove fear.
- A mentor knows what you don't even know you don't know.
- You will accelerate your performance by following a proven leader.
- Having an experienced mentor on your side can prove your credibility with lenders, brokers and sellers.

The cons:

- If you are an experienced real estate investor a formal mentoring program could duplicate some of the information you already know.

Multifamily real estate investing consulting

The pros:
- You can decide if real estate investing is right for you before you commit to high-priced programs.
- You can hire a consultant to help you analyze a specific deal; conduct due diligence on a specific property; put a partnership together; review contracts and financing terms; and conduct multifamily market analysis.
- By hiring a consultant, you will establish your credibility with multifamily lenders, sellers, brokers and managers.

The cons:

- If you're light on real estate investing experience consulting may be too specific or tactic focused.

Ask about their personal experience as an investor in apartment buildings. They should have expertise as both a buyer and a seller of investment properties. In other words, they should have ample experience on both sides of the investing deal making table. An investor who has bought and sold their own investment properties has a better understanding of investment exit strategies.

My recommendations

Much depends on you. Real estate investing is a business. The very first thing you must do is decide if this is the business for you. Some of the new investors with whom I consult decide not to invest.

Decide whether or not real estate investing is right for you before you take the plunge and invest a significant amount of your time and money. Take some time and talk with experienced investors.

Be cautious. You want to be certain that the person you're talking to doesn't have a vested interest in whether you proceed or not. Someone who is filling seminar rooms and hosting late night real estate infomercials might not be the best person to talk to. Also be cautious when speaking with experienced investors. They may not be forthcoming about the less successful deals they've done. Or about their near misses.

- If you are new to residential rental property investing, I recommend that you enroll in a full mentoring program.
- If you are a seasoned investor in rental properties, consider hiring a consultant.

For the new real estate investor

Read a multifamily investing book or two. Speak to someone who already owns multifamily properties to help you determine if real estate investing is feasible for you. Some of the beginning real estate investors I speak to are surprised to hear how much time is involved. Others believe they can easily buy an apartment building with no money down.

Many of the so-called real estate "gurus" suggest that you will not be managing your own property—that may or may not be true. It depends on the profitability and size of the property. A small property might not generate enough cash flow to pay you *and* pay a property manager.

Hire a mentor who will work with you throughout your investing career—a mentor who will be available to you after you purchase your first multifamily property.

Consider partnering on a deal. Get your feet wet first. You might be able to partner on a deal for an investment as little as $20,000-50,000.

The bottom line: Get the best education you can before you jump into multifamily real estate investing. Hiring a multifamily investing mentor will pay dividends for years to come.

For the real estate investor with experience in single-family rentals

A static and pre-determined mentoring program might not be for you. You'll want a program with some fluidity so that you're not spending time studying what you already know. An experienced mentor/consultant should be able to tailor a program that covers less time and less material—and costs you less money.

But also be clear that investing in single-family rentals is not the same as investing in multifamily properties. You are moving into a completely different world when you start buying multifamily properties and apartment buildings. Having the right education in a particular real estate niche is critical to your success.

And there's good news! You definitely have an advantage over the beginner real estate investor. You possess a degree of sophistication with property investing. You already know how to negotiate. You know how to network.

You know how to build a team. You know how to raise money. You're not afraid to make an offer—at least on smaller deals.

I would start by hiring a mentor/consultant to discuss your past experience to determine what you already know. Where is your expertise? Are you great at negotiating deals? Do you know how to study real estate markets? If so, researching multifamily markets will be easier for you than it will be for a beginner.

Pro tip: Hiring a multifamily mentor who can offer a tailored program around your strengths can get you to property ownership quickly.

Should You Be an Active or Passive Real Estate Investor?

"Should I be an active or passive real estate investor?" This question is the first and most important question you must ask yourself. When I work with my clients I ask:

- How much time and energy do you want to commit to your investments?
- Are you willing to commit to the education required to become an active investor?

If you're a new real estate investor you must decide if you want to experience the process of investing or turn it entirely over to someone else. For example, you will have little say in the management, operations and sale of an investment property when you invest in a Real Estate Investment Trust (REIT)—a passive investment.

When you invest in someone else's deal you are usually a passive investor. When you directly buy an apartment building or single-family rental you are making an active investment. You are the investor in charge of making all decisions that affect the property.

Residential real estate investing can be a tremendously rewarding experience. The financial rewards can be many. And you have an opportunity to positively impact the lives of others by providing a safe and secure place to live. You can start by making some personal decisions. Ask yourself:

- Do I want to be an active investor?
- Do I have a strong desire to take a leadership role?
- How much control do I want over my investments?
- How much time am I willing to spend?

You must also assess your aversion to risk. You'll read more on how to deal with risk in Chapter Eight: Accepting and Managing Risk.

Your first step

Before you make a real estate investment decision, decide whether you want to be an active or passive real estate investor. If you haven't decided on the active vs. passive question you will have no idea what your investment strategies will be.

If you don't know which route you want to take, you could become prey to less scrupulous investors looking for money. Lack of education can set you up to jump at every opportunity that presents itself. Or you can easily become discouraged.

111

In real estate the more active leadership role an investor takes, the better their returns. And sometimes, the greater the risk. When you invest in education then you are in a place to take an active rather than passive role.

Can you be both an active and passive real estate investor?

The answer is yes.

A good strategic mix of both passive and active investments can pay dividends for many years to come. A mix can also put less demand on you in terms of personal time and energy spent managing those assets.

I work with people at all levels—from the new investor buying a first real estate investment property such as a single-family rental or a duplex to investors who want to jump straight into a larger property such as an apartment building. Both are great strategies. Investment real estate can be leveraged over time into larger properties or by taking the profits and reinvesting into other asset classes.

I also work with investors who start their investment career as a partner in other investor's deals. They start by taking a passive role. It's a great way to learn the ropes from the inside.

What are the benefits of active vs. passive investing?

A benefit of passive investments, such as a REIT, is that you can invest in asset classes in which you might not otherwise have an opportunity to invest. This might include shopping malls, office buildings and hotels. You are also able to sell your share of the REIT—REIT shares are more liquid than real estate.

With a REIT you don't actually own real estate. You receive dividends and the benefits of appreciation (if any). A REIT is a paper asset, an interest in a security—similar to investing in the stock market. You also don't have the headaches of managing those properties yourself.

With education comes the courage to take bigger steps and to move into a more active role in real estate investing. With direct ownership an active investor has a greater opportunity to build wealth when done with the proper education.

With direct investing, where you personally buy and own a property, you can realize higher returns in the form of cash flow and appreciation, as well as principle pay down and depreciation (CATP!). However, you often must try to time the market before executing your exit strategies. It's all about how much control you desire and how much risk you're willing to accept.

How important is diversification?

Building a solid real estate investment portfolio over many years is a smart strategy. Most successful investors invest in a variety of asset classes. It's a good strategy for strengthening your risk profile.

It's possible to diversify within a single investment category. For example, real estate offers many assets classes such as single-family rentals, apartment buildings, mobile homes, storage units, retail store fronts, etc. Successful investors don't invest in real estate based on whims.

The diversification of these assets and the amount that you allocate is a personal decision. But you've got to be careful not to diversify for the sake of diversification. It's smart not to put all your eggs in one basket but at the same time you do not want to chase 50 small investments and lose control over all of all them just for the sake of having a "diversified" portfolio. It's to the new investors advantage to carefully invest in assets that give positive returns.

Chapter Five:
Market Research

Research is formalized curiosity. It is poking and prying with a purpose. – Zora Neale Hurston

~

Nine Multifamily Market Trends You Can't Ignore

In order to find the great multifamily investment markets, you'll need to start with some basic market research. Multifamily real estate should be a calculated investment combined with long-term vision.

Multifamily market neighborhoods and resident quality

In New York City, the Department of Consumer Affairs released a report on the ways neighborhoods influence residents' financial health. It states that grocery stores, financial services businesses, childcare, and affordable housing have a direct and significant impact, both adverse and beneficial, on a neighborhood's financial health.

There needs to be a balance for a market to perform over the long-term. Neighborhood trends and resident quality directly reflect that balance. So, how do you decide which geographic location has the best neighborhoods?

Following are the 9 market trends you cannot afford to ignore when investing in multifamily properties.

Pro tip: Commit these metrics to memory!

Trend #1: Steady employment growth

Look for a strong, growing market for employment. Companies and factories moving into an area is a good sign. Steady job growth will spur migration to the area and demand for multifamily real estate will increase. This will also have a positive impact on rental rate growth.

Trend #2: Well diversified employment

A high demand for workers increases an area's desirability. Look for a market that has more than one industry tied to its prosperity.

A mix of offices, factories and cultural attractions will ensure that an area has diverse, sustainable employment options. Do your homework.

Trend #3: Solid population growth

An increasing population in a target area is ideal. A decreasing or stagnant population trend is not favorable. Look at population growth trends for the past decade. It's especially relevant to determine what factors are driving population growth. Are new people moving to the area?

A growing population might also mean that people with stable wages have begun to have families. Some great places to find detailed information are census.gov, bestplaces.net, City-Data.com, and JLL's City Research Center (us.jll.com).

Trend #4: Proximity to employment centers

Urban growth is thriving, and people want to be able to walk, bike or have a short commute to work. The value of an easy journey to work cannot be over emphasized. Your prospective residents are looking for housing that is near their jobs.

Trend #5: Proximity to transportation

Good roads, train stations, bus lines and other mass transit are important to the growth of a community. Choose a multifamily market that is well situated along public transportation routes. Consider the walkability factor to bus routes and train stations. An isolated neighborhood is not favorable.

Trend #6: Low crime rate

Safety is also of paramount importance to renters. Young families will relocate and find multifamily properties that emphasize a safe environment. You can visit the local police station and get a premise history on specific properties within a multifamily market.

In addition, take a walk in the neighborhood. Look for vacant lots and buildings where crime might be conducted. Is there graffiti on buildings or trash in the streets? What is the overall quality of the street space?

Trend #7: Good schools

The quality of local childcare and schools are the determining factor for parents moving in or out of a neighborhood. Parents want their children attending above average schools. The end result is that the quality of a school means either long-term tenants or high turnover in your multifamily building.

Trend #8: Attractive, nearby retail

Convenient grocery stores, restaurants, and shops are important to a growing community. This is where community ties and daily family memories are made. A strong multifamily market will include a variety of retail shops and name brand chains. Access to basic shopping needs will determine the quality of your neighborhood.

Aesthetic beauty in and around the neighborhood also has an impact on the residents in the area and how they perceive the quality of their environment.

Trend #9: Cultural attractions and activities

Cultural attractions will draw not only local residents, but tourists from other communities as well. Museums, sports centers, arenas, parks, theaters, festivals and a range of restaurants are important to a market's vitality and growth. Public access along transportation routes to these activities should be factored in.

Five Exceptional Steps to Exploring Multifamily Markets

*"Twenty years from now, you will be more disappointed by
the things that you didn't do than by the ones you did do,
so throw off the bowlines, sail away from safe harbor, catch
the trade winds in your sails. Explore, Dream, Discover."*

—*Mark Twain*

You've always wanted to get involved in real estate investing, specifically in multifamily markets. Unfortunately, you may not know where to get started. Many people struggle, not with the process itself, but with deciding where and how they want to get that start.

Are you ready to dive in and get started investing in the multifamily real estate market? Here are some exceptional steps to checking out new markets.

Step #1: Get out in the streets

Sitting behind your computer screen sounds like the easy way out. After all, it's a great way to get a look at potential multifamily markets, research neighborhoods, and learn more about what you're doing. Research is great. Online property listing services like LoopNet certainly have their place. But just sitting at your computer is a good way to make costly mistakes.

From behind your computer, you will never really understand the multifamily real estate market at a local level. You'll miss what the competition is offering and who the local renters really are–and that means

119

you can't develop a solid investment plan or develop strategies that will help you succeed!

Instead, get out there. Go exploring. Visit actual local multifamily markets and neighborhoods. You'll learn so much more by checking out the market this way than you would just researching it online. This simple step can prevent you from spending a ton of money on things that won't generate the types of returns you need.

Step #2: Talk to multifamily brokers and property managers

A lot of investors are embarrassed the first time they speak with a multifamily broker or property manager. They're afraid they don't have the right knowledge, the right skills, or the right connections.

When you start checking out a new market, however, you need to talk to brokers and property managers in the area. It won't take you long to get over the embarrassment, and you'll learn a ton in the process.

Keep networking. Keep getting to know people. Remember, you're interviewing them. Get to know them and what they know. This can help you make the key decision between a great investment for you and a poor one.

Pro tip: Refer to the interview questions for hiring commercial real estate brokers in Chapter Four: Build Your Team.

Step #3: Learn the multifamily market industry jargon

Learn key talking points for evaluating properties and markets at a local level and the language used by professionals and renters alike. When you explore multifamily markets make sure your research includes:

- Average price per door
- Typical unit mix (1,2,3 bed)
- Rental amounts for each unit type
- Local demographics and natural market renters
- Local market cap rates
- Average rent per square foot
- Local in-demand amenities

Knowing all of this allows you to make an informed offer on a prospective acquisition. It's how you quickly tell a bad deal from a good one and an unrealistic seller from a realistic seller. For example, you'll spot an unrealistic seller when he wants $20,000 per door in a market where comparable properties list for $12,000 per door.

When you know the language, you can approach a deal with a little bit of swagger in your step: confident that you know what you're talking about and have the power to negotiate.

Step #4: Talk to local merchants and cops

Local police departments and merchants will be able to give you a very realistic picture of what it will be like to invest in this specific neighborhood. Merchants and cops know whether they work in a good neighborhood or a bad one–and they'll be able to share that information with you.

These individuals may also be able to point out local building styles and key pieces of information about the local amenities, which may shape the way you approach your building in the future. Merchants and cops also have a feeling for when neighborhoods are starting to deteriorate and what you, as a property investor, might need to watch out for, which will help you make better overall investment decisions.

Step #5: Visit the asset in person

See it with your own eyes. Touch it with your own hands. Walk through the halls and get a feel for it. You aren't investing in paper! When you invest in a multifamily dwelling, you're investing in a real property that you get to control and manage.

Drive by, walk by, and even tour properties you're interested in buying. Picture yourself owning them. Get a real, genuine feel for what the property looks like, what kind of maintenance it's going to take, and who already lives there. This simple step can go a long way toward allowing you to imagine yourself owning the property–and help you decide what you really want.

I have some great tips on how to tour an apartment building in Chapter Six: Finding Deals. You'll be touring properties like a pro.

Best Cities to Buy Apartment Buildings: Free Apartment Market Reports

When investigating real estate investment markets, it's important to start your research at the macro level by studying the national and regional markets. This will give you a solid baseline for comparison between regions and markets. Armed with that data you'll be able to knowledgeably drill down to specific data for individual metro areas and cities. In other words, a broad overview will help you see how each metro and city might perform in comparison to other areas.

Metro area data covers:

- Apartment investment market conditions and overviews
- Employment and payroll forecasts
- Construction forecasts: New development figures and absorption expectations
- Apartment rental vacancy forecasts: Including historical figures
- Apartment rent forecasts: Asking and effective rents
- Investment forecasts
- Sales trends
- Market cycles

Free national and metro apartment market investment reports

Integra Realty Resources (irr.com) publishes their IRR-Viewpoint annually. This includes an overview of:

- National real estate
- Capital markets
- Investment criteria: Market cycle phases and capitalization rates

Pro tip: While there you can also download the IRR-Viewpoint for each year of the past decade. If you are considering a particular market it would be very wise of you to look at how that market has performed historically.

Commercial brokerage firm Marcus & Millichap (marcusmillichap.com) has an annual multifamily investment forecast. This report offers both a national perspective and local market overviews. Their reports cover the:

- National economy
- National apartment overview
- Capital markets
- Apartment investment outlook

I highly recommend you download and read both the IRR Viewpoint and the annual Marcus and Millichap reports. All of these reports offer apartment market data on a national and local level and will help you narrow down your search for the best apartment and multifamily investing markets.

Pro tip: Once you determine which city you will invest in be sure to study the specific submarkets and neighborhoods within that city.

The Four Phases of the Multifamily Market Cycle

Investing in multifamily real estate is a process and over time, you learn how to gauge multifamily market cycles. When should you pick up a property to fix and flip? When should you renovate and sell? When should you refinance and hold on to a property, if needed?

It's imperative that you become familiar with the real estate cycles in your existing and target multifamily markets. Is the market moving out of recession and into recovery, or is it moving from expansion into hypersupply? It's possible to invest successfully across all phases of the market cycle, but better understanding of multifamily market cycles can help you make more effective investment decisions. This knowledge helps ensure that you don't make the wrong investment at the wrong time.

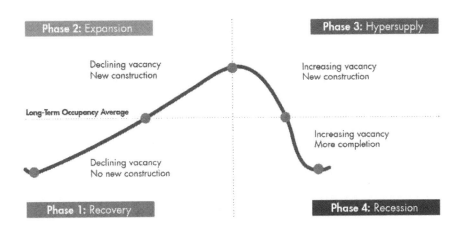

Multifamily-Market-Cycles-Quadrant Source: Glenn Mueller, PhD – https://daniels.du.edu/burns-school

Phase One: Recovery

During the recovery phase, there is no new construction. Vacancy rates in the area are slowly declining: the average multifamily property has a steady stream of renters but may have trouble keeping all of the units full. There are several signs your property is in a recovery market:

There is negative or flat rent growth. Rent growth remains at or equal to inflation rates, rather than increasing substantially.

Companies have just started hiring. Companies in the area are starting to slowly bring in new employees, which will in turn create a higher demand for housing. There's solid employment growth in the area, which means that people moving into the area won't have too much trouble finding jobs–and those jobs may also bring new people.

In the recovery phase, it's a cash buyer's heaven. Sellers are getting positioned to sell. This is a great time for strategic value-add for experienced operators, especially if you're able to hold the property until the expansion period. Cash is king during this stage, because it may be tough to get financing. You may have high carrying costs in the interim due to high vacancies, but you may also be able to buy more quickly and easily, and for a better deal than you would during other periods.

Phase Two: Expansion

During the expansion phase, the area is expanding and growing. You'll see several key signs:

Declining vacancy rates. There are fewer open apartments and other multifamily rentals in the area. Many apartment buildings may find it easy to keep renters in their apartments.

Rent increases. The market is reaching peak efficiency for owners. Rising rents are designed to support new construction and redevelopment of existing properties. Other owners may decide this is the ideal time to make those key renovations, and there's an upward pressure on rents as new construction pops up.

Unemployment in the area declines. Local employers have more openings, and fewer people in the area struggle with unemployment. People who lose their jobs have little trouble stepping into a new open position.

The expansion phase is both a seller's market and a buyer's market: sellers will benefit from selling at higher rates than the recovery period, while buyers will appreciate being able to snap up multifamily dwellings that are more likely to rent.

This is also an excellent time for value-add strategies that will help increase the value of your properties and raise rents. During the expansion phase, buyers are still banking on rental growth, which means they may overpay for an asset; however, stable properties and a stable community makes this an ideal time for development.

Phase Three: Hypersupply

The next phase in the multifamily market cycle is hypersupply: a period when the market is oversupplied with rental properties. New construction is still feasible, but the area is moving towards overbuilt. Look for these signs that your market is entering hypersupply:

Vacancies are increasing. It may be harder to find renters for properties, especially those with higher rents or less desirable areas. Properties will remain vacant longer.

There is declining rent growth. The price of rent may continue to grow, but it won't grow as fast as it did in the other phases.

New construction isn't being absorbed. Instead of new buildings filling quickly, they may take longer to absorb into the market. New properties may sit empty longer. The supply is increasing, making it a renter's market, rather than a landlord's market.

During the hypersupply period, it's a seller's market. Many people are looking to get out before the previous high values of the properties begin to fall. During this phase, savvy landlords start thinking hard about tenant retention and how to keep their existing tenants, rather than focusing on how to bring in new ones.

Phase Four: Recession

The market for rental properties is saturated, with supply outweighing demand. Are you worried that you may be looking at a property in an area during a recession period? These signposts in multifamily market cycles will put you on alert:

Construction stops. New product is still being delivered as former projects are finished, but no new construction is started in the area.

Vacancies increase. In many cases, they may fall below the long-term, 30-year average because of the high rate of available properties. Renters have their choice of properties, and they may look into new options if they aren't satisfied with their current lease.

There is negative rent growth. Rental rates grow slower than the current inflation rate. Interest rates, on the other hand, are on their way up. The recession market is a buyer's market, especially for distressed properties. This makes it an excellent time for people with cash reserves to renovate, reposition, and hold properties until the expansion phase.

Research Multifamily Market Cycles

IRR's annual Viewpoint publication shows the market cycle positions of major US cities for each asset class dating back to 1995. We encourage you to explore historical multifamily market cycles with this valuable tool. The Real Estate Market Cycle Report (daniels.du.edu/burns-school), compiled by Glenn Mueller, PhD, provides analysis of MSAs across 5 property types. Scroll to the bottom of the page to find their quarterly analysis.

I'll always look up a property on Google Street View, you never know what you'll see. But nothing beats actually getting out in the streets and doing your own research. I'll probably be saying this until the cows come home.

Opportunity Zones: Look Before You Leap

Multifamily investors are hearing a lot of hype around the Qualified Opportunity Zones (QOZ). Created by the 2017 Tax Cuts and Job Act, the program started as a way to encourage investments within economically depressed areas. The government, in turn, gives investors a deferment and reduction on capital gains taxes. The longer the investment stays in place, the bigger the tax break.

While there may a lot of interest in potential tax savings that come with these investments, there is a lot of uncertainty, as well. Investors have questions about whether QOZ investing is the right addition to their portfolio. There is also some concern about whether the program really benefits the areas it's hoping to help. So should you consider adding a multifamily property within a QOZ to your portfolio?

The challenges of investing in a QOZ

There are a few challenges that come with investing in areas identified as Qualified Opportunity Zones. First, the zones are largely located in Class C and D markets. These are properties that are usually 20 to 40 years old and located in low-income or economically disadvantaged neighborhoods. That means you'll be looking at a lower rental rate than you would get from other areas. It may take a significant amount of capital to get the building fixed up to the point you'll see any kind of ROI.

Managing a property in Class C and D markets can be operationally challenging, too. It's a good idea to have experience in these markets or to partner with someone who has.

The second challenge comes with finding a property in the first place. There isn't going to be a lot of low-hanging fruit in areas identified as opportunity zones. There is a big demand for these properties. You can see which areas around the country are designated as a Qualified Opportunity Zone on the CDFI Fund website.

You don't want to pick the first property you find in a QOZ, either. You'll need to find one that meets your specific investment criteria. That means finding a property matching your criteria for market class, style, demographics, ROI, and ease of operation.

What are the tax implications of a QOZ investment?

At face value, the tax breaks offered by a QOZ investment are pretty tempting. Investors must reinvest their capital gain, the profit they make off of the sale or investment in a property, in a QOZ within 180 days. At that point they can defer any taxes due on those capital gains until 2027. If the investment remains in the QOZ for five years, they get a 10% break on their capital gains tax bill. If they hold the investment for seven or more years, it's a 15% reduction on their capital gains tax. The Tax Foundation has a helpful guide and charted examples of potential tax savings under the QOZ program.

However, there is still a lot of uncertainty about the tax plan. There are a lot of open questions pending guidance from the Treasury Department and IRS, many of which you can read about online. If you decide to invest in a QOZ, make sure you have a CPA on board who knows as much as possible about the program. Ask them about other tax deferral strategies available, too, such as a 1031 exchange. This allows you to take the capital gain from one property and reinvest it in new property without paying capital gains taxes. They can help you decide which options are right for you and your specific portfolio.

Are there any downsides to QOZ investing?

There is some disagreement about whether the QOZ tax plan is helping do what it set out to do. The idea was to encourage investment in economically depressed and disadvantaged neighborhoods. Only a little over 60% of the investment needs to in the QOZ to qualify for the tax breaks. That means the investments could be significantly less than anticipated.

There is the issue of gentrification as well. As neighborhoods improve, they could force out those who can't afford to stay as rental rates start to climb. The cash infusion may not be helping the current residents, either, but instead bringing in new residents to the "up and coming" area. That's simply redistributing the economy instead of spurring on growth.

Andrea Riquier writes for Market Watch, "While the opportunities the program represents are clear to some participants, analysts and advocates around the country say there are very real questions about how effective it may be as a tool to broaden housing access and spur economic development, or whether it may, in fact, be detrimental to the needy communities it sets out to serve."

Looking for guidance on QOZ and other investment strategies?

So who should take advantage of Qualified Opportunity Zones and the tax breaks within? Are these purely for institutional investors or can the everyday investor benefit as well? QOZ properties could be a great addition to a multifamily portfolio. But the key is knowing which properties are right for your specific situation.

Not everyone has the experience needed to invest in these specific areas. And not everyone will be able to benefit from the tax breaks. The key is to work with an experienced team who can help guide you in this decision, including a qualified CPA.

How (and Why!) You Should Track the Multifamily Real Estate Market

Sir Francis Bacon coined the term "Knowledge is power" over 400 years ago. It's as true today as it was back then, especially when it comes to the multifamily real estate market.

Whether you are a developer, owner-operator or investor in multifamily properties, it's essential to keep up with the market both in your local area as well as across the country. This will help you maximize your investment and stay ahead of competition in the market.

Anticipate problems before they start

Staying informed about problems that other multifamily property owners are facing can give you a chance to assess your own property for similar issues. For instance, many property owners are experiencing issues with tenants subletting space in their rentals on sites like Airbnb.com. This could put owners and operators at risk of being liable for anything that happens on the property. That's a big issue, but one that you might not have anticipated beforehand. Knowing that others are dealing with this problem can help you proactively create clauses in your rental and lease agreements to avoid those same issues.

Know what your competition is up to

You need to know what your competition is doing. Industry newsletters, reports on local news stations, and local papers can help you stay up to date on what's happening with the market.

When you know what the competition is up to, you can create a strategy to protect your investment. Someone could be planning a new multifamily property development near your own, meaning you'll need to act quickly to attract and retain residents.

Likewise, you need to know what the competition is offering so you can stay competitive. A lot of multifamily sites now offer package delivery spaces. It's an in-demand trend and one you should be paying attention to. Knowing that your competition is offering it early on gives you time to consider investing in an Amazon locker service or possibly repurposing space in your lobby.

Stay up to date on legal changes that could affect you

You don't want to get caught out by changes to local and national legislation that has a negative impact on your investment properties. Knowing what local authorities are proposing can help you evaluate their potential negative or positive effect.

Staying informed can help you organize action protesting negative changes and potentially proposing alternative measure instead. For instance, many local authorities are introducing bills that could significantly impact the rental industry. In Colorado there are proposals to regulate tenant application fees, reduce the use of criminal background checks in screening tenants, and allow tenants more time to cure a lease violation.

This could end up capping the potential income from your property and tying your hands when it comes to cash flow and new investments. It's better to know that a proposal is on the table than to hear about it after the measure it passed.

Gain knowledge about when to buy and sell

Are you purchasing your first multifamily property investment? Are you ready to add another one to your portfolio? In either case, you need to know when and where to buy. Likewise, no investment is good unless you know when to sell it.

Staying informed about market trends can help you maximize your investment dollars. Developing your knowledge about the market can help you identify the next hot market as well as the optimal time to walk away from current developments.

Find out what people want (and what they'll pay)

Do you know what your residents want? Sometimes a relatively small investment in a trendy amenity can help maximize the market value of your property. But you have to know what those hot amenities are and what your residents will be willing to pay for them. This is where staying informed can pay off big.

Stay up to date on what amenities people want and what the hottest properties are offering. It may be something big like a business center or something as small and simple as a space for a trendy millennial game like cornhole. Finding out what people want in their rental property can help you get more from your investment dollars.

How to Efficiently Keep Up with the Multifamily Real Estate Market

Create Google alerts for key terms: Let Google news know what you want to stay up to date on and it will do the rest. Consider adding alerts for terms like "rental market + your town name" or "multifamily real estate market." Any news articles containing those terms will come right to your inbox.

Network with others in the real estate industry: Real estate brokers, builders, property managers are all a wealth of information. Take time to talk to them and get the benefit of their knowledge about what's happening both in your area and at the national level. You can network in person or through social media channels.

Subscribe to industry magazines and your local paper: Whether you read them online or get them delivered to your door, these are valuable resources to multifamily real estate insiders. I mentioned two of my favorite magazines in Chapter Three: Apartment Finance Today (multifamilyexecutive.com) and Multi-Housing News (multihousingnews.com), both are free and packed with industry news. Your local paper will have information on legislation, building projects, and housing market news as well.

Chapter Six:
Finding Deals

When people ask us how long does it take for something to manifest, we say, "It takes as long as it takes you to release the resistance. Could be 30 years, could be 40 years, could be 50 years, could be a week. Could be tomorrow afternoon." – Abraham-Hicks

~

How to Stay Focused When Looking for Investment Property

Babe Ruth said, "I swing big, with everything I've got. I hit big or I miss big."

Michael Jordon famously said, "I've missed over 9,000 shots in my career. I've lost almost 300 games. Twenty-six times I've been trusted to take the game-winning shot and missed. I've failed over and over and over again in my life. And that is why I succeed." He also said, "I can accept failure. Everyone fails at something. But I can't accept not trying."

Real estate investing means you will make a lot of offers that do not get accepted. Those swings and misses take time and effort, and they can be exhausting. It is easy to get frustrated and discouraged when looking for investment property.

Don't get emotionally involved

Real estate investing is a business. The numbers do not lie. When you have a passion for real estate, it can work for you or against you. Don't try to make the market what you want it to be. Find enjoyment in the process of searching for an investment property, even if you are not finding properties that meet your criteria as quickly as you would like.

Remember that some of the most valuable things in this world are rare. Not every available property will deliver a good return on your investment. If it were that easy, everyone would be doing it. You must put in the necessary time to learn the difference between a quality investment property and one that is not worthwhile. Always do your due diligence and make decisions from a financial perspective, not what you want to see.

Focus on the future

Bill Gates identifies why many people do not achieve their goals:

> *"Most people overestimate what they can do in one year and underestimate what they can do in ten years."*

This is why people don't stay with a healthy eating plan or exercise routine. Instead of being in it for the long haul and taking the necessary steps in the right direction, people want to believe they can work really hard for six months or a year to achieve their goals and then not have to work anymore.

All successful people have a vision.

Regardless of the slow markets or difficulties you may encounter in the short term, you can look forward to the future with confidence when you stick with the principles of investing that have been proven to work. You will make some missteps in real estate investing, but don't let them take your focus away from your long-term goals. Remember what you have accomplished and use both positive and negative experiences to become a better investor.

How to Use Multifamily Property Listing Services to Your Advantage

A new multifamily investor recently asked me, "Is LoopNet a good source for finding properties?"

"It's unlikely" would be the short answer. Yet CityFeet, LoopNet and other online listing services such as CoStar (whose acquisition of LoopNet was complete in April 2012) are the first stop for many new multifamily investors.

This may not come as a surprise to you but finding a great, never-before-seen deal on LoopNet will most likely never happen for a number of reasons.

- The property has already been "shopped around"—the listing broker's contacts have already had an early look.
- The property is, in all likelihood, overpriced or problematic.

Now for the good news

There are many ways to use multifamily property listing services like LoopNet to your advantage—especially if you are a new investor looking to buy multifamily properties or apartment buildings.

These sites are also a valuable resource for taking a look at new and unfamiliar markets.

How to utilize LoopNet and other major multifamily property listing services:

- Find a broker.
- Study average cap rates (with caveat below).
- Determine average price per door (with caveat below).
- Learn about property types, conditions, market sizzle and amenities.
- Practice analyzing multifamily deals.
- Sell a property.
- Find a multifamily commercial broker

Online commercial real estate listing services are an incredible source for finding active, experienced commercial brokers in your market.

If you're seriously considering a market as a potential investment area you definitely want to talk with at least three or four brokers who specialize in that market.

Visit sites like LoopNet to find commercial brokers who have listings in your market. Call them up or send them an e-mail and let them know of your interest in properties in their area. Start building relationships. And when you speak with them, don't forget to use the interview questions in Chapter Three.

Get a feel for average market cap rates, GRM and price per door

One of my biggest observations about online listing services is that properties are generally overpriced. Asking prices are frequently based on proforma financials that support inflated offering prices. As a result, cap rates, GRM (gross rent multiplier) and price/unit are also grossly exaggerated.

Nevertheless, you can still get an at-a-glance look at where these numbers are on an idealized basis. In my experience, they're generally not so far off as to be grossly inaccurate. So for example, if you've been told you can buy a property in a certain market at a 10-13% capitalization rate and most listings are averaging a 6-8% cap you know the number is most likely high.

Cap rates, GRM and other property screening tools are covered in Chapter 11: Preparing to Finance Your Property.

Learn about property types, conditions, amenities and "market sizzle"

Commercial real estate listing sites are also informative places to take a quick look at the types of listings that are in a particular market. This is especially helpful if you are new to an area. At a glance you can get an idea of the typical building styles common to that market such as:

- Property subtypes including garden/low-rise, mid/high-rise, duplex/triplex/fourplex.
- Year of construction.
- Number of bedrooms.
- Average number of units.
- Construction material such as solid brick or wood frame.
- Walk-up or interior entry.
- Converted single-family.

With a little more investigation into individual listings you can get a feel for:

- **Neighborhoods:** Is the market urban? Suburban? Close to cultural activities? Universities? Employment centers?
- **Average property amenities:** Do most properties have swimming pools? Offer in unit washers and dryers? Balconies? Wood floors?
- **Deferred maintenance**: Are properties listed as having major upgrades? Or do most seem in need of improvements?

Typically, the listing descriptions include information that you as new owner want to know about. They also promote the types of things your tenants are looking for., the market "sizzle."

Practice analyzing multifamily properties

Most listings include several ways to contact the listing broker. You can pick up the phone and call or you can e-mail right from the listing page online and request additional information about the property.

In most cases a broker will be happy to send you the listing brochure or offering memorandum. Here's a tip. Don't stop there. Ask for the seller's 12-month trailing financials on the property including a recent rent roll (you'll learn how to analyze a rent roll in Chapter Nine: Deal Analysis). Don't take "No" for an answer. Your lender will want this information. And so do you. I won't even visit a property or attend a property showing until I've had a chance to underwrite the property using the actual financials—not proformas.

If you're new to multifamily investing, or new to a particular market, it's your job to analyze at least a handful of deals in that market so that you are operating from a good baseline.

Sell a multifamily property

I think it goes without saying that if you are selling a property the more people who see your listing the better. The only reservation I've had with listing my properties with a service like LoopNet is if I feel the property won't sell right away. There's nothing worse than a "stale" listing or a property that appears online for months and months and months. If you've significantly overpriced your property you might want to think twice about putting it online. But if your property is priced right an online service can reach a worldwide market.

A last word about finding multifamily properties. Are you networking?

It's time for some honest soul searching here. Networking is your best friend when it comes to sourcing deals that others haven't already seen. Are you actively making contacts?

Through networking you may find multifamily owners who are ready to sell but haven't made a move in that direction yet.

Also know that in real estate investing patience is key. Start contacting everyone you can think of and plant the seed in their mind that you are actively looking to buy multifamily properties. Start here:

- Apartment building third-party property managers.
- Vendors and service providers to the apartment industry.
- Friends and family who know real estate investors.
- Accountants, certified financial planners, bankers and attorneys.

Using the property listing service to your advantage

Your understanding of a real estate market is critical to your success as an investor. Networking and connecting with professionals in commercial real estate is equally critical to your success. Don't stop at looking at a few listings online.

Start analyzing deals. Pick up the phone and talk to commercial brokers. Find and connect with successful multifamily real estate investors whether they are selling a property today or not.

How to Find Real Estate Deals in an Over-Heated Market

So, your real estate market is over-heated, and everyone is talking about it. People are saying, "Deals are overpriced. Good luck finding anything. The market is too hot to invest."

And you haven't found a deal yet. What do you do?

Don't panic.

Don't get in a hurry.

And don't give up.

Real estate markets are cyclical. Your market will turn around. It's your job to be ready and to have the confidence to make your move when it does. The first thing to remember . . .

Deals are still out there

In any market, up or down, deals are there to be found. You must continue to network and build relationships in any real estate market cycle. Hot or cold. Up or down. If you put your head in the sand and give up your search you risk a number of things:

- You'll miss deals that come on the market today. Good properties are out there. Motivated sellers come along every day.
- You will completely lose touch with your market.
- Professionals come and go. It's important to stay in the game so you know who the top players are. And you want those active players to know that you are "in the game." Let the other guys give up–it just makes for a smaller playing field.

The second most important thing is . . .

Don't give up your studies

Education should always be your first priority. Make it a habit to study your market on a regular schedule. Not occasionally. The best way to find real estate deals is to commit a certain amount of time each day and stick with your plan.

Read the real estate news sites and magazines. Look at the properties that are on the market. Run the numbers. How else will you get practice with analysis?

Study, study, and study some more. Meet with your mentors. Network with other real estate investors. Read books.

You definitely don't want to wait until you hear a market has turned around. By the time it becomes public knowledge the ship has already sailed. Seasoned real estate investors never stop thinking about real estate. They always keep an eye on their markets, local trends, demographics and economy. Some great ways to do that are:

- Get on local commercial broker's e-mail lists and review every listing.
- Read real estate investing magazines, blogs and news sites so you know the latest trends in financing; market sizzle (what rents units); demographics; popular amenities; employment; and jobs.
- Keep track of local market rents and concessions.

Become a student of your industry. This is the best way to truly become a professional real estate investor.

Become an expert real estate investor

When I first decided to move out of single-family investing and into multifamily, I invested just over one year in education and training to become proficient. It was a lot of work but also a lot of fun.

During that time, I:

- Looked at hundreds of listings on paper
- Attended a lot of property tours
- Met many commercial brokers and other apartment industry professionals (a priceless bonus in hindsight)
- Had a great time picturing myself as an owner of every building I saw

What's more? I started to get an excellent feel for the local market. In fact, I slowly became an expert on:

- Average price per door (a common measurement of price for apartment buildings and larger multifamily properties)
- Types of rental units on the market (such as one-bedroom, two-bedroom, studio/efficiency, etc.)
- Local market rent and concessions
- Local demographics and natural tenants in the market
- Common amenities
- Ideas for creating ancillary income
- Ideas for tenant retention and what renters want

By the time I found the perfect property I knew exactly what I wanted to pay for it and how I would operate the property the day I closed.

Adjust your strategy

You can also adjust your strategy by looking for other options within the multifamily asset class. For example, you might invest in:

- Smaller multi-units that can be converted to condos at a later time (hint, this might be sooner than you think).
- A good solid "buy and hold" property rather than a property that needs a ton of work today.
- A turnkey property that may provide less yield today than a value-add property, but value will be there over time.

What I want you to remember is that you can be flexible and stay within the same asset class of real estate.

Forget About Those Bright Shiny Objects

You probably know someone who is always chasing the newest sure-fire way to get rich quick. They jump around from one thing to the next never landing anywhere for long.

Forget about those bright shiny objects.

To succeed in real estate investing you must make a very real commitment and stick with it over the long haul. Choose a path. Have a plan. It's the only way to find real estate deals and to recognize the difference between a good deal and a marginal one.

As discussed in Chapter 5, real estate markets are cyclical. Markets repeat themselves over and over. When you have a plan and you commit to sticking around for a while you will succeed.

How Do You Find Those Pocket Listings Everybody Loves to Talk About?

As the real estate market heats up again, the industry practice of "pocket listings" is returning. The National Association of Realtors does not have an official definition for pocket listings. The term typically refers to a property with a signed listing agreement (Exclusive Right to Sell or Exclusive Agency), but the listing is not entered into the Multiple Listing Service (MLS).

Realtors are bound by a Code of Ethics to always strive for the best deal for their clients, and some say pocket listings violate MLS rules. Although most MLS boards do not like the practice and the NAR has no official policy on them, pocket listings can be done ethically and fairly.

Why would sellers want a pocket listing?

For commercial properties and multifamily properties, this is not that unusual. The owners might not want their residents and property management team to know they are selling. They may not want to have a lot of investors–who are considered their competition–traipsing through their property and seeing how they operate. Some just want to maintain their privacy.

When a listing goes into the MLS or on LoopNet or other internet listing service, all information about the listings is publicly available to every agent and practically anyone with a computer. Pocket listings of investment properties allow brokers to better qualify potential buyers and only show properties to people they know are ready, willing, and able to purchase.

Finding pocket listings

Network with the top commercial real estate brokers in your area. Attend their socials and cocktail hours. Let them know you are a serious investor with the capability to purchase investment properties. Make sure they know what you are interested in buying.

Some agents who have been in the business for decades do not get out and network much anymore, so call them. If you are a qualified buyer, they will take the time to speak to you. Start by inquiring about their listings in the MLS, and then ask if they know of any others that might be available or coming onto the market soon. Finding pocket listings requires patience.

Pocket listings are not always a bargain

Some sellers are willing to sell if they can obtain a ridiculous price. As an investor, you want to develop a relationship with one or more agents who will constantly be looking for properties that interest you.

Some listing agents are reluctant to share information on pocket listings with other agents because they want both the listing and sales side of the commission for themselves. Buying properties at bargain prices is more a matter of recognizing a bargain than going out and finding one.

How to Find Off-Market Multifamily Properties

Savvy investors know that a multifamily property will rarely have signs plastered everywhere that it is for sale, but that does not mean it cannot be purchased. Often these off-market multifamily properties offer great investment opportunities; you just need to know how to find them.

The direct approach

Sometimes the best approach is the most direct one, which means exploring the area you are interested in and looking for multifamily properties. Even if they are not for sale, you can still get in touch with the owners and find out if they are willing to let go of the property.

Be on the lookout for vacant or rundown-looking properties that you can spruce up as the owners of these might be more open to selling. Even if the owners are not willing to sell immediately, leave your details with them and they might get in touch with you if they ever decide to do so in the future.

Hit the auctions

Although they are not as common as single-family homes, multifamily properties do occasionally pop up at foreclosure auctions. Set yourself a reasonable budget for your bids and do as much due diligence beforehand to ensure that you get a good deal.

Do a little digging

If you are willing to take some time, you can find lots of potential multifamily properties by getting a list of properties from your local county assessor. In particular, you should look for out-of-town owners who might be tempted into selling. Other sources worth examining are foreclosure records and expired listings as these can also sometimes yield interesting results.

Build up your contacts

Although doing all the hard work yourself will pay off in the end, you can also make use of other people to ensure things go a little smoother. The best way to accomplish this is to build up your contacts in the industry so that you have access to information before it goes public. It is particularly beneficial to have solid relationships with lenders if you want to get on the inside track for good deals on multifamily properties.

Use the internet to your advantage

Thanks to the internet, you don't have to go out and get your hands dirty to find good deals. Join forums or groups on social media to keep your finger on the pulse of good off-market deals.

Finding off-market multifamily properties can get you some good deals but remember that the competition can be fierce. This means that some diligence and dedication from your side is essential if you don't want to miss out.

Unusual Ways to Find Investment Properties

When it comes to unique ways to find investment properties, you've got to think outside the box sometimes. Amazing deals don't always present themselves in typical real estate listings.

Before you set out to find your next property using one of the unusual ways covered below, decide what your tolerance for risk is so you're not looking at the wrong properties. For example, a fixer-upper will carry more risk than a property that is already stabilized and profitable. Chapter Eight: Accepting and Handling Risk has much more on this topic.

Drive for dollars

When you "drive for dollars," you're driving your car around the streets you want to find an investment property on and scoping out potential deals. In this method, a deal is usually a property that looks vacant, distressed or as if it's going through a negative transition. An apartment complex with grass growing more than a foot high, for example, usually signals the owner has checked out. A tarp on the roof of a multifamily property may indicate it has problems the owner can't fix.

Write down the address of each potential property, along with its condition notes and a photo. Dig around the property via public records to find the owner.

Talk to property managers

Property managers deal with investment property owners daily. They can be a surprising source of information about which rental properties will be up for sale, and these properties have already performed as rentals.

Consider direct mail

Direct mailing is still a solid way to advertise, as noted by Entrepreneur Magazine. With inboxes now being spammed with hundreds of emails, traditional mail grabs a bit more attention. Try direct mailing your intent to find investment properties in the areas that appeal to you. It won't cost much, and you may just strike gold.

Go boldly online

Just about everything is up for sale on the web today, and that includes real estate. Craigslist, for example, has real estate listings, and you can sort them by bedroom number to find multi-unit properties. If you decide to meet a potential seller through an online service, make sure you follow the posted safety rules, which usually include confirming everything you're told and verifying identities before handing over any money.

Focus on foreclosures

Just like single-family homes, apartment complexes and multifamily units do get foreclosed on. While the process varies by area, most municipalities have public postings of their foreclosure auctions prior to the sale. Find out where these notices are posted and review them frequently.

Whatever unusual method you use to find your next investment property, do your homework before buying. A little research now can save you a lot of trouble later!

How to Quickly Screen Investment Property

Let's say you have a lead on a property, but you want to do some due diligence before you decide to proceed. This checklist will help you quickly screen the property before you invest significant time and money.

Google Maps – Street View

Location makes all the difference in the world. A good quality investment property needs to be in a quality location. If the location is in a solid neighborhood then you can ensure less vacancy, a higher caliber of tenant and better rental rates. Think long term.

To visually screen investment property go online to Google Maps and take a look at the property with Street View. Is a motorcycle gang parked in front? Is there a bar next door? Basic safety questions need to be answered and Google Maps will give you your first snapshot of the area.

10 block walk

The very best way to get active in real estate investing is to get out in the streets. It's one of the best ways to research a market too.

One of my favorite commercial brokers referred to the concept as the "10 block walk." When you walk 10 blocks in every direction from a property, you'll learn what is really going on in the neighborhood.

How is the area evolving? Would you walk the streets at night? Are there streetlamps? Think about the kind of tenants you would like to attract and draw your conclusions.

Quick online market research

Before you even think about making an offer on a property you need to research the local market. Sperling's Best Places (bestplaces.net) is a great place to start. You'll find statistics on cost of living; crime rates; housing stats; employment & economy; population growth and other critical key metrics for identifying solid investment markets.

Police premise history

Call or visit the local police station in the area. Ask for a report on premise histories or service calls. This will give you a detailed look of how many times the police were called and what was addressed at the property. You need this valuable insight to the history of a property before you invest.

Screen investment property records

Liens against the property and taxes owed are important to know before you take one more step. It's also helpful to know the sales history of the property. You can easily check property records online or in person at your local assessor's office.

You'll find a history of the property and obtain recorded documents relating to the property via your local property clerk. The name of the office will vary by state. Search for: municipal clerk; town clerk; county clerk; county recorder; clerk & recorder; recorder of deeds; office of property records; assessor's office and other variations.

How to Tour a Multifamily Property

When it comes to investing in multifamily properties, knowing what you're getting yourself into is crucial to getting a good return on investment (ROI). Knowing about potential problems (and opportunities) with a prospective acquisition is key to helping you come up with an appropriate offer. That's why spending the time on property tours before you make an offer is so important.

Why attend property tours?

As an investor engaged in property tours, your job is to spot problems and to identify opportunities. It is especially important for new investors to get out in the market and tour as many properties as possible. It's how you build a baseline of properties for comparison purposes. For example, you'll gain a good understanding of typical amenities, average market rents and operating expenses for a specific submarket. Priceless knowledge!

So how do you look "under the hood" of a multifamily property? What are some things to watch out for? Let's start with the many benefits of in-person property tours.

The benefits of pre-offer property tours

- **Informs negotiations:** Checking the state and condition of a property can help you come up with a fair price during negotiations.
- **Discover costs to address deferred maintenance:** You'll be better informed about the potential costs of maintenance tasks that have been postponed by the seller.
- **Determine capital improvement planning:** Allows you to come up with a more accurate long-term plan to update fixtures and systems such as fire control systems, alarm systems, HVAC equipment, parking lots, etc.
- **Assess repurpose and reuse opportunities:** Can you add cool amenities, update the property and offer more market sizzle to attract residents?
- **Opportunity to check out tenants:** Will you need to reposition residents? And is it possible to find residents that meet your personal screening criteria in that market?
- **Determine seller's motivation, degree of honesty:** You won't really know the seller's true intentions or reasons for selling until you see the property for yourself.

The property tour

In most cases, the listing broker, or your buyer's broker, will conduct property tours. During the tour you'll discover that time will fly – an average tour could take as little as 20 minutes. So be sure you're asking to see everything listed below and that your broker is giving you ample time for your tour.

Don't be surprised if the seller and/or property manager are present for your tour. This is an excellent opportunity for you to ask casual questions about the current tenants and property operations.

Speak with everyone

When touring the property, make an effort to speak casually with tenants when possible. It's important to note that tenants rarely know that the property is for sale, but you could certainly ask what they like about living at the building. So be respectful.

Also, speak with employees or on-site managers when possible. They can provide you with some insight into what to expect when (or if) you purchase the property.

Make sure you look at your overall surroundings, including the outside and inside of the property.

Outside

Start by scouting the neighborhood. Arrive early and get in some exercise with a 10-block walk. How does the general area look? Once at the property, start with a walk around the entire complex. Here's what to look for:

- **Check out the cars.** Are they late model, in disrepair, on blocks, or parked on the lawn? If passing by during the day, are there a lot of cars? Ideally, a prospective property that is generating a successful income will have tenants at their jobs, not hanging out at home or loitering around the building.

159

- **Look for any signs of uncleanliness and neglect.** Is the trash overflowing? Are landscape and common areas being maintained, cleaned, and free of graffiti? Does the structure suffer from damage? Are there any cracks in exterior walls or foundation? Do you notice any shifting in the foundation or bricks in disrepair? Are sidewalks, railings, and steps safe for use? Does the property meet accessibility standards and requirements? Is there signage? Is the street address visible? Are windows open? No matter the season, open windows could be a sign of heating and cooling issues.
- **Ask to see the roof.** Does it need to be redone or has it been patched? When was the last roof work completed? Are drains and scuppers free of trash and debris?
- **Check building doors.** Are they propped open? This is not only a security issue, but it could be a possible sign of drug activity.
- **Look for other issues.** Are there any standing puddles of water or drainage issues? Are there any smells or odors noticeable around the property? Evidence of fire damage?

Inside

Don't hesitate to spend some time touring the interior. The building could look fine on the outside, but the inside may need work. It might also present opportunities.

- **At the very minimum, ask to see a residential unit of each unit type (studio/efficiency, 1, 2, 3 bed).** If you end up in contract, you will want to walk and make notes on every single unit.
- **Look at the entrance.** Is the entrance inviting? Is the lobby and mail area clean? Are unit numbers clearly visible? Is there an

160

entryway security system? Cameras and controlled access? Do systems meet life safety requirements? Is there proper lighting, egress, and exit signage? Is there a designated area for securely accepting package deliveries?

- **Check if common areas are clean and in proper working order.** Inspect property amenities and facilities like laundry and fitness areas. Check out the boiler room. Look for dated inspection notices, rust, disrepair, or safety hazards such as poorly stored flammable materials. Elevators and fire extinguishers should also have current inspection notices.

- **Once inside a unit, look for signs of wear and tear.** Look for cracks and stains on ceilings (always look up!). Are the windows old, floors warped? Doors and windows fit well? Do aesthetics like counters, flooring, fixtures, and hardware need to be updated?

- **Check other areas.** Don't forget the back stairs and storage units.

- **Look for bulletin boards and management signs**. Tenant notices can be very revealing.

- **Look out for any other issues**. Are there signs of pests or traps? What do you hear? Is it loud? How do the common areas smell?

Valuable networking opportunity

Be cool during your property tours, even if you are not completely confident, act like you are. You do not have to say much. You do not have to make an offer on the spot. Be sure to ask questions and show a genuine interest in the property and in the people you're meeting. Don't forget this business is all about building good relationships!

Resource alert: Download and print your own property tour checklist at theresabradleybanta.com/book_resources.

How Do You Know You've Found a Good Real Estate Deal?

Real estate that is situated in a good location is typically not a secret. Tennis star Boris Becker was fond of the phrase "Every minute of the day you are not practicing, somebody else is." The same is true of real estate investing.

There are a lot of people who want to be real estate investors, and a significant number of these people do invest in real estate. They are constantly looking for places to buy, and they are also driving up the price on a lot of properties that would otherwise be a good investment.

This leaves you with fewer potential properties to choose from and more competition for the few good investment opportunities that are available. When you do see one that is within your price range and meets most of your criteria, your inclination is to jump on it.
How do you know you've found a good real estate deal? Here's three signs.

The numbers add up

You have to analyze the property's profit potential without giving much thought to the listed asking price or current rent. It is a good idea to have a rent survey to determine the amount of rent that is appropriate for a particular property. If the list price is within striking distance of producing a Gross Rent Multiplier (GRM) that is acceptable to you, that is one indicator you should move forward.

The vacancy rate is dropping or less than 5 percent

When you have high demand and low supply, you have the essence of profit. It helps you build a stable portfolio that will continue to build long-term wealth. It improves your ability to obtain any needed financing. A desirable GRM number is less significant when the vacancy rate of the area is high. If you have a good GRM and low vacancy rate, you are moving in the right direction.

A stable or improving area

You might not be able to afford properties in prime areas but look for some signs of improvement. That does not guarantee the growth will continue, but if your knowledge of the area indicates a strong economy and the other factors line up, you have most likely found a good deal for you.

The last four words are crucial. A good deal for you might not be right for others. Conversely, you do not have the same financial resources and objectives as other investors. Keep in mind that growing areas often experience increases in utilities and property taxes. Such increases alter your operating expenses and profit.

Chapter Seven:
Partnerships

Ask for what you want and be prepared to get it.
– Maya Angelou

~

When Do You Really Need an Investment Partner?

It sounds impressive to tell someone, "Everything looks good, but I want to discuss this with my investment partner before we move forward." Beyond making your investment company sound a bit larger, there are some real benefits to having a collaborator.

There are times when it makes sense to partner with someone, and there are other times when it brings more aggravation than it is worth and can damage friendships.

When an investment partner makes sense

There may be times when you find a great deal but do not have enough cash available to buy it on your own. Perhaps you do not want to extend yourself further financially or take on a lot more debt at that time. If the only way you can make the transaction happen is with the additional resources of a partner, it makes sense to take this route.

Work-life balance

Having a partner can free up another valuable commodity that you have in limited supply: time. Real estate investing is demanding, and novice investors can quickly become swamped. Being rich with money is great, but if you spend all your time earning it, you discover that being money rich and time poor is more stressful than satisfying. A partner can help you maintain a proper work-life balance by sharing some of the duties and responsibilities.

A partner may also bring something to the deal that you lack. If you are a creative person, you most likely need someone logical and detail oriented. Novice investors can benefit from a partner with some established connections. However, for a true partnership, there must be balance in the equation. They can't feel as though they are carrying you and must appreciate your strengths and contributions to the partnership.

A partnership can become a sinking ship

A friend once told me, "All partnerships are sinking ships." You can tell he'd been burned once or twice. But his sentiment has some truth in it.

Working with an investment partner is something you should be very careful about. Do not feel obligated just because someone is a friend who wants to make some extra money. Each person must know what is expected of them upfront. Both parties should have the same level of commitment to the real estate deal. In addition to knowing their strengths, you should also be aware of their weaknesses and how they handle difficult situations.

If you do not really need a partner, there is no reason to get one. It is much easier to decline partnering with someone than it is to deal with the aftermath of a partnership gone wrong.

Be smart about who you choose to partner with and only do it if it will benefit the real estate investment you are making.

Benefits of Real Estate Partnerships

Not all real estate partnerships work out. You can't go into a partnership blind. For example, don't offer up your life savings, go home and expect checks in your mailbox. You must know what you are doing before any money is exchanged.

Prosperous real estate partnerships take work, time and sincere effort. Be thoughtful about who you partner with. Take the time to get to know the weaknesses and strengths of your partner. It will be worth your time. Successful real estate partnerships offer many advantages.

You merge superpowers

Like Superman and kryptonite, everyone has a weakness. You know it, you avoid it, and occasionally you try to improve upon it. The best business partner would be someone who supplements your weak points with strengths. Perhaps your strength is running the numbers, but the idea of negotiating makes you want to hide. Find negotiating champions you might want to partner up with.

Identifying your weaknesses and strengths will also help you define roles in the partnership. Expectations and goals should be set at the beginning. Do so in writing, so everyone is crystal clear on what needs to be done, by whom and when. Accountability and transparency are your watchwords.

You double your resources

When you partner up with like-minded individuals in real estate you can grow your own network of professionals. Building a solid team of brokers, contractors, legal talent, lenders, buyers and more is one of the most powerful, efficient ways to grow your business.

Take advantage of the horizon expansion to make sure everyone knows what you stand for as well. We can all benefit from collaboration.

Deeper pockets

The financial aspect of real estate investing is a stumbling block for some real estate investors. With a partner you expand your sources of financing and capital. The right partner can help increase the amount of capital going into a deal as well as doubling your borrowing ability.

Of course, there is always fine print to be written when it comes to money and real estate partnerships. There are many different kinds of partnerships. How a partnership is structured, the amount of money invested, and the risk involved are just some issues to consider when signing someone on.

Make sure all the details are spelled out in contracts first. This will save you sleepless nights of worry.

Use common sense

Good partnerships are similar to other healthy relationships in your life. Make sure you have shared values and goals. Be authentically you, not your internet persona. Communicate daily on progress. Respect the other individual for who they are, not who you want them to become. Focus on the big picture and don't forget to laugh.

How to Find and Network with Real Estate Investors

Finding opportunities to network with real estate investors can be a big boon to your own business in many ways, from the financial side to the creative angle. Partnering with someone else can help make your next dream deal become reality, and when you forge those connections, you'll be able to gain valuable insight and share ideas and strategies.

Since investors don't just fall out of trees, you'll have to do a little legwork to connect with them. Try the methods below to get your foot into the front door!

Look in your own backyard

Chances are, everyone from Jerry the real estate agent to Barb the REO attorney has had contact with other investors, and it's even better if you're connected to an investor through someone you actually know. Speak to the real estate professionals in your life right now and see if any names come up.

Make the time to meet any new investors you connect with this way. Even if you're looking for a partner on a specific deal and he or she isn't interested in it, you still might make a fruitful connection in other areas.

Try seminars and conferences

Investors do attend area conferences and seminars related to real estate investing. For some, these gatherings are continuing education and offer the chance to learn something new, while for others they're a solid opportunity to network with real estate investors. Either way, you'll have the chance to meet some investors and forge new relationships for a current deal or one in the future. Do take the time to check into the background of any investors you meet that you plan to do business with.

Check out local clubs

Look for real estate investors clubs near where you live. Investors sometimes form local groups for networking purposes, and their meetings are a great way to find, partner and brainstorm with other investors. Social media is usually the easiest place to start your local club search, and you can also scope out area real estate forums.

There are also nationwide groups, such as the National Real Estate Investors Association (NREIA) and the National Apartment Association (NAA). Look for chapters nearby by using the search feature on each organization's website.

Finding the right investor for your deal will take digging, but it's certainly worth it in the end. Always be upfront with your investor so you can foster a solid business relationship for this deal and other deals in the future.

What's the Difference Between a "Debt Partner" and an "Equity Partner?"

Many different terms come into play in real estate investments, but there are two very important ones that are sometimes misunderstood: debt partner and equity partner. What kind of partner you are in your deals affects your investment and how you get paid.

Equity partners have a piece of the pie: As an equity partner, you get a percentage of asset ownership. This means you may have a voice in some decisions, as set out by your agreement with the other parties involved and get part of the cash flow on a regular basis.

Debt partners have their initial investment: If you're a debt partner, you're loaning money and getting the agreed-upon interest rate in return until the debt is repaid. Unlike an equity partner, you don't have an ownership interest in the real estate, although you may end up with the real estate if the borrower defaults if it's the collateral for the loan you made.

A debt partner can be essentially "cashed out" once the loan has been fully paid back. An equity partner, on the other hand, isn't out once he or she receives the principal back; that partner is now an owner and entitled to an ongoing profit share.

Consider the deal-specific pros and cons

Which partner type is for you depends on the deal and the other people involved. In some cases, the other investors may not be willing to close the deal unless you're just a debt partner. Other times, both options may be available. At that point, you have to decide how much work you want to put in on this particular investment, how long you want to be tied to it, and how well you can work with the other investors.

Being an equity partner has a lot of benefits, but it also means you'll be more actively involved in the property and everything that goes with that. A debt partner has benefits, too. While you don't have a say in decisions and won't share in profits beyond your loan repayments and the return rate for that as a debt partner, you will make money without having to do much besides opening your checkbook.

Time is another consideration—equity partners are naturally often tied to an investment property longer than debt partners are.

Consider all the angles when you're deciding on a debt or equity partnership for your deal or as a part of someone else's deal. This isn't a decision to be made lightly; the future of your investment is directly affected by the choice you make.

How to Raise Money for Your Real Estate Deals

I'll bet if you talked to ten people, nine of them would say, "I'd love to invest in real estate if only…"

Take a minute to remember why you decided to invest in real estate. Why the idea keeps you up at night. Why you've invested time, money and energy pursuing your dream. The only thing holding you up is that you lack the funds to really get started. It might be easier that you think…

You already have the right attitude

You know you're committed. You have time. You have the desire to succeed. And you have the right amount of education to assure success. Think about those people who would love to invest in real estate (some of whom you don't even know yet!):

- Write down what they're dreaming of
- Make a list of the reasons that might be holding them back
- Consider how you can help them realize their dreams

This list will help you get clear on the benefits you can offer your investing partners.

Network with everyone you know

Let your personality shine through. Your excitement and belief in what you're doing is contagious.

Your potential real estate partners need you. They need your area of expertise. And they'll respond to your ideas. It's human nature. People love being around other people who are enthusiastic with life and have plans to make their dreams a reality.

Put the right real estate investing team in place

If you're light on experience, you're probably afraid to sit down with friends and family and admit you haven't actually done a real estate deal. Well… how do you think other investors got started? Not everyone has a rich uncle who's ready to dole out a million dollars. Many investors start from scratch.

Show your partners how smart you are. Build a team who knows the real estate investing industry. Have your team ready to step in when you close the real estate deal. For example, your partners will love to know that you've interviewed and found the premier property manager in town. And that you've hired the leading rental property renovation specialists. So will your bank or lender. Some lenders require that you hire a professional manager for the first year of ownership.

Let your potential partners know that you have the right team members and they're ready to go.

Learn and know what makes a great real estate deal

Real estate investing offers amazing benefits to you and your partners…

- Cash flow from rental units
- Market appreciation
- Tax benefits and deductions
- Pay down of loan principal over time (build equity)
- Forced appreciation (the value you bring to the property through improvements both financially and operationally)

Your partners might not be able to list the advantages above, but they've been hearing for years that real estate is a great investment.

You can show them why.

With current interest rates at an all-time low, there are a lot of people with funds just sitting on the sidelines. They'd love an opportunity to see higher returns on their money.

Find the perfect real estate deal

A great mentor once told me, "When you find a good investment opportunity, raising money for your real estate deals is the easy part."

And he was right.

How many people do you know who are able to invest the time looking for great real estate opportunities? Pretty short list, right? It's why most people don't invest in real estate.

Join investing clubs. Network with rental property owners. Meet and visit with local property managers. Talk to vendors and suppliers who offer services to rental property owners. Network, network and network some more. You'll be surprised at how many opportunities start appearing.

And the funny part? You'll find real estate deals that aren't getting done because the person who sourced the deal can't raise the money to do the deal. For you? Money is no object!

If you're new to investing, enlist the help of a mentor. A mentor or seasoned real estate investor can help you

- Analyze the investment numbers (income and expenses)
- Obtain lender financing
- Make a plan for what you'll do the day you close
- Structure a deal that will entice investment partners
- Put solid exit strategies in place (someday you'll sell or refinance)

Plan your pitch

Once you've outlined your plan, talking with potential partners is simple. Open the conversation by asking, "Have you ever thought about investing in real estate?"

If the answer is "Yes," take some time to explore why. Learn about your potential partner. Listen. Engage. Ask questions. The more the other person talks, the more likely they are to invest.

Briefly describe your investing plan…

- Your team
- The benefits of real estate investing
- Your plan for acquiring a property

I think you'll find that raising money for your real estate deals is easy. Talk to everyone you know—your friends, family and acquaintances. Share your dreams and enthusiasm for the future.

And if their answer is "No?"

You can bet they know someone who would be interested in hearing more.

Top Five Things Your Real Estate Investment Partners Love to Hear

There's a lot of talk around the Internet and at investment boot camps about how you can buy a multifamily property or apartment building with none of your own money. Most of the prevailing ideas are a stretch—if not outright hype to sell educational programs.

If you're investing in multifamily real estate, you're not likely to personally fund the entire transaction. In all likelihood you'll finance part of the investment property through a bank or lender and you'll turn to investment partners to help fund your:

- Down payment
- Closing costs
- Paid research
- Inspections
- Reserve funds
- Immediate renovation expenses

Chances are pretty good your real estate investment partners will be your friends and family members. Maintaining good relationships can go a long way to preserving your sanity.

Do you want happy partners? Here's the top things they'll want to hear:

1. "I've got money in the deal"

There's no better way to assure your investors and partners that you intend to make a real estate project or deal succeed than to let them know you have "skin in the game." If you do not have money in the deal, you will of course be investing a great deal of time. Be ready to discuss this with your investors or partners.

2. "I've done this type of real estate investment before"

Your partners want to know your track record and history in earlier or similar real estate investment deals. They want to know that your previous partners and investors realized the returns you promised them. If you do not have an investing history, you must have team that has experience.

3. "Here's your quarterly update"

The number one complaint of investors is they never hear from the business deal maker after they've put their money in the deal. Do you want happy investors? Communicate with your partners on a regular schedule even if you do not have much in the way of updates. Your business investors and partners want to hear from you.

4. "I'm proud to have you as an investment partner"

Let your business partners and investors know you appreciate their business acumen and their trust in you.

5. "Here's your check"

Need I say more?

A last word about investing with partners

The phrase "under promise and over deliver" could not be more applicable than when you are responsible for the money, assets and trust of your partners.

The best way to approach a deal is to ask yourself, "What type of return would make my partners happy?" Once you know the answer to that question you can decide if there is enough left over for you to make the deal worth your time.

Don't make the mistake of thinking about you first, partners second. If a deal is too skinny to satisfy investment partners with a certain element of surety don't do the deal.

How to Split a Real Estate Deal with Your Partners

An investment in real estate goes beyond finding and buying a good property. When you put a real estate investment together—especially a partnership—there's no question you have your work cut out for you.

When you're the deal maker you should be paid for your hard work and the skills you bring to the table. So, how exactly do you pay yourself for all that hard work? Especially when as the deal maker you must:

- Find the investment property.
- Put your team together.
- Raise funds and get financing in place.
- Oversee property improvements and upgrades.
- Operate the property.
- Create solid exit strategies to capitalize on your investment.

Now that you've taken a look at what's involved in putting together a solid real estate project do you see how you will earn the money the partnership is going to pay you?

The property details

We'll use the following property information for the two case studies below:

Purchase Price:	$2,500,000.00
Loan Amount:	$1,875,000.00
Annual Effective Gross Income:	$350,000.00
Annual Net Cash Flow:	$100,000.00
Sale Price:	$3,800,000.00
Equity at Sale:	$940,000.00

The following case studies are from real partnership pay out agreements:

Case Study #1: A nice clean way to pay yourself

Structure the deal so that you as the deal maker (sponsor) take 25% off the top—of everything. You pay yourself:

- 25% of all cash flow (net cash from operations).
- 25% of equity paid at sale or cash out refinance.

The remaining 75% of cash flow and equity is distributed to the partners based on a percentage of each partner's capital contribution. Note: If you have also contributed capital to the investment you will be paid your portion—in addition to the 25% sponsor fee.

This form of payout is simple to track in terms of bookkeeping and accounting.

How You're Paid:

25% Annual Cash Flow:	$25,000.00
25% Equity at Sale:	$235,000.00

This method of compensation is pretty straightforward. It involves little accounting and is easy for investment partners to understand.

Case Study #2: A more complicated way to pay yourself

Now here's an example of a much more complex payout agreement between a deal sponsor and the investment partners.
At acquisition and during the holding period pay yourself:

- **3% acquisition fee:** One-time "finder's fee" based on total purchase price.
- **1% asset management fee:** Percentage of Gross Income paid annually. (Note this does not include the property management fee.)
- **40% cash flow payout to sponsor.**

Note: The remaining 60% of cash flow is distributed to the partners based on a percentage of each partner's capital contribution, including you if you've also contributed capital to the deal.

At sale (disposition) pay yourself:

- 1% Disposition Fee: Paid to Sponsor upon sale of property (based on total sales price).
- 40% Equity Payout to Sponsor.

How You're Paid:

3% Acquisition Fee:	$75,000.00
1% Asset Management Fee:	$3,500.00
40% Annual Cash Flow:	$40,000.00
1% Disposition Fee:	$38,000.00
40% Equity Payout:	$376,000.00

Note: Asset management fees cover general property oversight. Asset management fees do not include payments for property management or property upgrade and renovation management. Read on.

Add a little compensation for your extra work and know-how

Now let's make it even more interesting. What if the physical property needs a lot of work? Somebody's got to be in charge of:

- Working with contractors to develop construction documents, plans, timelines, and budgets for each property upgrade or renovation
- Administering construction contracts
- Monitoring and approving of construction of each upgrade
- Other general construction management activities for each upgrade

Who's going to oversee property improvements? If it's you, you want to be sure you're compensated for your time and commitment.

Pay yourself a percentage (such as 10%) of all hard costs associated with property upgrades and improvements.

How you're paid:

When you spend $2,500 to upgrade an individual rental unit you receive $250 (10%) for managing the work done in that rental unit.

Note: Property upgrades should include work in all common areas and in individual rental units.

Which business model is better? It depends.

- How much bookkeeping or accounting do you want to take on?

- Do you want a payout agreement that's easy to understand?
- Does one method of payout compensate you more than the other? And is there enough left in the deal to make your partners happy?
- Can you find a happy medium?

Both models are perfectly acceptable. I've seen successful real estate investors use both fee and payout structures in the two case studies above. It's up to you as the sponsor to decide what you'll offer your partners.

The two most important questions of all

In every real estate deal I consider, I always ask myself, "Does this investment offer enough return so that my partners are happy?"

"Is there enough left over to make it worth my time?"

Pro tip: Pay out agreements should always be discussed up front.

Need Funds for Your Real Estate Deals? How About Syndication?

Many opportunities are available in the real estate market for investors, but without enough funds, your options tend to be limited. One of the easiest ways to gain access to the type of funds required for larger real estate deals is through syndication.

Real estate syndication can seem like a daunting option to somebody who has never made use of it before, but it does offer numerous advantages.

However, just like any business venture, making use of syndication requires a proper understanding of how it operates in addition to the pros and cons involved.

The concept behind real estate syndication

Real estate syndication enables investors to pool their financial and intellectual resources. This allows them to invest in projects and properties that are typically larger than what they would have been able to afford by themselves. This means that syndication is in essence a crowdfunding model for the real estate market. It is also an option that is favored by investors who want to invest in real estate but do not necessarily have the required skills or want the responsibility of property management.

A real estate syndication entails a sponsor, also called a syndicator, who is in charge of the acquisition and management of the real estate. Ideally, this person will bring a lot of experience in this area to the table.

Also part of the syndication are the investors who are investing with the sponsor in exchange for an ownership percentage of the real estate. In some cases, there will also be a joint venture partner who serves to bring the investors and syndicator together while also helping with financing, reporting and other tasks.

Pros and cons of real estate syndication

For many investors, the biggest pro of taking part in a real estate syndication is that they have a passive role and won't have to worry about the day-to-day operations. Other investors are drawn to the fact that they cannot lose more than the amount that they initially invested as their liability is limited. When it comes to property sales, refinancing and other major decisions, the investors also tend to hold voting rights.

For investors who like to be involved in the day-to-day operations, the lack of control will be a con. Of course, as with any investment, the real estate market can be volatile, which means value can increase and decrease depending on market conditions.

Always properly research the project and the people heading the syndication before making any commitments. If you're the syndicator, be prepared to demonstrate superior knowledge of your offering. Syndication can be a win-win situation for everyone involved, but only if it is handled properly. Always consult your attorney and CPA.

Chapter Eight:
Accepting and Managing Risk

*If you push through that feeling of being scared, that feeling
of taking risk, really amazing things can happen.*
– Marissa Mayer

~

Biggest and Costliest Mistakes Real Estate Investors Make

Whether you come from a completely different background or your family
has been investing in real estate for generations, you are going to make
some mistakes. It is important to understand that everyone makes
mistakes. Successful people know that and take steps to minimize the
severity of their miscalculations, recover, and move forward stronger and
wiser as a result.

Many new investors make understandable mistakes, get discouraged, and
give up. You are not going to do that. You already know that owning real
estate involves a lot of maintenance, preventative maintenance, and repair.
Your business plan and investment decisions are much the same way.

Real estate can create real and lasting wealth. It can provide enough income through cash flow to quit your day job. You've probably heard stories about how easy it is to get rich by investing in real estate. It almost sounds too good to be true, doesn't it? But there are caveats. Before you jump in with both feet think about how you can avoid these easy mistakes. . .

Mistake #1: Buying the "right" property in the wrong area

A client of mine recently came across an amazing apartment building that had the "cool factor" in spades. The all brick building was a former schoolhouse with incredible architecture. It had:

- gorgeous stairways
- crown molding throughout
- unique floor plans
- high ceilings
- wood floors
- stunning windows

It was a unique and beautiful property near the urban core and surrounded by boutiques and small shops and located in an upcoming neighborhood. Although the neighborhood had not quite "arrived," it was potentially on the verge of discovery. At least according to the broker and the current property owner.

Did my client buy the property without first investigating the neighborhood? Did he accept the claims of the listing parties as hard fact? No. Instead he visited with the police, local merchants and several property management companies who all (mostly) agreed on one important matter:

the area was rife with crime, drugs and tenants of a highly transient nature—and was unlikely to change for years.

What if he hadn't done his research? What if he had failed to see beyond the cool factor? The apartment building would have performed extremely well in the right neighborhood and with well-thought-out upgrades, but not today. And not in the current market.

Mistake #2: Hiring the wrong team for your property

As I said, the local professionals my client interviewed "mostly" agreed about the neighborhood. With a single exception. He interviewed a property manager who suggested he could replace the current residents with local college students and young 'upwardly mobile' professionals. A stretch, at best.

The property was not in a safe neighborhood. If young students and professionals agreed to rent units, they would be the first of their kind moving to the area. The neighborhood had potential, but it wasn't there yet.

So why on earth would a prospective property manager suggest this? Good question. Maybe he wasn't familiar with the market. Or, maybe he was just trying to get a new client by making outrageous promises (it happens).

Now here's the very scary part. What if my client had purchased the property and hired this particular property manager because he liked what he was hearing? And he wanted to believe it was true? Just because you want something to be true doesn't make it so. Your team must know and understand

- your market
- the reputation of the entire neighborhood
- local demographics
- current trends
- your ideal/target resident
- what sells units in terms of upgrades and amenities
- and they must have a proven track record.

Mistake #3: Lack of due diligence

In the story above my client exercised extreme care in conducting his due diligence of the rental market. He absolutely loved the property, but he didn't stop there. Believe me, he wasn't happy to hear that he could purchase and renovate the property only to end up with a very cool rental property with no tenants to appreciate it.

He did the right thing. He investigated. He listened. He did his homework. And he moved on to other opportunities.

Sometimes it's easy to fall in love with an idea. To believe everything you're told. To have a difficult time believing that a seller or broker might exaggerate the truth.

But it happens to all of us. The most important thing to remember is that you are not insulting the seller or the listing broker when you verify everything that's presented. This includes inspections of the:

- property (structural, mechanicals, property condition)
- financials

- neighborhood
- rental market
- historical income and expenses
- pro forma financials (projected income and expenses)
- existing leases
- and all documents on the property.

Mistake #4: Relying on pro formas

When you look at a property listing and you see a financial category under the heading "Pro formas" don't mistake these numbers for the current financials.

Pro forma numbers represent what would happen in a perfect world under your great management and rental property operations know-how.

Pro forma numbers suggest what you might get in the future.

In most cases pro forma numbers will show higher rental amounts (therefore higher income) and lower property expenses—used to "justify" a higher asking price for the property.

It's your job to ask for the historical income and expenses (a.k.a. annual property operating data, or APOD). Go back at least two years. I rarely visit a property until I've had an opportunity to look at two years trailing financials. If you're looking for financing, the loan underwriter will review these numbers as well.

Experienced real estate investors consider both sets of numbers—current and pro forma—before presenting an offer to buy.

The question is: Can you actually realize those pro forma projections in a reasonable amount of time without an unreasonable amount of cash outlay beyond the purchase price? If not, you should adjust your offer price accordingly.

Mistake #5: Believing real estate is a way to get rich quick

You can't. It's a measured process. It takes time, energy, education and good planning to get rich investing in real estate.

Have you heard of house flippers making a fortune in three months by quickly fixing and selling a rental property? Think twice before you believe claims of great profits. All but the most experienced flippers (like those with their own TV shows) end up over time and over budget. Many are lucky to come out ahead.

Real estate investing can be a job. Each step takes time. But you can succeed if you

- get an education
- find successful investors to mentor you
- locate good solid investment properties
- team up with experienced partners and professionals and
- successfully manage your property.

Think about this for a minute...

According to Forbes, after technology, real estate produced the largest group of self-made Forbes 400 Billionaires. And many support their wealth through real estate investments.

Mistake #6: Skipping a thorough analysis

While many novice investors know that real estate investments have tried-and-true formulas that must add up for a property to be profitable, they don't always pay them proper attention. They get excited when they get close to the action. Perhaps they get distracted by a shrewd seller or sales agent who takes advantage of their naivete. Maybe they are just impatient to get into an investment.

Don't skip doing a thorough analysis of the numbers. Don't bend the numbers just to make the deal work. The *numbers* don't lie. If you don't like what they tell you, check them twice. If they are telling you the property is not a good investment, move on.

Mistake #7: Trying to do everything themselves

People often overestimate what they can accomplish, which is why people abandon goals like exercising and returning to school. Once they do actually experience muscle aches, injuries, failure, and pain, they abandon their goals or push them out a little further into the future and procrastinate.

Real estate investors don't get the option of procrastinating. They have people depending on them and legal obligations. However, many do make the mistake of overestimating what they can do themselves. When they visualize things like lawn care, maintenance, answering phones, navigating legal documents, and managing tenants, they see themselves being able to take care of it all but soon appreciate the value of having a team of consultants and contractors.

Mistake #8: Underestimating costs

Once again, the numbers don't lie. You can't ignore them, and you must have adequate capital to cover operating costs, maintain insurance, conduct preventative maintenance and make repairs.

You will not be able to do everything yourself. You have to pay some people to help you get everything done. Make sure all necessary costs are included when you analyze an investment.

Common Landlord Nightmares (and How to Prevent Them)

Most people think real estate investors make a lot of money and do only a little work. That is the goal, but achieving it is difficult. While it is possible to find rental properties that are available at a good price and can be profitable for the owner, the parts people overlook are the pitfalls, headaches, and potential nightmares that come along with managing investment properties.

Here are three things that can be nightmares for landlords and how to avoid them.

Problem properties

What looks like a gold mine initially can turn into a money pit rather quickly. Many new investors feel they know enough to skip getting a professional home inspection. It is always a good idea to obtain a completely objective opinion from an experienced home inspector before buying. Most issues related to property condition can be avoided with proper due diligence before the purchase.

Terrible tenants

If you know many investors or have owned rental property yourself, you have probably seen what nightmare tenants can do to a place. Hoarders typically do not understand their behavior themselves.

There are also those spiteful, angry, or just outright disturbed people who intentionally damage properties. Terrible tenants are so common that there are some investors who seek out damaged rental properties that novice investors purchased, couldn't manage properly, and are then forced to sell at a significant discount.

The best way to prevent nightmare tenants is to not let them get in the door in the first place. Diligent screening is necessary. However, there is a right way and a wrong way to accomplish this. Be sure to consult with an attorney who specializes in landlord tenant law about your screening process to be sure it is fair and complies with all laws.

Legal landmines

A lawsuit is one of the worst nightmares a landlord may face, and it is possible to do everything right and still get sued. One of the best ways to prevent legal disputes is to maintain a positive relationship with tenants. That does not mean allowing yourself to be bullied by people who are highly skilled at being the squeaky wheel.

Demonstrate to tenants that you are a knowledgeable landlord who takes pride in providing a safe and top-quality living environment. Doing so requires that you know your state's and local area's landlord and tenant laws. You absolutely do not want to be in a position where a tenant or anyone else informs you of an issue that you were not aware is your legal responsibility.

By following this advice, you should be able to minimize your chances of encountering nightmare tenants.

Tips for First-Time Multifamily Real Estate Investors

When you're new to multifamily investing, the prospect can be both exciting and scary at the same time. The additional units housed in one building do offer more revenue streams than a single-family home, but they also come with their own unique issues.

A multifamily property comes with its own special set of benefits and potential problems. Here are some things you can do to be proactive:

Research the rent

The amount of rent you can get from the multifamily complex is the lynchpin of the entire deal. That rent, measured against the property's operating costs, is your profit and your cushion.

Check out local ads for units similar to yours to see what the average rent is. Look at how many units are for rent in the same area and what types of incentives are being offered; too many incentives could be a sign of high vacancies. One of the best tools for doing this is a rent survey.

Know your limits

If your money is entirely tied up into your investment, that leaves little room for emergencies. Don't assume rent will be coming in all the time to cover expenses and unexpected costs. Consider multifamily properties with an investment and operating cost you can handle even if all the units are vacant for a few months.

Check all expenses

As a multi-unit owner, you'll naturally have more expenses. Landscaping and snow removal may be new bills to pay, and there is also water and other utilities you may have to cover. Be sure you have an accurate and clear idea of all the expenses associated with the property you're considering. The only way to have a realistic picture of the investment is by considering all variables, particularly expected income and operating costs.

Have tenant plans and policies ready

You need to have a clear plan for attracting tenants to your units and keeping them there, in addition to policies for your rentals and procedures for dealing with problem tenants. Draft all your plans and policies before investing so you're ready to tackle the property from day one with a clear vision.

Know all applicable laws

Federal, state and local landlord-tenant laws must be followed to the letter if you want to avoid exposing yourself to fines and legal liability. Research and familiarize yourself with these regulations so you know what you can and can't do before you buy the property.

As a multifamily investor, you will face some new challenges, but the investment can be very much worth it in the end. Research and go in prepared for the best chance at success!

How to Reduce Risk When Investing in Multifamily Real Estate

Are you looking to invest in a multifamily property? Have you considered everything involved with owning a multifamily building or an apartment complex? Sure, you can get promising returns. There's less chance of losing value in a down market than with a single-family property and financing might be easier. And you can quickly grow your rental property portfolio.

But there are a number of risks involved with investing in a multifamily property. Luckily, there are a few ways to reduce risk with solid, diligent planning.

Reduce risk with smart planning

You should never go into a multifamily investment without a proper plan. You must prepare for the unexpected and have a solid idea about potential costs. Below are a few tips for developing a solid plan for your multifamily investment:

Perform thorough property inspections

A property in bad condition or full of poorly screened residents is bound to give you a financial headache, one that you can't afford. Go over all records with a fine-toothed comb.

Have the right team

Gathering a good team of experts for property inspections allows you to predict the costs of:

- Deferred maintenance (immediate cash needs)
- Capital improvements (cash reserve needs)
- Loss of income from vacancy and/or poorly screened tenants
- Renovations and improvements

Conduct market research at the micro level

Will improvements or new amenities result in higher rents? What do renters want, and can you give it to them?

Buy the asset at the right price, with the right financing

You don't want to find yourself over-leveraged and taking on too much debt, especially in a market downturn.

Hire a property manager

Having someone manage maintenance work, answer phone calls, offer customer service, and handle tenant reviews and complaints will make your life much easier. If you're a new investor, expect your lender to require professional third-party management throughout your first year of ownership.

Create a budget

It's important to put together a realistic look at property income and expenses during your first year or two of ownership. A pro forma budget analysis will help you avoid the dreaded cash call. Do this before you buy the property!

Have multiple exit strategies

Even before buying a multifamily property, it's important to have a detailed exit strategy or multiple exit strategies in mind. For instance, you might sell the property, refinance it, exchange it, or convert it to another use as in the earlier example of a condo conversion. Timing a market is difficult at best but knowing you have multiple exit strategies equals peace of mind.

Although investing in a multifamily property can be highly profitable, the market doesn't always do well. So, what do you do when your multifamily asset underperforms? If you can afford to wait, do it! You can hold the property until the market stabilizes. As the market picks up, rent will begin to rise, which can mean large profits for you.

Maybe your plan is to sell your property right away to avoid losing even more money and to reduce risk. Another option is to force property appreciation through strategic renovations and through the addition of inexpensive amenities. By renovating your property, and increasing income, you can raise the value of your asset.

It's always a good idea to perform a stress test on your property financials. What happens when vacancy increases? How much can you lower rent and remain afloat?

Stay up on regulatory issues

Government regulations may interfere with your profit margins. For example, rent control can regulate the amount you charge for rent (how much and how often you can raise rent), which could result in profit loss if the cost of rent goes down.

Other regulations like Denver's Green Roof Initiative could affect your multifamily property. The new ordinance requires that buildings over

25,000 square feet dedicate a percentage of a building's roof to green, vegetative space, or other options such as "cool roofs."

There are costs associated with installing new green or cool roofs, including more expensive insurance, which will greatly impact Denver multifamily unit owners. Preparing yourself for regulations like these is very important, whether you're saving funds to cover certain costs or doing research on geographical areas before investing.

Track changing social patterns and lifestyles

The multifamily industry is ever changing. The demographics of a particular area rarely stay the same. Baby boomers and millennials are constantly looking for homes that suit them, which means they won't stay in the same multifamily properties.

This could affect you as a property owner. With shifting consumer tastes, you can lose tenants to other more appealing properties. To combat this and reduce risk, you can create common areas that appeal to multiple generations and keep up with popular trends.

Buy properties with resilience

Your property should be able to bounce back from different challenges like financial loss due to mismanagement, climate change, and weather-related disasters. The best way to properly reduce risk with these issues is to prepare for them. The more resilient your property is to disaster the less it will cost you and the safer your residents will be.

You should thoroughly research the area in which you will make your investment. Some places are prone to hurricanes and tornadoes. Other areas experience blizzards, snowstorms, and fires. You might consider choosing an area with little risk of natural disasters. Doing so could save on repair costs in the long run.

Also be sure to ask the seller for copies of all insurance claims for the past 5-10 years. This is a great way to check for previous property damage.

Do not ignore tax planning

You can't forget about property taxes. High sales prices can make for some pretty high property taxes. Be careful not to underestimate property and income taxes at the time of purchase or sale. Mistakes could reduce your actual return.

The best way to take advantage of the many tax strategies available to real estate investors is to hire a Certified Public Accountant (CPA) who specializes in real estate investments.

Protect your property from exposure to legal issues

There are many things you can do to get yourself in legal trouble as a multifamily property owner such as:

- Breaking landlord-tenant laws
- Not adhering to fair-housing and habitability requirements
- Conflicts that expose your property to liens (contractor disputes)

It's important to be familiar with the law and local regulations to reduce risk and avoid such issues. Failure to do so could result in the loss of your property and even jail time.

Being a successful real estate investor involves many skills. It demands careful planning, thorough due diligence and a good dose of patience.

Watch Out for These Real Estate Investing Scams

Like any industry, investing in real estate comes with the risk of scammers. However, most issues can be avoided by being wary of anything that sounds too good to be true. The following scams are commonly used by con artists to try to dupe real estate investors.

"Get rich quick" seminars

Be wary of real estate investment seminars that sound too good to be true, especially if they promise to show you how to get rich quickly. The information provided is often readily available online for free, and their aim is to con you into spending more money on coaching or expensive books. In many cases, these scammers will try to pressure you into signing up for something or investing in specific properties by telling you that you only have a limited amount of time to respond.

Ponzi scams

Real estate Ponzi schemes involve the scammer convincing investors that they will receive extraordinary returns on their investment. The scammers then use the money for their own purposes and pay previous investors with money from current investors. These so-called "lulling payments" help prevent investors from becoming suspicious, but once the scheme collapses, the scammers disappear with the money.

Cold calling scams

Scammers sometimes cold call or email real estate investors and pretend to be brokers. They typically work from a script to convince investors that they can help with mortgage or real estate investments and mention offers that are hard to resist. Investors who fall for the promises of quick returns for almost no risk soon discover that the broker disappears once the money has been handed over.

Home improvement scams

This type of scam typically occurs on a smaller scale than other types of real estate scams, but it can be very costly nevertheless. It involves contractors approaching property owners with unsolicited offers for improving the property. These deals often sound too good to be true, and investors fall for it thinking it's a cost-effective way to boost property values. The scammer usually asks for payment by cash or check before starting the job and then disappears without doing the work.

Online sale scams

Scammers sometimes take legitimate property listings and then repost them on online classified sites while posing as the estate agent or property manager. This scam is common with rentals, but it is sometimes also used for investment scams. Be wary of promises that sound too good to be true and claims of urgency. The scammer will often ask for a down payment or deposit to hold the property until inspection and then vanish if the investor falls for the scam.

Chapter Nine:
Deal Analysis

What we hope ever to do with ease, we must learn first to do with diligence. – Samuel Johnson

~

Crucial Property Valuation Tips for Buying Apartments

Property valuation can be tricky, even for experienced investors. But there are key elements you'll want to consider when it comes to deciding what property is right for your investment. Knowing what those elements are and how they'll affect your property are vital to making a well-informed offer.

There are so many factors to consider when you are valuing a prospective multifamily acquisition. They will all inform your final offer price, and this is something you'll want to get right. Offering too much could reduce your profitability. Offering too little could cost you the opportunity of ownership.

Verify financial performance

For most investors, this is the first thing they'll look at when considering a property. How much money is coming in every month? And how much is going back out?

You'll want to look at the building's expenses and income closely. Additionally, take time to create a deal analysis spreadsheet. These can take a lot of the guesswork out of a real estate deal and help you feel confident about your property valuation and offer price. Finally, make sure you create a property operating budget. That can give you a realistic budgeting expectation for the first few years of operation.

Check physical condition

The physical condition of the building will inform you about what kind of expenses your building will likely incur in the coming years. Get a closer look at the condition of the building through a professional inspection process.

Inspections should encompass both the interior and exterior of the building. They should look at all the building's systems (plumbing, heating, electrical, and sewer) as well as general appearance.

Make sure that any inspectors or contractors you use are multifamily experts. Your inspection needs will be very different from those of a single-family property. And they should be thorough to give you the most complete picture possible.

Look for necessary improvements

Almost any property you invest in will have some necessary improvements. That could be anything from small deferred maintenance projects to large capital expenditures. But knowing what those improvements are ahead of time will help inform your property valuation.

Build in a budget for improvements by getting estimates from trusted multifamily contractors. Think about improvements you'll make in the next three to five years, as well. Taking these costs into consideration will help you build them into your operating budget. That helps you avoid a cash-flow emergency later on.

Identify value-add opportunities

Buying a property that needs a little work can be a very smart investment. Properties ripe with value-add opportunities can quickly increase in value with small investments of capital.

Look for cosmetic building renovations first. This might be modernizing community spaces, giving rooms a fresh coat of paint, or updating building signage. These are all relatively small projects that can provide big results. Raise the properties income while you lower your expenses and you'll increase the property's value in your investment portfolio.

Research submarket and neighborhood

Research the rental market. It's important to get detailed here. Not only should you have knowledge about the wider rental market in your area, but you should know the submarkets as well. Get down to the neighborhood level. Understand the current supply and demand of the market.

What are the market rents? What amenities are renters asking for? And what apartment trends are on the horizon? When you know your market, you'll know what the property does and doesn't offer that will make it attractive to prospective tenants (and to you as an investor!).

Examine documentation

You'll need to read the fine print. All of it. Documentation is where you'll learn the finer details of the property as well as find any warning signs. Read and review the full seller disclosure(s) and documents. Make sure you review the current leases, too. This will tell you more about your current residents and whether they will meet your goals for the property.

Resource alert: Use the due diligence checklist found in our resource document (theresabradleybanta.com/book_resources) to help ensure you have all the right paperwork to review. If you aren't sure about something you read, make sure you review it with your real estate lawyer and mentor.

Involve management team(s)

The property may be managed by the current owner or run by a professional property management company. Find out how the property has been managed in the past and whether their current operation strategies are working. Remember, you may be an investor, but it's also your job to lead the management team.

It's a good idea to engage your own manager during the acquisition stage. They may be able to see issues or opportunities that you don't. Their insight can be hugely beneficial when it comes to property valuation.

Struggling with property valuation on potential multifamily investments?

Valuation is one of the first steps you'll take when looking to expand (or start) your investment portfolio. It's a skill that takes time to perfect, and some investors struggle with it for years. You build your valuation skills through practice.

Multifamily Deal Analysis Mistakes to Avoid

I often hear new multifamily real estate investors ask, "How do I know if a deal is a good one or not?" It's a valid question.

Without experience and practice it's difficult to challenge the numbers in a property offering memorandum. How do you know if the income is correct? Expenses can seem pretty straight forward—but are they? You'll minimize investment risk by identifying common mistakes before they occur to you.

Underestimating capital expenses, repairs and unit turn costs

Don't overlook the fact that you may have to pay for major capital improvements from day one of ownership. You might also have to pay for general repairs and unit turn costs. Under the current ownership the rental market may have changed. You might inherit rental units that can't compete with the market without major upgrades and repairs.

It's extremely important to know if market rents and expectations have adjusted. Sometimes a buyer will discover, especially in a slow rental market, that renter's expectations have risen. Prospective renters will demand nicer rental units and amenities for their dollar. It might be necessary to bring newly vacant units up to market expectations to attract qualified residents.

In a hot market, with plenty of new construction, discerning residents will demand the latest and hottest amenities.

You might also have to finance repairs to major building systems. For example, a property that has poor drainage systems will continue to deteriorate without immediate upgrades to roofs, sidewalks and parking surfaces.

Assuming current unit rental amounts are at market rate

Buyers of multifamily properties love to look for opportunities to raise the current rents. But before getting too excited by the prospect of raising rents you must first decide if the current rental rates are truly at market.

For example, if a seller has offered concessions to their current residents you must take those concessions into consideration when calculating income. A concession could be a discounted rent given as a signing bonus such as free rent for the first or last month. The owner may have included free utilities. They may have waived payment of the security deposit.

You can also uncover other hidden issues. A seller might have high collection problems with their current residents—a problem that will become yours if you buy the property. And as dishonest as it may seem,

212

some buyers will fill a property with residents who are not properly screened to reach 100% occupancy just before the sale of the property.

Overlooking key operating expenses

When analyzing property historical financials, it's critical that you confirm all expenses when possible. The property taxes and insurance rates paid by the current owner will not necessarily be the same under new ownership. Check with commercial property insurance carriers and shop new rates.

A simple call to the local treasury division can answer your question about potential property tax rate increases and will confirm the amount the seller listed in her/her financials. You might also discover that the current property taxes are in arrears—there may even be a tax lien on the property. Good to know.

Before purchasing a multifamily property, you must verify utility expenses. Contact all utility companies and find out what the utility costs have been for at least one year. Pest control can also be a critical cost to investigate.

As a general rule of thumb, use a 35-45% expense ratio (the percentage of the property income used to pay expenses excluding debt service) when analyzing older apartment buildings and multifamily properties.

Neglecting to find the seller's motivation

Why is the seller really selling? Did you ask? Don't stop after asking this question one time. Ask it as many times as necessary to get to the real reason. Sometimes simply rephrasing the question can get results.

A highly motivated seller might negotiate price and terms. Or give you a credit for needed repairs—an agreed upon amount that you can deduct from the purchase price.

What does the property mean to them? An inherited property for example represents a huge payout to the seller. They are not emotionally attached to the property nor have they contributed financially to capital expenditures. They are less interested in recouping money spent than they are in a windfall at the closing table.

Neglecting to look at current residents and leases

Take a look at all current tenant leases and pay special attention to lease expiration dates. You may be forced to complete expensive unit turns for each new vacancy—especially when a property has significant deferred maintenance. The cost of unit turns can escalate overnight.

You might also find hidden problems within the community. I've seen buildings where the tenants run the property and the property management company has lost all control.

There's nothing worse than a mass exodus from a property, which can happen under a management change. If you introduce new community rules and regulations like tighter rent collection policies, you can expect to lose tenants.

You might also decide to implement stricter tenant qualification guidelines for all lease renewals which can create new vacancies—and more unit turn costs.

Do your homework

Before making an offer on a multifamily property you must examine all income and expenses presented by both the seller and the commercial broker. If you are light on experience get someone on your side who has experience analyzing multifamily properties—someone who is unbiased and doesn't stand to gain financially from the buy/sell transaction.

If you find yourself wondering if a deal is good or not don't do the deal without pursuing expert consultation. So you know, I offer multifamily deal analysis consultations. Interested in learning more?

Multifamily Property Deal Analysis

Looking to buy a multifamily property? How do you know what to offer? How do you know if you've found a great deal?

The key is in practicing thorough analysis. On every deal you look at. The only way you'll get good at multifamily property deal analysis is to practice. The more deals you analyze the better because you will:

- Become proficient with the use of deal analysis spreadsheets
- Develop a baseline for analysis using properties in your submarket
- Gain an understanding of what local renter's want—and what the competition offers
- Become practiced in the art of pro forma assumptions

Here are some tips on multifamily property deal analysis. When you carry out these tips you will start making offers on properties from a knowledgeable standpoint.

Grab a pen

Before opening your multifamily property deal analysis spreadsheets, grab a pen and paper (or open a new text document on your computer) and get ready to start taking notes as you review the deal. I do this every time I look at a new investment opportunity. Sometimes my list is two or three pages long.

Any question that comes to mind, no matter how small or seemingly insignificant, should make your list. For example, your property analysis might raise questions like:

- Why does the property have such a high vacancy rate?
- Does the potential to raise rents really exist?
- The property appears to need some upgrades. How much of the repairs and maintenance will be immediate? What are the immediate and long-range costs?
- Are major building mechanicals like the roof and HVAC system in good condition?
- Why is the owner selling?

Whatever your question or observation, write it down.

Pro tip: The CCIM Institute (ccim.com) offers some excellent excel spreadsheets via a quick search online. You'll also find information on their designation curriculum courses. Worth exploring!

Read the offering memorandum

What are your first reactions? What strikes you as odd? Marketing comments like, "A new major neighborhood development is underway!" or, "Great opportunity to increase rents!" should raise red flags. Neighborhood developments don't always materialize and when they do, they may have no positive affect on the property. If the current owner can raise rents why hasn't he/she already done it?

Hype is hype. Always question extraordinary remarks.

Keep adding to your list of questions. You can use your questions as you negotiate the deal or challenge the offering price if you think it's too high. And the answers to the questions will help you plan for what you'll do with the property if you actually acquire it.

Ready to run the numbers?

Open your property spreadsheets. I generally do three sets of analysis when I analyze a property. Here are the three ways I approach the numbers:

1. Analyze the property using the broker or seller's numbers

I like to run a property analysis based on the numbers provided in the Offering Memorandum (OM) because I want to see how the broker/seller has arrived at an asking price for the property. The OM will give broadly categorized data for income and expenses.

Income usually includes "Gross Potential Rents." This refers to the property's potential rental income at 100% occupancy. The broker/seller will also include "Other Income" such as laundry income, fee income and utility income (tenant reimbursement for utility expenses).

On the expense side you'll see:

- Real estate taxes
- Property insurance
- Utilities (electric, gas, water, sewer and sometimes trash)
- Repairs & maintenance
- Marketing & promotion
- Management & leasing fees
- Administration

Again, the data is broadly categorized. You'll see what I mean when you read the section titled *What Are Typical Apartment Building Operating Expenses?* in Chapter Eighteen: Maintenance.

In most cases you'll see two sets of numbers: the current property income and expenses; and the pro forma income and expenses. Challenge both. I've seen hundreds of offering memorandums where the current numbers are grossly exaggerated. It's not a good place to start when you're attempting to arrive at an offer price.

Pro forma numbers, which are based on assumptions, are often nothing more than calculated guesswork. For example, potential rental income is often based on "market rents"—the rent local competition charges for their units. However, the potential to realize "market rents" may not be realistic for the property you're analyzing.

Until you complete significant upgrades and repairs, you won't be able to command market rents. Or you'll discover that the property is in a small pocket of a neighborhood that will never realize market rents. Or the property has a poor reputation that only proficient management, time and great marketing will fix.

It's your job to investigate and challenge the pro forma numbers. As my favorite mentor says, "If the grass is green, someone's been fertilizing." A great place to start is by taking a look at where the property is today. And where it's been over the past two or three years.

2. Analyze the property using the historical operating data

A property's Historical Operating Data are the Year to Date (YTD) property financials. You get them by asking for them.

I like to run a property analysis based on the seller's current and historical operating financials because I want to see how the property actually performs today. Without assumptions and glorified pro forma numbers.

Also known as Annual Property Operating Data (APOD) these financials will include:

- Annual YTD profit & loss statement

- Property rent roll

These two documents are rarely included up front. You must ask for them.

On the income side:

You can use Gross Potential Rent when running this analysis. But do not base the rental amount on "market rents." Use the current rents listed in the property rent roll. (You'll learn more about using a rent roll later in this chapter).

Be sure to base your Gross Potential Rent at 100% occupancy. If some of the units are vacant find out what they would rent for or use your best guess based on the unit type. Also, don't forget to apply the market vacancy rate to your analysis. You might think twice about using the current, record-setting low vacancies of today—I use a 7% vacancy in my local market analysis.

Include any other income the seller lists in their YTD statements.

On the expense side:

Use the P&L statement provided by the seller. Rather than base your analysis on the broadly categorized income and expenses a seller/broker generally provides, use all the line item property expenses.

You want to arrive at a picture of where the property is today.

Does it cash flow? Is the owner self-managing or using a third-party management company? Can the rents be raised? Don't change your analysis based on what you will do with the property. Use the seller's numbers to get a good picture of the property under its current ownership.

You'll learn a lot from this analysis. For example, you'll know:

- If the seller is motivated to sell
- Whether the asking price is realistic

Don't forget to keep taking notes from your analysis of the property.

The art of multifamily property deal analysis

Obviously, a seller/broker will paint the best picture of a property in support of their asking price. After you take a look at how the property actually performs today you may not want to offer the full asking price.

Should you make a lower offer based on what you see in your analysis of the APOD? Many sellers are struggling with their property. They are not currently realizing the returns a property should get when managed and operated well.

Your job is to decide what the property is worth to you in the long run. What is an acceptable return for you and your partners?

Important: Don't forget to include the necessary capital expenditures that will come out of your pocket to upgrade a property to it's fullest potential. Money you may have to spend from the first day of ownership. Also, consider the time and cost (including lost revenue) to get the property fully operational.

3. Analyze the property from a pro forma perspective

Now it's time to look at the property as if you actually own it. How will this property do financially under your good management and new operations policies?

For this analysis you'll need to create or get a spreadsheet that includes categories for all projected income, expenses, debt service and capital expenditures over a 12-month period.

Resource alert: You'll find a sample pro forma spreadsheet in our resource document at: theresabradleybanta.com/book_resources.

On the income side:

Begin month one with the current occupancy and expenses. If the property is at 25% vacancy, start there. Make income projections based on your ability to begin to rent out the vacant units and increase rents over the next six to twelve months. However long it will take to reach market occupancy and market rents if possible.

Do the same with other income. For example, if the current residents are not paying for their utilities but you will be implementing a utility reimbursement program for all new leases and renewing leases, project that future income in your analysis. Do the same for new fees or other ancillary income you will introduce to the property.

Ancillary income would include fees such as: common area usage, trash, vending, parking, storage, guest suites for visitors, clubroom rentals, bulk telecom programs (bundle TV, internet and phone), renter's insurance, and pet deposits.

On the expense side:

This is where having a good baseline from similar properties comes in handy. Or having a good mentor in your corner. A multifamily real estate investing mentor can help you with pro forma assumptions. For some good tips on this topic read *How to Create a Reality-based Multifamily Pro Forma Budget* in Chapter Nine: Deal Analysis.

Start with the current expenses as provided by the seller. Now replace the expenses that will change under new ownership. For example, if you plan to hire a third-party management company at a 6% management fee, use that cost in your analysis. Other property expenses that will change under new management are:

- Insurance
- Taxes
- Debt service (mortgage payments)
- Leasing fees
- Maintenance fees
- Trash removal
- Legal and accounting

You get the idea. When you own the property, you will not be paying the same expenses or debt service as the previous owner.

You can get a good idea of expenses by shopping around. For example, check with your local tax assessor to find out what the new property taxes will be. Call your insurance agent and verify the cost of new insurance. Call local vendors such as trash removal companies and ask about their service fees. Talk with your property manager about their associated costs and fees.

This analysis will help you arrive at a fair offer price. Is the current reality so dismal it will take years and large infusions of cash for the property to reach its full potential? Or is the property worth the current asking price because it is well-managed and operated? Is there a happy medium?

When you thoroughly analyze a real estate deal you remove the guesswork.

Another benefit of multifamily property deal analysis is that you'll have a great strategy in place for what needs to be done the day you close on the deal.

Practice, practice, and practice some more

The best way to become great at multifamily property deal analysis is to practice. A lot. Thorough multifamily property deal analysis is the best way to avoid making costly mistakes.

Real estate is a game of negotiation. It's expected. Guesswork is not.

Multifamily Rent Roll Analysis

A rent roll is an itemized list of current residents by unit and the amount of rent paid by each resident in a multi-tenant property.

Two great uses for a property rent roll are:

- Analyzing a potential property for acquisition an
- Tracking your property management company's performance.

When you analyze a multifamily property for acquisition your analysis must include a thorough review of the rent roll. Most sellers and brokers will provide a summary of the property listing in an offering memorandum. Rarely does this documentation include a rent roll.

As a real estate investor, it's your job to get a copy.

A well-prepared rent roll can include:

- Unit number, unit type and square footage
- Resident name, move-in and move-out dates
- Lease term and lease expiration date
- Rent (current and market), security deposit and starting balance
- Additional income such as parking fees and storage fees
- All other charges (late fees, utility reimbursement, etc.)
- Amount paid and balance due

Note: The rent roll will show you the maximum rental income at 100% occupancy. This is also known as the Gross Scheduled Rents.

Resource alert: Following is a sample rent roll. You'll also find one in our resource document at: theresabradleybanta.com/book_resources

Rent Roll: City Apartments

Unit No.	Unit Type	sq ft	Tenant Name	Lease Start	Term	Move-in Date	Lease Expiration	Security Deposit
101	Studio	350	Linley, Thomas	3/1/20	12	3/3/20	2/28/21	$850.00
102	3br	1100	Millhone, Kinsey	12/1/19	12	12/1/19	11/30/20	$1,200.00
103	2br	850	Marlowe, Phillip	2/1/20	12	2/1/20	1/31/21	$1,050.00
104	2br	775	Spade, Sam	7/1/95	MTM	7/1/95	6/30/96	$1,200.00
105	3br	1200	Alleyn, Roderick	6/1/18	MTM	6/1/18	5/31/19	$1,200.00
106	3br	1200	Maigret, Jules	2/1/20	12	2/1/20	1/31/21	$1,200.00
107	Studio	350	Wimsey, Peter	2/1/19	12	2/1/19	1/31/20	$850.00
108	3br	1100	Marple, Jane	6/1/19	12	6/1/19	5/31/20	$1,200.00
109	2br	775	Poirot, Hercule	2/1/18	MTM	2/1/18	7/31/19	$1,050.00
110	2br	850	Homes, Sherlock	9/1/19	12	9/1/19	8/31/20	$1,050.00

(cont.)

Unit No.	Rent	Last Increase	Concession	Loss to Lease	Parking	Other	Amount Paid	Balance Due
101	$850.00		$0.00	$0.00	$50.00	$0.00	$850.00	$0.00
102	$1,200.00		$0.00	$0.00	$50.00	$0.00	$600.00	$600.00
103	$1,050.00		$0.00	$50.00	$50.00	$0.00	$1,050.00	$0.00
104	$1,100.00	6/30/98	$0.00	$75.00	$0.00	$25.00	$1,200.00	$0.00
105	$1,200.00	6/1/19	$0.00	$100.00	$50.00	$0.00	$800.00	$400.00
106	$1,200.00		$0.00	$100.00	$0.00	$25.00	$1,200.00	$0.00
107	$850.00		$0.00	$0.00	$50.00	$0.00	$0.00	$1,700.00
108	$1,200.00		$0.00	$0.00	$50.00	$25.00	$700.00	$500.00
109	$1,050.00	2/1/19	$0.00	$50.00	$0.00	$33.00	$1,050.00	$0.00
110	$1,050.00		$0.00	$50.00	$50.00	$25.00	$1,000.00	$50.00

Most multi-tenant property rent rolls will not include this level of data, but they should. Practical analysis of a multifamily rent roll will allow you to do the following.

Confirm the current property income stream

With a careful review of the rent roll you can verify the current rental income and income from other sources such as fees and utility expenses. Compare this to the numbers the seller or broker provided in their analysis of the property income. If you find a gross discrepancy between the income on the rent roll and on the offering memorandum it's time to start asking some questions.

In addition to reviewing the current rent roll you must get a copy of past rent rolls going back as far as 12-14 months. At the very least request a rent roll for the same period for the prior year. This will provide good baseline data for your income analysis.

Track the property management's performance

A rent roll will show you how long each resident has been at a property and when his or her lease term expires.

You will also be able to see the current vacancies and you'll know when to expect future vacancies. Take note if a large number of tenants have recently moved in. Some sellers will fill vacancies just prior to a sale. In order to fill a property quickly they may have lowered their tenant screening standards or made concessions that you as the new owner will be stuck with for the term of the lease.

If you see high turnover and collection issues it should raise some red flags. Late rent payments and unpaid fees will also raise red flags. All of these issues are a sign that further due diligence is required.

Use the data to analyze future opportunities

Sellers often advertise their property as having below market rents. They'll do this so that you will base your offer price on potential rental income.

Compare the current rental income (most recent actual rent) to market averages to arrive at your Potential Rental Income. Don't rely on the numbers provided by the seller or listing broker. You will not be able to command higher rental rates if the current rents are already at market.

227

Review all other fees (income) as shown on the rent roll. Look for opportunities to increase revenue. For example, in addition to raising rents there may be an opportunity to increase other property income. Are the current residents paying for their utility usage? Are paid services such parking being fully used by the current residents?

Use the data to analyze future expenses

A review of the rent roll for the past 12-24 months will show a vacancy history for the property. But don't let your analysis stop there.

You must review vacancies on a unit-by-unit basis. Look for "down-time" on each unit. A vacancy of several months could indicate that the unit was under renovation or it could indicate that the unit is difficult to rent. A submarket may have a demand for one- and two-bedroom units with very little renter interest for three-bedroom units.

It could also be an indication of a long drawn out eviction process—or the result of property damage such as fire, flooding or structural damage. Take note of any anomalies, both for individual units and the property as a whole, and ask the seller or listing broker for answers about why these anomalies occurred.

Structural damage, pest control problems, poor property management/maintenance can all contribute to historical high vacancy numbers.

You might find a property where tenants were given the last month's rent free of charge as a signing incentive. Be sure you are aware of all outstanding commitments. Find out if concessions such as discounted security deposits or other resident incentives were offered to the current residents.

A last word on rent roll analysis

The rent roll should be reviewed against all current leases in effect before closing on the property. Verify the rent roll for accuracy by checking resident names; rental amounts; lease terms and expiration dates; concessions; security deposits; all commitments made by the property owner; and any other agreements that will carry over to you as the new owner.

Your lender or bank will need a notarized copy of the current rent roll (provided by the seller) before closing.

If you are uncomfortable with your level of expertise with investment property due diligence, find an experienced investor or consultant and ask them to take a look at the property rent roll with you. This document is a critical part of your due diligence and should not be overlooked or taken lightly.

Don't Rely on the 50% Rule to Analyze Multifamily Real Estate

The 50% rule. Have you heard of it? There are some real estate investors who swear by it. A great many beginning real estate investors have not only heard of it—especially online and in forums—they use it when they analyze a prospective investment property. Often to their detriment. Why do I say that?

First . . . what is the 50% rule?

The 50% rule is a very quick and very rough estimate of a rental property's profitability.

It's a quick and simple formula used to determine what percentage of rental property income is used to pay expenses—excluding debt service. For example, say you find a property with a monthly income of $10,000 (all income including rent, laundry, fees, etc.). Using the 50% rule you estimate the monthly expenses at $5,000 (50% of $10,000). That leaves you with $5,000 to pay the mortgage and, hopefully, have some cash left for you.

Why don't I like it? Why do I feel adamant that new real estate investors should not use the formula?

- It promotes bad habits.
- There's a good chance you'll miss crucial expense information.
- Simple rule of thumb calculations should never be used alone.
- You might inadvertently arrive at an insulting offer price—and blow your opportunity to pick up a property right out of the gate.
- You might pass on an excellent investment opportunity.

It's a grossly inadequate tool when used as a stand-alone tool for analyzing a property—especially multifamily properties.

Here's some thoughts on why you shouldn't rely on the 50% rule to analyze multifamily real estate opportunities:

Crucial expense information

When you use the 50% rule, you assume 50% of rental property income is used to pay monthly property expenses. So what monthly expenses are we talking about? That's the million-dollar question.

Line-item investment property expenses include:

- Taxes
- Insurance
- Utilities (water, sewer, gas, electric, trash)
- Property Management
- Advertising and Marketing
- Leasing
- Legal Costs
- Capital Expenditures
- Maintenance and Repairs

Here's where you have to worry a little bit—especially if you're new to investing or if you're investing in an unfamiliar asset class. Did you know that most of the expense categories above also include sub-line item expenses?

For example, "Maintenance and Repairs" might include:

- Property cleaning
- Landscaping and snow removal
- Common area cleaning
- Appliance repair

- Painting rental units
- Carpet cleaning
- Cleaning supplies
- Maintenance supplies
- Pest control
- Window and screen repair

"Maintenance and Repairs" can also include:

- Leaking toilet repair
- Plumbing repair
- Drywall repair
- Flooring repair or replacement
- Electric repair
- Lock service
- Parking and sidewalk maintenance and repair
- Window replacement
- Unit turns (cost to make a vacant unit ready for the next tenant)
- Painting interior, exterior and common areas

As the new owner you will be responsible for paying all property expenses. Are you comfortable relying on a grossly simplified rule? You cannot properly evaluate an investment property until you have:

- Actual line item expenses (historical data at least two years back)
- An accounting of the current income (all sources) including vacancy

The 50% rule is never a good catch-all number

Even when you have a solid understanding of the long list of typical property expenses you can still miss things if you rely solely on the 50% rule.

You might miss:

Red flags

Let's say you have out-of-whack expenses—expenses that are way above average. For example, the property could be experiencing extremely high water utility expenses or pest control expenses. This could be indicative of serious issues at a property.

How will you catch these red flags if you rely solely on the 50% rule?

Who exactly is paying the bills?

It's not safe to assume that the tenants are paying 100% of the utilities—an expense that averages 8-12% of total income. Nor is it safe to assume the current owner is paying for third-party management—an expense that averages 6-8% of total income.

The 50% rule does not factor in variances from property to property. A guess could be costly. 6-12% is a big chunk of the 50% allocated for expenses!

What about deferred maintenance, capital expenditures and poorly screened tenants?

The proponents of the 50% rule say that over time most property expenses will be at 50% when you factor in capital expenditures (property improvements beyond general repairs). They'll claim that all expenses, including capital expenditures, will average 50% over time. But did you know that multifamily properties have an average expense ratio of 35-45% annually? That doesn't leave much wiggle room for your capital expenditures if you're already approaching 50% in annual operating expenses, does it?

Nor does the 50% rule tell you if a property has significant deferred maintenance, or costly ongoing expenses due to end-of-life building systems such as roof, heating and plumbing.

And if a property is full of poorly screened tenants chances are good that tenant turnover is high—resulting in higher (and more frequent) unit turn expenses.

All of the above factors can grossly skew your expense numbers.

A big risk to using the 50% rule

In my opinion the biggest risk to using the 50% rule is the temptation to be a know-it-all about a property you really don't know much about.

- You might pass on a deal because it doesn't look good at a glance.
- You might approach a seller with a low-ball offer and lose the deal.

- You might get stuck with a property that never provides cash flow.

Sure, the 50% rule is a really quick tool. It's a helpful tool to determine at a glance if you want to pursue a property—or pass. But the rule is only useful when you know the property type through years of successful real estate investing. And even then, you might miss nuances from property to property.

You'll quickly realize your mistake when you start pulling out your checkbook to pay for expenses you missed during your "quick and simple" analysis. Why not take the same "quick glance" at an itemized list of property income and expenses?

Don't rely on the broadly categorized numbers you find in the property listing data. Get the historical operating date (annual expenses and income) from the seller.

Wise investors spend a few extra minutes in their analysis of prospective deals.

Easy Steps to a Simple, Quick Multifamily Property Valuation

An accurate multifamily property evaluation is essential for the profitability and long-term success of your real estate investing business. Beginners should absolutely seek some guidance and input from a trusted advisor. Whether you are planning to purchase an apartment or a duplex, cash flow is crucial. Here are seven steps to simple, quick multifamily property valuation.

Know the market

To help you stay current on trends and determine value for multifamily properties in some major metropolitan areas, Freddie Mac provides the Apartment Investment Market Index. This free online tool is updated quarterly and gives you a better understanding of current conditions and where your local market may be heading.
Evaluate the local area

It is especially important for new investors to stay close to home with investments. You should know the location fairly well and have a good idea of what rents are being charged and if any new apartment complexes are in the works. You need to have a good idea of what locals can afford and what your competitors are offering.

Do some simple math

You should take the total rent a property is bringing in and divide it by the number of units. You have to consider what you can reasonably expect to get after you take ownership. For a quick evaluation, plan on expenses being 30 to 50 percent of your total income. It is better to be overly conservative with your estimate than too optimistic.

Estimate needed repairs

If the current owners have been neglecting basic maintenance and ignoring needed repairs, you must subtract the cost of bringing the property up to rentable condition from the value. Just like estimating expenses, you also want to estimate repair costs on the high side rather than the low end.

Know your capitalization (CAP) rate

Working out the capitalization rate of a property, is another way to determine whether you are getting a good return on rental property. The higher the cap rate is, the better the annual return on your investment will be. Of course, you should bear in mind that cap rates differ from city to city and even across neighborhoods.

The cap rate is simply the percentage return you get on your investment if you paid cash for the purchase. Take your net operating income (NOI), which is revenue minus expenses, and divide it by the purchase price for your cap rate.

Whether a CAP rate is good or bad will depend on your investment goals, with some investors happy if their CAP rate is as low as seven percent and others aiming for nothing less than ten percent.

Evaluate the unit mix

Unit mix is the percentage of units that are one-bedroom, two-bedroom, and three-bedroom. One-bedroom units are great for single people just getting started. Three bedrooms appeal to families. You must know what is in demand for your market.

Consider why the property is for sale

Regardless of how good something may look on paper, landlording takes place in the real world. You want a motivated seller, but you do not want to buy a headache from someone else.

Use the one percent rule

The One Percent Rule is one of the general rules of thumb used by investors to determine if a rental property is performing as it should. It simply states that the rent before expenses—in other words, the gross monthly rent—must be equal to at least one percent of the purchase price.

This means that the gross revenue of the property would be 12 percent of the purchase price each year, although after expenses, the net revenue is actually closer to 6 to 8 percent.

Some investors also consider it a good return when the monthly rent of a property is 2 percent or more of the purchase price plus repairs.

Know your gross rent multiplier

A gross rent multiplier is another rule of thumb for measuring whether you are getting a good return on rental property for a certain area compared to the other properties nearby. It is calculated by dividing the price or value of the property by the gross rent. The lower the resulting gross rent multiplier is, the better the investment. However, this method doesn't take into account other expenses and is more of a general way to compare rental returns.

These rent-to-purchase-price rules are useful for evaluating whether a property is achieving a good return, but they are all subject to a myriad of external factors that can influence their accuracy. Factors such as the type of property, location and amount of financing all play a big role when it comes to returns, so always look at the bigger picture.

How to Value a Multi-Unit Property

Multifamily properties can be a solid investment and a great addition to any portfolio. Benefits range from more reliable income than you'd get from a single-family to a lower price per unit than one-family properties provide.

All advantages aside, when you're considering multifamily properties—especially those with more than five units—you have to be careful when it comes to where you're investing. The state of your investment and your return is where you need to focus your attention, and that's usually something you can forecast by examining the seller's financials.

How value is determined

When you're looking at a single-family property, the value is determined by the appraiser looking at recent sales of similar properties in the same area. When you value a multifamily property, the return of investment the owner receives is front and center. It's difficult to find multi-units in the same area with the same features, so the money the seller is making off that property is largely what determines its value.

The value of a multifamily property can be changed internally by the seller raising rents or lowering expenses.

It's vital you know how to correctly value a multi-unit property so you don't overpay, which can prevent you from achieving a profitable cash flow.

Value determination: the basics

As you're reviewing the seller's financials, keep the basics of value determination for multi-unit properties as follows in your mind:

- **Income:** all the revenue the property generates
- **Expenses:** all the property's expenses other than capital expenditures and debt service
- **Net operating income:** the income minus the expenses
- **Debt service:** mortgages and other loans covered the property
- **Cash after debt service:** the net operating income minus the mortgage or other debt service

The net operating income is your biggest concern. The goal of a successful multi-unit property owner is to improve the NOI by decreasing expenses and bumping up revenue. The higher the NOI, the more cash that will be available after the mortgage is paid.

Still, you want to look at all aspects of the seller's current financial picture so you have a reasonable idea of what you're getting and what you're not with the property you're thinking about investing in. Check if the seller is carrying a lot of monthly expenses that eat into his or her profit flow and if so, find out why.

Carefully reviewing and assessing the seller's financial picture before you invest in a multifamily property can save you some unpleasant surprises and help shape realistic expectations before you buy. Always insist on a full financial disclosure from a multi-unit seller!

Purchasing a rental property can be a costly exercise thanks to down payments, loan fees, closing fees and other expenses. Even after the purchase, additional money will probably be required for maintenance, taxes, insurance and other unforeseen issues. To make all of this worthwhile, the rental property should yield a good return; otherwise, there would be no point in investing all this money.

How To Estimate Property Expenses in an Uncharted Market

A crucial part of analyzing potential investment properties is estimating your property expenses (operating expenses) as accurately as possible. These costs may include landscape maintenance, insurance, property taxes, payroll, and other management costs. Your operating expenses entail all costs except for any bank loan that was used to purchase the property.

Property expenses as percentage of gross operating income

When analyzing the financials of a rental investment property, operating costs should be between 35 and 50 percent of the gross operating income (GOI). For some high-end rental properties, the percentage may be higher. If your calculation puts operating expenses at less than 35 percent of the GOI, you should evaluate the projected numbers again. It helps to have someone else familiar with rental property ownership to review your estimates.

Maintenance costs

This depends largely on the age and condition of the property. Your inspector can provide some insight into what needs immediate attention

241

and other problems that will need to be repaired down the road. Budget for capital expenses such as lot paving, roof replacement, and upgrades to HVAC accordingly and you will most likely be able to handle some smaller unexpected issues.

Payroll and outside managers

When using outside management companies and other contractors, call around to see what the local costs are for the needed service. You may find that you are better off paying top dollar for the best service providers rather than having to constantly replace people who are willing to work for less. Keep that in mind as you figure your costs.

Insurance

You can contact your insurance agent with some specifics on the property and get a quote based on the coverage you need. Remember to encourage or require renters to carry their own renters' insurance policy, which can help you get a lower rate with your provider.

Tax deductions and other considerations

Have tenants cover as much of the costs related to their occupancy of the units as possible. When residents pay for water and other utilities according to how much they personally use, they are more likely to use less. You can promote the concept of requiring tenants to cover their own water and gas costs as a way to keep rental rates low for everyone. You can also deduct some necessary expenses on your tax return. Be sure to consult with your personal tax professional about what is best for your individual situation.

Poor operating cost calculations can mean the difference between a tidy profit and a significant loss, so be sure to take the time to investigate investment property expenses carefully.

Predicting operating expenses

The Operating Expense Ratio of apartment complexes can range anywhere from 25 to 50 percent (or higher) and is greatly affected by the building's age. Before investing in an apartment complex, it is imperative to figure out whether you are actually getting a good deal or not. Predicting your operating expenses for the year is important to help you create an accurate budget and identify areas where you can increase income and decrease spending.

Historical cash flow data

The sales listing brochure of an apartment building will typically list the operating expenses of the property in broad categories such as Taxes, Utilities, Insurance, Maintenance, Administrative and Property Management. This should give you a rough indication of what to expect for the coming year.

However, just like the bank, you should ask to see the historical cash flow figures for this property for the past two years to get a more accurate prediction. Take a look at the two years and compare the increase in expenses from one year to the next while remembering to take inflation into account when doing calculations.

Compare to other properties

Find at least five other property listings that are similar to the apartment complex you are looking at and ask for their property listing data and operating expenses. The operating expense data will give you an indication of the baseline for typical operating expenses in the current market.

Another useful source to get a baseline from is the National Apartment Association Survey of Apartment Operating Income and Expenses (naa.hq). Comparing the property to others will not only give you a more accurate prediction for the coming year, but it will also help you identify possible problem areas.

Do your own calculations

As soon as an apartment complex changes ownership, certain changes can affect your expenses in a big way. These can include taxes, insurance, property management, maintenance, repairs, and utilities.

For example, the property will be reassessed in most states after you purchase a complex and taxed based on the new value. This means that instead of looking at past figures, you should use your purchase price to estimate the taxes you'll be paying. With insurance, you could also get a better deal using your own insurer instead of the one currently used by the complex. With property management, you can check to see if better deals are available from different companies.

You can use different methods to predict an apartment complex's operating expenses for the coming year. In doing so, always try to get the most accurate data and compare your results to a baseline.

How to Create a Reality-Based Multifamily Pro Forma Budget

You're ready to invest in a new multifamily property. Before you get started, however, it's important to put together a realistic look at what income and expenses you can expect over the first year or two of owning the property. You do this by approaching your deal analysis from a multifamily pro forma budget point of view. In other words, what happens to property income and expenses once you own the property?

You don't want to get stuck with a property that is a constant drain on your resources; rather, you want a property that will help generate income and improve your financial portfolio. By taking a reality-based point of view as you pursue your investment, you'll discover that you're in a much better position to predict expenses once you take over the property.

Start with the trailing financials (T12)

The seller should provide a T12 when you're considering the property. If not, ask for a copy. A T12 is the 12-month trailing profit and loss statement for the property. It will allow you to evaluate profit and loss under the current ownership. But it won't provide a perfectly accurate statement of exactly what you can expect after you own the property.

Listing brokers will likely start by promoting profitability: a clear look at what you could make from the property in a pie-in-the-sky reality. Their offering memorandum will likely show the highest possible income and a low look at potential expenses.

Your ultimate numbers will not look like the seller's or broker's. Sure, you may have great results. You may be able to increase income or decrease expenses. That doesn't mean you should rely on those numbers in your own pro forma budget.

Multifamily pro forma budgeting from a reality based POV

Review the T12 and the brokers offering memorandum but take both with a grain of salt. Your multifamily pro forma budget should include your numbers, not the ones offered by the seller or broker. Ultimately, this will give you a better look at what you can expect from the property.

To arrive at your offer price, start by projecting your income and expenses through your first 12-24 months of ownership. The goal is to develop an understanding of your cash needs beyond the down payment and closing costs. This is especially important if you plan on having partners throughout your ownership. No one enjoys cash calls!

Ask yourself these key questions to help project and predict your income and expenses.

What rental income can we expect on day one?

Consider the current vacancies—or the ones expected at closing if there are tenants preparing to move in or out. Also review the current rent roll.

Do not use market vacancy to arrive at your numbers. If there are higher vacancy levels in the property, you may find that you struggle to fill those vacancies in a timely manner. On the other hand, if every unit is filled, you may be able to expect a higher level of income. A current rent roll is a critical part of your multifamily pro forma budget and should not be ignored or overlooked.

Will leases renew or expire?

How long do current leases on the property last? Do tenants usually choose to renew, or do tenants often move on after their lease has expired?

Scrutinize the leases that will expire soon after you take ownership. Often, tenants choose to leave under new ownership because they expect rents to increase. Consider how long units will be down during renovations, especially if you have plans for big renovations and changes throughout the building.

You can't count on the same occupancy numbers that the property currently has, especially if you know that you're going to make significant changes to the building or to the individual units. Noise and consistent disruptions across the property can also lead to new vacancies.

What property expenses are likely to change?

Some expenses will remain relatively consistent even when a property changes ownership. Others, however, you can expect to change such as the following:

- **Liability, hazard, and umbrella insurance:** You can't know when you look at the seller's insurance expense whether they are over- or underinsured. During your due diligence period, speak with an insurance broker and get a quote effective for your closing date. Make sure that it is based on your specific needs and includes

247

the appropriate riders for your loan: flood insurance, hurricane insurance, earthquake insurance, loss of rents, code changes, and so on. Your insurance is the first line of defense for risk management and asset protection, so make sure you don't let it fall by the wayside!

- **Personal property taxes.** Some jurisdictions will tax non-real property that is included with an asset. Make sure you're taking this into account.

- **Utilities.** Do you plan to introduce a tenant utility reimbursement program as leases renew or are signed? If so, your utility income and costs will change. Utility usage may change. You may also find that utility costs change if you introduce significant improvements to the building or due to weather differences from year to year.

- **Property taxes.** Sometimes, sales trigger a tax increase. Contact the assessor's office to get a better idea of when you can expect from property taxes.

- **Property management.** Is the seller self-managing? If not, who do they use as a property manager? You might want to continue working with that individual. Chances are, you'll bring in your own property management company. As a result, management expenses may change drastically. Also, your rates may differ based on the number of buildings you own or a range of other factors.

- **Debt Service.** Do you intend to pay all cash for the property? Or will you finance a portion of the purchase? If financing, you'll want to include the debt service expense when arriving at total cash needed.

What are our immediate cash needs?

As you prepare to take on a new property, make sure you have ready cash on hand to handle immediate needs. This might include:

- Unit renovations
- Unit refresh costs (basic repairs and maintenance)
- Addressing common area deferred maintenance
- Additional leasing fees and commissions
- New signage and marketing materials

You'll also want to be sure that you really know your market before you take over the property so that you can adequately prepare for potential expenses, including giving potential tenants more of what they want. Some questions to ask are:

- What do prospective tenants want? What will they pay for it? And can you give it to them and still be profitable?
- Can you expect to fill vacancies quickly?
- Is your renovation budget accurate?
- How quickly can you turn units? Raise rent?
- How much cash will you need to keep in reserve?

By answering these questions, you'll get a better idea of what changes need to be made quickly in order to help the property reach its full potential— and therefore put together a better multifamily pro forma budget.

Resource alert: Following is a sample multifamily pro forma spreadsheet. You'll also find one in our resource document at: theresabradleybanta.com/book_resources.

Description	January	February
# Occupied Units		
# of Vacant Units		
Occupancy		
Annual Operating Income	January	February
Gross Potential Rent		
Rent Collected		
Laundry Income		
Parking Income		
Pet Rent		
Pet Fee		
Application Fee		
Utility Reimbursement		
Other Income		
Other Income		
Total Income	0	0
Annual Operataing Expenses	January	February
Resident Manager		
Maint & Repairs		
Landscape		
Snow Removal		
Pest Control		
HVAC Repair and Service		
Paint & Decorate		
Make Ready Expense		
Water & Sewer		
Trash Removal		
Gas		
Electric		
Telephone; Cell, DSL		
Waste Water		
Leasing Fees		
Advertising		
Bookkeeping		
Professional Management		
Legal		
CPA		
Insurance		
Taxes		
Total Expenses	0	0

Description	January	February
Net Operating Income (NOI)	0	0
Debt Service		
2nd Note		
3rd Note		
NOI After Debt Service	0	0
Capital Expenses	January	February
Appliances		
Carpet Replacement		
Heating / AC		
Landscape		
Electrical Update		
Plumbing Update		
Roofing		
Halls, decks, stairs, railings		
Asphalt/concrete Repair/Replacement		
Total Capital Expenses	0	0
NOI after Debt and Capital Expenses	0	0
Cumulative Cash Needs	0	0

The Do's and Don'ts of Real Estate Investment Pro Forma Analysis

A real estate investment pro forma is a pretty important document in real estate investment that covers the expected cash flow of the subject property. Before you sit down and take a closer look at the pro forma for your next deal, here's what you need to do—and what to avoid.

Do ask about the source

Sometimes, sellers or brokers will inflate the investment pro forma by estimating items based on something not yet proven. For example, a building may call for higher rent than what is currently being charged, so the broker goes ahead and makes the pro forma based on potential rent figures. However, in this case, the rent hasn't been raised yet, and there's no guarantee that higher rents won't lead to a higher vacancy rate.

A pro forma based on real numbers is far better than one based on projections, so always ask for the data sources for all figures.

Don't take the vacancy rate at face value

There are two things to watch out for when it comes to the vacancy rate: underestimating and overestimating. A statement with a vacancy rate of 2 percent, even if that is what the seller is currently experiencing, isn't very conservative. To better prepare yourself for the variables, recalculate the figures using a vacancy rate between 7 and 10 percent.

251

An overestimated vacancy rate on a pro forma, on the other hand, is more of a red flag about the property, as it could mean the seller wasn't able to attract or keep tenants. For a more realistic view of vacancies, ask the seller for rent records over the past five years.

Do get additional income detail

Your pro forma may have a listing for additional income, which is revenue generated by the property in ways other than rent. A complex that charges for parking, for example, has that extra income coming in. If additional income is listed, get documentation of its source. Extra revenue is good to have, but you need to evaluate the stability of that stream before you consider it.

Don't take listed expenses as the final word

A pro forma may not include all the expenses that it should. It's easy to forget occasional expenses, like snow removal fees in the winter, but these costs absolutely factor into the overall investment. There may be expenses associated with additional income items that are not factored in, too. Dig deeper around the property's expenses and try to get as much information as possible from the seller.

While an investment pro forma is a good way to get a snapshot of the prospective properties you're considering, don't completely rely on it. Do your own research before buying your next property.

Chapter Ten:
Due Diligence and Negotiation

Negotiation in the classic diplomatic sense assumes parties more anxious to agree than to disagree. – Dean Acheson

~

Due Diligence: What It Is, and Why It Matters

You learn early as a real estate investor that there are no shortcuts to success and no guarantees. The same is true of due diligence. Investing involves a lot of hard work and some degree of uncertainty.

Due diligence requires time and effort, but it does serve to reduce your risks. That makes it well worth the upfront time investment you make on any property you are considering. The majority of costly mistakes investors make could have been avoided through proper due diligence. Maintaining a profit is difficult in any economic climate, and it is more difficult when you have a lot of unanticipated costs.

Determining property value

There are a lot of moving parts to any real estate transaction. Investment properties have even more factors affecting the value. If a property is making money for the current owner, why are they selling it? Something must be motivating them. One of the first things you should assess is why they are selling. It could be because there are some upcoming costs associated with the property that will derail its profitability and throw it into the red.

Be sure that any contract you sign provides ample time for due diligence and a clause that allows you to renegotiate the terms of the contract or exit the transaction if necessary, based on what is discovered during the due diligence period. Use a due diligence checklist and begin all inspections as quickly as possible.

Resource alert: Download and print your own due diligence checklist at theresabradleybanta.com/book_resources.

Do your footwork

In addition to personally inspecting the property, you should also make an effort to speak with as many tenants as possible and interview employees when possible. They can be greatly informative and provide you with some insight as to your possible upcoming role as landlord. Keep in mind that a seller usually does not want the residents to know the property is for sale. So, be discreet during your casual conversations.

Financial due diligence

This is a tedious and time-consuming process. You do not want to learn as you go. You should engage the assistance of an experienced investor or mentor in your specific real estate investment niche. You also should be using a CPA who specializes in investment property.

Call upon them for this phase of due process.

This can involve reviewing available operating statements, property financials and leases. Be sure there are no special clauses in any lease that may lower the monthly rent for some tenants. The seller should be able to provide a full accounting of security deposits.

Review existing insurance policies and check for lower cost options. Ask for information about insurance claims made in the previous five years. There should also be a complete inventory of all property being transferred in the sale. And be sure to obtain copies of the trailing financials covering the past two or three years. These financials are also known as Annual Property Operating Data (APOD), or Profit and Loss Statements.

Proper due diligence takes patience, effort, and utilizing a team of professionals. It provides you with an understanding of the property's construction, maintenance history, and potential for profitability.

What to Look for When Buying an Apartment Building

As someone looking to invest in apartment buildings, you'll want to keep the following checklist in the front of your mind. Keep in mind that apartment buildings meeting some of the following requirements will fall under the "value-add" category. In other words, a property that needs improvements to management, the physical building and sometimes the occupants or staff.

It's a good and often profitable strategy—but not one for the faint of heart in spite of what you read on the Internet. For example, a value-add property requires someone who can:

- bring the skills to take over for troubled property management
- make improvements and repairs to the property
- reposition the tenant base
- improve overall property operations

It's easy to bite off more than you can chew when dealing with a value-add apartment building. But if you're ready to do some work, a value-add property can be a rewarding experience both personally and financially. Always look for the following in a prospective acquisition.

Central location, desirable to tenants

The property is within walking distance of grocery, restaurants and retail. Is located in a major metropolitan area, near centers of employment and within immediate vicinity of mass transportation.

Property is poorly managed

The current manager is just mowing the lawn and fixing leaks, there are multiple sources of untapped income (laundry, parking, storage, community services, vending, etc.), and multiple opportunities for shopping new services and lowering expenses.

Verifiable upside in existing rents to market

The current rents are below the average market rent rate. The current management has a poor collection history (the party's over). Marketing improvements and enhanced resident screening will attract new residents at higher rental amounts.

Motivated seller

The property has had the same owner for the last 15-20 years. An owner who is looking to off-load the property and motivated to sell (see #2).

Needs some TLC and not a total rehab

The apartment building has no major deferred maintenance. There's a 1-2-year proposition to bring the property to market standards, such as: new carpet, shower surrounds, lighting, paint, parking, appliances, etc.

Occupancy at 70% or above

There's a maximum two to three-month period to bring the building to market occupancy. An occupancy below 70% spells trouble and will need significant financial reserves on the buyers' part.

Good unit mix

Look for an apartment building with a unit mix of one, two- and three-bedroom unfurnished units. Note this will vary by market and renter demand – avoid all studio units.

Full financials are provided and verifiable

Rent rolls, leases, maintenance records, P&L, capital improvements, etc. are readily available for the past 12- to 24-month period.

"Free" utilities and separately metered units

The opportunity exists to easily introduce a Ratio Utility Billing System (RUBS) where tenants are billed back for utility usage.

A Class C property in an area that supports Class B properties

New management and cosmetic improvements (paint inside and/or outside, hardwood flooring, new lighting) may improve properties from a class C to a class B property.

Be methodical in your approach

Purchasing an apartment complex can be both exciting and stressful. On one hand, you are taking steps toward accomplishing your goal of real estate investing and doing something you are passionate about. However, along with the possibility of living the life you have long envisioned for yourself, there are many potential pitfalls that might be encountered in the process. Be methodical when you do your market research and property inspections.

Property Inspection Tips for Purchasing Apartments

Whether you are a first-time investment property buyer, or you have successfully closed several transactions, the following property inspection tips will help improve your likelihood of making a profitable investment. And if you're new and somewhat overwhelmed, prefer to these lists to help with your step-by-step inspections. Do not hurry through the process.

Start at the top

Roofs are costly to replace yet very valuable for protecting the interior and structure of your buildings. It's important to have a good estimate of the remaining useful life of a roof so you can budget for a replacement.

Foundation

Foundation problems are not always easy to spot. It is best to use an experienced professional who knows what to look for and where to look. Purchasing new construction is no guarantee you will avoid foundation problems – it only means they will not be noticeable for a few years.

Mechanical systems

System inspections should also be conducted by certified professionals. The National Association of Realtors recommends discussing in detail what your inspector will assess prior to ordering the inspection. You should only use inspectors with thorough commercial property inspection experience.

Each unit

You should walk through every unit yourself to note the general condition of each one and any issues that need attention. This also gives you an opportunity to note the quality of existing tenants and how to budget for turn costs, which are the costs you incur preparing units for new tenants when the units are vacated.

Review service contracts

Your service contracts with landscapers, trash removal, and HVAC contractors should survive the sale. If they do, read the details of each. You want to be aware of what is being done on your property and of the contractors' responsibilities. You might consider hiring new providers.

Verify utilities

Be sure all utility bills are paid, and you know which utility bills you will be responsible for paying. This typically includes gas, electric, water and sewer, but there may be additional costs and fees imposed by the local municipality.

Audit existing leases

It is a good idea to review background checks and look for any tenant-specific variations in the rent roll. You want to be sure collected rent amounts match the lease and that there are no special clauses allowing some tenants discounts or free rent for some duration.

When You Buy a Property, You Inherit the Tenants

When you invest in a rental property, you'll probably inherit the tenants at that property. They'll become your tenants, at least for a while. It helps to be prepared.

Here are five crucial questions to ask:

1. Are the "inmates running the asylum?"

If the current property managers are not enforcing lease terms, policies and procedures, expect real challenges to implementing new rules—even if you are the new sheriff in town.

2. Will property improvements equal new tenants?

The new tenant profile you are banking on might not exist in your market. Submarket research is critical to your success.

Who exactly are the renters and potential renters in your small submarket? If you don't know, find out. Talk to the people who work in that specific submarket, namely: real estate brokers; local police; local merchants; property managers; and experienced, successful residential real estate investors.

261

3. Will I inherit collection and delinquency problems?

It's not unusual for a seller to "stuff" a property with unqualified renters prior to selling the property in order to reach a high occupancy level. Do the existing residents meet your tenant screening guidelines? And are they current on security/damage deposits, rent and fee payments?

4. What are the lease renewal dates for each tenant in the property?

Unless you're investing in an asset class such as student housing where it's common for leases to renew at the same time, look for staggered lease renewal dates for the tenants in your new property.

Think about what will happen to your bottom line if some, most, or even all, of your residents move out at the same time.

5. What about concessions, side agreements and hidden deals?

In tougher rental markets leasing agents will frequently offer special deals in order to attract new tenants.

These tenant concessions can include items like:

- waived damage deposits;
- waived application fees;
- waived pet fees and damage deposits;
- monthly rent discounts; or
- agreements such as free rent for the last month of tenancy.

Note: These concessions and agreements aren't always in writing.

The bottom line (and this is really important)

Don't guess. Don't make assumptions about the current residents. Do your homework. Ask for copies of current and trailing (past months) rent rolls early in your property analysis.

Always obtain copies of tenant files before you close. The requested tenant documents should include applications; leases; written agreements; records of oral agreements; credit check and other screening information; deposit receipts; and more.

Steps to Making an Offer on a Multifamily Property

You've done your research. You've selected a solid real estate investment market. And now you're ready to start taking a hard look at potential multifamily investment properties within your chosen investment market. You may even have some properties in mind.

Where do you go from here?

Here are the key steps to making an offer on a multifamily property:

Review the listing brochure

Contact several multifamily brokers who specialize in your chosen investment market.

You may find brokers who push for an exclusive arrangement as your representative, but that loyalty has to be earned. Work with multiple brokers until you find one you trust and work well with.

Review each listing brochure (a.k.a. offering memorandum) and make a note of any questions. There's no such thing as a stupid question.

A listing brochure will give you pertinent information about the property:

- Property address
- Building style
- Number of units and unit mix (1 bedroom, 2 bedrooms, etc.)
- Current and pro forma financials (rent, other income and expenses)
- Proposed financing
- Financial analysis (proposed investment returns)
- Asking price
- Sale and rent comparables and other market data
- Other property highlights the seller and broker consider important

It's all good information to have. But be aware this is a marketing brochure that's designed to promote the property and to support the asking price. It's equally important to look for what the brochure doesn't cover.

What's missing? For example, if the marketing copy covers the wonderful location and neighborhood but doesn't mention anything about property improvements, then chances are the property needs work.

Pro tip: If you are working directly with the seller of the property, without a broker to act as an intermediary, be aware that diplomacy will be the key to your success. It's important to approach negotiations with a win-win attitude.

Your reputation: When I do a real estate deal my goal is to acquire the property but I also want to be able to leave something on the table for everyone. When everyone is happy, and no one feels as though they've just been "taken to the cleaners," you've done a good job as a real estate investor. And your reputation will reflect that.

Get a copy of the historical financials

Now it's time to get a good a look at the property's current and historical financial performance. Ask for copies of the Profit and Loss Statements (aka annual property operating data, or APOD) for the past two years.

Very few listing brokers in my experience will offer the historical property operating data—but most will make it available to you if you ask for it. This is part of your due diligence as a smart real estate investor. Always ask for the trailing financials and never accept "No" for an answer.

Also get a copy of the current rent roll. See if you can get a copy of past rent rolls as well.

Complete your initial financial analysis

If you've read my book Invest In Apartment Buildings, you'll know that I like to do two sets of financial analysis.

I like to look at the current numbers as presented by the listing broker or seller and I like to complete an analysis using the historical operating data for the past year. It may surprise you to know that these numbers often tell vastly different stories.

It becomes your job to decide where the happy medium is likely to be. If you are new at multifamily property analysis get an experienced mentor to give you a hand.

Schedule a property tour

If you're new to multifamily investing, attend as many property tours as possible. Get to know the:

- Market and local neighborhood
- Building styles
- Average unit mixes
- Typical common areas and amenities
- Natural tenant demographics
- Local brokers and property managers

Once you're familiar with your market you can be more selective about the time you spend looking at physical properties.

During a showing you can expect to see the common areas such as entryway, basement, halls, laundry, boiler room etc. I always ask to see the inside of at least some of the rental units too—I don't care if the unit is occupied or vacant.

Take a good look at the exterior:

- What kind of cars do the tenants drive?
- Is the parking lot full during the day? Do the residents have jobs?
- Does the property show signs of exterior structural damage?
- How do the grounds look?

Tour the interior of the property:

- What's the condition of major building mechanicals like: roof, boiler, HVAC?
- How do the common areas look? Are they clean? And in good repair?
- Do you see proper life safety features (exit signs, fire extinguishers, etc.)?
- Will you need to update the property? New flooring? Windows? Paint?

Pro tip: Refer to Chapter Six: Finding Deals for a refresher on touring properties.

Submit Your Offer

It's time to make an offer to buy. I can hear you say, "But wait a minute! We haven't had the inspectors in. And I haven't seen the tenant leases. Or completed thorough due diligence!"

After an initial offer is made and accepted, the real negotiations have just begun!

267

With multifamily properties or apartment buildings, most negotiations begin after you are in contract. This is the time you will conduct your:

- Inspections
- Due diligence
- Negotiations of final purchase price, seller credits, and seller financing
- Lender financing agreements

If you are light on experience, talk with your mentors and broker about arriving at a beginning offer price before making an offer on a multifamily property. Practice as much financial analysis as possible. The more you practice the easier it will be to arrive at an offer price.

The Art of Negotiation

The negotiation process is usually a part of any real estate deal or transaction. Good negotiation skills must be a strong part of your game.

You will become skilled in the art of negotiation when you have a solid understanding of the strategies that can be used by you—or on you. These six rules will help you look at negotiations in an entirely new way.

Rule #1: Everything's negotiable

If you don't fully embrace Rule #1 you will not become skilled at negotiation. You must believe that everything is negotiable. For example, I recently asked my phone company to waive my service charges for three months because I had been a customer for years. They said yes. If I hadn't asked, I would not have received the bonus months.

In a purchase of a mid-size apartment building I negotiated several items before we agreed to close the deal. The seller carried a large unsecured note on the property, gave us a seller credit for repairs which bought us a new roof, asphalt and sidewalks, and accepted a significantly lower purchase price.

Whether a deal is small or large most people and companies are willing to negotiate.

Rule #2: Be willing to walk from the deal

You must be willing to walk from the deal—and the other party must believe it. That means you need to believe it.

If you're buying an investment property and you've completely fallen in love with it (you absolutely must have it) negotiations will not be as successful if you ignore Rule #2.

If you must have the house or property use a "partner" as the one who could do without. In this instance you could say, "I doubt my partner will agree to that. She doesn't really need to buy this particular house. I'll ask her." In either case, the other party must know, without a doubt, that you are willing to walk from the deal with zero regrets.

Once you have these two rules down it's pretty much smooth sailing. But you've got to believe Rule #1 and Rule #2. They are non-negotiable (in spite of Rule #1!).

Rule #3: Agree on everything else

Use your people skills, no need to be pushy. Negotiations can and should be about people. Take your time. Find out what motivates the other party through conversation, questions and listening.

Ask yourself, "What does each party need to accomplish?" This will give you an opportunity to navigate towards a solution where each party realizes their desired goal (ideally).

You might say, "Let's sit down and talk and see if we can come to a mutually beneficial agreement."

This is an important strategy to fully understand.

Let's say from our example above that the seller of the house you looked at had already told you she would accept nothing less than a full price offer. Rather than let this kill the deal your goal will be to say, "Let's put that aside and see if we can agree on everything else."

There are still many scenarios where the seller could get her full price but not in the way she might be seeing right now. For example, you could end up negotiating a seller credit for repairs, or the seller could carry back a small second. In both cases, she could still get the full asking price, or close to it, but the actual dollar amounts would be categorized at closing as something other than the purchase price.

Rule #4: "You'll have to do better than that"

This is a simple and effective strategy. When the offer is made you simply reply, "You'll have to do better than that." This is particularly effective when the other party clearly realizes that you are not desperate to get the deal done and are, in fact, willing to walk. The key here is to make your statement and then stop talking! Give the other party an opportunity to make a better offer.

Rule #5: Don't play the high-low game

The High-Low Game is an old, dated strategy that is unnecessarily confrontational. You start low, the other party starts high, and hopefully you meet somewhere in the middle. This is generally not an effective strategy. It's a game where the focus is solely on the money and all other elements of negotiation are set aside.

It's a game of chicken that is time-consuming and can damage relations between the parties. There may be issues of more significant value to both parties when the simple dollar amounts are removed from the negotiations.

Rule #6: Know when to quit

If the other party refuses to negotiate further and you have not reached an acceptable deal, always remember you can walk away and come back later. You could offer to resubmit an offer in a week, or a month. This accomplishes a number of things. It reinforces Rule #2 (you are willing to walk from the deal), it provides a break from negotiations and gives both parties an opportunity to think about what they've brought to the table so far. It also allows for some distance that will help you reevaluate your desire to see the deal through to completion.

Negotiate Seller Credits When Buying Multifamily Properties

You're investing in real estate as a business. To make money. To find the best and most profitable deal. You may even be accustomed to negotiating a purchase price. But do you find yourself reluctant to ask the seller to chip in for property repairs? After all you don't want to rock the boat.

The negotiation process is a challenge for most people. It's human nature. We don't like to be told "No." Do you hate the idea of negotiating? Well, here's a different way to look it. Negotiations do not need to be unfriendly or hostile.

Imagine you're the seller for a minute

Put the shoe on the other foot. Pretend you're the seller of the property. Say you've owned the property for five, ten or fifteen years. You're intimately familiar with it. Right? You know about the blemishes. You remember every single time a contractor has made repairs. You're fully aware of the deferred maintenance—the stuff you keep meaning to fix but haven't got around to yet.

Now let's say you've found a buyer for your property. Do you hide that information? Hope the buyer doesn't discover the imperfections? Hardly.

Typically, what comes out in an inspection is no surprise to the seller. And even if it is a surprise there's no question the problem exists. When you ask a seller to credit you for some of the essential repairs, it's really no great surprise. They may even feel you've caught them in the act of not disclosing every little item.

So, why wouldn't you ask for a credit?

Asking for a seller credit for repairs

There's more good news.

Here's a way of thinking that will eliminate the pressure of negotiating. Property inspections are normal during a real estate transaction. In commercial real estate, the inspection process is part of the contractual obligations of both the buyer and the seller.

The seller knows you will inspect the property and they expect to see your follow-up about the items that you find unsatisfactory. You are not calling the seller on the phone and saying, "Hey there's a bunch of things I don't like over at your property." Nothing so crude as that.

Your findings from your inspection of the property are provided to the seller in an Inspection Notice. It becomes part of the contract. It's standard procedure to negotiate seller credits when buying multifamily properties. And when you put those items in black and white, they're hard to deny. It's the power of the written word—with personal remarks removed. Simple and clean.

The contract language reads…

BUYER'S NOTIFICATION OF UNSATISFACTORY PHYSICAL CONDITION

Notice to Correct. Pursuant to [section] of the contract, Buyer notifies Seller that Buyer requires Seller, on or before [date], to correct or resolve the following unsatisfactory physical conditions of the Property or Inclusions: Buyer to receive credit at Closing for the following items: (List each item and the cost of the repair.)

If both parties agree in writing to a credit, it will appear as a miscellaneous adjustment (credit) on the buyers closing statement. Typically, the end result is an agreement to meet somewhere in the middle. Again, this is standard business procedure. And what's the worst thing a seller can do? Say "no," right?

List of non-aesthetic, essential repairs:

- Roof restoration, roof coverings, gutters, scupper drains, downspouts
- Sidewalk, asphalt, courtyard surface
- Parking and car port structures
- HVAC
- Plumbing
- Electric
- Boiler and other large mechanical systems
- Main sewer line
- Pool
- Elevator
- Building structural integrity

- Individual units (such as units with extensive damage)
- Leaks and water damage
- Plumbing back flow
- Common area flooring, walls, ceiling, entryway and doors (severe damage)
- Common area appliances such in laundry facilities
- Doors and windows (severe damage)
- Wind, fire or hail damage
- Damage to asbestos and lead-based paints containing materials

Take note of the language, "non-aesthetic, essential repairs." I've had buyers ask that we remove graffiti (aesthetic) and winterize the sprinkler system (non-essential).

Ask for repairs to the big stuff like a roof that's at the end of its useful life or a boiler system that's on its last leg. Don't nickel and dime the seller. If you do, you can easily insult the seller and jeopardize the entire transaction.

A last note. The negotiations for repairs are done while in contract—after an offer is made and accepted. You'll conduct your inspections during the due diligence phase of the contract.

Negotiation Techniques to Sway Real Estate Deals in Your Favor

Often it is the unspoken conversation that carries the most weight. For example, say you walk into a store and talk briefly to a salesperson about the weather outside. You are really testing out the salesperson at the same time, the unspoken questions being, "Can I work with you? Are you going to offer me a fair deal?" The questions and answers to these unspoken conversations are often unconscious.

In real estate investing, an awareness of unspoken conversations will improve your deal making abilities. The following negotiation techniques might just sway real estate deals in your favor.

This is powerful information, not to be used to take over small countries or take candy from children. Lady Karma has a way of catching up with all of us, so consider yourself warned.

Comfy seating

Our first example was published in Science. Researchers simulated the negotiation process by having participants imagine shopping for a new car. They noticed there was a difference in behavior between those who were sitting in a soft, padded seat and a hard, unpadded seat. "Buyers" were more likely to increase their offer up to 40% while in the cushy seat. (Think of the implications!)

The chance of a 40% increase will make anyone double check for soft seating arrangements around a negotiation table, right? Just make sure your seat is cushion-less so you stay firm on your numbers.

A hot drink

Our second example demonstrates the powerful effect of a hot cup of coffee or tea. Researchers Lawrence Williams and John Bargh suspected that there might be a connection between physical warmth and regarding someone in a warm way.

They proved their theory by asking people to hold a cup of coffee for a short time as a favor to the research assistant. The participates had no idea that holding the cup was part of the experiment. Some cups held iced coffee and others held hot coffee. The participates were then asked to rate a total stranger's personality.

Williams said, "what we found was that there was a significant difference between the two groups, and their ratings of person A on the warm traits, such that participants who held the hot coffee cup saw person A as being more generous, more sociable. The people who held the cup of iced coffee saw person A as being less generous, antisocial, selfish."

So, the takeaway is that physically cold objects promote psychological coldness and by the same principal, physical warmth promotes psychological warmth.

How can you use these negotiation techniques? Make sure to bring hot drinks to the table while getting to know potential clients.

A light touch

The third study focused on physical touch. Researchers at the University of Mississippi and Rhodes College ran an experiment studying the effects of interpersonal touch on tipping in a restaurant. They had waitstaff briefly touch customers on the hand or shoulder as they were returning their change. The waitstaff who touched their customers earned much larger tips than the ones who didn't touch their customers.

277

I discounted this study at first, crediting the effects of flirting, but then reread the fine print. The waitstaff touched some of the customers on the shoulder so lightly it was considered barely noticeable. Researchers concluded, "The tipping rate for the two types of touch did not differ from each other and did not differ according to the customer's gender. Both tipping rates were significantly larger than a control, no-touch condition."

It was concluded that touch effects can occur without awareness. In further investigation, I found similar research studies have come to the same conclusions.

Use commonsense

I want to stress that unwanted touch can be considered harassment and completely creepy, so please take this study with a grain of salt. Use this information in the context of your situation.

Subliminal touch occurs when you touch a person so lightly that they barely notice. For example, tapping someone on the shoulder or touching their back can make them feel more positive toward you. So, for your next deal bring hot coffee, choose a smart seating plan and greet your prospect with a handshake as well as a slight touch.

Chapter Eleven:

Preparing to Finance Your Property

When you combine ignorance and leverage, you get some
pretty interesting results. – Warren Buffett

~

Terms All Real Estate Investors Should Know and Understand

It can be very intimidating to a novice investor who feels otherwise confident in their intellect to become lost in a conversation because the agent or seller is using terms they have not heard before.

Those agents and sellers are probably just trying to throw you off your game and rattle your confidence, so ask for clarification if someone tosses out a term you don't understand.

Here are a few key real estate investing terms to get you started.

Real Estate Owned (REO): This refers to real estate owned by a corporation such as a bank or asset management company because it was taken back by a lender through the process of foreclosure. REO properties are not owned by individuals who have an emotional attachment to them. You can sometimes get a good deal, but they also come with elevated risks of title issues and other problems.

Net Operating Income (NOI): This is the amount of income a property can theoretically produce via rent and other income collected from operations if the property does not have a loan against it. The NOI equals all revenue such as rent and other income from operations, minus all operating costs such as maintenance, insurance, utilities, and property taxes. All costs are subtracted except mortgage payments to determine a NOI.

Debt Service: This is one of those terms a real estate agent or other person might throw at you just to make you feel out of place. Often calculated annually, it is the cash necessary to cover interest and principle on the mortgage for that time frame.

The Debt Service Coverage Ratio (DSCR): The DCSR is a measurement of the cash flow that is available to pay the property's current debt obligations, such as a mortgage. Put more simply, it is the number of times a property can pay its mortgage after all other expenses have been paid. Lenders typically want a DSCR of at least 1.25. You need to know your lender's threshold when evaluating properties.

Gross Rent Multiplier (GRM): The GRM is a rough screening tool used to determine if a property is in line with similar properties. The ratio is determined by taking the purchase price divided by the annual gross rents of an investment property. For example, a $2 million-dollar apartment building with annual gross rents of $250,000 has a GRM equal to 8 ($2,000,000 / $250,000).

The GRM is very fast to calculate but ignores vacancy, expenses, repairs, etc. It should always be used in conjunction with other screening tools.

Personal Guarantee: When you sign a personal guarantee on a loan, it means you are putting up your own home, bank accounts, and other assets to cover the loan, even if the loan is made to your LLC or other business structure. Be very careful about signing a personal guarantee.

Capital Expenses (Cap Ex): These are large expenses that contribute to the long-term value of the property. You need to have capital expense reserves to cover major costs such as roof replacement, HVAC upgrades, and parking lot resurfacing. Be sure to set aside money each year to cover these necessary expenditures.

Benefits of Financing Your Investment Property

You are already aware that owning investment property has many benefits. However, it also comes with some potential pitfalls. Unfortunately, many novice investors have been led down the wrong path by some late-night infomercial about buying investment property with no money down.

If you are struggling financially, don't expect ownership of investment property to turn your life around. You should be well positioned financially and able to devote the necessary time and research required for each property. Only then can you determine the best strategy for building your portfolio and recognize the best financing options.

Here are just a few benefits of financing your investment property.

Appreciation of your highly leveraged property

With a small down payment and a conventional mortgage, you can purchase a valuable investment property by using very little of your own money. You are buying the property primarily using debt. This is referred to as being highly leveraged. The actual purchase price of the property can be five, ten, or even 20 times the amount of your out-of-pocket money.

Any appreciation of the property is on the total value of the property, not just your cash investment. It remains one of the best ways to accumulate wealth and continues to be done by people of every income bracket.

Renters pay down the debt for you

This key benefit to financing and owning investment property is also where many investors get tripped up. They try to live off the rental income and pay down the debt at the same time. These people often end up hoping the property will quickly appreciate in value so they can sell it for a huge profit to bail them out of their dire financial situation.

In time, you can pocket a portion of your rental income and sell the property for a profit, but you need to be financially stable enough to wait for the right time to do this.

Tax benefits

As a landlord, you can deduct interest on loans used to purchase, repair and maintain your investment property. There are many other expenses related to your property that qualify for deductions. Be sure to discuss travel expenses, legal fees, and other payments made to professionals with your tax advisor.

One of the best deductions involves using a depreciation schedule based on your purchase price of the property. You can depreciate the purchase price of the property even as it increases in value.

Speak with your tax advisor before choosing which method of financing is best for you. Hard money loans often have longer terms, but soft money loans typically come with more flexible payment plans.

Creative Financing for Your First Rental Property

If you are buying your first rental property, take some lessons from toddlers who are just learning to walk and taking their first steps: it is not going to go perfectly.

Don't expect to be as successful as other investors right from the start. Take baby steps. It is important that you are able to recover and try again.

Don't be too proud to accept assistance. Toddlers often master the skill of walking by leaning on a walker or tightly gripping the fingers of a parent. You will benefit from having a mentor you can turn to as you navigate your first real estate investment. Consider the excitement toddlers have as they experience walking for the first time. Be enthusiastic and creative!

Creative financing

The term creative financing refers to anything other than traditional financing from a bank or lending institution. Most of the time, investors are using as little of their own money as possible to purchase investment properties so they can stretch their investment dollars further and earn income from multiple properties rather than just one.

Even if you can make a significant down payment or pay cash for a property, it is ideal to purchase with little or no money out-of-pocket if you are financially stable and not strapped for cash. That way, if you do need to put additional money into the property for any reason to maintain or fuel profitability, you can.

"Subject to"

This method refers to the purchaser continuing to make payments on the loan that was obtained by the seller. The purchase is "subject to" existing financing remaining in place. The contract is executed, and the title is transferred, but the loan remains in the name of the previous owner and the new owner is responsible for making the payments. This is beneficial to purchasers because they are able to buy a property with no down payment and refinance the loan in a few months. It is most commonly used when a seller is struggling to make payments, falling behind and heading toward foreclosure. The "subject to" lets them get out from under the payments immediately.

Your first deal will most likely be your most difficult. You will always remember it and the lessons you learn from it. It is understandable to be nervous and experience some anxiety, but do not be afraid. You have done your homework. You are prepared and this is what you should be doing.

Forgive yourself when you make a simple mistake. Always keep in mind that the biggest mistake is to let nerves prevent you from moving forward.

How to Meet with a Real Estate Lender

Finances can make or break your real estate plans. Without the right resources in place, you'll have a harder time swinging your deal no matter how great of an opportunity it is.

A real estate lender is one such valuable resource, but you've got to be prepared before you meet with them so you're seen as a strong borrower. Before you meet with a lender about your real estate deal, here's what you need to do.

Outline your success

If you've already owned rental properties, gather property statistics so you can build credibility with the loan officer. This includes occupancy rate, cash on cash return, tenant longevity and your gross yearly rental yield.

285

Be prepared to demonstrate how you currently manage your properties or bring a certification that shows your contract with a property manager.

Detail your needs

Be ready to explain how much you need and why you need it in a clear and concise manner. The lender will want to know where the money is going, and if you can't provide a detailed answer, you're going to be in trouble. Be prepared to show commitment

You're going to be expected to have a down payment that shows you're committed to and serious about the deal. You'll need at least 20 percent of the purchase price as a down payment, but be ready to put up more if necessary to close the loan or get a lower interest rate.

Have property specifics ready

Have all the details about the investment property you want to buy detailed and analyzed on paper. At the very minimum, you should be able to show the lender estimated renovation expenses, your estimated gross yearly rental yield, and the property's fair market rent.

Because of the lender's underwriting criteria, their assessment may differ from yours, so you need to be able to professionally explain your information without becoming upset or angry.

List some questions

Have a list of questions ready to bring with you to ask the lender. It's vital that you fully understand the lender's criteria, what they need from you, and what potential snags could arise in the future.

Remember that no two lenders are the same, so what one lender requires may be different from the next. If you're as prepared as possible before you step foot in that loan officer's office, you'll stand a much better chance of landing your funding.

How to Prepare for the Multifamily Loan Application Process

For years, borrowers looking to finance multifamily properties have been led to believe

- their credit is not relevant
- lenders look exclusively at the cash flow of a property
- they are golden if the property income covers expenses (including debt service)
- financing requirements are met as long as the numbers work

That's not true anymore. When you approach a lender or commercial mortgage broker for financing, your lender will want to know about you. They'll want to know that you are able to finance the property; guarantee loan repayment with minimal risk; and successfully operate the property.

I know borrowers who fight the multifamily loan application process at every step—kicking and screaming all the way to the closing table.

If they actually make it to the closing table.

But why not have a rewarding experience?

The multifamily loan application process does not have to seem like a trip to the dentist. If you prepare in advance of the loan application date you will have time and energy to address other issues that might come up during the underwriting process. And you'll be ready to concentrate on your business plan of multifamily ownership.

When you arrive at your commercial mortgage broker or lender's doorstep with the documents and information below your lender will love you and your chance of funding your deal is greatly increased.

Your Statement of Experience (résumé)

Your lender is likely to ask for a copy of your real estate investor résumé. Your résumé is a typewritten document that summarizes your real estate investing skills and experience.

If you do not have a track record of successful multifamily real estate investments, show a lender that you have transferable skills.

Transferable business skills will include

- employee/team management
- sales, leasing and marketing
- bookkeeping
- collections

- budget forecasting and
- property maintenance and business ownership

If you have skills from the single-family side of real estate investing such as landlording, be sure to include those skills.

Here's a sample Statement of Real Estate Investment Experience:

***

Statement of Real Estate Experience For: [name and contact info]

John Doe is an experienced real estate investor. His investing experience includes single-family and multifamily real estate investments, self-storage, and commercial land development. His current investment focus is multifamily real estate, specifically apartments.

Real estate experience:

- Qualified Real Estate Professional under IRS guidelines since 2007
- Owns and operates a professional real estate management & investment company; duties include but are not limited to:
  - o Profit & Loss Statements, Balance Sheets
  - o Bookkeeping
  - o Forecasts
  - o Property acquisition, rehab, marketing & sales
  - o Property management and leasing
- Experienced in owning and managing single-family rentals & small multi-unit properties as follows:

- o Properties in New York, Pennsylvania, Arizona and Mexico
- o Properties include buy & holds, flips, land, re-fi's and short sales
- Instrumental in creating and currently operating Advisory Committee and Homeowners Association (HOA) for land development project in Scottsdale, Arizona.
- Multifamily experience:
  - o Owner-operator of two small multifamily investments
  - o Extensive national market research & knowledge
  - o Expert in multiple national submarkets
  - o Expert in evaluating rents, cap rates, market values, vacancies, market cycles, etc.
  - o Extensive education and practical application in multifamily deal analysis
  - o Direct marketing to owners – includes offers & contracts
  - o Created local teams to stabilize properties, including management, rehabilitation and maintenance
  - o Preparation of offering memorandums, deal structuring & finance
- Current portfolio:
  - o Acquired a total of five income producing properties over the past ten years.
  - o All properties are stabilized, fully occupied and located in appreciating Class B markets.
  - o We have increased revenue by 35% and lowered expenses by 27% across the entire portfolio and aggregate property values have doubled since acquisition.
  - o Aggregate LTV is 65%.
- Team members include:

- o Commercial property management company: [company name and contact]
- o Real estate attorney: [name], partner in previous deals
- o Renovation group: [company name and contact]

***

In your résumé, list the names and contact information for all the skilled professionals who will manage and run your property. These professionals can include leasing agents; renovation specialists; trade contractors; and an experienced commercial property maintenance team.

Pro tip: Some lenders may require that you hire a third-party management company for your first year of ownership.

Resource alert: A sample Statement of Experience can also be found in our resource document at theresabradleybanta.com/book_resources.

Real estate investing team

Also let your lender know that you have team members with multifamily real estate investing and property operations experience who are ready to step in the day you close.

Don't be surprised when your commercial mortgage broker or lender asks for your tax returns for the past two years. Scan these documents and be ready to deliver them as an electronic file.

Your lender will also want to see a Personal Financial Statement. This statement is an itemized list of your assets and liabilities. You don't need a fancy financial statement—a text document or spreadsheet will work.

Your list of assets will include:

- Cash
- CDs
- Securities and stocks
- Notes and contracts receivable
- Life insurance (cash surrender value)
- Personal property
- Retirement funds
- Real estate owned (market value)
- Other assets such oil and gas and businesses owned

Liabilities will include:

- Current debt (credit cards and other accounts)
- Notes payable
- Taxes payable
- Real estate mortgages or debt and
- Other liabilities such as automobiles

Deduct your liabilities from your assets to arrive at your current net worth. A thorough personal financial statement will also include an attachment listing the specifics of each individual liability and asset. For example, the two lists below itemize the assets and liabilities for a single piece of real estate owned.

Real estate owned (asset):

- Property description/location
- Market value
- Amount owed and
- Original purchase price and date

Real estate mortgage or debt (liability):

- Name of creditor
- Amount owing
- Original amount paid
- Monthly payment
- Mortgage interest rate and
- Items securing the property

Historical operations

Historical operating data also known as *Annual Property Operating Data (APOD)* or *Trailing Financials*, lists all property income and operating expenses. This is information you probably already have from your early analysis of the property.

You *must* ask the seller for copies of all trailing financials for the past two years—more is better.

You'll also want to ask for copies of the property rent roll for a trailing period of at least one year—more is better. The loan underwriter will need a notarized copy of the current month's rent roll.

It's also a good idea to offer a list of any capital improvements made to the property in the past several years.

Stabilized pro forma

Your lender will want to know how you plan to operate the property especially if you're buying a building with low occupancy, collection problems, high expenses and low income.

It's a great strategy to buy a property that you can add value to but—and this is a big but—you need to show the lender that you know how to make immediate improvements to the property operations.

An annual operating budget is the perfect way to prove your plans for maximizing profitability. I show you how to prepare an operating budget in Chapter Seventeen: Property Management. This level of preparation for the multifamily loan application process will set you up for success.

Are You Shelling Out Too Much for Hard Money?

Hard money loans can undoubtedly be very useful when it comes to investing in real estate, but hard money lenders typically desire above-average return rates on their money.

As an investor, there are compelling reasons to resort to hard money loans as they are typically not dependent on creditworthiness and often come with quicker approval.

Having access to cash also means it is easier to take advantage of bargains and close deals before the competition can get a jump on you.

Caveat emptor

When resorting to hard money loans, it is very important for you to remain cautious and do your research. Remember that the real estate is usually provided as collateral to the lender, so if your investment goes wrong, it could result in the lender gaining possession of the property.

Define your strategies

In order to avoid shelling out too much for hard money, you first need to determine your goals. For example, if your goal is to buy and hold on to the property, a long-term loan usually works better than a short-term one. When it comes to the interest, you need to ask yourself whether you are still getting a good deal on your investment.

By making your calculations ahead of time, you are not only in a better position when dealing with potential lenders, but you can also avoid loans that could cut too deeply into your profits.

Stick within your asset class

When opting for hard money, it is usually beneficial to deal with lenders who have experience in the types of property that interest you. Some lenders specialize in multifamily properties and apartment buildings and will have a better understanding of what can work best for both parties compared those who specialize in single-family residential.

Shop around

As an investor, hard money is essential to your growth and for landing better deals, but this does not mean you can be reckless. Hard money lenders take a bigger risk than banks, so it is no surprise that their interest rates will be higher than those of conventional loans. However, the rates will differ depending on the lender, the region and even competition.

Other factors, such as whether the loan is determined by the current value of the property or the after-repair value, also come into play.

Do your homework and compare how much you will be paying to what other investors are paying so you can be confident that you are still getting a good deal.

Essential Things to Know About 1031 Exchanges

Real estate investors can find a surprising tool in the most unlikely of places: the Internal Revenue Code, specifically §1031. Within the 1031 exchange, you can reinvest your proceeds from your investment real estate sale into the purchase of another property. This eliminates or limits the tax you'd normally have to pay on those proceeds on your taxes that year.

The 1031 exchange is a powerful tool in the right investor's hands, but it does come with some caveats. Keep reading for three essential things you need to know about the 1031.

There's no such thing as a free lunch

A 1031 exchange defers tax, but it's not eliminating that tax forever. According to the Internal Revenue Service, the tax on your gain from the sale is postponed if you're using that money to reinvest into another "like-kind" property. You can keep doing these exchanges, however, and defer the tax indefinitely as long as you follow all the rules.

Keep an eye on the properties

The definition of "like-kind" property is a little broad, but real estate is usually considered like-kind to other real estate even if they're not the same type, such as a multifamily home versus an apartment building. One thing to note here is that all of your cash proceeds have to be reinvested in the replacement property. If you sell an apartment complex for $500,000 and use $300,000 of that to buy a replacement multifamily home, you can still be taxed on the remaining $200,000 (minus the closing costs you're allowed to deduct from the multifamily sale).

There are hard and fast deadlines

1031 exchanges have two timing rules. First, you have to put the replacement property you're planning to buy in writing and deliver it to your qualified intermediary (QI) within 45 days of your property sale. The intermediary is the person or institution you gave the cash from the sale to hold; you're not allowed to have that cash under the 1031 rules.

The next deadline is 180 days after your sale, which is all the time you have to close on the replacement property. Note that these two deadlines run concurrently, so if you give your QI the replacement property designation

50 days after the sale of the property, you have 130 days left to close on its replacement.

There are a lot of rules in 1031 exchanges, but the end result is well worth it! Make sure you work with qualified professionals so you don't end up holding the tax bag at the end.

Chapter Twelve:

Real Estate Investment Strategies

Believe you can and you're halfway there.
– Theodore Roosevelt

~

Strategy vs. Tactics in Real Estate Investing

Successful real estate investors usually have a clear vision of what they want to create. They focus on their passion. They design a clearly written strategy. They know the why of what they are creating. They begin with the end in mind.

I read an interesting quote by Roman philosopher Lucius Annaeus Seneca the other day…

"Luck is what happens when preparation meets opportunity."

It's a good quote, but perhaps falls somewhat short of being very helpful. I'm not a firm believer in sitting around waiting for opportunity to knock or one to credit success with luck. Are you? I doubt it.

I'm sure you'll agree that preparation is a good thing. But I see too many novice real estate investors who fail to realize their vision, in part, because they get caught up in the tactics, a.k.a. preparation, when they're uncertain about what they're trying to create. They fail to see the forest for the trees.

Apply this thinking to real estate investing

Here's the perfect example…

You want to invest in real estate. Why? What do you want to create? Gobs of cash? A nice safe place for your residents to call home? A legacy for your kids? Awards and accolades? All good reasons.

Here's where the forest and the trees come in.

Instead of looking at every step you must carry out, all the education pieces, why not hop in the car and drive around picturing yourself owning real properties? Think big. Look at the 100-unit apartment building or even the high-rise down the street and picture yourself owning it.

What would owning the property mean to you? What would your day be like? Who would you meet? What types of people would be on your team? Who are your residents? Can you picture them in your mind?

What do you want to create?

I love this quote credited to Billy Sunday,

*"More men fail through lack of purpose
than lack of talent."*

When you have a dream and the passion to see it through, when you have a clearly written mission statement and strategy, you'll find the tactics become fluid.

Here's the difference. Tactics can be rewritten; they can be course corrected. Your vision and purpose—your "why"—and your long-term thinking are where you will find success. Talent, skills, education can all be gathered along the way. I think life is supposed to work that way.

Start with the end in mind

I'll agree it might not be your best strategy to start with a 100-unit property—although some have done it. But you can work your way to realizing your dream. Start with small properties. Learn the ropes. Trade up to bigger and bigger deals.

You're probably saying, "Well that's fairly obvious, Theresa." But think about this. What if you invested in a 4-unit rental property…and then stopped? Simply because you didn't envision more?

How to Find Your Real Estate Investing Niche

Most people associate "single-family home" with the word "real estate" but you and I know a different world, don't we? The field of real estate investment has a dazzling number of options to specialize with.

For a new real estate investor, deciding on a real estate investing niche can be a bit overwhelming. Should you invest in raw land? Apartment buildings? Student or senior housing? Condos and town homes? How about specializing in self-storage or industrial? You might even consider investing in oil & gas (yes, that's also a real estate investing niche!).

Where to start? Where are you?

You start with what you know and where you are. Do you live in a college town? Does your town get seasonal traffic? Are you near a beach or lake? Are you close to an industrial area? Maybe you live in a commuter town. Just by living near this feature you are more familiar with the ebb and flow of this niche.

What do you know?

Sit down and focus on what you know about this area. What does the local industry need? How is this area shrinking or growing? What do people want when they come to the area? What does local or state government plan for the area? Are there any big building projects underway?

You'll become knowledgeable about your area with some internet research and a few phone calls. Use my free real estate market checklist as a guide.

Get educated in a specific real estate investing niche

After narrowing down what your area offers it is time to get educated in that real estate niche. Get on the ground floor and talk to your market. For example, if you live near a college town, then find out how much local housing costs for students. Talk to some students. What are they looking for in housing? Is it a washer and dryer? Maybe they want proximity to classes? Discover what they really want.

Everyone, of course, has different needs, but there will be a common thread among the population you speak to. Now you want to give the population, your market, what they want.

That's your niche!

Read, watch and listen

Depending on how much experience you have in real estate, you would be wise to read a few books and blogs. How-to real estate investing books, videos and articles will help you narrow down the type of real estate to buy. They can also help you raise funds and become familiar with what is important to know in local real estate transactions. My free Fast Start to Real Estate Investing Program is an excellent place to begin.

Real estate investing podcasts are another goldmine of information for learning about real estate investing. The time you spend getting educated will help you avoid costly mistakes in the future.

Find a mentor within your real estate niche

Another prudent step would be to find a real estate investing mentor. Reading books and listening to podcasts are excellent tools but you don't know what you don't know, right? That's the fear that usually stops people from becoming real estate investors.

People have coaches and teachers to guide them through uncertain waters in every stage of life. Sometimes you need a mentor to give you the practical, insider's guide to the industry. Other times mentors are important to keep you true to your goals and dreams. Together, you can plot a practical, achievable plan for your real estate dreams.

Find the voice of a real estate professional you enjoy and reach out to that person.

Time to take action

Finding your real estate investing niche takes education and action but you don't have to take that journey alone. There are guides and resources all along the way that will make you feel like we are in this adventure together!

Are Short-Term Rentals a Good Real Estate Investment?

A woman shouted in front of me, "Short-term rentals like Airbnb are bad. They're putting local B&Bs out of business and ruining my neighborhood!" Emotions were running high at the town meeting. It was sounding like a witch hunt, all misplaced blame and zero logic. Fortunately, economic logic and common sense prevailed in the end.

No doubt, short-term rentals have been a touchpoint for hot debate in many communities. Whatever your opinion, Airbnb, VRBO (Vacation Rentals By Owner) and HomeAway represent a short-term rental trend growing across the world and you might want to cash in on it.

I'll focus on Airbnb because it is the largest mover in this real estate niche. Here are some tips you will want to keep in mind.

State and local compliance

Each state and town have their own short-term rental laws. They will differ from your long-term rental in definition and legal specifics. It is possible that your locality does not even allow Airbnb rentals in specific terms. New York City is the famous example for this.

Many condominium complexes prevent short-term rentals in their bylaws. If short-term rentals are allowed, read the fine print.

Towns are usually very clear about what codes and regulations need to be followed. Make sure you are compliant before you post on Airbnb because your listing photographs will plainly reveal you.

Fees, taxes, the IRS and short-term rentals

Airbnb charges 3% for their services with each guest. That's the easy part. More difficult, each locality and state have different tax laws for short-term rentals. Contact your local government to find out what you are responsible for.

How you're taxed in the U.S. for short-term rental income is even trickier. Your own personal taxes vary based on your income, how often you rent out the home and how much you charge. If you are operating as a business entity, then that's another ball of wax.

Just know that you will be responsible for paying taxes on whatever income your short-term rental provides. Airbnb sends tax forms directly to the IRS documenting income. Your bottom line is to keep good records and consult with an accountant and/or lawyer.

Insurance

Airbnb's insurance policy offers "primary coverage for Airbnb hosts and landlords, as additional insureds, in over 15 countries. Our program protects against liability claims up to $1 million USD that occur in a listing, or on an Airbnb property, during a stay."

Nice, but we all know that having an insurance policy and actually receiving money when something happens are two very different things. I would recommend getting an additional short-term rental insurance policy, just to be on the safe side. You never know, right?

How to set up your Airbnb account

Setting up an account with Airbnb is easy. They require all hosts and guests to provide identification with a photograph, usually a driver's license. You then must pass facial recognition software, verifying that you are indeed the person on the license.

Once verified you can set up your bank account, credit card or PayPal account. Research says these are the two elements that make homeowners feel comfortable with welcoming strangers into their home. That the identity of the guests has been verified, and no money will be physically exchanged.

Setting up your listing

The written part of your listing is self-explanatory. Get all of the specific details of your property in black and white. If one burner on your stove doesn't work, then be up front about it. Be honest and transparent. Don't give unspoken promises. That thing you don't want to mention will come up.

Manage peoples' expectations in your listing and then you can exceed them in person. Good reviews are worth gold.

The most important element in your listing

Good photographs are, bar none, the most important element in your listing. Make sure you have clean, uncluttered rooms to begin with. Post the best quality photographs. Photograph every room in your home, with different angles to each one.

Think of a friend coming to your home for the first time. What landmarks will assist in recognizing your rental as guests arrive? Include photographs of your front door, the building from the outside, your street and anything else that might be helpful in finding your rental. Once your listing is live, promote it with social media.

The rest is fairly easy

Now you know the basics of starting a short-term rental business. First do your homework with short-term rental laws, compliance, taxes and insurance. After that heavy lifting, the rest is fairly easy.

In comparing notes with other Airbnb hosts, overall, guests have been respectful and considerate of their property. It can be a financially rewarding endeavor.

Tips for Putting the Sizzle into Your Short-Term Rental

Looking for ways to jazz up your short-term rental? Would you love to exceed the expectations of your guests? Do good reviews sound wonderful to you?

Short-term rentals like those offered through Airbnb are a hot market all over the world. Their appeal will only grow during the vacation months, so get ready. Competition is fierce.

Use the best possible photographs

First, view your short-term rental listing from your prospective guest's point of view. You want your home to seem inviting through the photos you choose.

Let your potential guests imagine themselves in your space by posting photos that demonstrate how comfortable your home is. For example, include a photo of a chair next to a table with a cup of coffee and a laptop.

Or, include a photo of your kitchen with a bowl of fresh fruit on the counter.

Clean your place thoroughly. Don't forget the basics. Make your windows sparkle and your floors shine. Take 50% of the stuff off your kitchen counter and store it somewhere else. Get rid of clutter. Fluff the pillows.

Offer more photographs than needed

Make sure you have plenty of photographs of your property, inside and out. Photograph each room at different angles. Document what the property looks like in different seasons.

Imagine you are giving directions to a friend who is visiting for the first time. Include photographs of the surrounding area, with landmarks, to help guests easily locate your space.

Price competitively

After photographs, reviews are usually the second stop for interested guests. Before you receive your first good reviews, consider setting your price lower to attract business. Good reviews are worth every dollar of your discount.

After you have accumulated some positive reviews, research the prices local hotels and other short-term rentals are charging and price in the same range.

Make contact count

Respond promptly to inquiries. Compose your email replies in a friendly and warm tone. Reach out to guests a week before they arrive to finalize arrival times. Review any special needs they might have. Be flexible with check-in times.

Also, provide information about the neighborhood. Where is the best place to get coffee? Who serves the tastiest regional dishes? What is the best place to soak up the culture? Let guests feel like they are in the know before they arrive. Share your insider scoop about the area.

Exceed expectations

There is increasing competition in short-term rentals, so go the extra mile for your guests. Besides offering the basic soap, fresh sheets and towels, offer something in addition.

Have the fridge stocked with how they like their coffee/tea. Leave a hand-written thank you note with chocolates. Offer a complementary bottle of wine and/or water. Leave a bowl of fruit to enjoy. Share your gym membership. Leave soothing music turned on for a relaxing arrival atmosphere. Whatever you do, that extra effort will make your short-term rental listing shine.

Have an instruction book to your short-term rental

Airbnb encourages hosts to create a House Manual for their guests and with good reason. Your property is more complicated than you think.

Include notes on how to work all of the electronics. Explain how to turn the shower on and get hot water. Detail check-out procedures and expectations. As always, include photographs to illustrate your instructions.

Help your guests get around

Leave your guests with a sheet of information about buses and transportation, museum information, and short local day trips to take. Include travel books, brochures, and menus of local attractions and restaurants. Airbnb hosts can create city guidebooks for guests to see once they've booked their reservation.

Also provide discount coupons that might save your guests some money during their stay. Point guests to local places off the beaten path. City guides for your short-term rental guests

Use a key-less lock

Make your guests stay as hassle-free as possible. If you will not be there to greet your guests, then use a key-less lock. Set a code and use a keypad.

Each code will be personal to the guest, which makes it easy for the guest to remember. It also offers your guests additional security. They'll know the guests before them do not have continued access.

As a bonus, it allows for check-ins when you are not home, and you don't have to worry about lost keys.

Keep it simple

Keep your short-term rental property meticulously clean and uncluttered. Clean your space professionally if possible. A clean, safe, cozy space is what guests want. Don't go overboard with decorating, remember, less is more, but be authentic to who you are. Decorate for the holidays as you normally would.

Use fresh flowers from the local Farmer's Market and art from the area. Your guests want to live, and experience the area, like a local.

Make them feel at home

Keep an umbrella by the door for unexpected rain. Leave soft blankets on the couch and books to read by the bed. Put a deck of cards and a stack of fun games to play in the living room.

Just in case, organize an emergency kit with an extra toothbrush, toothpaste, disposable razors, band-aides, a flashlight, and medicine kit. Most guests won't use the kit, but it is good to know that it is there if they need something in the middle of the night.

Multi-Unit House Hacking 101

If you ask any seasoned real estate investor what their most difficult deal was, they will invariably say it was their first property. Not difficult because of the size of the property, getting funding or the players involved. It was hard because it was their first deal. That's human nature. We are hard wired to avoid risk and the unknown.

What is house hacking?

"House hacking" is a trendy term for a small multi-unit investment property (1-4 units) where the investor actually lives in one of the building units. If you try this strategy, you must go in with your eyes open. You can lose money if you haven't done your research. Start your research by asking the following questions.

Why is the owner selling?

The first, lynchpin question you need an answer for is: Why is the owner selling? Your first and second response will be something mumbled or vague. Keep asking. Why is the owner selling? Ask until you get an answer that sounds plausible. Then check the answer if you can.

Is the seller going through a divorce, a lawsuit or another legal disaster? Do they have trouble keeping decent tenants in the property? You never know what you might find. Knowing why the owner is selling will give you power as a buyer. Power is good.

Access your state court system and type in the seller's name and the property address or legal description for the property. Do a little digging for property information with these screening resources. Multi-unit house hacking requires answers to a spectrum of questions.

Gather some basic property information

You'll use the following information in deal negotiations.

- What is the age of the property? What building materials were used in its construction? As an investor it is your job to know every inch of the property that is on the selling block. You will be responsible for all of it.
- How many units are on the property? Go see them yourself.
- What is the square footage of each unit?
- Are all units legal and up to code or is the seller hedging?
- Are life safety systems such as exit signage, CO/smoke detectors and firewalls properly installed? What are state and local requirements for such systems?
- Has anything been remodeled? If so, when?
- Ask what, if any, capital improvements have been made over the past 5 years.

If no property improvements were made, then you know the seller has been putting a few things off. It is your responsibility to be certain the building is compliant with applicable building codes and approved for occupancy.

Who are the current residents?

This might be one of your most critical areas of research. After all, you'll be living right next door to your residents.

- You must get a rent roll of the current tenants. Go as far back as you can. (Read: At least two years.)
- Find out how long the residents' leases run, any concessions they received and how long they have been at the property.
- What is the average turnover time for a vacant unit?

- How long does the average tenant stay?
- Do residents generally get their security deposits back or do they leave in the middle of the night?
- What is the profile of the average resident? Do they meet your screening guidelines?
- Search for online reviews and discover what past and current residents think of the property.

What about the neighborhood?

Do your homework and you'll have a more realistic understanding of the market and how the property will perform. Start with these steps.

- Walk in a 10-block radius around the building. Do you see pawn shops and liquor stores or nail salons, coffee shops and restaurants? What does that tell you about the future of the area?
- Visit the property during the morning, afternoon and evening.
- What is the flow of foot and car traffic?
- What is the closest public transportation?
- Go to the police station and get a premise report on the property. Ask about the reputation of the area. How long do people stay in the neighborhood?
- Research what type of unit rents best for the neighborhood: one, two- or three-bedroom units? In other words, which unit type has the highest demand in this market?
- What are the rents in your area for one bedroom, two bedroom and three-bedroom units?
- What are the current rental rates for the area?

- Ask around and find out what the neighbors think of their neighbors. People love to share their opinion.

Your homework will give you a more complete picture of the situation.

You can use all of your research to do your own multi-unit house hacking. When you know the neighborhood, the natural market resident and comparable buildings, you can estimate what you could ask for and get in rent. Based on the neighborhood and the rent roll you know how long your tenants will stay in your building.

What updates could you complete to command higher rents? What amenities or concessions motivates this market?

Reduce landlord risk

Exposure to risk is what keeps many people from investing in multi-unit properties. You eliminate risk with education, like anything else. It's important to know what questions to ask to mitigate your risks.

For every vacant unit you should know what the related costs are for

- Tenant screening fees
- Legal fees
- Evictions and related court costs
- Lost rent
- Leasing fees
- Turnover expenses for cleaning, trash, repairs, and maintenance

To avoid a few of these costly issues make sure you have a proper tenant screening system in place. Running a potential tenant through a basic credit check will cost time and energy but avoid headaches down the road.

Look for tenants with stable employment and higher disposable income instead of taking the first person that applies. You'll find a list of apps that can help you with landlord responsibilities in Chapter Twenty-Two: Technology.

What are typical unit turnover costs?

Everyone has heard stories about tenant damage. It doesn't always happen, but security deposits do serve a purpose. Get ahead of the game. Know that when a tenant leaves you will incur turnover costs. Get acquainted with professionals in your area so you know what a reasonable price would be for making a unit ready for a new tenant.

Since each unit is different, but measured in square footage, break down the price to a square foot average and use it as a formula. With each vacancy you may be paying for:

- Carpet cleaning
- Carpet/floor replacement
- Interior painting
- Full unit cleaning
- Trash removal
- Pest treatment

Do a little digging on landlord costs

Your expenses will include the upkeep of common areas, and payment of taxes, insurance, debt service and possibly property management.

- How are wastewater and sewer charges tallied and paid? Are they paid by the tenants or the property owner?
- Is the owner responsible for any tenant defaults on utilities?
- Who pays for utilities such as gas, water, and electric?
- How often is pest treatment required?
- Will taxes be reassessed?
- Will your property insurance cover replacement value or market value?
- Do you need liability coverage?
- Do you need a property manager? What are their fees?

Don't skip property inspections

Another risk lies in large maintenance items. Ask to see the paperwork on each unit. Hire professionals to inspect all units before you start negotiating. If the units are damaged or in poor repair, then they will have to be renovated immediately. This is where doing your due diligence pays off and saves you sleepless nights of worry.

While considering the property give close inspection to the

- structural integrity of the building,
- roof,
- furnace,

- hot water heater,
- windows and
- HVAC system

Make sure everything is in good working order. If not, their replacement costs should be included in your negotiations.

Cash flow

Long-term, to manage your risk, you will need a monthly and annual cash flow budget. (You perked up at the word cash flow, didn't you?) A portion of this cash flow needs to be saved for unexpected needs. It is a reserve fund for the property, not your lifestyle.

Let's face it, things will go wrong. You don't want to build a house of cards. Cash reserves are the only thing that will help you weather any unforeseen issue. You need to know how much the property is producing and how tight your expenses will be. Analyzing the numbers is vital.

Your team

Now you are armed with solid questions for any multi-unit house hacking. Use them! Don't think that you have to become an expert in every area. That's why you have a team, remember? You are the leader of your team and should be cognizant of the questions that need answers.

Multi-unit house hacking has a lot of dimensions to the process and you should be fully informed before any purchases are made. Spend time getting to know the process and you will be wiser in your next multi-unit house hacking deal.

Most Common Expenses with a Real Estate Flip

Perhaps the term "flipping" is not the best way to describe purchasing a house with the intention of selling it for a profit. Calling it flipping makes it sound almost effortless. In reality, flipping a house is a time-consuming process that requires research, money, and knowledge about construction and the local market. If you have all of that, you can set about to do the hard work. Here are five common expenses associated with the process.

Purchase price

This is the most important cost you will pay and will determine whether you make a profit or prepare a nice home for the next owners at a loss. You want to find properties available for purchase below their market value; the amount of work needed is really secondary. If the repairs needed are intimidating to most buyers, that can bode well for you. Find a home that meets your criteria and make a low-ball offer.

Real estate commission

Agents have a wealth of knowledge about properties on the market. They can quickly look up how many times a property has been listed, at what price, and its sales history. A real estate agent saves you a lot of legwork and provides valuable information. For an ongoing relationship with you, an agent may be willing to work for a flat fee rather than a percentage.

Repairs and upgrades

Before you can determine an acceptable purchase price on a property, you must know how much you can sell it for after repairs. To determine the after-repair value (ARV), look at similar homes in the area that have sold in the previous three months. Then you can look at the repairs needed to bring the house to that value. You may have to make low-ball offers on several houses before you find a willing seller.

Taxes

You are going to be responsible for property taxes for the time you own the house and for taxes on your profit. Consult with your tax advisor on what expenses qualify as deductions.

Utilities and lawn care

Potential purchasers will need water, electric, and gas turned on for their inspections. Some homes that have been vacant for a long time may have substantial costs to activate utilities. Many municipalities will mow neglected lawns and attach a lien to utilities. You must maintain the property within compliance of local codes.

Flipping a house might not be as easy as the name sounds, but with proper research and realistic expectations, you can still make a nice profit with a real estate flip.

Make Multifamily Your First Priority

If you're thinking about investing in real estate, take a good look at acquiring multifamily assets. The unique economic trends, potential revenue streams and tax incentives alone make them an attractive long-term investment.

Multifamily real estate is advantageously poised in the US economy. Here's why.

Baby boomers and millennials combine forces

Money follows the trends of the generations. Baby boomers and millennials are a powerful duel force in the economy. Both generations are focused on apartment living. This unique situation puts a premium on multifamily properties.

Economic trends show that many millennials aren't buying homes. Instead, they're opting to put their money into apartment living. They want the option of freedom and travel. Baby boomers are downsizing their single-family homes to move into smaller apartments for freedom and savings. Both generations are trending towards multifamily properties. And where the trends are, the money flows.

Positive cash flow from investing in real estate

If you own a single-family property you have limited options for creating positive cash flow from your investment. Multifamily properties offer multiple ways to create positive cash flow beyond basic rent.

Multifamily property owners often charge for extra amenities such as:

- laundry facilities
- parking
- party rooms
- shared workspace
- bike lockers
- fitness centers
- doormen
- pet services
- storage

Each new service adds an additional source of revenue. Not only that, these services and amenities will attract new residents to your property. There are many ways to create additional revenue based on your location and market.

Tax breaks

Providing safe, clean housing for residents is a wonderful service. Of course, not everyone is willing to do it. The risk you take also has its rewards. There are many tax strategies and incentives for those who own or own a part of multifamily real estate. Laws vary depending on if you are owner-occupied, but the principal is the same.

When investing always consider mortgage interest; property taxes; operating and capital expenses; and depreciation when planning your tax strategies. A tax professional who is fluent and savvy in real estate investments will help you maximize your tax savings and protect your revenue stream from the unexpected.

Multifamily in your portfolio

Real estate investment has a wide field. There are endless angles to play when investing in real estate. Multifamily real estate should be a consideration because of economic timing, cash flow and tax incentives.

You will find that the right apartment properties are powerful investment vehicles.

Things You Probably Don't Know About Multifamily Real Estate Investing

If you've read my book *Invest in Apartment Buildings: Profit Without the Pitfalls,* then you know I like to repeat something a mentor told me years ago. He told me that what most people know about investing in real estate, especially beginners, is easily summarized into three categories:

1. What you know you know
2. What you know you don't know, and
3. What you don't know you don't know

In a way, hearing this was somewhat terrifying. Was there really that much I didn't know? Stuff I didn't even know existed? Whoa. But my favorite mentor taught this, so I chose to believe him. This concept is especially important for new real estate investors to fully grasp. Knowing that your education is incomplete is the first step towards reducing risk.

You simply can't know everything. No worries. You'll tackle this. How? Find team members that *do* know. Buddy up with, or hire, a mentor. Network with industry professionals namely brokers, property managers, vendors, service providers, and other successful multifamily real estate investing pros. Read. Read. Read.

You don't need to be an expert to invest in real estate

Say what? But didn't I just say you should learn all those things you don't even know you don't know? Or, did I?

Here's what you do. Surround yourself with experts. Choose a really great property manager. Hire a broker you like and trust. Find mentorship with like-minded successful investors (but don't chase every bright shiny object you see, have a plan and stick with it). Decide whether you want to personally experience the process of investing or turn it entirely over to someone else.

Assumptions are allowed

As long as you know the source of the data used in analysis, and you've vetted those numbers, it's okay to make financial projection assumptions. (Always remember garbage in, garbage out.) For example, use the following assumptions to predict property performance.

- Vacancy (7%)
- Income Growth (5%)
- Expense Growth (3%)
- Cap Rate (7%)

- Expense Ratio (40-45%)

Use assumptions to plan budgets for the long term. For instance, make 24-month, 36-month, or even ten-year projections to determine best- and worst-case scenarios. It's always a good idea to run several scenarios using both conservative and aggressive assumptions. Note: Determine your own investment market variables through market research and by connecting with experts in your market.

Sellers will sometimes "stuff" a property just before sale

It's not uncommon for a multifamily property owner to fill vacancies just prior to listing a property for sale. They do this in order to reach occupancy levels that are more palatable for the buyer and the lender. It also allows them to make a case that supports a higher asking price.

And if they started with a large number of vacancies? You can probably put money on the fact that if they needed a lot of new tenants fast, they most likely rented to any tenant they could find. Hard to believe, isn't it? It happens.

The problem is, those tenants are now yours. You'll know them well. They're the tenants who can't pay rent. A lease audit (be sure to review tenants' applications, too) will shed light on the current tenants. You can then plan accordingly. The last thing you want to do is to begin property ownership while buried under massive debt collection.

One problem tenant can affect the entire community

A few years ago, I had a property manager who was a relative rookie. But he was a likeable, outgoing, energetic rookie with an entrepreneurial mindset. Things were going along well until he started renting units to renters from the coalition for the homeless program. He believed this would solve the problem of late rent payments because the government paid like clockwork.

While it made his life easier, renting to the coalition was a disaster for our rental community and us. Some, not all, of the new coalition tenants introduced activities to the community that frankly terrified current residents. Those current residents broke leases and left.

Questions You Should Ask About Your Multifamily Investment Strategies

"I want to invest in a multifamily property." I probably hear this statement about half a dozen times a week.

What I usually don't hear are statements that demonstrate a good understanding of multifamily investment strategies. There's simply a desire to invest in real estate without much thought regarding long-term investment plans once a property is acquired.

Solid investment strategies and market knowledge are the keys to your success. Your multifamily investment strategies should be in place before you invest in your first property.

Your strategies affect your:

- Real estate investment portfolio
- Operations policies and procedures
- Ability to attract partners
- Ability to be proactive
- Exit from your investment

What are your investment goals? Are you looking for cash flow? Appreciation? Short-term or long-term holding periods? Are you able to carve out time for your real estate investment business?

These are important questions you must answer. As are the following:

What type of multifamily property will you buy?

How much time do you have to devote to your real estate investment business? The following two property types will put vastly different demands on your resources.

- **Turnkey:** A property that is stable or has already been stabilized with competitive occupancy and rents, a solid tenant profile, and no deferred maintenance.
- **Underperforming:** A property with deferred maintenance, below market rents, unrealized income, poor management, and above average expenses.

Clearly an underperforming asset will demand much more of your time and resources.

What will you do with your property once you own it?

The following exit strategies can be applied to both performing and underperforming assets.

- Flip to another buyer through a means such as wholesaling or assumable financing
- Add value with renovations and asset repositioning
- Refinance
- Convert to another use such as condos or long-term senior care
- Hold
- 1031 exchange into larger investment properties

Your tactics will vary for each property type. For example, you might want to add value to an underperforming asset by addressing deferred maintenance, increasing net operating income (NOI) and putting top-notch management in place. But even a turnkey property has value add opportunities. For example, you might increase income with the addition of new ancillary amenities or through the implementation of new operations policies.

What strategies will you implement to increase NOI?

Raising property income and lowering expenses will increase NOI. In the multifamily investment arena, property value is directly related to NOI. Chances are pretty good you will have opportunities to increase income and lower expenses at your new property.

Here are some strategies for increasing NOI:

Raise property income

- Implement RUBS (Ratio Utility Billing System)
- Raise rents
- Change tenant profile (reposition resident base)
- Add new ancillary services and amenities
- Increase fees and service charges
- Implement new leasing policies
- Implement proactive maintenance policies

Lower property expenses

- Hire top-notch third-party management
- Rewrite operations procedures and policies
- Establish tenant retention strategies
- Conduct vendor and service provider reassessments
- Appeal property taxes
- Shop new property insurance, look for discounts to industry
- Install energy efficient building systems

With the proper education it's not difficult to outperform your competition.

The very best thing a new investor can do to fine-tune their multifamily investment strategies is to work with a mentor who is already in the business. Talk with successful multifamily real estate investors. Most will be happy to have a conversation about your investment strategies.

Going Solo? 5 Steps to Setting up a Real Estate Company

Real estate investment offers a lot of opportunities for building your wealth, but the risk involved also means that it is a daunting experience. It is an industry with plenty of legal and financial issues that must be fully understood, so it is not something for people who are not willing to put in the effort.

However, for those with the drive and determination to succeed, the following steps can lead to success.

Step #1: Decide what type of investor you want to be

First, decide what type of investor you want to be. Some investors are in it for the long haul, while others are more interested in flipping. The latter usually offers quick returns, but it can be a money pit if you are inexperienced or don't have enough knowledge of the market.

Long-haul investments tend to offer better stability, but they can take a while to bring in profits. Do your research and think very carefully about what type of investment makes sense for you.

Step #2: Sorting out your financing

If you are independently wealthy, financing is not a concern, but most people are not that fortunate and have to look to other avenues for the money required to invest in properties. Many first-time investors opt for finding a wealthy partner, but if you want to go your own way, there are also lenders that offer good loan terms.

When it comes to financing, it is always better to secure more money than you think you need because it can be used for refurbishments.

Step #3: Take care of legal matters

Instead of simply buying properties in your own name, create a real estate company to do everything properly. The business options available to you depend on the tax status you feel comfortable with, but most real estate investors opt for LLCs.

Although the process is relatively straightforward and will allow you to legally separate yourself from liability, it is still wise to find proper legal advice.

Step #4: Insurance is a must

Whether you opt for long-term rental properties or short-term investment properties, insurance is a necessity. It is the only way to safeguard your real estate company from accidents or unsafe conditions. Make sure that your policy for rental properties specifies exactly what the responsibility of the renter is and what is covered by insurance. For investment properties, don't tie yourself to a long-term contract.

Step #5: Get expert help

When you start out with your real estate company, it is better to work with a mentor or experienced investor for your first few purchases. Not only does a real estate expert usually understand the market better, but he or she can provide you with a lot of useful advice for building your company.

Chapter Thirteen:
Today's Renters

The best type of investment property 15 years ago
is not likely to be the right property now
or even 15 years from now. – Theresa Bradley-Banta

~

American Households are Changing

You choose your tenants when you choose your building. Most investors look for a property that some other real estate investor is selling in order to reduce their portfolio of properties. They figure that if it has been used by someone else as a rental property for years, it should also work for them. But, the right investment property for someone else may not be the right property for you.

Households are changing

The U.S. Census Bureau (census.gov) reports that American households are changing. The number of households that have a married couple with children has been decreasing steadily since 1960. As the number of households with married couples has declined, the percentage of unmarried couples with and without children has increased significantly.

Another key change that is important for real estate investors is the percentage of one-person households, which has gone from approximately 12 percent in 1960 to almost 30 percent in 2011. With many Americans living longer, more active, and busier lives, they are appreciating the convenience of living near shopping and healthcare without having to take care of property maintenance themselves.

It is important for real estate investors to understand their local market. Many people who rent are not doing it because of credit problems or other financial issues. Instead, many responsible people choose to rent a nice place to live rather than go deeply in debt on a home that will also take much of their free time to maintain.

There is a need for well-maintained rental properties that suit all household types. These households include young people with no children, older Americans looking to downsize, and couples with and without children.

What all renters want

Regardless of their current household composition, there are certain things all renters tend to look for when choosing where they will live.

- **Responsible management:** The most common complaint from tenants is lack of responsiveness and basic respect from property managers.

- **Security:** There are no guarantees, but people prefer communities with adequate lighting, background checks of residents, and management that responds quickly to security concerns.
- **Convenient location:** Millennials and people over 65 are not big on driving. These demographics like having things within walking distance.

In addition to having as many of these features as possible, it is important to showcase that your property cares about all of your tenants. People want to feel welcomed and appreciated. It might be your property, but it is their home.

How the 2008 Post-Recession Housing Market Has Changed Multifamily Investments

If you talk about real estate investing to most people these days, they will probably shake their head and shudder at the thought. The Great Depression changed how the United States economy functions. Recovery was slow, and those who survived it lived the remainder of their lives with a unique perspective that no other generation will ever have.

Most people alive today remember the collapse of the housing market. They grew up believing that real estate is always a good investment because they aren't making any more of it. The 2008 housing market collapse completely obliterated the traditional American dream of home ownership for many people.

As people recover financially and feel more optimistic about their future, they do so with an altered perception of the term "home" and real estate.

The millennials factor

These young people are more community-minded than any previous generation. Many of them prefer living within walking distance of work and shopping rather than having a large luxury vehicle to transport them from point A to point B. These same millennials make paying down college debt a higher priority than home ownership. They appreciate the many amenities of apartment and condominium living.

This shift in attitude toward renting has provided sustained momentum for multifamily investments. Renting an apartment is not viewed as a dreaded first step they must take prior to actually owning a place of their own.

Many of these young people watched their parents lose a home they had spent years working to maintain. Even if their family home did not fall into foreclosure, these millennials saw the amount of stress that can come along with a mortgage. As a result, many of them see renting an apartment as freedom from the financial burden that comes with owning a home.

Investors must understand what is important to millennials

Millennials understand the importance of higher education. Many of them earn a comfortable living well above the median household income for the United States.

Millennials embrace living near employment and entertainment centers. They look for ways to live green and leave a small carbon footprint. Owners of multifamily properties must consider the amenities and features that are important to these young tenants if they wish to remain profitable in the current and future housing market.

Renting to Boomers and Millennials: They're More Alike Than You Think!

The demographic groups known as boomers and millennials are the largest populations renting apartments, so it is vital to know what they value. Knowing what resonates with both demographics will help you craft a powerful leasing and marketing message. Here's how to go beyond their differences and focus on what qualities they share.

A beautiful lobby

Having an attractive, inviting lobby is always key. Keep your lobby and common areas clean and uncluttered. Millennials and boomers want a lobby that feels open and arranged like a lounge.

Use high-end touches for this high trafficked area. You want residents to feel like they can linger and socialize in this space. The initial look and feeling of a building is important to both groups. Make it count.

Common spaces to work and socialize

Beyond the lobby, residents want comfortable common spaces like internet lounges and rooftop terraces. If you are successfully renting to boomers and millennials, you'll quickly realize they all want to be engaged in their community.

Open and flexible common spaces create value with their recreational opportunities. Create a landing spot around an activity like a golf simulator, a chess board or ping pong table.

337

Foster a sense of community by planning monthly social events for residents. Form a craft beer club or a book club within your building. Send out a newsletter to highlight activities.

The experience of life

Online event planner Eventbrite (eventbrite.com) found that millennials and boomers are more likely to spend money on events, social gatherings and concerts rather than physical items. A growing number of Americans overall care more about the experiences of life and don't want to miss out on life's opportunities.

As a landlord, you can help your residents hunt for experiences by sharing local concerts, classes and festivals with them. Make sure you are tapped into the events held at your neighborhood libraries, parks, and universities. Create a calendar of local events on your web portal. You may attract tenants just because they appreciate the close distance to activities.

Location is key when renting to boomers and millennials

Location has always been vital. Make sure to emphasis your close proximity to conveniences and entertainment. Highlight entertainment venues such as bars, restaurants and coffee shops.

Nearby transportation opportunities are also important. Bus routes, major highways, and train stations will appeal to boomers and millennials who value easy access to all of the places they work and play.

Walkability to everyday conveniences is highly valued. Both groups want the ability to walk to a local market or cafe.

Smart technology

Boomers pioneered the rise in technology. Millennials grew up with technology, so it is second nature to them. Offering solid WiFi connectivity and cell phone service throughout your building is understood as a given by both. All community living spaces are expected to be wired and up to date.

Make sure you have enough bandwidth for streaming videos, tablets and smartphones.

Smart-home automation is a step up and would be a marketing asset. Residents can control the temperature, lighting and security of their apartment from their smart phone. This sense of control will create a better apartment living experience for all of your tenants.

Sustainability and energy efficiency

Smart home technologies are energy efficient. That is important because becoming environmentally friendly is mandatory for millennials and important to boomers. At a minimum your building should have a recycling program in synch with your local requirements.

Retrofitting your building has a wide range of applications and can be as painless as installing LED lighting in common areas. You could go all out with solar panels on the roof. Either way, increased sustainability means increased visibility for your building through your marketing message to prospective renters.

339

Don't forget, boomers and millennials read online reviews

Don't forget to maintain and monitor your online reputation when renting to boomers and millennials. The internet is one of the first places both groups seek out when determining where to live. Online reviews work to market your building while you sleep. These days online property reviews mean lost or gained business.

If you are renting to boomers and millennials, emphasize your community amenities throughout your social media sites. Be sure your marketing message incorporates any or all of the features above. You'll have a stronger and more diverse community for doing so!

Chapter Fourteen:
Your Brand

You already have a brand whether you realize it or not.
– Theresa Bradley-Banta

~

Apartment Complex Branding 101: Who Are You?

Although it is a current buzzword, branding has been around since humans starting trading shiny rocks. Branding is the public's perception or image of your product and services.

Companies can spend thousands of dollars shaping their brand, but the public always has the last word. So, the real question is: What is the public's perception of my company? Yes, that's right, you already have a brand whether you realize it or not.

Sample case

Many years ago, before branding was a verb, my friend lived in an apartment complex that had threadbare carpets, discolored banisters and a vibrant mold colony. When the residents got together, the perennial starting conversation was to debate the origin of the rotting cabbage smell in the buildings. Did it come from the damp basement or the mossy roof? You get the picture. The publicly understood brand for the complex was "slow decay" or "absentee landlord."

Despite the brand, people lived in the complex for three reasons. The rents were below market, the apartments were a good size, and everyone else lived there. These were quality features that could have been used to refocus the branding, specifically the community element.

Time for a reality check

In 2019, visual content curator Stackla (stackla.com) conducted a survey which found that 90% of consumers say authenticity is important when deciding which brands they like and support. You must be honest about what you are starting with.

Go out on a limb and ask your residents what they really think. Just asking for feedback will enhance your reputation. Yes, you are going to get some snarky responses, expect it, but you will also get some real pearls of insight as well. When you have a handle on what your actual public brand is, then it is time to build on the positive. Keep it real.

New refrigerators and countertops would not have convinced the residents in my friends old complex that they were living in a "Luxury" complex. In fact, the brand would have been openly mocked. Instead, it would have been very easy to capitalize on the "Friendly Community" brand to residents and potential customers alike. Planning a few resident barbecues or brunches would have redirected conversation from "What is the best way to get rid of mold?" to "When is the next event?"

The Clean and Safe Brand

At a bare minimum, what you need to start with is the "Clean" brand

Power wash the outside of your buildings. If the paint comes off with the power wash, then you know that it is time for a fresh coat of paint. Use pest control services on a regular basis. Replace the carpeting in the entryway every 6 to 10 years. Do I need to say it? Vacuum the carpet daily. Get rid of the old onion smell. Yes, it is there, you just can't detect it anymore. Use odor-absorbing paint for unit turnovers and in the common areas. Plug in an air-freshener.

Eric Spangenberg, Dean of the College of Business at Washington State University, has been studying the effect of scents on people for years in retail and real estate situations. Spangenberg advocates using simple scents, such as orange, lemon, basil, vanilla, green tea, pine and cedar. Don't be overpowering; less is more. At the very least, put out a bowl of white vinegar overnight to neutralize unwanted odors.

"Safe" is the other brand that must be addressed

Women, even women who are total strangers, will warn each other if a complex feels unsafe, especially if there are children involved. Take extra precautions to establish a "Safe" brand and secure your complex. One crime could mar your reputation for years.

Make sure you have adequate night lighting around parking lots and entryways. Keep all shrubs around doors 3 feet or under so there is no hidability factor. Install security cameras and assign fines if people prop entry doors open. Ask the police to drive through your parking lot on a regular basis in the evening.

If you have a property maintenance company, assess their reputation. Anyone acting remotely inappropriate will be a subject of wildfire conversation among residents. Provide an open channel of communication to residents regarding safety concerns. Respond to their worries and make sure your residents feel heard. Be assured that every effort you make to ensure a "safe" brand will be noticed.

Pro tip: The first step in branding is self-awareness. Make sure you can own the "clean" and "safe" brand before you move onto Branding 102.

What Is Brand Marketing, and Do You Need It?

In the highly competitive world of property investing, proper marketing can make the difference between success and failure. For long-term success and a stable business model, branding is also important.

The purpose of marketing is to motivate potential customers to take action. Branding is necessary to build a base of loyal customers. An essential part of effective brand marketing is utilizing your current customers and tenants to generate new tenants from word-of-mouth and glowing reviews. To turn your existing tenants into your raving fans, you need brand marketing.

Establishing your brand

Your brand is what distinguishes you from your competitors. Your branding clearly conveys your values and company characteristics. Branding is the foundation and launching point for all of your marketing efforts. Think of your brand as solid and stationary. It is there for your tenants and is consistent and reliable. Marketing is more fluid. It goes out and finds new tenants and motivates them to move to your brand.

Do small investors need a brand?

Large corporations spend millions and have entire divisions devoted to developing, maintaining, and protecting their brand. Small investors do not have that luxury. It is understandable to feel that branding should be low on your list of priorities and that you already have many things competing for your time.

The best way for a small investor to view branding is not to think of it as a task you complete, like doing taxes or mowing the lawn. Think of your brand as your reputation. Businesses of all sizes have a reputation and identity. While you may not give much thought to brand marketing or branding, you do care about your reputation.

This means that you devote some time to thinking about the impression people have of your company. What is the first thing that comes to mind when they see one of your properties? Do they recognize it as a property owned by you because it looks fresh and well-maintained?

Your personal style, standards and values

You want your properties and brand to convey a positive impression to everyone. You do this by applying your personal style, standards and values to everything your company does. That includes things like how the company vehicles are maintained and the landscaping. Think about other companies that make an impression on you.

You are making an impression on others with your company, and you want it to be a good one. You must be proactive in taking steps to control and influence the impression people have of your business.

Creative Ways to Improve Your Apartment Brand

So, what's your brand? It might something you're just beginning to think about, but your apartment building already has a brand. Your brand comes from the image your property is portraying to both the people living there as well as the general public.

Your brand comes from your building's appearance, reputation, community, and external marketing. It should help distinguish you from your competitors. A great apartment brand will also help convey your company's core values and characteristics. It will become the foundation and launching point of your marketing campaigns.

The benefits of apartment branding

- **Focuses your marketing efforts.** When you know what your brand is, your marketing becomes stronger and more effective. For example, if you want to target millennials, then you'll want to take to social media. Focusing your marketing to a demographic is a smarter use of your budget and will lead to a higher conversion rate. When you start to brand through marketing, remember to filter your marketing efforts through the requirements of the Fair Housing Act which will help you avoid problematic terminology.

- **Helps build a solid community.** Great multifamily property branding will focus on targeting a particular demographic. When you brand for that demographic, the people moving into your property will share common interests and values. That can create a stronger community in your building. The result is people living there longer and becoming more invested in their home.
- **Increases your revenue potential.** People pay more for the brands that they love. That's true whether its coffee, shoes, or an apartment. When your property has a brand that excites people, they are willing to pay more money to become a part of it.

How to Brand Your Apartment Building

It's up to you to take charge of your brand and ensure it's a good one. Maybe you didn't realize you needed a brand. Maybe your current brand is old and dated. Or maybe you are simply looking for ways to rebrand. Whatever the reason, there are many easy and creative ways that you can improve your apartment brand and increase your revenue.

Update the appearance in line with your brand

The appearance of your building should be in line with your brand. That includes the exterior as well as the public spaces such as lobbies and

347

courtyards. Once you've identified your brand, carry that over into the design. Consider elements such as:

- **Integrating your brand's dominant color scheme into the design.** You can do this with feature walls in the lobby or even canopies on the outside. This helps potential renters connect the physical building with marketing that they've seen. This will help build your brand and attract your target demographic to your space.
- **Update your signage.** Use similar fonts in both your building's signage and marketing. That will strengthen brand identification. This can be a great opportunity to rename the building, too, bringing it more in line with your brand (for instance, Shady Acres isn't a great building name for a place targeting millennial renters!).

Branding your building's appearance doesn't have to be a huge financial investment. There are many ways you can update on a budget.

Design with a single demographic in mind

What demographic are you targeting with your brand? If your apartment complex is in an up-and-coming area of town, it might be young working professionals. If it's in a quiet established community, it might be baby boomers. Many baby boomers are in the market for luxe urban apartment living and are looking for key amenities in their property. Knowing who your target demographic is and what they are looking for, then designing your space with them in mind, is key to your success.

You might find it helpful to create a profile of your ideal renter and keep them in mind while making design decisions. Think of that profile when designing your communal spaces and choosing amenities to include in your apartment. Would they prefer a business center or a community room? Hot tub or a dog park? Extra storage or a party area? Knowing who you are designing for can make these decisions easier. Again, be sure to adhere to the Fair Housing Act requirements when targeting demographics.

Market lifestyle, not living space

Focus your apartment brand on selling a certain lifestyle. People choose where to live because it fits the sort of lifestyle that they want. Prove to them you can deliver it through a boutique-style service versus mass-market appeal. That's exactly what Portus (boutiqueapartments.com) is doing with their buildings in Denver, Colorado. They have branded their buildings as eco-friendly, artsy apartments for professionals. It's been a huge success for the company.

Brand your property through lifestyle shots in your marketing. Include residents enjoying certain amenities, entertaining friends and family, and enjoying the local area. While residents will still want information on the home itself (such as room sizes, monthly bills, etc.) that's not what will get them through the door. Branding through lifestyle will help attract motivated renters to your property.

Use Social Media to Promote Your Apartment Complex

Social media is in the fabric of everyday life. Are you using social media to brand or promote your apartment complex? If done right, you can engage your residents in the social media effort and get positive testimonials. Read:

Free advertising. You could increase your retention rates and allure prospective residents interested in your buzz.

You may already know about Eric Brown of Urbane Apartments fame. Under Brown's leadership the company started a resident-written blog recommending favorite local destinations and events. Urbane Apartments (urbaneapts.com) has a social networking site exclusive to tenants. Of course, they also have active YouTube, Facebook and Twitter profiles. The traffic to these sites has doubled and tripled even though the Urbane Apartments complex only offers 300 apartments in total. Impressive, right?

How to create an online community

So, what amazing content drives traffic to these social media sites? You already know the glossy, disingenuous feeling to avoid. People want real information they could use in their daily life, not thinly veiled advertisements. For example, who do you think serves the best cup of coffee in town? Explain the why of your opinion. Use your voice.

Tapping into resident participation means creating an online community all about the residents, all about their world. What do the residents care about, want to know and want to share?

Keep your media feed authentic, useful and fun. Profile a local baker whose passion is chocolate cake, recommend a dry cleaner that doesn't eat buttons and highlight a safe place to walk your dog. Ask questions to start conversations but make them good, real questions. Engage residents about their favorite local gems and ask them to share.

Hip, community-driven and media savvy is the branding Urbane Apartments has now and you could replicate that success. Keep publishing your updates in a consistent manner, daily or weekly. Remember to focus on community locations and events. Reach out and ask for participation from residents.

How to get your residents involved

When your residents move in give them a welcome gift bag with some token items to make them feel at home. Gifts like toilet paper, a box of chocolates, paper towels, tea or coffee are always welcome items when moving into a new place. In the bag include a card with the addresses of your social media sites.

Display your addresses in the lobby or anywhere else residents might take notice. When you send out an email to residents, create a social media optimized email signature.

You could easily get a QR (Quick Response) Code, the code that smartphones can scan. Put that code up in poster form anywhere in your building. Utilize the code on promotional material, your front door and the lids of coffee cups. Put your code where people are really going to see it. That QR code will take anyone right to the social media site of your choosing. Use it.

Remember…

Keep it foremost in your mind that the entire world, present and future, can see what you post on social media. Permanently. When residents post complaints or get obnoxious, and they will, then you need to respond to the complaint in a quick, professional, business-like way. Criticism is not always a bad thing. See it as an opportunity to shine.

Always take the high road and rise above. You will earn immediate respect for keeping your cool, addressing the issue raised and resolving the problem to the best of your ability.

Based on a study from the Neilson Norman Group (nngroup.com) only 1% of your social media users participate regularly, 9% engage occasionally and 90% of the community is just reading and observing, not participating at all. That is a huge percentage. You should always remember the silent 90% in the background assessing your posts and your reputation.

Your reputation is evolving. That is the upside and the downside. Social media is a tool but like any tool you should use it wisely. Make your posts genuine, fun and engaging. Pay attention to your audience and ask them to participate. Your time and effort using social media to promote your apartment complex will be rewarded.

Turn Your Residents into Brand Ambassadors

As a landlord, you have an excellent opportunity to turn your tenants into brand ambassadors. Every company wants to have its customers become a willing part of its marketing department. Consider the loyal customers of Apple. Many of them would not consider switching from a Mac to a PC or a different smartphone.

You may have high demand for your rental units, but do people camp out in anticipation of a new opening in your apartment complex? That loyalty and passion takes time and effort.

You have a great opportunity because your tenants already have a very close connection to your brand—it provides them with their home.

Value their opinions and input

People can sense when their thoughts are respected. You have spent a lot of time studying the real estate market and trends, but do not overlook feedback from your tenants.

Hearing negative comments can be difficult, and some of your tenants may not be as tactful as they should be, but they may still have a point. Ignoring what they say will only distance you from them and reduce the likelihood that any tenants will become your brand ambassadors.

Identify your most likely ambassadors

Some people are natural leaders and serve as a source of information and counsel to everyone who knows them. These people are typically curious by nature and like to be involved. They will read every post you make on social media and absorb as much helpful information as you will provide. By being an authority and a reliable source of information on real estate, you will earn their respect. Be mindful of these people, and you will be in an excellent position to convert them into your brand ambassadors.

Make them part of your team

People like being part of a team and feeling like they are involved. They want to be loyal to a brand. People appreciate and respect companies that care about more than just making a profit. They want to do business with real people they trust. Personalize your communications with them and be proud to have your name and image associated with your brand.

Look for opportunities to make your tenants feel involved. Go beyond the standard feedback forms and communications on social media. Actively engage with them and ask for their thoughts in person. If they love their home, they will convey that to others when they speak to them about your brand.

It doesn't take a lot of effort to turn your tenants into brand ambassadors, and the rewards can be tremendous, so start taking these steps today!

How to Generate Traffic to Your Apartment Community

The hands-down, best way to get new tenants into your building is through word of mouth. How do you get people talking? Make sure that your current apartment residents really do have a sense of community. There are many ways to create that feeling.

One idea would be to bring the residents together through promoting a One Book, One Community event. Make it a promotional event, create a buzz and partner with the local library or community center. On a publicized day bring all of the participants, residents and guests together by hosting a brunch in your facility to discuss the book. This will create good will among residents and the community. It is also an excellent opportunity to showcase your building. The same day you could offer tours of open apartments.

Continue planning events that your apartment community can talk about and anticipate. Soon they will do the advertising for you.

Community events don't have to be so broad; it depends on the net you would like to cast. Think of the demographic you would like to attract. Where would they go to have fun? The local coffee shops? Story hour at the library? The golf club? Target where your demographic traffic would show up and market that area. Create tailored events that would appeal to your audience and promote your apartment community.

Make sure you have a physical presence

If your building is hidden from view, make sure the local community knows about your existence. Share promotional magnets or brochures to the human resource departments of local companies. Bring cookies to local agencies that might refer your apartment building to customers. Depending on your pet policy, you could create a pet goodie bag with your business card and distribute them to local veterinarians or shelters.

Generating traffic to your apartment community can be tricky if your building is literally out of sight, down a driveway or hidden behind another building. Your property signage should be large enough to be seen from a distance. Make sure you have wonderful curb appeal to invite potential residents inside once they actually see your building. You get only one chance to create a wow impression.

Get an online presence

As everyone knows from experience, most physical traffic starts as online traffic. Create an inviting website and make sure it is mobile-friendly. Post current promotional events, updates and vital information. Give the potential client a feeling of what it would be like to be a resident through the website. Post an attractive photograph of your building and positive testimonials from your residents. People shop online for everything, including places to live.

Post informational content on your website, anticipating the questions a potential resident might ask. Videos are the easiest way to engage visitors. Post walk-through tours of your available apartments. After enjoying a video of an apartment, a potential client is much more likely to visit your building. After viewing the videos, invite visitors into your building with monthly promotional events. Give them a reason to walk into your apartment community.

Generating traffic to your apartment building should be approached as a win-win situation for yourself and the local community.

Chapter Fifteen:
Leasing and Marketing

Make the customer the hero of your story.
– Ann Handley

~

Powerful Leasing and Marketing Tips

Starting out at as real estate investor is difficult enough, and on top of all the other challenges, you have to compete with some big companies for tenants. These large corporations can spend hundreds of thousands of dollars on marketing and bring potential tenants in with incentives and enticing bonuses for signing a lease.

You do have options beyond a "for rent" sign with a couple of balloons attached. Get creative and utilize that passion you have to attract top-quality renters to your properties. Here are a few leasing and marketing tips to get you started.

Referrals from current renters

Good word of mouth is one of the most valuable methods of marketing out there. Major corporations have entire departments devoted to retaining current customers and building brand loyalty.

This is one area where you have an advantage over the large corporations. No matter how they try, corporations cannot establish the strong connection individuals can with people. Make sure your current residents know they are appreciated and you're grateful they chose to make their home with you.

Consider an annual tenant appreciation barbecue. This is a low-cost and enjoyable way to retain the tenants you currently have and bring new renters through their referrals.

Go the same places your future renters go

When it comes to real estate, people want to deal with a person they already know and trust. You won't be able to saturate the local media with your name to gain name recognition. This does not mean you shouldn't utilize radio and other advertising mediums but be aware that it might take a while for you to begin seeing any substantial results from those dollars spent.

Networking with your targeted demographic is a low-cost method that pays off quickly. There are local groups for community activities, charitable causes, and leisure activities. When you know who your targeted renters are, go to where they spend their time and do not be apologetic about letting them know what business you are in.

358

Cross-promotion with other small businesses

It's tough for any small business to go up against multi-million-dollar companies. Let some of the other locally owned businesses know that you are on their side. These butcher shops, produce markets, fitness centers, car washes, and other outlets all benefit from new residents moving to the area in which they are located.

Many will appreciate a new way to advertise their business and will be glad to partner with you on coupons, flyers, or perhaps sponsoring that tenants' appreciation barbecue.

There are lots of possibilities. Be creative and be enthusiastic—you will be surprised at what you can accomplish! Read on for more creative ideas.

Extraordinary Ways to Market and Lease Apartments

When it comes to marketing and leasing apartments Craigslist might be your best source—but it's not the only game in town.

Zillow.com, HotPads.com, Rent.com, Apartments.com, your own website and social media can all generate good traffic. But have you explored new resources and strategies lately? Try these ideas for great results:

Market where your target renter hangs out

Take a minute right now and think about where your target market likes to spend their leisure time. You can find some unusual places to advertise.

Often these are places that your competitors haven't thought of like:

- Movie theaters (place an ad during the "pre-show entertainment").
- Concert venues.
- Ridesharing apps such as Uber and Lyft (enormous advertising potential).
- Local schools and universities.
- Coffee shops (put your property ad on cup sleeves).
- Bike sharing stations.

For example, Denver B-cycle (denverbcycle.com), which was the first large-scale municipal bike sharing system in the United States, is a hugely popular program especially among young urban residents. This wouldn't happen to be your target market would it?

Getting the local community engaged in promoting your multifamily property is easier than you might think. Getting the word out to your community is key.

Local community events

Baseball teams, dance competitions and 5K events all need sponsorship from community businesses to make them happen. Sponsor an event and get your name on a tee-shirt. Name recognition and good will, will come from everyone who reads it.

Classes and recreational outlets

Start a yoga class, a volunteer club or a bowling team to engage your residents. Print tee-shirts with your name and brand and build a team atmosphere. Post fliers around your community promoting your events. Invite everyone to join in and have fun.

Chamber of Commerce

Join your local Chamber of Commerce. It's a great way to network locally, get to know other helpful members of the community and promote your apartment building. Learn local politics, makes friends and create allies.

Coffee shops and delis

Most communities have a coffee shop or deli where all of the locals go to pick up the morning paper or something hot to drink. These touchstone locations often have a place for fliers, a bulletin board or a designated space on a wall.

Ask permission first, and then post a flier of your building. Naturally, it should highlight your amazing move-in incentives.

Moving companies

There's a certain synchronicity here. It just makes sense. Join forces with a local moving company. Offer a discount for residents who are referred from the moving company and perhaps the moving company can offer discounts to people using their services on your referral.

Local animal shelters

People who own a pet are often in search of a place to live that is pet friendly. Consider allowing for pets based on these excellent pet rental policies. Once established, let your local animal shelters know that you welcome certain types of pets.

Toys for Tots

Worthy programs like Toys for Tots are rewarding to be involved with. Host a drop-off location in your lobby to create increased foot traffic and community connections. Use the extra traffic to show off your lobby. Make sure brochures are out and current lease incentives are posted.

Grocery shopping carts

People often spend more time in grocery stores than they expect to. You've been there, filling up your cart, reading the signs on the carts. You can't help it. They are a perfect place to advertise your apartment property.

Your own events

If you have an attractive lobby or an extra meeting room, allow your fellow Chamber of Commerce members to host events in your extra space. You could charge a small fee or negotiate to leave promotional items at their place of business.

Make sure to host tenant events in which your residents invite friends and family to participate. Open a staged apartment nearby for guests to visit.

Experiment and have fun

These are just a few creative local apartment marketing ideas to get you started. Engage the community. Make your marketing message a win-win, and momentum will increase traffic to your door.

Develop mutually beneficial relationships with local merchants

When a local merchant learns that you will promote their business to your community, they will embrace the idea of cross promotion.

Local employers are especially happy when their employees live in close proximity to work. Proximity to work contributes to less tardiness and fewer missed days due to bad weather.

Offer to waive your application fees for employees of participating merchants. Other ways to support your local merchant in exchange for free advertising are to:

- Include coupons or flyers of the local business in new resident welcome packages.
- Put a "Welcome to the community! Enjoy dinner (or a discount etc.) on us!" note in all new resident welcome packages.
- Offer local merchant discounts or gift cards to new and renewing residents.
- Offer a referral fee to merchants.

In exchange your local merchant can:

- Post your apartment building ad on notice boards or shopping carts.
- Include your ad in company flyers and mailings.
- Provide word of mouth advertising.

The extra effort spent in meeting your local merchants can be rewarding on both a personal and financial level.

It's time to update your curb appeal

There's nothing worse than seeing prospective renters keep driving right on by at 30 miles an hour after a quick glance at your property. Five seconds is all it takes to make a negative, and lasting, first impression.

Curb appeal is one of the most important things in property marketing and leasing. Presenting an exterior that meets your target markets' standards must be one of your biggest priorities.

You can develop incredibly creative ads that draw potential renters in droves yet lose them before they reach your front door if your apartment community has no curb appeal.

Here are some inexpensive ways to make your property more attractive and welcoming:

- Touch up the paint.
- Add outdoor planters that are stuffed full of colorful flowers.

- Add a canopy.
- Install inexpensive landscaping.
- Put up modern signage.
- Offer mobile friendly ways to contact your leasing agent.

And don't forget the people who walk by your property every day. If they're walking, chances are they live in the neighborhood.

It's a great idea to hold an open house at your property—especially if you have fantastic curb appeal. Put out a sandwich board with balloons and grab the auto and foot traffic on busy weekends.

Send a "feel good" letter to your current residents

Your current residents can be your most influential marketing group. Sending occasional thank you letters to your residents will help establish a sense of community.

But it goes beyond creating happy feelings. When your resident loves where they live, they will tell their friends and family. Establish a referral incentive program at your property where each referring resident gets a gift, bonus, or rent discount.

Some effective ways to get the word out are by:

- Hosting a resident referral party.
- Sponsoring a community yard sale.
- Holding open houses with tours of the property.

When you receive a compliment from a resident be sure to ask if they would be willing to share it online.

Pro tip: An on-site manager can market and lease apartments. In fact, he/she may be your best asset. You can read more about hiring and managing an on-site property manager in Chapter 17: Property Management.

Pick the "right" property management company

Some property management companies have amazing branding. Find out who they are and hire them—or watch them closely so that you can model their branding. These are the management companies that offer the "cool" factor to their residents.

Sometimes the branding is as simple as offering a "green" element to living at their communities. For example, recycling programs are a very inexpensive and desirable service to offer at your property.

You can create your own buzz and cool factor by offering something as simple as pre-leasing. Include text such as "Now Pre-Leasing for Large Two-Bedrooms" in your online advertising and on your property signage.

It may not seem like a big deal, but pre-leasing can tell prospective residents that they are with a proactive management company. It also implies that your property is a desirable building to live in because people want to sign leases months before they are able move-in.

Why I Never Use a "No Vacancy" Sign

Is your multifamily property or apartment building fully leased? Excellent!

Why not put out a "No Vacancy" sign so everyone in the neighborhood knows that you're doing a fantastic job at your property? And who wants pesky potential residents bothering on-site managers and leasing agents? They've got more important things to do right? Of course, I'm only joking.

Smart multifamily property owners are *always* ready, willing and happy to talk to potential renters. Take a minute and think about your strategies. What are you trying to do? You want renters. You want income. And you want to keep your property at full occupancy.

A "No Vacancy" sign says, "Go away! We're full. We don't need you!"

Here's an alternative: Invest in a "Now Pre-leasing!" sign. A pre-leasing sign:

- Delivers the message that your property is full—without turning away interested renters.
- Implies that your property is a desirable place to live. People are getting in line to rent from you!
- Creates a sense of urgency.
- Helps potential new residents plan. They can pre-lease a unit from you while waiting for their current lease to expire.
- Keeps your managers on their toes. There's nothing worse than a manager who loses contact with the local rental market.
- Builds a pre-qualified waiting list for your upcoming vacancies.

367

Give it a try the next time your property is at 100% occupancy. You just might be pleased with the results.

Genius Marketing Ideas to Fill Apartment Vacancies

Investing in multifamily real estate can be a highly effective way to create wealth and achieve financial freedom. As the British economist John Stuart Mill said, "Landlords grow rich in their sleep." Wise words, assuming, of course, that the landlord has no problems attracting quality tenants to fill apartment vacancies.

Using innovative social media strategies to market real estate vacancies is an effective, smart way to leverage your efforts.

Use social media to target your ideal renter

Study your rental market to predict what population demographic is going to be interested in your apartment building. Don't waste your time on fire hose marketing. Nothing can pinpoint advertisement like social media. Use social media to target your ideal renter

Do your research; one size does not fit all. For example, Facebook is used by seven-in-ten adults. 73% of adults report using YouTube. Instagram and Snapchat are used by 67% and 62% of 18- to 29-year-olds, respectively. Of course, numbers fluctuate.

Dig into the most recent social media stats and discover where you can maximize your efforts. The Pew Research Center offers online fact sheets on social media and mobile use (pewresearch.org).

Expand your social media reach

Look beyond the Facebook world and capture new audiences through Instagram, Pinterest and Snapchat. Post professional photos of your available units along with contact information.

Side note: photos are everything when it comes to marketing your apartment listings. Before you go any further, make sure you have high quality, professional images.

Beyond just adding killer photos of your apartments to Instagram and Pinterest, you can cultivate those accounts to widen your reach.

Instagrammers who respond to comments and engage on other relevant posts by liking or commenting tend to get more traffic. On Pinterest, create different topical boards that are appealing to your target client.

Motivate residents using online reviews

Personal resident reviews are one of the most effective forms of marketing. You cannot beat the power of online reviews, positive or negative. Google, Yelp, Zillow, apartments.com and B.B.B. (Better Business Bureau) are only a few sites that have reviews to learn from.

Start a tenant referral program if you haven't already. Incentivize the program in a way that will motivate tenants to promote your apartment community with online reviews or with engagement on social media. Offer small gift cards or entries to win rent discounts or other prizes.

The power of the review

Apartment seekers will read your online reviews. That's pretty much a given. Be sure they get a positive impression by encouraging current residents to share their raves online.

Your tenant incentive program will reward residents for writing positive reviews on sites like Google, Yelp, Zillow and more.

Other than an incentive program, don't forget to simply ask for reviews. Of course, if you are providing stellar service, your residents will be more inclined to leave those five-star reviews for you, so if your reviews are on the less-than-positive side, it's time to do some reflection about how to improve.

Freshen up your Facebook presence

Facebook is still an extremely powerful social media outlet, with over a billion users.

Currently, Facebook is the largest social media site. Your apartment community should have its own Facebook Business Page as a springboard. Once set up, you'll buy advertising on Facebook that controls who sees your ads.

Experiment with different kinds of graphic design and see which one pulls the most traffic. Once you have a formula down you can use it over and over again.

Advertise your available units on Facebook Marketplace

Marketplace has essentially replaced Craigslist in most markets, so you'd be wise to get your properties listed ASAP. Users love Marketplace for its easy search function, excellent mobile view, and convenient contact options.

Facebook Live for business lets you provide a behind-the-scenes look at your available unit with 360-degree photos and videos.

Create Facebook events to garner more visibility for your property

Run regular open house events, host community events like free yoga classes, outdoor movies, or a toy drive for the holidays. As people search for upcoming things to do, your property's event will be front and center.

Use Facebook Events to promote an Open House for your vacancy. Post photographs, send out invites, create a party atmosphere and generate a buzz around your apartment building.

Encourage community engagement through a Facebook group for residents

In addition to fostering a positive sense of community, you can advertise events and run contests to encourage people to share about the property within their personal networks. Also, take advantage of Facebook Groups to promote any updates to your business page.

Fill apartment vacancies with #HashtagPower

Each time you post on social media sites like Instagram, Twitter, Pinterest, or even Facebook, strive to include several relevant hashtags to drive traffic to your post. Don't overdo it, though, or you risk looking spammy. 10-15 hashtags will be plenty for Instagram; pare it down for the others.

Your hashtags should be relevant, engaging, and on brand. Do you have a tagline or slogan? Hashtag it! Harness the power of trending topics by including those each day, like #MotivationMonday #tbt, or #WeekendVibes.

Before slapping any old hashtag on your post, check a site like hashtagify.me to research how that tag performs and to find others that are trending.

Video marketing

Pair your resident referral program with video marketing. Here is a statistic that you can use: YouTube reaches more 18-49-year-olds than any cable network in the U.S. That is a huge, growing slice of the population. Utilize this platform to highlight your property.

Record positive resident testimonials about your property in a video and upload them to your apartment website and link it to a YouTube channel as well.

That is only the tip of the video iceberg. You can upload videos about staged apartments, event promotion and lease-signing incentives. The possibilities are limited only to your imagination.

Everyone loves a story

With over 300 million active daily users, Snapchat is an underutilized social media platform in the multifamily marketing world. You'd be wise to pay attention to it now, especially because Gen Z is entering the rental marketplace, and they definitely aren't using Facebook anymore.

Highlight your property through Snapchat stories and ads and encourage residents to follow your account and share their own content about the property.

Use Snapchat to promote apartment turnovers. When residents vacate a unit, create a Snapchat story showcasing the unit's transformation. Illustrate the cleaning, painting and prep for the new residents.

Then use photos to highlight tenants moving into their new home. Show new residents receiving their welcome package. Get a final photograph of the apartment community coming out to welcome the new residents.

A picture is worth a thousand words

Post polished apartment photographs to Pinterest and Instagram. Remember to link your appealing photos to your apartment website and Facebook page.

You can start a Halloween apartment decoration contest on Instagram or Pinterest. You get the idea. Ask residents for creative competition ideas on your account and increase your community involvement.

Include Twitter in your social media strategies

An excellent way to engage on Twitter is to have tenants post pictures of their apartments using a branded hashtag, then allow everyone to vote on their favorite. Ask residents to vote for the ugliest holiday sweater or their favorite dish in the chili cook-off. Resident involvement is the key.

Use Twitter to highlight local events in the community surrounding your apartment complex. This will increase your social following and builds the local community. A win-win.

Blog It!

Many successful apartment communities publish their own blog with relevant local content. By using local keywords and publishing regularly, your apartment website will rank higher in search engine results. Not sure what to write about? Some ideas include tips for first-time renters, highlights of local attractions, and features on area events.

Start a YouTube channel

Create your own YouTube channel that highlights fun and practical tips for renters as well as videos featuring your property. You can upload walk-throughs of your available floor plans, highlight fun events at your community, or feature resident testimonials.

Your videos can then be easily shared via social media or on your website. Vlogging, aka video blogging, is set to be a major marketing trend. Share snippets of daily life in the community to build an even bigger audience of potential renters.

Sure, you may have to get a little creative to crush the marketing game for your multifamily real estate, but the right mix of savvy and good old-fashioned hard work will fill apartment vacancies faster than you can say #WelcomeHome to your new renters. Earn those dollars while you sleep!

Let your imagination out of its box

No matter where you post your apartment listings, make them entertaining. Generic listings are a dime a dozen, so get creative and make your listing stand out. Think out of the box and infuse your description with fun details.

The most creative apartment listing I've come across was written in song form by Jonathan Mann. He posted a music video on YouTube when he was looking for a roommate, titled Come Live with Me in Brooklyn.

Social media sites are powerful tools limited only by your imagination. Be different; make people curious, smile and engage with your content. Do your homework on where your targeted demographic is hanging out the most and maximize your social media strategies with videos, photographs and playful content.

Creative Ways to Hold a Multifamily Open House

Holding an open house for a multifamily residential complex can be challenging, but there are lots of ways to do it creatively. The process doesn't have to cost a fortune, either.

Holding an open house is still one of the best ways to expose a listing to a wide audience, so it is not something that should be overlooked.

Take advantage of technology

Technology can be used in a multitude of ways to make your multifamily open house more appealing and informative, not to mention fun. Be sure to showcase the features of your open house listing on your website and keep the people on your buyer leads list updated via regular emails.

Social media is another avenue that can be used to promote your open house because you can post photos, videos and even virtual tours of the property. The goal is not to provide an alternative to attending the open house, but to create interest and awareness about it.

Apps such as Open Home Pro will also enable you to connect with the tech-savvy people who attend the open house.

Involve different groups

While the aim of your open house should be the prospective buyers, they shouldn't be your only focus. Don't forget about the people already living in your multifamily residential complex because they're able to provide great word-of-mouth marketing for the open house.

You can also hold a brokers' open house that is only for real estate agents. Create a list of all the top-selling agents in the neighborhood for the past year and invite them. You could even consider getting a charity involved to make those typical raffles a little more unique. This will add a feel-good element to the proceedings as everybody loves helping out worthy causes.

Grab attention on the day of your event

When holding a multifamily open house, it is vital that you grab the attention of people passing by and entice them to come take a look. To increase visibility, you can use traditional methods such as balloons or get a little more creative and employ other gimmicks.

One of the most eye-catching methods is renting a drone to display an open house banner over the property. After all, if people cannot find the open house, all your other efforts will have been for nothing.

Consider putting up a welcome sign with relevant information about the properties at the entrance and also look at unique ways to serve refreshments to those who attend.

Making a good first impression still counts, so get creative and make sure that you leave a good impression on everyone attending the open house.

Are You Offering Free Rent Concessions to Attract Tenants?

One way to avoid vacant properties and attract more tenants is to offer rental concessions. In some cases, concessions are also offered by landlords to tenants when it is time for them to renew their lease.

Rental concessions can even be used by landlords as a way to compensate tenants for problems that cannot be changed. These can range from the neighborhood in which the property is located to a lack of nearby amenities.

A variety of different rental concessions can be offered depending on the situation. Although these can sometimes mean lower income for the landlord, it is better than the alternative, which is the property standing vacant and not bringing in any money.

Do you need to pay people to live at your building?

Before you decide to give money away via free rent concessions, examine your property for weaknesses and strengths. Perhaps a few of these problems will ring a bell.

- The laundry area and other amenities are not being used.
- Signage—what signage?
- Dinosaur-sized weeds surround your building.
- The lobby has a frayed carpet and a dingy look.
- Your leasing office is open part-time and closes at 3:30pm.
- Police lights are your only outdoor lighting.

Start with the basics

Sure, free rent is an easy way to rent a unit fast but in order to improve your leasing efforts some underlying issues may need to be faced and addressed. Here are a few ideas and resources to get you started!

- Offer creative move-in specials instead of free rent.
- Brainstorm ways to put the sizzle back into your rental units.
- Focus on your community brand.
- Meet with your team and ask for their feedback on what practical improvements could be made. Use your frontline for insight.

- Shop your competitors. Experience apartment shopping through the eyes of a potential renter. What are the marketing ploys that have sizzle?
- Compare your prices and amenities to the marketplace.
- Offer community events.
- Review each of your units. Consider their strengths and weaknesses and price competitively for your marketplace.

Before you offer free rent concessions, take a hard, unbiased look at your property. Make sure you are poised competitively in your area to maximize your bottom line.

Free month's rent concession

A free month is one of the most common rent concessions to offer potential tenants. One way to do this is to amortize the cost of the free month over a 12-month period. This means that tenants will pay slightly less per month than what the gross rent would have been.

Alternatively, the free month can be added on to the beginning or end of the lease while the tenant continues to pay the gross rent during all of the other months. Adding the free month at the end of the lease will also help to safeguard you somewhat against the lease being broken early.

A free month is also safer than offering a reduced security deposit because a tenant could damage the property and then disappear before the lease is up.

Free perks

If your property has any optional amenities, such as garage parking, washers or dryers in the unit or other extras, these can be leveraged as rental concessions. Free use of a fitness center, if available, also makes for a good rental concession.

In reality, not many tenants opt for paid amenities, so including some as rental concessions can serve to draw in renters without making a dent in your rental income.

Small renovations

Offering smaller renovations such as refinished floors or new appliances as rental concessions enables you to entice renters without sacrificing rental income. While it does cost you a bit more upfront, the renovations will also increase the rental value of the property, which is beneficial in the long run.

No need to break the bank

Bear in mind that depending on the type of property and its location, there is no need to go overboard with concessions. Some renters are happy with a gift card or gift certificate, so use good judgment when deciding what to offer and don't put yourself at a disadvantage.

First get potential residents through your door!

Remember to use your own staff, residents and local businesses to help increase your apartment complex profile.

- Incentivize your resident referral program.
- Train your staff on telephone techniques and sales skills.
- Make sure your advertising has an identifiable brand in the marketplace.
- Focus on community building. Plan events for and with your residents.
- Have a personal touch. Write (with a pen) and deliver birthday cards for residents.
- Network! Invite local charities or businesses to resident events as a win-win.

Make sure the entryway to your lobby is inviting, fresh and clean!

Creative Move-In Specials for Leasing Apartment Units

If your competition is offering the dreaded "first month free" rent concession, then it is time to up your game. But why give away rental income when you can generate new leases with the following 17 move-in specials? These creative marketing specials are easy to implement and adapt for your market.

17 creative move-in specials to lease units

1. A free phone cover, coffee mug or fidget box—with your branding!

2. A few months of free parking, gym membership, laundry, extra self-storage or another waived amenity fee.

3. Tickets to a local professional sports game, waterpark, art museum or music festival.

4. A new nightstand or end table with a smart phone charging station built into the surface.

5. A gift certificate to a local restaurant, grocery store, hairdressing salon, batting cages, or movie theater.

6. The no-stress move in option: Let residents move their furniture in, set up cable and utilities over the course of a week instead of one single day without charge.

7. A new appliance such as a washer/dryer, ceiling fan, refrigerator, stove, mounted flat screen television or dishwasher.

8. A free Fitbit, iPod, iPad or tablet.

9. Discounted security deposit.

10. Free renters' insurance for one year.

11. The ability to pick an upgrade of their choice: crown molding, new fixtures and/or paint color.

12. Different payment options: Offer online payments, Apple Pay, credit cards or PayPal.

13. Smart home technologies to control apartment environments from a phone.

14. A built-in bedroom closet organizer system.

15. Free use of a truck for moving-in day. Include moving boxes and a pizza.

16. An Amazon Prime membership or a Netflix or Hulu subscription.

17. A few months of house cleaning!

Offer move-in specials and reward tenants during a memorable event!

Host a "new residents night celebration" and give the move-in specials away with fanfare. When giving resident referral incentive gifts, make it a party for your community! People will talk, document with social media and remember the community feeling of the party longer than their takeaway gift.

If, in the end, you are going to give a straight rent concession, then make the offer off the first month of rent instead of spreading it over the course of the year. That way sticker shock is avoided when it is time to renew the lease. Of course, all rental concession activity should be recorded on your rent roll.

Scents that Work Magic in Apartment Marketing and Leasing

"Smell is a potent wizard that transports us across thousands of miles and all the years we have lived… odors, instantaneous and fleeting, cause my heart to dilate joyously or contract with remembered grief." — Helen Keller (Blind and deaf educator, 1880-1968)

As your potential residents walk through one of your properties, they are consciously examining their environment but there is unseen magic at work. Unconsciously, they are being transported to positive and negative associations through the scents in the air. You can weld that power to your own advantage if you know how to use it.

383

Memories and emotional associations

Smell is one of the first senses to form and develops deep connections in the brain, one area being the amygdala, an area that forms memories. When we smell something, we unconsciously associate it with emotions from the memory.

For me, the smell of Hawaiian Punch recreates happy childhood memories. I cannot consciously explain why my elementary school brain locked onto the scent of Hawaiian Punch. All I know is that, for me, it means pure, childlike excitement.

You could name your own associations, as everyone can. This is called the Proust phenomenon, the ability of odors to spontaneously trigger emotion through personal memory.

Thank you, advertising industry

Frequently, these memories and emotional associations are not consciously considered, but instinctual responses. Retailers know this and scent their stores appropriately. They call it "environmental fragrancing" and it means increased sales. It works for big business and it can work for you.

Start with the bad scents

First you have to get rid of any bad odors. People can tell if you are masking a scent, especially if it is a bad one. You have been next to someone wearing too much cologne, attempting to mask an unpleasant odor, haven't you? It's the same thing. You must thoroughly clean the property.

384

- Plug in a dehumidifier and/or a HEPA air filter.
- Mop or vacuum floors.
- Wash any fabrics in the unit that absorbed odors.
- Paint walls with "odor absorbing" paint.
- Make sure all food and liquid has been emptied from cabinets and fridge.
- Clean all surfaces.
- Use products that neutralize odors like baking soda, vinegar or Febreze.

Marketing with scents

Now that you have set the stage you should plan on using one simple fragrance for the rental unit. Researcher Eric Spangenberg found that, "cash register receipts revealed a significant bump in sales when an uncomplicated scent was in the air." Spangenberg used a simple orange scent to create the sales increase.

Choose a scent that would be appropriate to your market and season. Keep the scent understated, not overwhelming. Sometimes a little goes a long way.

Recommended simple scents:

- Orange or lemon
- Rosemary
- Vanilla
- Baking cookies

- Fresh air
- Cucumber
- Recommended simple holiday scents:
- Pumpkin pie
- Apple pie
- Pine
- Cedar

Once you choose a fragrance that will "brand" your property to the brains of potential residents you are on your way. Let scent work its magic in the mind for you. Keep it simple and keep it understated.

Chapter Sixteen:
Renovation

Nothing great was ever achieved without enthusiasm.
–Ralph Waldo Emerson

~

First Multifamily Property Renovation? Avoid the Single-Family 'Experts'

All advice is not created equal, especially in the world of real estate and renovations. These days, it seems anyone who binges HGTV and feels a close personal connection with Chip and Joanna Gaines has a strong opinion on how to renovate properties. Of course, armchair "experts" are a bit easier to ignore than actual professionals within the real estate market.

Multifamily property investors, especially newcomers to the industry, run the risk of accepting the wrong advice from well-meaning single-family property investors. Multifamily investments are an entirely different beast, so think twice before you make decisions based on the advice of single-family friends and family.

An expert at multifamily property renovation will help you:

Choose wise renovations

Single-family property investors have a tendency to follow a "go big or go home" game plan. When you're renovating a single-family home that needs to dazzle prospective buyers, that can be a good strategy. Not so in the multifamily property market. You can only charge so much in rent, so adding expensive countertops and high-end finishes to multiple units may not get you the same return on investment (ROI).

Experts in multifamily property renovation are able to identify selective renovations that will appeal to your target market while keeping costs as low as possible. Whereas a single-family property investor may be attracted to granite and stainless steel, a skilled multifamily expert can steer you to less expensive but still attractive options.

Attract renters with the right amenities

Experienced multifamily property renovators have their fingers on the pulse of the market at all times. They can let you in on the hottest upgrades and amenities creating market sizzle today.

You'll always want to ask what amenities are most attractive to your target market, and how you can get your highest return for a low capital investment. These pros will have ideas for your local market and neighborhood.

Identify new revenue sources at a property

Multifamily property renovators are pros at finding new ways to increase profits at an investment property. Can you repurpose a space to attract more renters from your target market? Could you find a way to profit from a repurposed space through rentals or service fees? For example, many apartment communities offer pet washing stations or bike repair shops in exchange for a small usage fee. Not only does this add value to your residents, it brings in another stream of income.

Beyond that, an expert eye can spot existing features to highlight and maximize. Perhaps the entryway could be spruced up with a quick coat of paint and some simple landscaping. Is there a unique entryway that you could incorporate into your marketing, or an outdoor feature that is particularly appealing?

Spot hidden costs and maintenance pitfalls

A skilled multifamily property renovator will help you identify and budget for costs you may not be aware of. For instance, you may need to plan for the following:

- Lost revenue from vacant units during renovation.
- Management overhead for planning, managing, and inspecting the renovations.

- Disruption to revenue throughout the property—will you have to offer financial incentives for current residents who may lose access to amenities or be inconvenienced by construction noise or equipment?

In addition, a multifamily expert will help you generate a plan for operating and maintaining major building systems. A thorough inspection and maintenance plan of the following systems can help you avoid the disaster of unexpected emergency repairs:

- Boilers and HVAC
- Roofs
- Landscaping
- Plumbing
- Parking
- Windows and insulation

Network for deals and information

Your multifamily property renovation expert has a serious advantage over single-family folks when it comes to networking.

Your bottom line will benefit from valuable connections gained from a multifamily insider. They have connections with vendors and service providers who cater specifically to the multifamily industry. Perhaps most importantly, they know reliable contractors and other service providers who understand economies of scale and price their services accordingly.

Before you get in over your head, make sure you have the right people in your corner.

How to Hire Multifamily Property Contractors

Do you wish there was an easy way to find the right contractor to handle repairs and renovations at your multifamily investment property?

What if you could just follow a few easy steps to find and hire great help? Well, you're in luck. I have some great tips on how to hire multifamily property contractors. But first, a word to the wise about multifamily renovations. This crucial piece of information will save your sanity…

Skip the single-family renovators

I've already mentioned the perils of accepting the wrong advice from well-meaning single-family property investors. With multifamily investing, it is critical that you hire the right contractors for the job. Be careful. If you bring in a property renovator or contractor who has experience only on the single-family side of property renovations, there's a 98% chance you've got the wrong person on the job.

The mistakes are subtle…until it's time to rent a unit.

Let's say you and your single-family contractor have done a magnificent job with renovations. You've installed granite countertops; gorgeous, high-end cabinets; the latest stainless-steel appliances and you've installed wood flooring throughout the unit. Stunning and pricey renovations.

Then you discover you can only raise your monthly rent by $50. Your local market simply won't open their wallets to pay the price you think your units are now worth. Think about how long it will take to pay for those high-end renovations with an additional monthly income of $50!

Most single-family renovation specialists don't understand the multifamily market. And why would they? It's not their job to know what rents multifamily units while staying within budget.

How to find multifamily renovators

Chances are you know a lot of contractors who are highly skilled at their jobs. They've probably done work at your house or at a neighbor's house. It's easy to pick up the phone and ask for help. But first be clear about what your goals are.

It's time to use some common sense:

- Do the contractors you are considering have experience working on multifamily properties?
- Are they willing to show you their other jobs?
- Will they give you great suggestions about what your target rental market desires?
- Will they add the "sizzle" that rents multifamily units?
- Can they tour your rental unit and confidently tell you, "This lighting has to go but these cabinets are great and we can spin the 'vintage' look to aid in your marketing?"

You get the idea. Ask for referrals within the multifamily industry. Commercial brokers, multifamily property managers, apartment and multifamily associations, and multifamily investment property owners are all excellent resources for finding good contractors.

Pride goes before the fall

You and I could have long conversation about how important it is to lead your team. After all, the buck stops with you. But it's okay to admit you need and welcome advice. As American oil well firefighter Red Adair said, "If you think it's expensive to hire a professional to do the job, wait until you hire an amateur."

Use clear examples of what you want to do through property renovation.

- Is life safety an issue?
- Do you want to increase property income?
- Make specific repairs?
- Maximize the efficiency of building mechanical systems?

Be as specific as you can. But don't be so certain that you are right. Don't make it your goal to impress your contractor with your superior knowledge. Ask for suggestions. Be open to creative ideas and advice. A good multifamily contractor may have ideas that will improve the operations of your investment property. Ideas you've never thought of.

How to hire multifamily property contractors

Follow these suggestions when working with multifamily contractors:

Getting bids

- Get written estimates from 3 or 4 contractors.
- Ask for customer references. And check them!
- Require copies of insurance certificates and licenses.
- Get everything in writing (guarantees, warranties and promises).
- Don't pay the full amount up front.
- Include start and completion dates.

Your job

- Be there.
- Make decisions quickly.
- Treat contractors with fairness.
- Ask for opinions/ideas.

Be available for your contractors. Keep your promises. Work as a team. Before you know it other multifamily investors will be coming to you for advice on contractors.

Common Misconceptions About Dealing with a Bad Contractor

Having a bad contractor working on one of your multi-unit properties can be frustrating, and it can become expensive pretty quickly. This type of situation requires immediate but careful action to protect your investment and your wallet. Following are some common misconceptions people have when it comes to dealing with a bad contractor.

You can immediately "fire" them

Once a contractor has made a major mistake they're not acknowledging or rectifying, it seems logical to just fire them and hire someone else. However, you must keep in mind that you signed an agreement before they started, and it is likely a legally binding contract.

To avoid exposing yourself to liability in court should they sue you for breach of contract later, document all of the times they failed to meet the contract specifics. And document your contact attempts.

Follow the correct procedures outlined in your state laws for advising a party of a breach of contract and terminating it and follow those rules to get the contractors off the project. If you've paid for things in advance, you might lose this money, but it may be worth it in the long run if the work so far needs to be redone anyway.

There's no agency to contact for help

If your contractor is licensed, you can contact the entity that issued the license and explore your options. You may be able to file a formal complaint or ask for help from the license issuer. The contractor will want to keep their license in good standing, so they may respond to your concerns if the issuer is involved. Other places you can file a complaint include the Better Business Bureau and any local contractor organizations.

A lawsuit is not the first answer

Lawsuits against a contractor could cost you more than what you lost in the end. There is not really a price tag on personal satisfaction if you do take a bad contractor to court and win, but in terms of your property investment, it's in your best interest to try to work out the issues first. Put all the problems you have with the work in writing and meet with the contractor to create an action plan.

Always research contractors before you hire them, and make sure everyone on the project is on the same page. Investing a little time before you hire a contractor can help you weed out the bad ones.

Biggest Renovation Mistakes Investors Make

Most people think they are smarter than average. This phenomenon is referred to as illusory superiority. People often overestimate their own abilities and think they possess certain characteristics and traits that others lack.

Perhaps you are more intelligent than most people. After all, you now know the psychological term for this cognitive bias of superiority that can so easily trip people up in many areas of their lives. You are also learning how to avoid the biggest renovation mistakes that many investors make.

Underestimating the true costs of renovations and repairs

People often think in broad terms when evaluating properties. They might get some input from the inspector and then just use a round number like $60,000 for all renovations. When the actual bids for needed work are itemized and repairs reveal hidden defects or unanticipated costs, the bill often ends up being twice what they had in their renovation budget.

Your accuracy improves over time, so err on the side of caution and don't let how much you might like the location cloud your renovation budget estimates.

Thinking the value will always increase by at least the costs of renovations

Real estate is a speculative business. The market changes and some people lose money. You can minimize your risks with prudent decisions and due diligence, but there is always some risk. If you want a guarantee, put your money in a FDIC account.

Skipping the profitability analysis

Investors must calculate profitability before purchasing a property. Much like the stock market, there are always sellers and buyers in the real estate market.

As an investor, you should be considering several possible deals at any given time. You are going to move forward with some, but you will walk away from others. The profitability analysis helps you compare deals and consider various possibilities within the same property.

Cutting corners on renovations

Always use the services of licensed contractors with suitable experience. Many people are tempted to cut costs by using low-grade materials and unsafe contractors. You are liable for what happens on that property before, during, and after renovations.

Carrying out the wrong renovations

Renovations can be a particularly enjoyable aspect of real estate investing for many people. Nevertheless, you should not renovate based on your personal tastes. Instead, you should base renovations on your target market and what will bring you the best possible return on your investment. Shopping at home improvement stores is great, but you don't earn money indulging yourself. Be selective about what renovations you do and stick only with those that add value.

Inexpensive Landscape Makeovers for Your Rental Property

When it comes to investing in real estate, you do not want to spend any money unless you know it will provide a return on your investment. You can significantly increase the appeal and the value of any property with a landscape makeover.

Many investors focus only on the building and neglect the lawn and other outdoor common areas. You can be sure that every property you own looks fresh and appealing by spending some time and money enhancing the landscape.

Courtyards, barbecue areas, and garden areas

Talk to a landscape designer about the best low maintenance plants for your area. Screening plants will provide an inviting outdoor space and make the area appear more spacious than the look you get with a privacy fence. Many species of screening plants grow quickly and require only minimal care.

398

When you think about cost-efficiency, you must consider ongoing upkeep in addition to the initial costs. These areas enhance the value of the property to your tenants and do not cost much to create or maintain. When renters get more usable space for their rent, they feel better about paying each month.

Shade structures vs gazebos

Everyone loves a gazebo but building one can cost a lot in terms of lumber and time. Unless you use expensive composite materials, they also need routine painting and maintenance. Shade structures are low cost, easy to install, and do not need gutters or downspouts. These shade areas provide occupants with a cool place to get some fresh air and enjoy the outdoors while staying protected from the harmful rays of the sun.

Update concrete patios and sidewalks

If your investment property has one of those ugly grey concrete slabs for a patio or courtyard area, you can economically spruce it up with paving paint. There are also many low-cost paver options available.

Long lasting stamped concrete, also called textured or printed concrete, is another option. It comes in unlimited colors and can be made into a variety of shapes and patterns. By choosing a color, you can create the illusion of more space. Border the patio with some stones or edging plants for a neat, manicured look.

Landscaping tips for landlords

Include usable outdoor features to make your properties stand out from other available rentals. Fire pits, outdoor cooking areas, and play areas wow potential tenants and have them picturing themselves enjoying many good times at home.

Consider working with a professional landscape designer to enhance the curb appeal of your properties. Just like interior designers, they know how to make the most of whatever space is available. Provide something tenants can't find anywhere else.

A garden area, edible landscaping, and plants selected to attract birds help tip the scales in your favor when wooing top-quality tenants.

Putting the Sizzle Back into Your Rental Units

Rental units that are fresh and stylish in appearance are the ones people want to occupy. You should strive to maintain your units with the latest upgrades but stay at a monthly rent that the majority of people in your target market will pay. There is no point in spending money if you do not know what return you will get on your investment.

Some upgrades save money

Vinyl siding and composite decking may cost more up front, but over time they can reduce ongoing labor costs for painting and staining. New windows can justify an increase in monthly rent because they save your tenants real dollars in heating and cooling costs. Energy-efficient windows can also extend the life of your HVAC units by reducing the start and stop cycles needed to maintain a comfortable temperature.

Consult with a designer

You want long-term tenants who take pride in their place of residence. You should avoid chasing the latest trends and aim for warm, bright colors that go with any decor.

Durability often trumps style when it comes to carpet, but floor coverings need to be replaced often in rental properties. Look for attractive floor coverings that hold up to heavy use. You want to remodel and upgrade due to wear and tear, not just because the style trend has changed.

Keeping up with technology

No interior design trend changes as quickly as new innovations in technology. You may like being an early adopter in your personal life but equipping all of your apartments or rental houses with the newest smart home equipment would be foolish.

Speak with your insurance provider about which security features will help you get a lower rate. Parking lot cameras and exterior lighting have come a long way in recent years. You can reduce the likelihood of property theft, improve security for your occupants, and lower your insurance premiums with some affordable LED lights and quality exterior cameras.

Consider other perks

A complimentary alarm monitoring service included with their lease can add another layer of security and tip the scales in your favor with new tenants. Upfront costs are always a concern for people moving.

Having a moving van available to new tenants is a perk that has worked for landlords for many years. If you do not have an on-site gym facility, offer a complimentary gym membership to a nearby location.

Be sure all of these perks are available to new and existing tenants who sign a one- or two-year lease. Your goal is to entice current occupants to stay and attract new tenants—to put the sizzle back into your rental units.

How to Budget Capital Improvement Expenses

Your big-ticket—or capital improvement expenses, as the IRS refers to them—property upgrades aren't always the easiest thing to budget for. Capital improvements are any major property improvements that add significant value to your property, such as updating your electrical or plumbing systems or replacing your roof.

Even though these types of improvements only happen occasionally, you still need to be prepared to cover the cost without straining yourself financially. By putting some money aside in your budget for improvements, you'll stand a better chance of being fully prepared.

Know what you need

Decide what improvements can't wait. If your parking lot is in rough shape, that's an improvement that can't be put off until next year. The same thing applies to outdated components in your major HVAC systems you now have concerns about. Perhaps the system still works and doesn't need to be completely replaced, but you're feeling an upgrade is due and repairs won't address the issue.

Know what you want

Evaluate your property to determine which big improvements you want to make and when. If you'd like to upgrade the laundry facilities, for example, but the current appliances are functional and the tenants aren't having problems, that's a want but not an immediate need.

Get realistic estimates

Work on creating realistic estimates for your needed and desired improvements. Price the fixtures, equipment, labor and anything else you'll need for each project.

Always overestimate, as big updates have the potential to go right over what you had planned. If there's a possible snag in a project that may or may not hike up the cost, include that possible expense hike in your project total.

Look at the numbers

Decide what you can afford now and what you cannot based on the project totals. For example, if your necessary parking lot paving is $35,000 and your new laundry facility is $25,000 but you don't have more than $45,000 to spend, go with the lot this time around.

Add in your estimate

Once you've got the project estimates for the improvements you're going to do, budget them in by dividing the total needed by the number of months until the month in which you want to start work. For example, if you want to start a $25,000 laundry room upgrade eight months from now, you need to set aside $3,125 each month.

Even if you're not planning any improvements, you can still budget ahead for when one is needed or wanted. Review your property to identify possible improvement needs and wants for the next three to five years. Use that information to guide your budget creation.

Reduce Multifamily Operating Costs with Green Strategies

If you are a multifamily housing investor, you're already helping create denser, transit-friendly communities. However, there is likely more that you can do in the area of energy-efficient multi-unit investing. In addition to helping the environment, it also benefits you in a variety of ways.

ENERGY STAR for your existing buildings

According to the Environmental Protection Agency (EPA), owners of multifamily housing units can reduce multifamily operating costs by 30 percent by making some energy-efficient improvements to existing structures. You can even earn an ENERGY STAR (energystar.gov) certification for your building. This will improve your position among the competition and demonstrate to potential tenants and current tenants that you are doing your part to help the local community and the environment.

Would you like your property to be the first choice for the many millennials who make living an environmentally conscious lifestyle a top priority?

Here are some things you can do right now to reduce your multifamily operating costs:

- Convert common area lighting to LED
- Install low-flow toilets, faucets and showerheads
- Repair leaking plumbing fixtures
- Upgrade to energy efficient appliances, hot water heaters, furnaces and air conditioners
- Use low VOC (volatile organic compounds) paints
- Weatherproof windows
- Check caulking and weather-stripping
- Install WiFi enabled thermostats
- Use green materials in apartment finishes (recyclable carpet, tile, wood flooring, backsplashes, countertops, cabinets, etc.)

- Look into alternative energy sources such Xcel Energy's WindSource®
- Offset electrical use with renewable energy credits
- Offer recycling programs to your residents
- Use natural cleaners that are good for the environment

The important millennial demographic

If you are staying up to date on the latest news about millennials, you probably know that many are opting to pay down debt rather than purchase their first home.

The National Association of Realtors (NAR) annual survey of home buyers and sellers found that in 2019, the share of first-time home buyers was 33 percent, holding steady from 33 percent the previous year. This is good news for you as a multifamily investor if you have the green features that are important to them.

Green features attract members of this important demographic and keep them happy. They are the sharing generation and appreciate the benefits of multifamily unit buildings.

Tax savings and resale value

The U.S. government offers incentives to businesses that incorporate green technologies and processes into their operation. Start by checking the Database of State Incentives for Renewables & Efficiency (dsireusa.org).

When you can show significant operating savings, your green apartment building becomes more attractive to buyers. For every $1.00 per square foot that you save in operating expenses, you can increase the net present value by approximately $10.00 per square foot.

In addition, if your project is certified by the U.S. Green Building Council's LEED program (usgbc.org), you can back up your green performance claims.

Pro tip: Do your homework. Make sure the return on investments is worth the upfront cost. There are many options to consider, and not all green features carry the same ROI. If you take the time to carefully research and choose the best ones, you will reap the benefits for many years to come.

Profit-Maximizing Design Makeovers for Older Apartment Buildings

Investing in older apartment buildings can be a smart move for your portfolio. But there are risks that come with an older apartment building, as well.

The first is the market appeal. If your older building is competing against newer, more modern multifamily properties, you'll end up at the bottom end of fair market value. The other big issue is operating costs. A lot of older apartment buildings look like a good buy until you look at the cost of lighting, heating, and maintaining them.

But that shouldn't scare you away from purchasing an older building. There are many profit-maximizing makeovers you can do to your property. These updates will help increase the appeal and decrease operating costs. Plus, you'll be able to use "green" and "eco-friendly" in your marketing. And that's a feature becoming more important to potential residents.

Here are some important updates you should consider for your older multifamily property.

Upgrade the design aesthetic

The design aesthetic of your space is your building's first impression. An aged impression can turn off potential renters. It can leave your building feeling drab and dated. Upgrade the look with designs that fit your building's brand.

- Lobbies should be intimate or sleek and stocked with new furniture.
- Install updated signage, inside and out, and keep it on-brand.

Modernize the kitchen and bath

Kitchens and bathrooms can make the difference between a rented unit and one that sits empty. The trick is to update these rooms at the same time. If you do one and not the other, the one you don't update will look even worse by comparison. Sparkling clean is the name of the game here.

- Use light color palettes in these spaces.
- Go for stone or concrete for durable and low-maintenance surfaces.
- Install touch-free fixtures for resource savings.

- Replace all old hardware and lighting fixtures.
- Refurbish cabinets.
- Reglaze or replace the tubs.

Install new lighting and lighting controls

New lighting and lighting control technology will help reduce energy consumption within your multifamily property. That's good news for you as the property owner of an older apartment building, as common areas won't cost you as much to light. But it's good news for your residents, too, who can look forward to lower monthly energy bills.

- Replace all traditional lightbulbs with LED bulbs.
- Install dimmers and timers to decrease energy consumption.
- Use motion, occupancy, and photosensors in public areas to lower operating costs.

Embrace green building strategies

There is a reason green building strategies are so popular. They are good for the planet and the people living in your buildings. But sustainable practices reduce operating costs, too. They also appeal to renters, who feel good about their living space and are more likely to renew (and be referrers, too!).

- Research LEED certification for ideas about how to make your building more sustainable. You can find information on the U.S. Green Building Council website (usgbc.org).
- Reduce water waste with ultra-low-flow showerheads and toilets.

409

- Use healthy, energy-efficient materials when doing any remodeling or upgrades to your building.

Install building automation systems

Smart home technology and building automation systems (BAS) are great for residents and property owners alike. These systems help reduce operating costs and energy consumption, even in older apartment buildings. They can also increase security by giving tenants and owners more control over the property even when they aren't on-site.

- Smart locks provide more control over who goes in and out of the property. Additionally, they end the need to rekey the property after a tenant moves out.
- Smart thermostats. Smart thermostats learn when to raise and lower the temperature, providing huge energy savings.

Add in-demand amenities

Tenants care about the amenities available in public spaces. Adding in-demand amenities can be a huge boost to your appeal on the rental market. Research amenities available in similar properties in your area and see where you are lacking.

Also, look at what amenities are in the most popular properties and see where you can improve.

- Create natural spaces for a park-like atmosphere close to home.
- Build community gathering spaces available to everyone.

- Invest in recycling programs.
- Set up a fitness center.
- Provide modern amenities like docking stations, building wide WiFi, and package delivery systems.

Replace aging building systems

As you upgrade aging building systems, look for energy efficient replacements. Make sure you also work on preventative maintenance planning. This will help you mitigate costs associated with your older systems and work towards replacing them.

- Replace your roofing with something more energy efficient. Duro-Last® (duro-last.com) offers a commercial roofing system. It's certified sustainable and great at lowering cooling costs.
- Replace older boilers, plumbing systems, and windows with energy efficient options. Sometimes the energy savings will help offset the installation costs.

Research your funding options for older apartment buildings

Don't assume these updates are going to cost you a fortune. There are funding options available at both the local and national level. They offer cost-cutting incentives like rebates, tax credits, and low-interest loans.

Below is a list of national funding resources that may offer incentives you can use. Be sure to research funding options with your local and state government agencies as well, as they may offer extra resources.

National funding sources:

- Center for Rural Affairs Commercial Property Assessed Clean Energy (C-PACE at cfra.org)
- Energy Star's Rebate Finder (energystar.gov)
- Fannie Mae's Green Financing Loans (fanniemae.com)
- EPA's Green Infrastructure Funding Opportunities (epa.gov)
- HUD's Green Retrofit Program for Multifamily Housing (hud.gov)

Great Ideas for Modernizing an Apartment Complex

When you have an aging apartment complex, it is only natural to want it to look more updated. Tenants are attracted to many things when it comes to an apartment besides rent and building and unit appearance is one of them.

Giving your apartments a more modern look is one way to please potential renters and even increase rent, but you've got to find that ideal balance between project results and cost. Try these inspiring apartment updates to boost your appeal without sailing over your budget and into all your profits!

Harness the power of the accent wall

Accent or feature walls are a newer design idea and a definite break from the all-neutral wall look seen in older apartments. For about $50 in materials, you can update apartment units by painting one wall in the living room a different and bright color.

Make sure you choose the wall in the room that is the natural focal point, advises Realtor.com. If you can't decide, go with the wall that has the smallest width so it doesn't overwhelm the room. Choose a color that fits in with your existing scheme or sets off a feature in the apartment.

You can also use feature walls in your common areas and lobby or entrance hall. Just like with units, find a color that sets off a positive feature in the room, such as a fireplace or rich woodwork. Super bold colors, such as fire-engine red, are no longer popular choices, so go with rich but more subtle hues of greens, purples and blues.

Instantly update your kitchen and bathrooms

You don't need expensive new appliances or flooring to bring your unit's kitchen and bathroom up to date. Replace cabinet doors and hardware with newer items to instantly give the rooms a more modern appearance.

Countertops can also visually date an apartment, so replace these if it fits into your budget.

Look to the lights

If you've got outdated lighting fixtures, your unit and building are immediately showing their age to prospective renters. Light fixtures tend to draw the eyes, so replace any relics you've got from the 1970s still hanging around with sleek, newer models.

An outdated apartment is always harder to move, so don't hand yourself a disadvantage by having units and a building that feel old and worn to potential tenants. By trying the simple and inexpensive apartment updates mentioned above, you can give your apartment complex new life almost instantly.

How to Update Your Apartment Building Exterior and Lobby

Keeping your apartment complex current with market trends means looking at the building and grounds with new eyes. Putting an investment into updating your apartment building will help retain good residents and attract new potential residents.

Have you ever been in an older person's home in which all of the furniture is 30 years old? Yes, you know what that feels like. Would you want to live there? It might be fine for that older person but no one else wants to live in a time capsule.

Start outside

First look at the outside of your building with a critical eye. What jumps out at you? Brown patches in the lawn? An uneven gutter? Fading paint? Naturally, your tenants would prefer a green lawn leading up to beautiful flowerpots next to the entryway.

If the building needs cosmetic work, then you know that everyone else has noticed the issues as well. People assume that if the outside of a building is unkept, then the inside of the building must be neglected as well. Get the outside of your building in shape. Take care of the basics.

The psychology of arrival

LandscapingNetwork (landscapingnetwork.com) breaks the psychology of arrival into 3 elements. The first one is the vehicular experience. Where do your residents pull their car in to park? Are the parking spots clearly marked? Do the parking spots have standard parking dimensions? Are the residents cursing you every time they pull in because of bumper damage? These are all elements that create their experience coming home to your apartment building. You want to make it a positive experience.

The pedestrian experience is the transition from the car to the apartment building. Is the parking lot well-lit in the evening? Are hedges trimmed for safety? Is there a well-defined walkway from the parking lot to the building? If there are steps, are they well illuminated? This should be an easy navigation, even in the dark.

The last part of the arrival experience is the entryway or lobby. This area is critical. Focus on providing an environment where your residents are proud to have their friends and family visit your community.

Your lobby

For a full house of residents, you must make residents feel good the minute they walk into your lobby. Even if your lobby is small, you can make a positive impression. Use your lobby as a showcase for the rest of your building.

You only get one chance to make first impression. Is your lobby clean? Free of odor, trash, junk mail and packages? Are there signs of deferred maintenance or of wear and tear? Can your colors be updated? Have you posted a clear way for prospective residents to contact your leasing agent?

Think about the lobbies of boutique hotels that create a private, intimate feeling. For reference, visit a boutique hotel or take a look at a few lobbies online. Note the floors, walls and arrangement of the furniture. Consider how you can recreate that feeling in your building.

Flooring is one of the easiest ways to make a statement. Consider hardwood or laminate hardwood, porcelain tiles that can resemble wood or luxury vinyl. For wall colors use warm, soft, neutral colors, like grays and browns, which appeal to the largest audience and wear well. You can add a dash of color for a smart accent.

Safety first

Safety should always be a concern in the lobby and is noted by the residents. Obviously positioned video cameras can record traffic at all points of entry. There should be a buzzer system for visitors at the outer door. Make sure all entry doors shut and lock securely. Good outdoor lighting is invaluable, keeping residents safe in their comings and goings.

In addition, a corner of the lobby would be a perfect place to have lock boxes for resident mail and packages. Leaving packages out in hallways is a cause for concern for residents. All mail and packages should be secured.

The exterior of the apartment building and lobby is where you want to focus improvements. You are advertising all day with your building. Let your building and lobby sell itself.

Improve Energy Efficiency in Older Apartment Buildings

Most of us in the multifamily real estate industry are dealing with dinosaur-era properties. Okay, a slight exaggeration. The research says that over 78 percent of the multifamily buildings in the United States were built prior to 1990.

We all know the issues with projects that enhance energy efficiency. Split incentives, the maze of codes and permits, and the perennial lack of funding or profitable results. That's the perception.

Energy efficiency will save you money

The truth is that retrofitting your building even in small ways can save you money. Admit it, your building isn't as energy efficient as it could be. Yes, some retrofits are a long-term investment but there are other quick fixes that can help your bottom line this month.

Capital is out there. You might have to do some digging but there are grants, rebates, tax incentives and other ways to find the money. Just think of the ways you can market your building after your retrofit!

Target how you need to retrofit for sustainability

First you must evaluate your building's performance. Look at the property with new eyes. There is help out there to make sense of the areas you should address.

- EZ Retrofit is a free tool for multifamily owners that offers an "easy way to identify cost-effective water and energy efficiency upgrades." (sahfnet.org)
- Energy Star offers free analyzing tools. (energystar.gov)
- Green Button helps you access your utility usage data. (greenbuttondata.org)

Conduct a nighttime audit to find out what's on after hours that shouldn't be. Remember to calculate the expected utility inflation so you know what the best return numbers would be.

Retrofitting options

Once you know where you can save money, then you can zero in on your options. For example, there are several wide areas you can improve energy efficiency.

- Building envelope improvements—doors, windows and insulation
- Energy efficient products and appliances—lighting, refrigerators
- Heating, air conditioning and ventilation—HVAC improvements
- Installing solar photovoltaic (PV) panels
- Landscaping—using grey water irrigation or drought resistant gardens
- Plumbing upgrades—low flow adjustments, pipe insulation

Financial assistance for going green

There are financial resources to help you at the federal, state and local levels. Read the fine print in these offers. You need to do your research to make sure the retrofit products you buy match the specific requirements for the rebates, tax-incentives, lower interest rate loans, deals for trade-ins and other special offers.

If you are using a contractor make sure they are fluent with the specific requirements for your area to maximize your savings advantage.
Start your research with the big federal players and narrow down to your state and municipality.

- Energy Star (energystar.gov)
- Fannie Mae (fanniemae.com)
- EPA (epa.gov)
- HUD (hud.gov)
- Department of Energy and Environment (doee.dc.gov)

Depending on your budget and the scope of your project you should plan for bottom line profit with your retrofit.

Think of going green as another feather in your marketing cap. Yes, there will be a financial reward, but you should also give yourself credit for doing good for the environment and doing good for the economy. It's a win-win.

Want an Energy Efficient Rental Property? Here Are 18 Things You Can Do

Renters are becoming increasingly engaged with sustainable living. Demand is high for energy efficient products. Retrofitting your multifamily property for green sustainability can mean small changes or large changes but you should start somewhere.

There are no one-size-fits-all answers because every property is different. Start by measuring your energy efficiency and thinking about where you can improve.

18 tips to make your property energy efficient

1. Replace fluorescent and incandescent lighting with energy-efficient lighting systems.

2. Use drought-resistant, native plants for landscaping. Use grey water, irrigation sensors and timers.

3. Utilize lighting controls that offer timers, bi-level switching, dimmer settings and motion sensors.

4. Replace drafty single pane windows with double or triple pane windows.

5. Install ceiling fans to maximize heated or cooled air flow. Change their direction seasonally.

6. Use the Energy Star Online Bulk Purchasing Initiative (energystar.gov) and purchase energy-efficient appliances in bulk at discounted prices.

7. Install solar panels and obtain a Section 48 tax credit—a 30 percent tax credit for the Solar Investment Tax Credit (seia.org) otherwise known as ITC (investment tax credit).

8. Change and clean your HVAC filters every month during the high cooling and heating seasons. Practice regular monthly maintenance of your cooling and heating equipment to stay energy efficient through the year.

9. Upgrade your HVAC systems to energy efficient models. Replace chlorofluorocarbon chillers. Aim for modern energy efficient standards in your equipment.

10. Utilize insulated blinds and shades to control sunshine. This can be used in the summer and winter seasons to encourage or reduce heat increases through sunshine.

11. Adequately insulate the interior of your building. Apply insulating panels to the building's exterior to increase insulation. This will aid heating and cooling efficiency.

12. Windows and doors frequently cause significant heating and cooling losses so be sure to install caulk, glazing and properly seal.

13. Reflective roofing reduces the heat island effect in urban settings. Investigate the cool roof or the green roof as ways to cut the heat effect and deal with storm water runoff.

14. Install a recirculation pump to your recirculating domestic hot water system. Insulate all exposed hot water piping and turn down water heater/boiler thermostats to the minimum temperature required for hot water needs.

15. Install low-flow plumbing fixtures including new shower heads, faucet aerators, flush valves, and dual-flush systems. Make leak detection part of regular maintenance.

16. Use LED exit signs.

17. Use sleep settings on all office equipment. Printers, copiers, scanners can automatically enter a low-power sleep mode while they are not being used. Refer to their service manuals for instructions.

421

18. Install programmable, smart thermostats.

Even if you're not planning new improvements, you can still budget ahead for when one is needed or wanted.

Chapter Seventeen:
Property Management

Always do right. This will gratify some people and astonish the rest. – Mark Twain

~

Ten Brilliant Apartment Management Tips

When you own an apartment complex, management is key. You want to be sure that you're effectively managing your apartment complex, whether you self-manage or prefer to hire third-party managers.

Leading your team is also key. Appropriate apartment management can help you avoid financial and legal disasters. The following tips will help keep you out of trouble. They're also a high-level view of many of the topics covered in detail throughout this book.

1. Pay attention to life safety

Keep up with your inspections, and make sure that you're in compliance with local guidelines. You want to be sure that your apartment complex is as safe as possible for all of its residents, whether you have college students, families with small children, or predominantly seniors living in the complex.

Life safety standards include appropriate, clearly labeled fire doors, smoke and carbon monoxide detectors, exit signs, emergency lighting, and a wide range of other elements that help keep your residents safe. Never skimp on safety–and check yourself to be sure that you're taking care of regular inspections.

2. Include clear tenant policies in your management plan

Managing tenants requires clear policies and standards. You want procedures and policies in place that are clear, easy to understand, and readily available to everyone. Make sure you know the regulations governing your apartment complex such as rules about pets, noise limits after a certain hour or how many tenants can reside in a unit.

Your apartment management policies should answer the following questions.

- What are the rules and regulations guiding the use of common areas and amenities?
- How do tenants communicate with staff members?
- Is it easy for tenants to get in touch with the right individuals, or do they often struggle to make connections?
- How are disputes managed with tenants or between tenants and other members of the community?

You should also have clear tenant screening and leasing practices in place. How will you screen tenants? How will you decide who to lease to? The clearer these protocols are, the greater the likelihood that you will fill your building with stable and long-term residents.

3. Review legal policies regularly

Your apartment complex should always be on the sunny side of the law–and you want to be sure that you aren't missing any important elements. Good apartment management requires working knowledge of issues like how to handle evictions, fair housing compliance, and how to handle accessibility throughout your complex.

By reviewing your local landlord-tenant laws with your attorney, you can be sure that you won't miss any important legal details that could come back to bite you later.

4. Take a look at your leasing and marketing strategies

How do you handle keeping your apartments rented out? Whether you work with a third-party apartment manager or you handle this task yourself, as a complex owner, you will become a marketer. It's crucial that you pay attention to marketing information, including how to best reach the target market for your complex. Develop a solid marketing strategy that will keep the majority of your units rented.

5. Set a budget every year

Every year take the time to sit down and review your annual budget. Look at expense management: where were your biggest expenses last year? What expenses do you anticipate in the coming year?

Evaluate your revenue projections for the coming year. Set out any major capital expenditure plans and take a look at your cash reserves. The better you understand your finances, the easier it is to make savvy financial decisions.

6. Take care of financial reporting

All too often, apartment management falls into trouble when it comes to financial reporting. Not only do you need that information for your personal records, you will need to report it come tax time. Make sure you keep up with the books. Regularly conduct banking and budget reviews.

Putting effort into financial reporting now will make things far easier on you when you file your taxes each year or when you look for a loan for a future property purchase. Work closely with your property manager and stay current on your property rent roll, monthly profit and loss statement and quarterly budget forecasting.

7. Take care of preventative maintenance

Just like any building, your apartment requires preventative maintenance in order to look its best–and in order to stay safe for your tenants. Pay attention to common areas as well as your units. Take a look at wear and tear over time and make sure you have projections for that maintenance. Some types of maintenance, including taking care of HVAC units and fireplaces, may need to be taken care of seasonally to maximize your investment. Plan out your seasonal apartment management early in the year so that you aren't surprised when it's needed.

8. Stay on top of market research

Get to know your local area. What are other local apartments renting for? What amenities are other apartment buildings offering? Pay attention to the local economy as well as to local trends and market cycles. Keep up with your competition in terms of what rent and amenities you offer. When possible, increase your rents to help you improve your community.

9. Prioritize major building systems inspections

Every year, you need to take care of regular building systems inspections. This includes:

- The roof
- Windows
- HVAC maintenance
- The boiler
- Electricity
- Plumbing
- Life safety and security systems
- Lighting
- Landscaping
- Garage/parking
- Stairs and Balconies

Inspect these items on a regular basis to ensure that there are no safety hazards or ongoing problems. By identifying those problems and taking any preventative measures early, you can decrease the odds that you'll face more expensive repairs down the road.

10. Choose the right staff members

As an apartment complex owner, you also become the boss. Create clear hiring processes. Know what you're looking for in team members and set a policy in place for training. You'll need leasing agents, on-site managers, and maintenance, cleaning, and construction crews throughout your time as a complex owner, and you want to make sure that you choose the right apartment management team for your property.

How To Manage Your Multifamily Property Manager

As you can see, apartment building ownership is not for the faint of heart. Managing multi-unit properties presents its own special list of challenges and required skills and talents.

When it comes to managing your property, you have two choices. You can manage the property yourself or you can hire a third-party management company. If it's a small property, less than 50 units, chances are you'll be managing it yourself especially if you want a property that cash flows.

You, your team, or your manager, must have skill sets and experience in at least the following areas:

- Accounting.
- Leasing and marketing.
- Maintenance and renovations.
- Community and resident relations.
- The know-how to increase income and lower operating expenses.

Great multifamily property managers are hard to find. But know this: your property manager is the number one person on your team.

Managing your multifamily property manager

Your level of involvement with the management of your property is up to you—it is not a decision your manager should make. You determine what protocols and procedures will be set forth in your management agreement. And you determine how often your manager reports to you.

The key to successfully managing your asset is to put solid systems in place. The best time to do this is at the beginning of your relationship with your manager, not as potential problems develop. It's much harder to make adjustments after your manager has had a free hand and is accustomed to managing your property his/her way.

You're less likely to hear your manager say, "Well, we've always done it this way, I'm not changing now" when you've established upfront how you want things done. Here are some great systems to put in place:

Rental property accounting

There are many multifamily property management software programs on the market today. Most commercial property managers use software programs such as Yardi, AppFolio, Rent Manager, RealPage and Tenant Pro.

Be sure your manager actually knows how to use the software. Before hiring a property manager ask to see and review sample reports from the properties he or she is currently managing. Property management software programs are designed with integrated accounting systems and comprehensive reporting—but the old adage "garbage in, garbage out" still applies even when your program has all the bells and whistles.

Pro tip: Request online access to your property reports. Most property management software programs have an owner portal. Have your manager give you the appropriate log in information so that you can access your property rent rolls and reports 24/7.

Here are the reports you must receive and review regularly:

- Cash flow statement
- Balance sheet
- Profit and loss statement
- General ledger
- Monthly A/R collection report
- Rent roll

These reports will cover all property income collected, all invoices and expenses paid and the status of your tenants. Plan to review these reports as needed. For example, you may want to review them on a weekly basis at the beginning of your relationship then monthly or bi-monthly as you gain confidence in your property manager.

Pro tip: Your manager should also provide an annual budget forecast. These are your projections for income and expenses over the next 12-months. Do not prepare an annual operating budget for your multifamily property or apartment building and then file it away and ignore it.

Multifamily property rent roll

Along with leasing reports I like to see a rent roll on a regular basis—at least bi-monthly. Your property rent roll should be kept current at all times and available to you online. At a glance you can see, among other things, your vacancies and collection status—two items you must always watch closely.

A good rent roll will include: Unit number, unit type and square footage; resident name, move-in and move-out date; lease term and expiration date; rent (current and market); security deposit; starting balance; additional income such as parking fees and storage fees; all other charges (late fees, utility reimbursement, etc.); and amount paid and balance due.

Leasing and marketing residential investment properties

It's up to you how often you receive leasing and marketing reports. Leasing is such a critical part of property management that's it's a good idea to ask your property manager for weekly updates especially if you've purchased a property with high vacancies.

Your weekly leasing and marketing updates should include:

- **Leasing status updates:** Be sure your manager gives you accurate and detailed information on leasing activities at your property. For example, don't let your manager simply say, "We leased two units this week." Your reports on newly leased units should include all of the information found in a comprehensive Rent Roll as described above.

- **Marketing activities for the week:** Where has the property been marketed and what are the results?
- **Market rent:** Your manager must keep current on the rental market. What are comparable properties charging in rent and utilities for similar rental units? Can you raise the rent on your units and stay competitive?
- **Collections:** Be sure your manager lets you know of any collection issues with your current residents. If a resident is having difficulty paying rent you need to know about it immediately.

Responsive property management: Maintenance and renovations

Establish a system for resident maintenance requests.

How will your residents contact your property manager when they have a maintenance request or other questions? Who will follow-up with your residents? And when? Set established procedures for your residents and manager to follow. Your manager should be on top of resident complaints and requests for maintenance 24/7. Set deadlines for returning calls and written requests.

You should approve all property renovations. Here's an example of not leaving it up to your property manager. I had an 18-stall carport at a property that was in need of a new roofing membrane. A simple repair. I asked our property manager to get a bid on repairs, which he did. However his bid included complete gutter replacements, new downspouts and replacement beams in addition to the new roofing material. All but the roofing material were unnecessary improvements.

The lesson here is don't leave renovation decisions in the hands of your property manager. You can put a clause in your management agreement that states the manager must secure your approval for any expense that exceeds a certain dollar amount—a dollar amount set by you.

Community and resident relations

Plan to have periodic conversations with your manager about your property's community. How would your manager summarize the residents at your property? And more importantly how can he/she positively influence relations with your residents?

Some of the things your manager should be proactive about are:

- **Resident rewards:** Offer a small reward to your current residents for telling their friends and family about vacant units at your property. You might want to host community barbecues or events from time to time.
- **Premise history:** It's possible to request a premise history from your local police department. Much of the activity that involves the police can occur at night when your manager is not around. It's a good idea to check the premise history periodically. It's an even better idea to have an on-site manager who lives at your property if financially feasible. A good on-site manager can dramatically enhance resident relations.
- **Online property reviews:** What are current and past residents saying about your property online? Are they posting complaints or

compliments? Respond to every review your property receives including those left by residents prior to your purchase of the property.

- **Ask for reviews:** If your manager (or you) receives a compliment from one of your residents ask them if they would be willing to share it online. And let them know you plan to share it with the rest of the management team.

The know-how to increase income and lower operating expenses

Property managers who have experience as both a manager and a multifamily property owner can bring a lot to the table in areas such as:

- Operations consulting.
- Value added strategies: Improvements that can raise the value of your property.
- Industry vendors and service providers: An owner/operator of multifamily properties will have good industry contacts for vendors and service providers for multifamily properties. Review your current service providers annually for cost and service.
- Increasing revenue.
- Lowering expenses.

It's been my experience that the best multifamily property managers own multifamily investment properties. Look for this type of manager and make good use of their talents. A good owner/operator manager can help you improve your property revenue, decrease property expenses and increase the value of your property.

Legal issues

From time to time legal issues will arise at your rental properties. Be certain your property manager uses attorneys who are experienced in real estate law and residential and commercial landlord representation.

Put procedures in place for:

- Handling evictions and completing proper eviction documentation such as SDRs (security deposit return letters).
- Property inspections for compliance with state, city and local codes.
- Fair housing compliance.
- Collections.

The key to establishing a good working relationship with your property manager is to have open and frequent conversations about how your property is performing. Even bad news can be manageable if you stay on top of it.

Don't let your manager dictate how you work together. You'll be far more successful when you take leadership and an active role in your property management.

How to Lead Your Multifamily Property Manager Starting the Day You Close

Here are proactive things you can do to lead your multifamily property manager. Knowing this information puts you in the driver's seat—exactly where you should be as the property owner.

Multifamily property management checklist

Some property management items will be of immediate concern such as "life safety." Determine if you need to arrange for inspections or service. Are the following functioning as designed?

- Building and individual unit security systems
- Common area and entry cameras
- Common area lighting including parking, front and rear halls, stairways, exits and entries
- Smoke and CO detectors in all resident units and required common areas
- Proper fire safety equipment (to code)

Verify that all testing and certifications are current. Also verify that the building is in compliance with local, state and national housing codes.

Other items, while not as critically important on day one, should be addressed as soon as possible. For example, you'll want to create a marketing and leasing plan covering:

- Leasing fees and bonuses
- Tenant lease renewal procedures and fees
- Vacancy analysis: Average market rents and target rent increase timeline
- Market and submarket research such as local leasing trends; demographics; market sizzle (the in thing that your market renter wants); and a targeted leasing campaign

Your immediate goal for week one is to get rents collected; assess vacant units and develop a plan to bring them online; get the property clean looking and presentable; and initiate marketing with front signage, website and flyers.

Before you begin any management activities at your property, be sure you have a signed property management agreement. A quick note about this. Your property management company will have an agreement they like and use with all of their clients. That doesn't mean it's a good contract. In fact, I've seen managers who don't really understand their contracts.

You have the right to make changes to a property management agreement, or to substitute an agreement you are willing to sign. Be clear about costs, fees and how the parties can terminate the agreement.

 We like to use our own property management agreement. Here it is:

***

Sample Multifamily Property Management Agreement

This Apartment Management Agreement (the "Agreement") is made this _____ Day of September 20__ by and between _____ ("Agent"), and [your company name], LLC ("Owner").

1) PROPERTY - That certain property consisting of the multi-family apartment complex known as _____ located at _____ in the city of _____, County of _____, State of _____ together with all personal property of Owner attached thereto, located thereon or used in connection therewith (The "Property").

437

2) AGENCY - In consideration of the property management services to be rendered by Agent pursuant to this Agreement, Owner hereby designates Agent as the exclusive Agent and representative of Owner for the purposes of management and operation for Owner's account of The Property.

3) TERM - This Agreement shall become effective as of the ___ day of _____ 20__ (the "Effective Date") and, shall continue in full force for ___ months. This Agreement shall automatically renew for a term of twelve (12) months unless written notice is received by Agent, from Owner, a minimum of thirty (30) days prior to the expiration of the term. Either party shall have the right to terminate this agreement by delivering written notice thirty (30) days prior to termination.

4) MANAGEMENT FEE – (a) The agent will be paid a fee of ____% of the monthly collected revenues from the Property. Revenues include rent, pass through costs to tenants, vending income, and forfeited security deposits applied to rent (excluding damages). Revenues do not include insurance proceeds or other revenue sources not listed above. Agent will be reimbursed for all expenses directly related to the management and leasing of the Property. The Agent will not be reimbursed for Agent's general office overhead and expenses. Projects including, but not limited to, property renovation, reconstruction, or damage recovery are outside the scope of the normal management fees and will require additional compensation to be agreed upon by all parties prior to initiation of work. (b). Upon signing a new tenant into a new term lease, the Agent will be paid a one-time fee of ___% of monthly rent per unit. (c). Upon signing a current tenant into a new term lease of 6 months or greater, the Agent will be paid a one-time fee of ___% of monthly rent per unit. (d). Agent will be paid $___/hour for maintenance performed at the property.

5) POWERS AND DUTIES OF AGENT - The Agent shall (a) use its best efforts to keep the Property rented by procuring tenants for the Property, (b) collect the rents and other income due the Owner on a timely basis, (c) deposit all income, including security deposits, in a separate Broker Account on behalf of Owner, (d) pay normal reoccurring operating expenses on a timely basis from the trust account, provided funds are available, (e) hire employees, vendors, contractors, and suppliers to provide services, materials, equipment, and supplies for the benefit of the Tenants and Property, (f) secure Owner's approval on any expense, other than normal reoccurring operating expenses, that exceed One Thousand Dollars ($1,000.00) except for emergencies to protect property, health, or life, (g) enforce the tenants' lease obligations and rules and regulations, (h) provide monthly operating statements, (i) keep the Owner informed of any potential problems, hazards, and code violations existing at the property, and (j) perform other reasonable duties or tasks requested by the Owner.

6) DUTIES OF OWNER – Owner shall be responsible for providing funds, or causing funds to be provided, for the Operating Account to meet on a timely basis, the cash requirements of Agent for the proper operation of the Property. Owner agrees to review monthly financial statements for any errors or discrepancies within 120 days from the close of the respective month.

7) OWNER'S AGENT AND SECURITY DEPOSITS - Pursuant to _____ [state] Real Estate Commission requirements; all security deposits received from tenants are transferred to Owner and are not held by Agent, owner has full financial responsibility for return of the security deposit to tenants. Owner authorizes the Agent to return any deposit due the tenant from the Owner's operating account. Owner appoints Agent as the Owner's representative for service of legal notices affecting the property. Upon notice of any dispute from the tenant, Agent will not unreasonably withhold the Owner's true name and current mailing address.

8) INSURANCE OBLIGATIONS – (a) Owner shall obtain and keep in force adequate insurance against physical damage (e.g., fire with extended coverage endorsement, boiler and machines, etc.) and against liability for loss, damage or injury to property or persons which might arise out of the occupancy, management, operation or maintenance of the Property. Manager shall be covered as an additional insured on all liability insurance maintained with respect to the Property. Said policies shall provide that notice of default or cancellation shall be sent to Manager as well as Owner. (b) Agent will procure and maintain insurance against the misfeasance, malfeasance, or nonfeasance (errors and omissions) management of the Property, with limits of not more than One Million Dollars and with a deductible of not less than Five Thousand dollars.

9) OWNER'S INDEMNIFICATION - Owner hereby warrants and represents to Agent that it has the lawful and proper authority to employ Agent as provided herein. Except in the event of the negligence or willful misconduct of Agent, its officers, directors, employees, successors, assigns or other persons acting on behalf of Agent, Owner shall indemnify, defend, and hold Agent harmless from any and all costs, expenses, attorney's fees, suits, liabilities and damages from or connected with the operation or management of the Property by Agent or the performance or exercise of any obligation, power or authority herein or hereafter granted to Agent. Owner also agrees to hold harmless and defend Agent from any and all claims arising by reason of Agent's employment of any Property employee, including all costs of Agent's employment of any Property employee, including all costs of defense. Owner shall further indemnify Agent against, and hold it harmless from, all damages, claims, loss, cost or expense, including, without limitation, attorney's fees and costs arising out of defects in design or construction of the improvements in the Property or any breach of any legal duty or obligation which is by law or under this Agreement the responsibility of Owner.

10) ALTERNATIVE DISPUTE RESOLUTION (ADR) - Any controversy or claim arising out of this Agreement shall be settled by mediation or another form of alternative dispute resolution (ADR). The mediation or ADR shall be held in (your state and city). The expense of the ADR proceeding shall be equally split between the parties, except that each party shall be responsible for their own expert fees and related costs. Each side shall be responsible for its own legal fees. The parties agree in good faith to first seek resolution of any dispute between them prior to invoking this ADR provision.

IN WITNESS WHEREOF, the parties have executed this Agreement the ___day of _____, 20___.

Owner: [your company name], LLC
By: _____

By:_____

Agent:

By: _____

By:_____

441

Resource alert: Our property management agreement is included in our resource document at: theresabradleybanta.com/book_resources. Feel free to download and use the document but be sure to run it by your own landlord/tenant attorney for local compliance.

It's *your* job to lead your multifamily property manager

Now that you've given your immediate attention to the items above, here's the rest of the property management checklist.

Review these items with your property manager. And always remember, most property managers are professionals and may have some excellent management ideas that you haven't thought of. Be receptive to the ideas and suggestions of your team.

Building and common areas

- Curb appeal and common area cleanliness get immediate attention
- Order new signage, banners and marketing materials such as leasing flyers
- Ascertain that all common areas are free of obstruction and all flammable or hazardous materials are properly stored

Property operations

- Establish communication protocols for weekly and monthly property management reports; in-person meetings; maintenance, leasing and staff; and community relations

- Set policies and procedures covering pets; guests; rent payment due date; late fees and collections; rental concessions (if any); common area rules; property emergencies; and security and life safety matters
- Set eviction policies
- Set rental policies. Will you allow pets? Assisted housing or Section 8? Smoking? Etc.
- Establish tenant screening guidelines
- Approve tenant forms: tenant application; tenant lease; notices to evict; collection letters; and management announcements or notices; etc.
- Define duties and goals of on-site manager, if any
- Define duties of maintenance and leasing personnel

Residents

- Distribute change of management letter to residents covering where and how to pay rent; resident incentive and referral programs; and any exciting management news or developments
- Provide online tenant portal for rental application; rent payment; resident lease agreement; and other documents
- Create tenant welcome packages
- Send balance due letter to tenants, if needed
- Establish community rules

Maintenance

- Draft property maintenance plan covering repairs, unit turns, resident notification systems and response times
- Review status and consistency of preventive maintenance efforts

- Review mechanical system functions including staff familiarity
- Ensure mechanical systems and piping are properly labeled and functioning at high efficiency

Marketing and leasing

- Design marketing materials for property website, print and online rental ads and flyer
- Develop property branding
- Include marketing material such as floor plans, photos (exterior and interior), and the contact person for leasing inquiries

Additional sources of income

- Introduce resident utility bill back system upon expiration of tenant lease(s) (monthly flat fee or variable charges for utility usage).
- Identify untapped sources of revenue such as fees for services like storage, parking, bike repair, pet cleaning, etc.

Accounting, financials and reports

- Review and approve all property reports currently in use by management: rent roll; profit and loss statement (P&L); balance sheet; cash flow statement; delinquency and collection report; aged accounts payable report; etc.
- Set annual or monthly caps and expense thresholds at which approval is needed such as a dollar cap for any single repair or expense

- Approve property rent roll which should include rent paid; delinquency or balance due; current and market rents; and lease expiration dates
- Conduct a rent roll audit against leases, look for discrepancies and solve. Check that all leases are dated (otherwise a case could be made they never expire at all); tenants have received lead paint disclosures (if not, it could mount to large fines); and security deposits and other fees have been collected
- Open operating and reserve account(s). Also, complete bank signature cards
- Open escrow account for tenant security deposits
- Prepare historical utility consumption analysis

Miscellaneous takeover items

- Prepare notification of new management to vendors, advising them of intent to review and rebid contracts
- Review lease renewal dates with third-party services such as laundry facility services, roof advertising, etc.
- Notify all utilities of change in management
- Obtain full lease files from prior management
- Issue master keys, secure key box
- Complete unit inspections: CO detectors, appliances, bath, toilets and tub, water damage (if any), plumbing, electric, heating/cooling controls, etc.
- Review pest control history, determine treatment plan if needed

Your property manager should have a takeover checklist too. It may include items such as:

- Arrange to have management company's name included in policies, worker's compensation, public liability and other forms of liability coverage
- Obtain new vendor insurance certificates naming new management company

Don't forget, you are the property owner. It's your job to manage your investment asset and to manage the team you've entrusted to care for that asset.

What Makes an Awe-Inspiring Property Manager?

If you think about it, property managers are part of the customer service industry. Whether they're talking with a prospective tenant or handling the property's vendors, great customer service skills are an absolute must.

Of course, excellent customer service skills are just one part of the awe-inspiring property manager package. To captivate potential tenants, meet the needs of all current tenants, owners and guests, and run the property seamlessly in all areas, a property manager must possess and develop some specific qualities.

Attentiveness in all areas

Managers must pay attention to what residents, staff and vendors say. And listen to each word without becoming distracted by phone or email. The best property managers are aware of the obvious and unspoken needs of property owners and residents, and the only way to do this is by getting the details.

Maintains a positive mental attitude

In property management using positive language and staying upbeat even when presented with an extremely challenging or frustrating situation is crucial.

Property managers meet confrontation head-on and sometimes without any warning. You just don't know who will enter your office and for what reason, so your manager must approach each situation with a good attitude and a smile in order to resolve problems more quickly.

Personable yet equal in approach

A property manager must be able to empathize with tenants and put themselves in someone else's shoes to better understand and handle unique situations, but empathy must be balanced with objectivity.

While one tenant may be reminiscent of a favorite aunt and another of a past coworker who made life miserable, property rules must be applied equally to both.

Able to keep calm

Property residents, staff and others might enter the property management office in a state of distress, and your manager has to be ready to respond in a calm manner no matter how stressful the situation happens to be. Have staff try role-playing potential scenarios with coworkers to practice staying calm under pressure.

Start by setting the stage for calm by keeping a clean office. A messy space can make people feel more anxious and stressed out. Having an organized, clean office will make your space more peaceful and inviting to visitors from the get-go.

Early Warning Signs Your Property Manager Has Lost Control

Even the most dedicated and professional property managers can get into trouble. And sometimes you—the property owner—are the last to hear about it. Here's what you should watch for:

Excessive cash calls

A cash call is when your property manager contacts you and says, "Hey, I hate to bother you, but we need a couple thousand dollars to get caught up on operating expenses."

Multifamily real estate is an income-producing asset. When operated properly, income should be sufficient to cover expenses. Cash calls should rarely occur.

Pro tip: Prepare an Annual Operating Budget for your property. Review it with your manager on a monthly or quarterly basis. Your manager should also provide an Accounts Payable Aging report that includes invoice amounts and days in aging period (30, 60, 90 days).

High delinquencies and collections

When tenants fall behind on rent payments it frequently becomes very difficult for them to catch up. You will continue to lose revenue the longer the delinquency persists—often revenue that can never be collected, even through legal proceedings.

Often the best course of action is to take immediate action and serve the tenant with a Notice to Quit. Be certain you and your management company are on the same page about how to deal with tenants who fall behind in payments.

Pro tip: Your monthly reports should include a master rent roll that shows rental amounts collected and the balance due for each rental unit in your property. You should always request that your management company prepare monthly collection and tenant aged accounts receivable (A/R) reports.

Increasing vacancies

A property that is 100% occupied is nice although you might not always reach that pinnacle of perfection. Your property should at minimum match the vacancy rate for your local rental market. The minute the vacancy rate at your property falls below local market averages, talk with your property manager.

Pro tip: Review your property rent roll every month without exception. Review your leasing and marketing plan with your management company at least semi-annually.

No new lease renewals

As you review your rent roll and tenant reports, look for lease renewals. These are tenants who choose to renew their lease and continue residing at your property. If your tenants are moving out at their first lease anniversary date, rather than renewing, you need to know why.

Pro tip: Your operations policies should include plans for lease expiration dates and unit turn management. Are residents being contacted 60 days before their lease comes up for renewal? Do you have a plan for quickly turning units once a tenant has moved? And don't forget to offer pre-leasing to prospective residents. You'll build a waiting list for units at your property.

Tenants are approaching you with problems

Have you ever visited your property and had tenants run up to you and ask if you are the owner? And when they do, are they complimentary about your property or are they bringing a long list of complaints to your attention?

Residents should never have to wonder who to contact.
The fix: Establish maintenance response times and a work order management system at your property. Create and distribute a community rules and regulations handbook that includes the proper procedures and channels for tenant complaints.

Online complaints

When was the last time you searched online for your property address? It is critical that you implement policies for policing online reviews and comments about your property. Your policy should include a plan for responding to every comment posted online.

And speaking of policing, do you know what the police are up to at your property? Most police calls happen at night when your property manager is not around. Many police departments offer premise history reports for a minimal fee.

Your job

The most critical foundation for managing your property manager is good, timely and accurate reporting. Read the reports. Meet with your manager on a regular basis to discuss property operations and proactive management strategies.

Think of it this way. Your property manager oversees daily operations. You, as a smart investor, manage your asset—this includes managing your team.

How to Ensure Your Property Manager is On Top of Things

Your property manager represents you with your tenants. Whether that's for better or for worse comes back to how well you're up to speed with him or her. The right property manager will keep tenants happy while keeping expenses down and staying on top of repairs, the wrong one will cost you in one or more of those categories.

While you can't follow your property manager around all day every day, here's what you can do to make sure he or she is on top of the game.

Get monthly reports

Your property manager should be able to give you comprehensive reports once a month that provide a current snapshot of your property when combined.

Reported items should include rents received, money spent, money owed, tenant complaints, vacancy rate, complaint resolution details, and other information related to your property's physical and financial condition. Gathering the information for the reports regularly will help your manager stay on the ball, and the information provided will keep you updated on your investment.

Perform periodic inspections

Your manager should carry out regular property inspections and provide you with a copy of the associated reports, but you should also do one yourself occasionally. If you're relying solely on your manager's inspections, you could be unaware of something seriously wrong in your property.

At the very least, inspect common areas, building exteriors, vacant units and any area of the building besides occupied tenant units on occasion. Don't tell your manager you're coming beforehand as you want to see your property as your tenants normally do. Tenant-occupied unit inspections do require a heads-up, as local and state laws likely require you to give tenants advance notice.

While you're there, speak to your tenants. They can be a valuable source of information on areas where your manager is falling short.

Keep communication open

Strong, solid communication is the foundation upon which a firm owner-manager relationship is built. A manager who feels as if he or she can come to you with ideas or problems will perform much better than one who believes you don't care. Make yourself available to your property manager as needed and take their suggestions and concerns seriously should any arise.

All of these suggestions will help you monitor your property manager's performance, but you should consider an immediate change if you notice some obvious red flags. If tenants are leaving in droves or you've had major repairs due to your manager's inattention, it's time to cut your losses and find someone else.

How to Create an Annual Operating Budget for Your Multifamily Property

A multifamily property annual operating budget allows you to compare the actual financial performance of your property to your long-range projections for future income and expenses.

It's important to prepare an annual income and expense forecast for your property whether you manage it yourself or if a professional third-party management company manages it for you.

Pro tip: Do not prepare an annual operating budget and then file it away and ignore it. The following will give you some great ideas for using a budget to your advantage.

Benefits of creating an annual property budget

A budget allows you to establish or identify:

- **Performance targets:** Covers projections for things like lowering expenses and increasing income.
- **A baseline for property management reviews**: Is your manager on target?
- **Income and expense projections based on market drivers and assumptions:** Are market rental rates increasing or decreasing? What about vacancy rates? What annual percentage increase can you expect for expenses?
- **Capital improvements planning:** Cost projections for your really big projects like new windows, boiler or roof.
- **Problems:** Are units sitting unoccupied for long periods of time? Are expenses exceeding expectations? Have we missed opportunities for additional revenue?

Importantly, a budget can help you maximize profitability and avoid unforeseen major repairs and expenses.

Third-party property manager performance baseline

The best use of a property budget is to track how your manager is performing. Ask your third-party property manager to prepare an annual budget forecast with side-by-side quarterly comparisons of actual vs. budgeted income and expenses.

This budget then establishes a baseline for your property manager's performance reviews. It's a great idea to have regular meetings with your manager to review these comparisons. How are they doing in meeting projections? What can be done to course correct when and if your targets are not being met? Some of the items to review are:

Multifamily property income:

- **Vacancies against leasing projections:** Is your manager on target for leasing new units or maintaining the average occupancy rate in your market?
- **Lease renewal (rollover) projections:** These are leases that are due for renewal during the budget period. Make initial contact with residents no later than 60 days prior to lease expiration. If there is not a renewal commitment from your tenant there should be a follow up in 45-days.
- **Future profit projections from increased revenue:** This could include rent increases, laundry revenue increases, the introduction of a utility reimbursement program (RUBS) where tenant pays utilities, etc. Where are you able to increase revenue at your property?

- **Future revenue projections from new sources:** Where can you find previously untapped revenue? Can you charge for amenities such as parking, storage, recycling or business/entertainment centers? Can you install vending machines in your common areas?
- **Cash flow projections:** With accurate cash flow projections you'll be able to make strategic decisions about the allocation of revenue for improvements.
- **Replacement reserves:** Determine what percentage of gross scheduled income can be put aside for future use. For example, you might want to hold back 5% of all scheduled revenue or you can allocate a certain dollar amount annually per unit in your property.

Multifamily property expenses:

- **Projections for lowering current expenses:** Are your mechanical systems operating at peak efficiency? You may be able to lower utility bills with systems that operate efficiently. Can you contest your current property tax payment amount?
- **Review third-party vendors and service providers:** Conduct annual reviews of your property vendors such as services that provide lawn care, common area cleaning, trash removal and property insurance. Let them know they will be up for annual review for cost and service. Do your service providers have pending increases?
- **Utilize the know-how of your service providers:** Ask your vendors for efficiency/cost saving suggestions (property improvements or services they can provide) and budget accordingly.
- **Property management:** Review all fees such as leasing, maintenance and on-site management (if applicable). Are you

satisfied with the performance of your manager? Are their fees as projected?

Most multifamily and apartment building management software programs will generate a budget-to-actual income and expense report for comparison. Ask for this report.

Pro tip: A budget is nice, but you must review it alongside actual property financials on a quarterly basis.

Investment property analysis assumptions (a.k.a. drivers)

Using the following or similar assumptions, you or your property manager can project all income and expense increases over a 12-month period beginning with the current month. You can change these variables at any time. It's a good idea to run several scenarios using both conservative and aggressive assumptions.

The following assumptions are used for example only. You will need to determine your own variables based on your particular investment market. A good, experienced multifamily property manager can help you determine your local numbers. Most multifamily brokers will provide local statistics as well.

- Vacancy (7%)
- Income Growth (5%)
- Expense Growth (3%)
- Cap Rate (7%)
- Expense Ratio (40-45%)

These assumptions will help you determine the best- and worst-case scenarios and will assist you in planning budgets for the long term. You can create 24-month, 36-month or 48-month projections using assumptions. This planning can help you set targets for increasing revenue and lowering expenses. By doing so you can predict your property value over the long term.

Pro tip: The National Apartment Association conducts an annual Survey of Operating Income & Expenses in Rental Apartment Communities. You'll find the survey by searching naahq.org.

Investment property capital improvements planning and projections

In addition to predicting regular, recurring expenses your budget should include projections for major capital improvements. For example, you might want to paint your common areas (halls, stairs, entry, mail room, laundry, etc.) every three years.

Planning for long-term improvements allows you to stagger the improvements over time. By doing this you can avoid surprise expenses. These funds are commonly referred to as replacement reserves and include:

- Common areas improvements such as new paint, lighting, vinyl, carpet, parking lots and driveways.
- Major building systems repair or replacement such as windows, roof, boiler and air conditioning.
- Individual unit upgrades.

Pro tip: Use your annual operating budget as a tool. Plan to hold quarterly budget reviews with your property manager and/or your team. An annual budget can drastically maximize your profits when used as designed.

How to Hire and Manage an On-site Property Manager

An on-site property manager is responsible for the day-to-day operations of your multifamily property. But it doesn't stop there. Because your manager lives on the premises, he or she becomes the "face" of your property.

Your manager interacts with current residents; prospective residents; service providers; the fire department and city building inspectors; your lender's inspectors; and all other visitors to your property. Your manager is your ambassador to the outside world.

An engaging and competent on-site property manager can:

- Act as your diplomat and public relations person.
- Have a dramatic and positive influence on community relations.
- Attract the type of resident you want to see in your property.
- Be your 24/7 eyes and ears.
- Increase leasing activity and,
- Give you peace of mind.

Here are some of the things you'll want to consider when hiring an on-site manager:

459

On-site property manager compensation

You, as the owner of your property, determine the salary, credits, fees and bonuses paid. These amounts should be negotiated at the beginning of your relationship with your on-site manager.

Many on-site property managers receive free rent. And nothing more. Others receive a base salary in addition to a rent credit.

On-site property manager monthly salary or rent credit

Base salary rates will vary based on condition of property; building style, age, and class; location; competition; supply and demand; and overall economy. And compensation packages will vary from market to market.

- **Monthly salary:** The monthly salary is a base pay commensurate with the duties required, the size of the property and the local market.
- **Rent Credit:** Rather than pay your on-site manager a salary, their compensation comes in the form of free rent, or a credit for a portion of the normal monthly rent.

Pro tip: Depending on the local demand for good on-site managers and the duties required of your manager it may be necessary to offer a salary in addition to a rent credit.

Multifamily unit leasing bonuses

In addition to base salaries and rent credits, multifamily on-site property managers frequently receive leasing bonuses. It's a great idea to give your resident manager the incentive to keep your property at full occupancy.

- **New leases:** Your on-site property manager receives a percentage of the monthly unit rent for all new leases signed as a result of their direct marketing efforts. For example, if the unit rents for a monthly amount of $1,000 your manager will receive 30% of the monthly rental amount, or $300. This is a one-time fee.
- **Lease renewals:** Your on-site manager receives a set dollar amount per lease renewal. For example, you might pay $125 for each lease renewal if the lease term is 12-months or greater. This is a one-time fee.
- **Performance bonuses:** Performance bonuses are especially useful if you own or have acquired a property with high vacancies. Your manager will receive an additional bonus if they meet a certain volume of new leases. For example, if your manager leases four or more units in a single month, you will pay the normal 30% of the monthly rental amount plus an additional 20% leasing bonus. Using the example above if a unit is rented for $1,000 you will pay a one-time bonus of 30% ($300) plus a bonus of 20% ($200) for each unit leased.

Pro tip: You can stipulate that your on-site manager rent to new or renewing tenants in "accordance with the owner's tenant screening guidelines." If a tenant fails to meet those guidelines your on-site manager will forfeit those leasing bonus.

Other on-site property management fees (if qualified)

In addition to the general duties described in your management agreement your on-site property manager may qualify for additional compensation.

Some of those duties might include:

- **Market research:** Often an actively engaged on-site manager knows local leasing trends better than anybody else. Duties could include market rent research (what are other similar units commanding in rental amounts and can your rents be raised?); market amenities (what does the competition offer and can you do the same at your property?); or rental unit upgrades (what is your competition offering in order to attract your target renter?).
- **Community relations:** The duties could include hosting an annual resident barbeque or semi-annual resident get together (such as an ice cream social); publishing a bi-monthly apartment community newsletter; or designing a community flyer or bulletin board.
- **Creative marketing:** Your on-site manager can find new, previously overlooked avenues for reaching your target rental market.
- **Property maintenance:** If your on-site manager has handyman or construction skills why not pay him/her to handle the small maintenance items at a much lower rate than your traditional third-party property management company charges?

All of the duties above can be paid at an hourly rate. Again, the amount you pay your on-site manager is up to you as the owner. You may be able to have your on-site manager handle the duties that a third-party property management company would otherwise provide—at a significantly lower hourly amount.

Pro tip: Always remember that it will be someone's responsibility to manage the on-site manager. Your on-site manager might report to your third-party manager, they may even handle the hiring and firing. A system for reporting and frequent performance reviews *must* be established in advance. As your on-site manager's duties and responsibilities increase, so does the need for the oversight of your manager's performance.

Sample multifamily on-site property manager duties

Here are some of the duties you can assign to your on-site property manager, depending of course on their qualifications to conduct such tasks. Be sure to include your list of responsibilities in your on-site property manager agreement.

- Answer calls, meet and greet residents, prospective residents and property inspectors.
- General office administration.
- Keep accurate up-to-date records of expenses from property operations.
- Submit timely expense reports.
- Inspect vacant units for make ready status.
- Synchronize the time clocks, turning backwards and forward as necessary. (This includes outdoor and indoor security lighting and sprinkler systems.)
- Check and maintain boiler water levels and oil pump.

- Clean the laundry room, mail room and entryway a minimum of twice per week.
- Clean the property exterior and common grounds which includes snow shoveling, plant watering and courtyard care.
- Pick up trash from the grounds regularly.
- Water, maintain and mow the lawns regularly during the season.
- Clean the common areas every three days or more often as needed or conditions warrant.
- Clean the common area windows and hall carpets as needed.
- Coordinate tenant service and maintenance requests.
- Communicate with residents in a responsive, positive and direct manner.
- Arrange for carpet installers, plumbers, electricians, appliance deliveries, etc. to get into the apartment units or building to repair items as well as meet with pest control people to spray the building.
- Show apartment units to prospective residents. Accept rental applications and non-refundable application fees and forward to owner or third-party management company.
- Travel to and be a liaison between property management office and community residents.
- Handle all unit make readies: This includes wall prep, paint and paint touch up, all cleaning and hauling including stoves and refrigerators, carpet shampooing if necessary, wall plate replacement, light carpentry, window repair, window coverings, small repairs, etc.
- The on-site manager with the exception of the application fee collects no money, checks, cash, money orders or any other form of payment. (It's up to you whether you allow your manager to accept

payments from your residents. As a rule of thumb, I, or my third-party managers collect all funds at my properties.)

Final note

Not all properties will be able to financially support an on-site property manager. However, there are some alternatives you can consider. Hiring a qualified and competent on-site manager might be a viable substitute to engaging the services of a full-blown third-party management company.

For example, it might not be necessary to hire a third-party manager if you have a competent on-site manager and you self-manage by personally taking on the duties a third-party manager might otherwise handle such as: property bookkeeping; financial reporting; and major capital repairs and improvements. Independent contractors can also handle these services.

Stable Predictable Cash Flow: The Sirens' Song

Stable predictable cash flow. That's the siren song of the multifamily real estate investing gurus. The song that promises you tons of cash. A tune that will let you laugh at money worries. Lyrics that promise the leisure life—a life where you live like a king while multiple tenants pay for your investment property.

But there are some tricks to avoiding shipwreck. I know this from personal experience and from the experiences of my consulting clients.

Multifamily properties offer stable predictable cash flow because your income comes from many tenants. They offer a definite advantage over single-family properties. If you lose a tenant in a single-family rental you've lost 100% of the revenue for that investment property.

But don't forget. The song of the siren is irresistibly sweet. Greek mythology says that if you don't hear the song you can outwit the siren. You can play a sweeter song, one that drowns the voice of the siren, by following these tips:

Adhere to tight tenant screening policies

Good tenants equal stable predictable cash flow.

Establish solid tenant screening policies, put your policies in writing and make sure your team follows them to the letter. Include the following:

- All new residents complete a tenant application.
- Tenant references are checked including with current landlord.
- Prospective tenants meet income guidelines.
- Criminal and credit reports are pulled.
- Legal judgments such as court ordered evictions or payment delinquencies are verified.
- The application includes the resident's rental history.

Pro tip: Have an attorney review your tenant screening policies for compliance with local landlord-tenant and fair housing laws.

Make sure your lease renewal policies are in place

Establish a routine for tracking pending lease expiration dates. When a tenant is up for lease renewal contact the tenant to discuss their intentions of renewing their lease. Set a schedule for contacting each tenant with a renewing lease at least 60 days before the lease expiration date.

If your tenant does not plan to renew their lease, schedule a thorough make ready inspection of the unit. Make ready inspections will help you plan and budget for unit turn costs. It's also an opportunity to make some improvements to the unit that might allow you to command higher rents. Also, there's always the possibility that your visit with your resident may uncover issues you can address. A good tenant may decide not to move after all.

Stagger your rental unit lease expiration dates

To stagger leases simply means that your leases do not all renew at the same time. Monitor your pending lease expiration dates and make a plan to have tenant leases renew throughout the entire year. This will help you keep the number of vacancies at a low at any given time.

Keep in mind that you may not want leases renewing during times of low rental activity. During the holidays most prospective residents are not looking to find new lodging. In cold weather climates, January and February see slower leasing activity.

If you're currently stuck with a large number of units with the same lease expiration date you can address the issue as you turn units. For example, when a unit becomes available, suggest that your new tenant sign an 8-

month lease today and renew for a 12-month period at their next renewal date.

Offer incentives if necessary, for shortened lease terms. Give your signing tenant a discount on the first month's rent or agree to keep the renewing 12-month lease at the same rental amount. It's good business to invest a little money to avoid having a large number of vacancies at the same time.

Avoid tenant collection issues

Collection problems are the number one killer of cash flow. When your tenants aren't paying rent, you're not making deposits. Multifamily properties are communities. If word gets around that you're not enforcing rent due dates and late payment fees the problem will grow.

Establish strict payment policies and discuss payment terms with each lessee so there is no confusion. Be sure to outline your policies in your lease agreement and enforce those terms. No exceptions. It's your job to rent to residents who can afford to live at your property. It's not your responsibility to make exceptions for tenants who fall behind.

Post notices to evict as soon as a resident fails to pay rent when due. Payment plans can work to get a tenant caught up but, in my experience, once a tenant falls behind in payments, they rarely get whole again.

Track your local real estate market

Smart multifamily investors stay on top of what the competition is doing, and they plan for contingencies. Keep an eye on what the competition is offering in terms of rent, leasing bonuses and concessions such as free rent, waived deposit fees and utilities charges.

Spend some time on craigslist.com, zillow.com, and apartments.com to track the other multifamily properties in your immediate rental market. You don't want to discover that rental prices have fallen in your market and you've lost residents because you were unaware of rental trends.

And if rental rates are on the rise? Good to know, isn't it?

Know your renovation costs and ability to pay

Major capital improvements and expensive property repairs have a way of eliminating cash flow. Planning for long-term capital expenditures allows you to stagger the improvements over time.

An annual operating budget will help you with

- capital improvements planning and projections
- establishing performance targets for your property
- setting aside some of your cash flow for replacement reserves

With careful planning, multifamily properties will offer years of stable predictable cash flow. It's one of the benefits of having a large number of residents paying rent for the privilege of living in your property.

How to Create Revenue in Your Multifamily Property

When was the last time you had a conversation with your property management company or yourself about raising the rent on your rental units? What was your goal? Increased revenue? A desire to see improvements to cash flow?

I have good news. When you start talking about ways to create revenue in your multifamily property, you're on the path to success.

You might be surprised at how many multifamily property investors do nothing but collect the rent and occasionally glance at the profit and loss statements. I want to be sure you do more than that. The best way to be sure you're not leaving money on the table is to create and implement new and creative revenue generating resources.

Don't become complacent with your vendor contracts

Put in the effort to make sure that you are still getting the best deal on your insurance, janitorial, trash, landscaping and other vendor contracts each year and make a switch when needed in order to improve your revenue.

Let your vendors and service providers know that you will review their fees and services annually. Also, that you will be shopping around and comparing them to the competition. Don't make this an idle "threat." Put your annual review process on your calendar and do it.

Your reviews should cover your providers of:

- Insurance
- Trash removal
- Pest control
- Cleaning
- Property management
- Leasing
- Marketing
- New and refurbished appliances
- Carpet and flooring replacement or repair
- Laundry leasing
- All third-party skilled maintenance providers for painting, electric and plumbing, HVAC, etc.

Pro tip: This is also a great opportunity to get input from your providers on ways to lower costs and streamline services. They may have ideas you never thought of.

Be sure to review any third-party leases the sellers may have signed with a laundry vendor (or any other vendors). Are you locked into a long-term lease for washers and dryers? Are you better off buying your own laundry appliances? Pay special attention to revenue sources where you split the proceeds with a third party.

Change your offer to prospective residents

When was the last time you or your team studied local market rents and concessions? Can you:

471

- Raise rents?
- Decrease rental concessions? (Concessions are enticements to new tenants such as free lease signing bonuses, a reduction in rent or security deposit or other perks that decrease property revenue.)

Ancillary income: add new amenities, services and fees

You might be sitting on a gold mine of untapped revenue sources. Consider charging fees for:

- Parking
- Storage units
- Whole building WiFi
- Recycling programs
- Bike storage
- Pet rent
- Late rent payment
- Community events
- NSF

Install your own vending machines and coin-operated laundry

Don't underestimate the earning potential of laundry machines on the premises. These not only generate constant income, but they can also entice new tenants to move in because of their convenience. The same goes for vending machines. They are a great source of additional income without too much extra work.

You might also consider renting common areas for special uses such as parties or even leasing your rooftop to the local cable or telecommunication companies for installation of communication towers.

Implement new leasing policies

Your operations policies should include lease expiration and unit turn management. You'll increase revenue by decreasing the time a rental unit sits vacant.

- Stagger lease expiration dates and keep vacancies to minimum
- Implement a system for contacting residents 60 days prior to least expiration
- Streamline the make-ready process
- Establish pre-leasing strategies for upcoming vacancies
- Offer incentives to your leasing team for new and renewing leases

Implement proactive maintenance policies

Catch potential problems early. Establish a regular property inspection schedule of:

- Rental units (occupied and unoccupied)
- Common areas (indoor and outdoor)
- Major building mechanicals (roof, boiler, HVAC, etc.)

Pro tip: A simple proactive fix can often eliminate expensive repairs down the line.

Utilities and green building practices

Today's residents are looking for properties with the latest green building practices. Not only will new systems increase revenues through lower costs and rebates they can be implemented in your marketing strategies.

- Implement a Ratio Utility Billing System (RUBS)
- Install energy efficient building systems such as a Durolast reflective roofing system
- Install energy efficient windows
- Cover windows with awnings to lower heating and cooling expenses (this is a great way to improve curb appeal)
- Install energy efficient lighting
- Take advantage of ENERGY STAR products and rebates

Consider charging pet fees

Pet fees can be a great source of additional income as most owners consider them to be a part of the family and actively look for complexes where pets are allowed. Either a one-time pet fee or a monthly pet fee can make a big difference to the revenue from your apartment complex.

Add a valet garbage service

Adding a doorstep garbage valet service such as Trash Butler (trashbutler.com) for the apartment complex not only helps to keep the property clean and improve curb appeal, but it can also help to improve your bottom line. Residents will appreciate the convenience, and it is also a great marketing tool to differentiate your complex from those of the competitors.

Sell advertising space

There is a lot of ancillary income to be made from blank space by selling it to advertisers. Just make sure that when common areas, laundry rooms, elevators or the sides of buildings are used for advertising, you don't annoy renters by going overboard.

Look into parking costs

Premium parking and electric car ports are services that many renters would gladly pay extra for. You can even rent out bike racks for tenants to store their bikes in a covered, secure area instead of taking up space in their homes.

The bottom line is that there are usually multiple ways to generate new revenue at your apartment complex while still providing value to your residents. This makes it a win-win situation for everyone involved, without the backlash that comes with simply raising rent prices.

Your number one job as a real estate investor

You've got to constantly stay in the conversation about how to implement new ideas for increased revenue. You can't just visit the topic once a year.

Whether you manage your property yourself or a third-party management company does it for you, operations policies that affect the bottom line must be implemented and monitored constantly. A monthly review is a great idea.

Be creative. Raising the rent is one thing, finding new sources of income can be more of a challenge. Seasoned real estate investors continually challenge themselves and their team members to come up with new ideas, policies and ways to implement changes to operations.

Best Places to Find Free Landlord Rental Forms

Whether you are renting apartments or single-family residences, you need to use a written contract and forms. There are several forms you should have on hand at all times. These include, but are not limited to, lease application forms, lease agreements, lease renewal notices, notices to vacate, eviction notices, and receipts for any payments received.

There are many sources for finding free forms, such as your local library, real estate agents, and your real estate investment club or professional association. And state real estate commissions forms are often available online.

You want contracts and rental forms to be as concise as possible while still containing essential terms that protect you and your property. The purpose of contracts is to avoid any misunderstandings. The landlord and tenant relationship is not an adversarial relationship. You want your residents to also feel that they are protected and appreciated in the agreement.

Professional associations

Start with this group when thinking about forms and where to source them. Experienced landlords will have insight on paperwork and often-overlooked clauses that you will not think of until the need arises. These professional associations also provide publications to assist with tenant issues and help you remain in compliance with all laws pertaining to landlords and tenants.

Real estate brokers

You should already have an established relationship with a few agents who specialize in rental properties. These real estate brokers have access to standard landlord forms and other useful publications through the National Association of Realtors (NAR). Contract requirements vary by state. They should be familiar with the content of these forms and know from past experience any additional terms that should be added such as policies for drugs on premises or other illegal activities.

Your attorney

Using these standard forms is perfectly legal and binding to all parties. You may still wish to create your own lease agreement, which can include your company name and specific clauses pertaining to your properties. It is well worth paying your attorney to draft such a contract. Your attorney will be sure the contract includes all necessary disclosures and complies with the laws for your area.

Be sure you have thoroughly read any form you plan to use. You want to be prepared to answer any questions tenants may have and address any concerns. You do not want to frighten away good tenants with numerous pages of fine print. Give them adequate time to read all required forms before signing.

The execution of a lease agreement should be the beginning of a long-term, mutually beneficial relationship for you and your tenants. Take the time to get it right so you can start off on the right foot.

The Importance of Performing a Rent Survey

To ensure your continued success as a real estate investor, you must know that you are making the maximum available profit from each of your properties. One of the best tools for doing this is a rent survey. It should be done on any new property and as a part of managing the properties you currently own.

In addition to telling you the current rental rates for the area, it can give you occupancy rates, identify which features are attracting tenants, and indicate where the rental rates for the area are heading in the foreseeable future. A rent comparability study is an essential part of determining the value of a property you are considering for purchase.

Rent surveys by appraisal companies

Rent surveys are typically completed by an appraisal company because a thorough rent survey is needed for assessing the inherent worth of a rental property. You want to be sure you use the services of an appraisal company that has extensive experience in rent surveys on your type of property and that they know the area. Collecting and compiling the necessary information for a thorough and reliable survey is not easy. You need someone who knows what they are doing.

Here are some of the variables that will go into a rent survey:

- **Rent:** Average rent for the market area and the current demand for rentals.
- **Typical lease duration:** The amount of time you can expect a tenant to rent your property is key to knowing the amount of rent you can expect.
- **Assumptions and disregards:** This applies to commercial rental properties. For the purpose of the rent survey, the assumption is a clause stating something assumed to exist with a hypothetical tenant. The disregard is something that will not be taken into consideration when determining the rental value, such as any improvements made to the property by the tenant.
- **Type of property:** The rent of a property will vary based on whether the property is used for commercial or residential purposes.
- **Anchor tenant:** Another vital aspect is whether or not there is an anchor tenant that will attract customers to the location, who will then be shopping at other stores in the same location. You'll find this variable in mixed-use multifamily properties.

DIY rent surveys

Some investors complete their own rent surveys on apartments and residential rentals by collecting the data themselves and inputting the information into a spreadsheet for comparison. If you do the rent survey yourself, be sure you are comparing truly comparable properties.

You may want to enlist the services of a local Realtor or broker who specializes in rental property to obtain the information and help you with the survey.

Market trends and research can also be found at:

- The National Apartment Association (naahq.org)
- Your local housing authority
- Investment advisory brokerage firms such as Berkadia (berkadiarea.com), JLL (us.jll.com) and IRR (irr.com)
- National Multifamily Housing Council (nmhc.org)
- Paid data and analytic services like the Urban Land Institute (uli.org), Axiometrics (axiometrics.com) and CoreLogic (corelogic.com)

For excellent regional information take a look at:

- RealPage (realpage.com)
- National Association of Realtors (realtor.org)
- Zillow (zillow.com)

An online search will bring up additional resources. Try a search that is specific to your investment market or property location.

Don't Run Afoul of Fair Housing Laws

You probably already know it is against the Fair Housing Laws to discriminate against potential tenants due to their race, gender, and age. However, you should know that the Fair Housing Act of 1968 and the later amendments cover several protected classes and categories of people. To avoid any accidental violations of Fair Housing Laws, you need to be familiar with how these laws cover your entire relationship with all potential renters and active renters. This includes everything from advertising to managing your rental units.

Family status

This is one of the most common ways landlords unintentionally run afoul of Fair Housing Laws. You can't discriminate against any renters based on whether or not they have children, are pregnant, or may be trying to adopt. Actions that may be considered discrimination include declining to rent to tenants with children, charging a higher deposit, or limiting children's access to common areas.

You also are prohibited from putting families with children on certain floors or otherwise isolating them. Be mindful that saying things like, "You may enjoy living in an area with more children better," or "These units are best suited for adults," are considered verbal violations and are actionable.

Disability or handicap

The Fair Housing Act protects people with mental or physical impairment. Additionally, the law stipulates that landlords must make reasonable accommodations for individuals with a handicap, those with past disabilities, and those who are perceived by others to have a handicap.

For a house rental, the tenant must pay for modifications themselves and return the house to its original condition prior to moving out. As a landlord, you must allow service animals regardless of your existing pet policy if they meet the following three criteria: the person must have a disability, the animal must serve a function related to the disability, and the request to allow the animal must be reasonable.

Gender

It is very easy to unintentionally discriminate against tenants based on gender. If you decline to show a rental property to a woman because you don't feel it is a safe place for her to live, you are violating Fair Housing. There is an exception for renting a room with a shared living space. While the Fair Housing Act does not specifically cover sexual orientation and gender identity as protected, it may still be covered by the Fair Housing Act.

It is crucial to be familiar with the Fair Housing Laws if you want to avoid problems. You should also read your state's laws to be sure you are in compliance with them.

Pro tip: Hire a landlord/tenant attorney who specializes in your local area. Have them review your tenant documents, especially your lease agreement, and all tenant screening and eviction practices. This attorney can also handle your tenant evictions.

When Do You Really Need a Pet Policy?

People really love their pets in the US. In fact, the American Veterinary Medical Foundation reports that 36.5 percent of American households have at least one dog, and just over 30 percent own at least one cat.

At one point as an investment property owner, you will have to decide whether to allow your tenants to have pets. While pets can definitely pose a damage risk, permitting residents to have them can attract more tenants who are willing to pay a higher rent for the privilege. If you're going to go the pet route, you need to have a policy in place to protect your property and set out the responsibilities for those animals for your tenants. You might consider requiring a pet damage deposit.

Your pet policy musts

Any pet policy you use must spell out the type of animals allowed, the responsibilities of the owner, and any other conditions you've set. Make sure all your terms are permitted under any applicable federal, state and local laws. Note that different regulations apply to service animals because they're not considered pets and shouldn't be banned by your pet policy.

A good policy will spell out what types of animals are allowed and how many are permitted per unit. Obtain information about the animal from the tenant so you have a profile that includes its current vaccinations and any applicable license status.

One requirement worth considering is only allowing spayed or neutered animals when it comes to cats and dogs. The Humane Society of the United States says that spayed and neutered animals are less likely to roam, howl, spray or urinate to mark territory, behaviors that could lead to problems and repair expenses for you as the property owner.

Check with your insurer

Some insurance companies won't cover certain dog breeds, such as Pit Bulls, Rottweilers and Doberman Pinschers. These dogs are viewed as dangerous by the insurer, so if you're in that situation, you may want to limit what breeds you accept in your rentals. While you may not be liable for harm to someone else caused by a tenant's dog, there is no guarantee, and you shouldn't open yourself up to any potential lawsuits.

Ultimately, a clear pet policy can save you a lot of time and trouble. Create yours today if you're allowing or going to be allowing pets on your properties, and make sure you apply it equally across the board.

Creative Apartment Operations Hacks for Multifamily Property Owners

Running an apartment community is no easy task. The size of your multifamily portfolio will dictate apartment operations policies and how many employees and contractors are needed to do the job. It takes a full team including the property manager, leasing staff, and maintenance crew who must all work in harmony to keep your tenants happy and your property in great condition.

One item all apartment communities have in common are the challenges that management encounters during day-to-day apartment operations. Here are the top topics that plague property owners and managers, along with easy tips and solutions to tackling those problems.

Apartment crime

Instances of community and neighborhood crime can drive away prospective renters. As more and more prospective residents scan online reviews, they are making decisions about the safety of a property before their first visit. How many leases are lost due to crime?

It's a fantastic idea for you, or your manager, to search online reviews for your property on a regular basis. Often, you can correct online reviews that might be plaguing your community.

There are many different types of crime that can occur on your property. Here are some to watch out for:

- Car break-ins
- Domestic violence
- Property damage
- Apartment break-ins

Start by getting a local police department premise report on your property. A premise history will help you decide which steps to take to rectify criminal activity. For instance, if your property has a high amount of car break-ins, adding additional lighting in dark areas might deter burglars.

Resident complaints

Property owners and managers must act quickly and judicially when residents lodge complaints. You cannot willingly pick sides. Your standard response to resident complaints must be clearly covered in your apartment operations policies. And you must consistently adhere to those guidelines.

Complaints often cause inefficiencies, interrupt the daily flow of work in the leasing office, and can cause morale to drop. Residents most commonly complain about:

- Repairs
- Noise
- Rent increases
- Security deposit refunds

A good solution is to add tenant exit surveys to your apartment operations policies. Exiting residents are quick to point out any complaints they may have. A tenant exit survey will show you how you can improve on the experience for your remaining tenants. If response rates are low, offer some sort of giveaway.

Resource alert: See our sample tenant exit survey in Chapter Twenty: Tenant Retention and also in our resource document at: theresabradleybanta.com/book_resources.

A revolving door of staff

A property manager certainly has a multitude of duties overseeing apartment operations. Bringing in income, interacting with staff, and making sure that everything is in place so residents' expectations are satisfied, are just a few of the tasks at hand.

Turnover among leasing staff and maintenance technicians are also a potential problem. There is a cost to constantly retraining staff.

Maintenance

As apartments age and wear down through the normal wear and tear residents place upon them, repairs are seemingly never ending.

Maintenance covers a wide range of topics. Repairs will vary depending on which part of the country your community is located. For example, according to Terminix (terminix.com), the southeast region of the United States is most susceptible to termite infestation. Apartment owners should hire a company that tests and treats accordingly if applicable.

Newer apartment complexes are outfitted with more technology and social spaces with media rooms and computers. Of course, this requires more staff training and potential repairs. Some of the areas where you can expect repairs are:

- Heating and air conditioning systems
- Plumbing (clogs, leaks)
- Pools
- Elevators
- Computers and other building-wide technologies (WiFi, smart locks, security systems, etc.)
- Fitness centers

Make sure you, your staff and property managers are properly trained. Your apartment operations policies should include a preventative maintenance plan. Managers may also want to consider earning their Cam credentials.

Declining neighborhoods

Not necessarily a product of apartment operations, but equally important, is location. Less fortunate or economically disadvantaged parts of town will generate some of the lowest prices per square foot. Apartment buildings have a long shelf life. It's common for certain areas to be gentrified while others are left to fend for themselves. If you are in the former group, you'll be able to reap huge profits in such cases.

However, your property may see falling rents if it's located in a declining area. You often have tough choices to make that might include selling or potentially remodeling your property. Also, properties that are located in poor neighborhoods may be subject to a higher crime rate.

Chapter Eighteen:
Maintenance

Don't start today by doing yesterday's work.
– Deniece Schofield

~

What are Typical Apartment Building Operating Expenses?

"How do I know if a deal is a good one or not?" I hear this question more than any other. But this question is almost impossible to accurately answer without:

- Detailed property operating income and expenses.
- Comprehensive capital expenditure projections.

Let's talk about expenses.

The apartment building listing brochure

Apartment building offering memorandums typically list property operating expenses in general, broad categories such as:

- Insurance
- Property Management
- Property Taxes
- Utilities
- Repair and Maintenance
- Administrative

As I said, these are fairly broad categories. Until you get your hands on the seller's historical profit and loss numbers—a.k.a. APOD or annual property operating data— it's almost impossible to get an exact understanding of the property. And it's your job to get this information.

Your bank or lender will want to see historical cash flow figures for the property going back at least one year, preferably two. And so should you. How do you get them? Simple. Ask for them. Don't take "no" for an answer. When I analyze deals, I ask to see these numbers up front. Before I agree to a property showing and before I consider making an offer.

Hidden expense numbers

The problem with broadly categorized property expenses is that you cannot drill down to specific costs. Without itemized line item expenses, you can miss red flags. And some expenses can be left out completely.

For example, the simple category "Utilities will include:

- Gas,
- Electric,
- Water,

- Sewer and,
- Trash (sometimes included in utilities).

Without line item expenses it's almost impossible to knowledgeably analyze a deal. And to accurately assess potential problems and opportunities.

Operate from a good baseline

When I look at properties in any market, I analyze at least five similar deals to the one I'm interested in purchasing. This gives me a good baseline for typical property expenses. For example, when I see an atypically high cost for "water" I know I need to investigate further. This could be a red flag for serious plumbing issues.

But without a baseline I might completely miss the water bill is high in comparison to similar properties.

Here's another example. The price for pest control is often included under the "repair and maintenance" category. Pest control is a common property operating expense, but the cost is typically fairly low. An unusually high cost for service could be a red flag for a serious problem such as bed bugs, which can infest an entire property. Bed bugs are becoming more and more common. Even five-star hotels and new Class A apartment buildings can—and do—become infested.

Again, without historical numbers and a baseline to compare expenses to, you might miss noticing an abnormally high pest control number.

Always get a property's historical operating data

As I've already said, always, always use the T12 historical annual property operating data when analyzing properties. I cannot emphasize this enough. It is not enough to rely on the broadly categorized expenses presented by a seller or by a commercial broker.

Unexpected apartment building operating and renovation expenses

As a new apartment building owner, you will incur unexpected expenses. That's a promise. It's almost impossible to foresee every eventuality. You might simply overlook an expense. That happens. But with some practice analyzing deals—as many as you can—you will be become more educated and less likely to miss something.

Until you become proficient with property analysis, work with a multifamily mentor or apartment building owner/operator to analyze any deal you are considering making an offer on.

Resource alert: You'll find a spreadsheet with sample operating expenses in our resource document at: theresabradleybanta.com/book_resources.

Common Areas Maintenance and Management Tips

As the owner of a multifamily property, you have plenty of things to keep up with–including maintaining the common areas. Do you know what's really necessary to take care of the common areas on your property? Who's responsible for it? Equally importantly, can you find a way to profit from that basic maintenance?

Knowing how to effectively manage maintenance on your property, including those common areas, can help set you up to manage your property more successfully.

Why maintain common areas?

Common areas of your multifamily dwelling are the areas that are used by everyone, rather than belonging to a specific unit. These might include the pool or clubhouse but can also include hallways and stairwells exterior to the units.

In short, a common area is any area that is used by more than one family of tenants. The maintenance of common areas is critical for five key reasons.

1. **It's the law!** In Colorado (and most other states), you must provide a habitable space for your residents, including safe, secure premises that do not compromise the safety of the residents.

2. **Keeps everyone safe:** Regular maintenance helps provide for the safety and security of residents, staff, and visitors.

3. **You'll avoid fines and unnecessary exposure to liability:** Because of your legal liability as a landlord, you can receive fines from the city and the state if you don't keep up with maintenance on your property. Not only that, you may face expensive legal bills if, for example, a resident has a trip and fall accident on poorly lit stairs.

4. **Extends the life expectancy of your carpet and flooring:** It just lasts longer when you take the time to maintain it! Dirt in your carpet wears away at the fibers, so each step on dirty carpeting can decrease its life expectancy.

5. **Delivers better leasing and marketing results and increases your overall profit:** Let's face it. The way the outside of an apartment complex looks matters. Potential tenants start forming an opinion of the property long before they actually look in an open unit. If you want great curb appeal and better renters, take the time to fix up those common areas!

What are common areas in your building?

In your multifamily complex, you may have several different common areas. As you're planning maintenance, consider:

- Exterior walkways
- Community gardens
- The parking lot and carports
- Laundry facilities
- Mail areas
- Package and storage rooms
- Community areas, including clubhouses
- Courtyards
- Corridors, halls, and stairwells
- Entryways
- Decks and railings
- Pools
- Lighting

- Doors
- Elevators
- The barbecue, fire pit, or grill in a social gathering area
- Trash disposal and recycling areas

Typical common area maintenance expenses

When you're focused on providing a high quality of maintenance for your tenants, you may have a number of expenses that need to factor into your operating budget. Make sure you're including these common area maintenance expenses:

Repair and maintenance: You'll need to keep everything clean and tidy and take care of any repairs necessary throughout the year. Previous maintenance records will give you a better idea of what it will cost to maintain those areas in the future. If the building is new to you, you should also consider how well-maintained previous owners kept those areas. If you plan to offer more maintenance for your residents, your costs may increase.

Snow removal: Contact local snow removal companies and ask about the expense of maintaining your parking lots, sidewalks, and other outdoor common areas.

Utilities in the common areas: Tenants need clear, safe lighting in common areas. As the landlord, it's your duty to provide that lighting. You'll also need to consider common area utility expenses such as:

- Water for the pool, fountains, community bathrooms, laundry room equipment, sprinkler systems and landscaping

- Electric and gas for heating and air conditioning

Trash and recycling removal: In most multifamily dwellings, the landlord takes on the cost of removing waste from the premises. Look for a provider that will take care of both trash and recycling, ideally with minimal restrictions. For example, will your provider take away large furniture and other items that might not fit in the dumpster? What about brush that builds up outside?

HVAC maintenance: You must heat and cool your common areas; or, you might use a large unit to run the entire building. Regular HVAC maintenance can help you avoid expensive repair costs.

Janitorial and housekeeping services: Who takes care of cleaning up, whether you've just had a community event, or the carpets are simply in need of a quick vacuum? Employing housekeeping services will keep your complex looking its best.

Insurance and taxes: Insurance on your building can help pay for expensive repairs. And of course, you'll owe property taxes every year.

Security systems: Providing security can help increase the safety of your residents as well as increasing the overall quality of the residents in your building.

Pest control: Don't rely on tenants to take care of pest control themselves! Instead, make sure you include pest control to keep bugs and mice to a minimum.

Property signage and door numbering: Make it easy for visitors, residents and emergency responders alike to tell exactly where they need to go.

Staff and service providers: For some large complexes, you may need to employ people or companies specifically for tasks like housekeeping, maintenance and repair, laundry room servicing, inspections, and exterior window and building cleaning.

Do not ignore these key common area requirements

As you calculate your maintenance costs and complete your common area management planning, pay special attention to the following:

- **Cleanliness and curb appeal:** You only get to make a first impression once!
- **Disability access:** Make sure the building is up to code!
- **Building code compliance:** Everything from adequate lighting in stairways to an appropriate number of unblocked exit doors can help you avoid expensive fines.
- **Emergency procedures:** Make sure everyone in the building knows what to do in the event of an emergency–and that you're taking any necessary steps to protect your residents.

Saving money on your investment

As you consider your property, make sure you're taking the necessary steps to save yourself–and your tenants–a little money.

Try some of these key tips:

- Source vendors who offer volume discounts

- Set up a plan for long-term capital improvements and sustainable initiatives–one that fits your income flow
- Hire an on-site manager to help take care of these tasks for you
- Reduce operating costs and save energy by implementing green strategies throughout your building
- Create and implement a preventative maintenance schedule
- Write a property operation manual and include standardized maintenance practices

Pro tip: Maintaining your building is one of the most important parts of being a landlord. Fortunately, with this guide, you can make it easier to include all of the important elements.

Preventative Maintenance Planning

One of the best ways to keep tenants happy is to quickly repair items that are reported as broken or damaged. However, it is also vital to avoid operating solely from a reactive position. On many occasions, repairs are avoidable when adhering to a preventative maintenance plan. Without such a plan in place, the cost of repairs or replacements can quickly mount.

A preventative maintenance plan involves replacing items instead of simply using a temporary fix. Although this can be more expensive in the short term, it will safeguard you against avoidable big-ticket expenses.

Common areas

The appearance of the common areas on your property can greatly affect prospective tenants' perception. Inspect all common areas including parking lots, halls, entryways, entertainment centers, mailrooms and storage rooms weekly.

Repair any damaged flooring or sidewalks immediately and check exterior walls for any damage. Check the signage to ensure that it is clean and visible at all times. Check that all machinery for communal use, such as the pool pump and washing machines, is working properly.

Lawn, trees and vegetation

For trees and vegetation, keep an eye on branches and root growth. Trim branches before they become a hazard to the building or power lines. Roots should also be monitored because they can result in costly repaving if the overgrowth goes under concrete surfaces.

Check that the water drainage system is functioning properly and kept clear of debris or vegetation. Inspect the irrigation system weekly and replace irrigation heads when needed.

Lighting and electrical

Regular inspection of fixtures will ensure that the light quality of the property remains high and that proper energy savings are maintained. You should also be on the lookout for overloaded or damaged sockets as these can turn into fire hazards.

Individual unit inspections

Carry out regular individual unit inspections once every three to six months. Check that the plumbing, lights, electricity, HVAC system, smoke detectors, carbon monoxide detectors and gas meters are all functioning properly. Be sure to also check the gas meters, gas lines and valves to ensure that there are no leaks.

Seasonal maintenance

Certain maintenance tasks must be scheduled for certain seasons, such as ordering snow melt in time for winter. Get exterminators to the property once or twice a year to keep them free of pests. Check the roofing before and after the rainy season and winter. Ensure that all gutters and rails are cleared to prevent blockages or leaks.

Improper maintenance can result in safety hazards for tenants and also damage the property, so the sooner a proper preventative maintenance plan is set in place, the better off you will be. Adopting a wait-and-see approach might save some money over the short term, but it will inevitably result in serious financial repercussions later.

How to Conduct a Thorough Property Inspection

If you use a third-party management company to oversee operations at your multifamily property—or even if you manage it yourself—it's a good idea to conduct a physical property inspection every six months.

Depending on the size of your property, a walk-through should take you no more than 60 minutes.

During your property inspection examine:

- All common areas
- Model units
- Leasing office
- Storage and mechanical rooms
- Parking lots and structures
- Rooftop(s) (don't skip this)
- Front and back stairs
- Front and back entryways
- Hallways
- Laundry

Walk the entire property inside and out. Make arrangements with your on-site or third-party manager to see the inside of several rental units, too. This is something that should be scheduled in advance, as the residents will need proper notice of your brief visit.

What do you look for during a property inspection?

As you walk the common areas take note of the following:

- Is the property clean?
- Do you notice any funny odors?
- Are the common areas in good repair or in need of a refresh?

Also determine if you are in compliance with local ordinances and life safety requirements. For example, your inspection should include life safety systems such as:

- **Smoke and CO detectors:** Are units installed in all common areas and rental units? Are they regularly checked?
- **Exit signs:** Are they working and properly located?

If you are the owner manager, put on your property manager hat so that you can inspect the property from an unbiased, receptive point of view. If you were your own boss would you keep yourself on the job? Or would you give yourself the boot?

Multifamily property inspection checklist:

- Janitorial and housekeeping are doing a good job. The property is clean and common areas are free of obstruction.
- Lawn and landscaping are regularly maintained and free of trash and debris.
- Appropriate indoor and exterior security lighting exists in halls, laundry, mail, entry/exits, parking, pool and all other common areas (indoor and outdoor).
- Exit signs and egress are clearly marked and in working order.
- CO detectors are installed in all units. Verify working condition and establish a schedule for testing and inspections.
- Fire extinguisher inspection and testing is current and future inspections are scheduled.
- Disability access is ADA compliant (Americans with Disabilities Act)

- Common area doors and windows are properly secured.
- Entry doors remain locked at all times.
- Mechanical/boiler room doors remain locked at all times.
- Hallways and stairwells are clear of obstruction.
- Emergency vehicle access/fire lane is clearly marked.
- Verify working condition and establish scheduled testing and inspections of:
  - Secure entryway system
  - Domestic hot water system
  - Boiler system
  - Plumbing
  - Electric
  - HVAC (heating, ventilation, and air conditioning)
  - Roof
- Laundry room is regularly cleaned. Washers and dryers are properly serviced; lint screens are checked on an established schedule.
- Mailroom/mailboxes have working locks, the tenant names are clearly visible, and the room is regularly cleaned of junk mail and trash.
- Elevator has a regularly scheduled maintenance check and the logbook is current and up to date.
- Storage room is securely locked with no improperly stored flammable or hazardous materials.
- Pool area has non-slip surfaces, is properly gated, the rules and regulations are visibly posted. There are no improperly stored flammable or hazardous materials.
- Boiler/mechanical rooms are securely locked with no improperly stored flammable or hazardous materials.
- Ensure all mechanical systems are property labeled.

- Master keys access (locked key box) has been granted only to authorized personnel and is locked and secure at all times.
- Trash dumpsters are properly located and emptied on a schedule that assures the area remains clear of debris and overflowing trash at all times.
- Barbeques, fire pits and grills are compliant with local ordinance.
- Pest control inspections and preventative treatments are regularly scheduled.
- Property signage is visible and provides contact information for property management and leasing offices.
- Street address numbers are clearly visible to emergency services.
- Resident doors are clearly labeled with unit numbers.
- Establish and map access to crawl spaces, roof, storage, plumbing systems, main water shut off, utility meters, outdoor lighting and sprinkler controls, mechanical rooms and master keys.
- View property with an eye to structural integrity. Look for signs of shifting, cracks, uneven surfaces, etc.
- Power washing, window and blinds cleaning and general building envelope upkeep is scheduled.
- Loitering rules are enforced.
- Decks and railings are properly secure.
- Bulletin board postings are in compliance with rules and usage guidelines.
- Asphalt/sidewalks, parking curbs and line painting are in good condition.

Pro tip: While it might be tempting to assign the multifamily property inspection checklist to someone on your team, think twice about doing that. You've invested a lot of money in your real estate portfolio. It's your job to manage your asset and to manage the managers. Don't become complacent over time. Put your inspections on your calendar in advance and keep those appointments.

Resource alert: If you like operations checklists (and who doesn't?) you'll find a complete multifamily operations checklist in our resource document at: theresabradleybanta.com/book_resources.

How to Ensure a Cool & Safe Summer for Your Residents!

In between seasons is a perfect time to get ready for the extreme temperatures of summer. With some preparation and few energy efficiencies tips you can be ready for a cool drink under a shady umbrella in no time.

Information is key

Let's get the worst possible summer situations out of the way first. As the weather warms up your residents need to know what to do in case of a weather emergency. Depending on your geographical region, hurricanes and tornados are summer events. Often there is little advanced warning, so clarity is vital. The best way to avoid panic is to know exactly where to go and what to do.

- Inform your residents how to prepare ahead of time.
- Tell them where to go during the event.
- Let them know what cautionary measures to take after the event.

You'll find resources for handling emergencies at your property in Chapter Twenty-One: Life Safety.

Summer A/C test run

Have a professional run a basic maintenance on your A/C unit(s) now so that they will be ready when you are starting to sweat. We all know summer cooling costs are expensive.

Appliances and equipment in multifamily buildings can save you money each year or add to the utility bills. Energy Star labels are an easy way to identify energy efficient units.

The yellow Energy Guide labels also detail yearly operating cost and electricity use for appliances. Make sure your appliances are set up properly to save you money in the long run.

Here are some year-round energy saving tips:

- Equip apartments with programmable thermostats.
- Set the water heating system to 15-120°F.
- Do not position dishwashers next to refrigerators.
- Properly maintain systems with annual inspections.
- Make repairs quickly.
- Replace outdated components.

Check your windows

Insulation will save you money in the winter and the summer. Caulking and weather-stripping are effective methods of sealing for air leaks. Check caulking around the door and window frames.

You can apply Low-Emissivity Film (Low-E film) a product that can be applied to windows to block 97% of UV rays. This effectively keeps heat out during summer. In the winter months the film helps to retain heat in homes.

The materials used for the framing and windows themselves will impact the energy efficiency of your building. When it comes time to replace windows, purchase windows that have low-e, double glazing and/or insulated frames.

Increase air flow

If you don't have ceiling fans you might want to consider installing them. Check that your ceiling fans are turning counterclockwise. The blades are tilted upward as they spin to push air downward and create stronger air flow. In winter you will want the ceiling fan to rotate clockwise so the warm air that collects at the top of the room gets circulated. A win-win.

How can your residents help stay cool?

There are recommendations you can make to your residents, especially in urban areas that are prone to black outs during the summer months. Skip the washing machine's heat dry cycle and air-dry dishes instead. Also, line-drying your clothes can save a lot of energy and is so easy to do during the summer months.

Try to limit usage of all heat-producing appliances like the dryer, dish dryer, stove, or oven. Encourage residents to use big appliances at night when it won't be necessary to increase the A/C in a temperature competition.

Everything runs more smoothly when you plan ahead. Prepare your residents for possible weather-related emergencies. Look for ways to save money in the long-term on energy efficient appliances. Insulate to conserve cool A/C air this summer and heat this the winter.

Now get your patio umbrella out of storage and you are ready for that cool drink! Can you work while relaxing in your lounge chair? Yes!

The Complete Fall Maintenance Checklist

Managing a multifamily property is all about planning. With the right fall maintenance plans in place, emergencies are either dealt with swiftly or are prevented before they can happen. You make plans through your vendor leases and agreements, your maintenance schedule, and with the seasons themselves.

The fall is an important time to pay attention to your multifamily property. As the cold weather blows in, there are a few things you'll want to take care of both in terms of fall maintenance and business management.

Leasing & marketing

The holidays are a tough time to find new residents. If that's going to happen, you want to know ahead of time. In the fall, you'll want to check on all resident lease dates and send renewal notices to those whose leases end during the holidays. This way, you'll get a clearer idea of who is staying and if you'll need to tackle holiday tenant turnover.

If you do have residents leaving in the fall, now is when you want to start marketing for a new tenant. Prospects are thinner in the winter so getting started early is the best possible plan. Be ready to do your between-tenant work lightning fast or, if a unit does stand empty for a while, consider any pending renovations.

Pro tip: In the future, try to avoid signing leases that end between November and January. Consider offering lease incentives and flexibility for tenants to end their leases before or after that time. They don't really want to be moving during the holidays so this is not a hard pitch to make.

Drills and safety

With the cool autumn winds, the fall is a great time to do your annual fire drills and safety checks. Why? Because your tenants won't be baking or freezing while they march calmly to the parking lot and back to show they know how. Fire drills cause everyone to roll their eyes and remember being 14 again, but they are also a necessary part of responsible property management.

Designate a safe distant area where tenants will be safe in the event of a fire. Assign tenant-buddies for any residents who are too elderly or handicapped to get themselves out.

Property

The fall is also a good time to check in on management performance. Assess how efficiently you're spending your operating budget and whether you're hitting your target metrics.

Fall gives you enough time to correct your course and get your financial books in order before the end of the year. Plus, you'll have some great ideas for your property new year's resolutions. Assess your performance with our multifamily property operations checklist.

Resource alert: Again, you'll find the operations checklist in our resource document at our site, theresabradleybanta.com/book_resources.

Pro tip: Fall is also the time to get serious about any holiday party plans for the resident community.

Asset management

Next, ask yourself about how the business is doing. Fall is when we start thinking about endings, so let that guide you to smart business decisions. Set aside time each fall to review your asset management plans. Start with a review of your:

- **Tax strategies:** Speak with your CPA to take full advantage of the current tax benefits for your specific tax needs.
- **Exit strategies:** Is it time to refinance, sell or 1031 exchange? Are you ready for new assets? What are current property values and interest rates and where are they going?
- **Local market rents:** Is it time to raise your rental rate?
- **Competition and tenant trends:** Is it time for renovations, new amenities or capital improvements?
- **Partnerships:** Do you need better communication, a new plan, or a new partner?

Fall is a great time to think strategically about your income-producing assets. Consider taking your portfolio through a SWOT analysis. This is a powerful tool used to identify the strengths, weaknesses, opportunities, and threats within your multifamily property portfolio. Find out how to do your own SWOT analysis in Chapter Twenty-Three: Pro Tips for Success.

Fall maintenance & inspections

Last but certainly not least, remember that fall is a great time to take care of all inspections and maintenance concerns before the chill sets in. You want everything in ship-shape so that the first freeze has no chance to do damage and your building's furnace & water heaters last all winter long.

Outdoors

- **Roof:** The roof should be at the top of your fall maintenance list every fall. Check roof, scuppers and downspouts for:
  - Leaks

o Obstructions
o Wear and tear

- **Drainage:** Keep an eye on your drainage after a heavy autumn rain. Watch anywhere for pooling water or lingering dampness. Check the drives and parking area for cracks or low places that puddle. Check the casings for water seepage and basements for signs of potential leaks and flooding.
- **Debris:** Why do we call autumn "fall?" Because everything trees can possibly drop, they drop onto your lawn. Now is also the time to clean up before the first snow. Keep your property clear of dead leaves, weeds, and branches. If you have leaf removal or snow removal equipment, have it inspected and repaired. Touch base with your landscaping and snow removal companies about your fall and winter maintenance schedules and costs.
- **Landscaping:** Plant fall bulbs, cold weather resistant plants like pansies, marigolds. Follow a leaf clearing schedule. Blow-out and turn off sprinkler systems. Store water hoses. Insulate spigots.

Indoors

- **Windows and doors:** Anywhere the building has an aperture, check it. The fall rains and the winter snows will try to get in. Followed by cold winds and condensation. Caulking, insulation and weather stripping are your best friends and can help you reseal any apertures that are loose or have a loose fit in their frames. The name of the game is energy efficiency, keeping the cold air out. Crooked frames can indicate foundation issues.
- **Lighting:** While the weather's still nice, gather up your bulbs and make a round of the outdoor lighting. Inspect each light for

integrity and take care of any minor repairs. This will all make sure you're not trudging through the snow to replace a dead light bulb in December. Remember to change the timers in outdoor and other security lighting.

- **HVAC:** Finally, never to be underestimated during your fall maintenance inspections, get your building HVAC checked. Heat is the single most important utility during the winter, so you'll want to have that locked and assured before the first freeze. Change the filters, adjust temperature settings, and take care of any necessary tune-ups. Now is also a good time to "put away" your AC in top condition.

Pro tip: The fall is an important time for multifamily property owners and managers. Whether you are taking care of fall maintenance preparations or reviewing your business goals, now is the perfect time to get all your property ducks in a row.

Easy Property Winterization Steps: Get Ready for Winter!

And now we arrive at winter. As the last days of autumn depart, now is the time to prepare your apartment complex for the winter ahead. Taking a few property winterization steps now will keep you toasty when the thermostat starts to drop.

The basic property winterization steps

Boiler and furnace maintenance should be first on your list. Everything should be double-checked and overhauled before the snowflakes start falling. Making an emergency repair call for hot water or heat in the middle of winter will be considerably more expensive than a routine check in the fall.

If it is time to replace a heating unit, then look for a new one with an Energy Star label. There are state, local and federal incentives that would help defray costs with rebates but read the fine print before you buy. Make sure you purchase the right unit for the rebate.

Don't forget to stock up on sand, rock salt alternatives, or other environmentally safe products to melt ice on walkways and improve traction. Plan to check with the National Weather Service regarding winter storms and wind chill warnings.

Young children and the elderly are especially vulnerable during this time of year. Share with your residents the best practices during snowstorms and extreme cold to stay safe.

Air flow

Your building's first defense against the weather is the exterior. You already know those problem spots where your building is leaking or damaged. It's time to call the professionals who can address those issues.

Another place for drafts might be outlets. Check the outlets on the outer walls of the apartment. Seal the outlets up if you feel a draft coming from them. Turn off the power, remove the cover plate and spray expanding insulating foam around the outlet box.

Now that you have eliminated unwanted air drafts, consider flowing air in the right direction. We all know warm air rises. Ceiling fans can help push warm air down to residents. Check that your ceiling fans are turning clockwise during the winter months, keeping the warm air moving throughout the room.

Drainage

It is also time to clean the gutters and any other drainage system your building uses. Leaves, seeds and small branches can clog your gutters. Don't let water accumulate and freeze, leading to load bearing problems on and around your building. Freezing and melting ice will create problems so make sure your drainage systems are clear and in good working order now to prevent problems later.

What can your residents do?

Make sure to stay in communication with your tenants. The easiest way to inform them of property winterization steps is through online sources and your social media outlets.

Approach energy efficiency as a win-win situation. If it is possible you should consider installing digital thermostats in units. Heating costs can be cut in units when residents are at work.

Suggest to residents that they hang insulated drapes. These drapes can keep the cool, air-conditioned air in during the summer and the warm air contained in the winter. The drape investment would aid their comfort all year long. Also encourage tenants to open their (insulated) drapes during the day to let in sunlight. The sun's warmth can naturally raise temperatures in a room.

Your residents may want to contribute to property winterization with a few energy tips of their own. Winter is coming. Be proud, you have gone through your checklist.

Chapter Nineteen:
Tenant Management

Listen to understand, not to reply.
– Natalia Butenko

~

Building Trust, Credibility and Rapport with Tenants

You put a lot of time and money into finding the right property, but there is no guarantee that tenants will come just because you build it or buy it. Marketing costs big money. Paying for marketing and still having a high vacancy rate will cost you even more.

Keeping your current residents is far more cost-effective than constantly acquiring new renters.

It all begins with good tenants

No matter how much you try, you can't fake the level of respect you have for a person. Unscrupulous real estate investors build their business on owning cheap properties and renting to desperate people. Perhaps their renters have no other option due to poor credit or low income. A typical workday for those investors involves equal parts chasing rent and badmouthing their renters.

Make it clear that you will maintain a good home for all of your renters. Maintenance bills, utility bills, property taxes, and loan payments do not pause just because you do not have tenants occupying a property.

The prospect of having money constantly going out without any or insufficient money coming in has led many real estate investors to accept tenants against their better judgment. Doing so will prevent you from building trust, respect and a positive relationship with your tenants.

Building trust with your tenants

People who are adept at reading the market, analyzing numbers and deciphering which properties have the greatest potential for profit are not always outgoing and personable. That's fine. People appreciate a good listener more than a good talker.

In this fast-paced world where time-saving products are highly valued, it is a rare thing to have someone take the time to genuinely listen in a one-on-one conversation. People appreciate it.

Establishing credibility

While you are listening to people, they are watching you. They notice how you dress, how well your vehicle is maintained, and how you interact with others. People who are always in a hurry come across as arrogant, disorganized, and unprepared. To establish credibility, you have to look the part and walk the walk of a prepared, organized, and confident person.

Maintaining rapport

Providing an opportunity for people to communicate with you is crucial. This is where social media and routine property inspections come in.

When people feel they have an opportunity to be heard and involved in what is going on around them, they feel more comfortable and are less likely to look for another place to call home.

New Tenant at Your Property? Here's Your 30-Day Plan

As a landlord your job is to find good residents for your property. Let's be clear; good tenants pay the rent on time and take care of their housing as if it was their own. Good residents are a rare and precious commodity. You'll set a positive tone early with your new tenant by listening to their concerns and taking action.

Here's what to do during your first 30 days with a new tenant:

Get your new tenant online early

After the leasing documents have been signed direct your new resident to your website and the social media addresses you use to communicate with your residents. On your website should be links for

- maintenance requests

- online rent payments
- basic orientation for new tenants
- social media sites for your community
- up-to-date information regarding your complex

Your new resident may or may not tap into your online resources before she moves in, but it is important to set the tone that the most effective method of communication is via your tenant portal. You'll read more about websites and tenant portals in Chapter Twenty-Two: Technology.

Before the move-in

Avoid hassles on moving day and run through the basic maintenance checklist prior to residents moving in. Make sure

- all appliances are in working order
- the unit is bug-free
- filters have been replaced
- the fresh paint is dry
- the unit is clean, odor free and vacuumed

Move-in day

Moving is a stressful experience but you can make the day easier for your residents. Your new tenant will notice your efforts! Prepare

- a spot for the moving van
- a tenant welcome letter and tenant package
- bottles of water waiting in the fridge

- a print copy of the tenant handbook

Sometime during this day, you or your property manager will need to go over the apartment with your new tenant, making sure you are both on the same page regarding the condition of the unit.

With the use of video all of the details can be documented and signed off by both of you in no time.

There are apps for landlords that make the inspection process quick and easy. Property inspection apps like Happy Inspector (happyco.com) and Inventory Pro (inventory-pro.co.uk) are covered in more detail in Chapter Twenty-Two.

Within 7 days

It's time for your maintenance and property management teams to send a welcome email introducing themselves. These messages will include information you have already covered with your new resident, but we all learn through repetition. In your communication review the standard expectations for

- rent payments
- late fees
- maintenance requests
- emergency procedures
- life safety matters
- tenant handbook compliance

Include links for each topic. Invite your new resident to join your online community via your social media and web sites.

After 14 days

Send your new resident a friendly email inquiring if she has any questions regarding the tenant handbook, any procedures or building protocols.

Also, in your email include a surefire way to win friends and influence people—ask your new resident if she has 1 priority maintenance request you can address for her. Read that again: One. Yes, limit just one top priority. Despite the limit, you are addressing her needs and just the offer should go a long way in establishing happiness.

Now you must hold up your end of the deal and address the maintenance issue within the week.

Send new tenants a rent payment reminder prior to the next rent payment due date. Include your instructions for easy payment and provide a contact person.

After 30 days

If your resident has not already engaged in the online community, then invite her to join with links to your social media sites. If there is one strong element that will keep good residents feeling safe at home, it is a feeling of belonging or community.

Develop a monthly online newsletter and ask tenants to contribute articles or tips. Host events that tap into the whole apartment complex. A strong community helps with building trust, credibility and rapport with tenants.

Communicating with your new tenant

Please note it's important to keep a record of all communication between you and your new tenant. Companies like AppFolio (appfolio.com) offer online property management software with two-way texting and customizable email features where all conversations are automatically logged in the program.

Any changes to your lease agreement and lease terms must be done in writing and require the signatures of all parties to the lease.

In order to keep the residents that pay rent on time and take care of their apartments, you have to keep the stream of communication ongoing. When your tenants are happy, then news will get around. They will attract more residents to your building.

The Do's and Don'ts of Accepting Online Rental Payments

Some people will live out their life only paying their bills by check or cash, preferably in person. Many of those folks are part of what is often called America's "greatest generation." They should be respected, honored, and appreciated as tenants.

There are also millennials, who are accomplishing some great things themselves and working to ensure that future generations can reach their fullest potential. These folks embrace technology, and you should appreciate them as tenants, too. That requires you to accommodate their comfort level with using technology for things like rent payments.

Benefits of online rental payments

For you as the manager and bookkeeper, the benefits of accepting online payments are numerous. It simplifies rent collection, reduces the possibility of lost or misplaced payments, allows automatic recurring payments, and makes record-keeping much easier.

The tenant also benefits from the convenience of making payments day or night and getting instant verification of the rent payment. Some rent payment tools even furnish their payment history to Experian, allowing young tenants to easily build credit history.

Some best practices regarding online payments

With the many benefits of online rental payments, you may want to only accept the electronically processed payments. Do plan to accommodate everyone. Cash is legal tender for all debts, both public and private. However, according to the U.S. Department of the Treasury, unless there is a state law that says otherwise, businesses can set their own policy for acceptable payments.

You can refuse checks, cash, and money orders, but this is not a good course of action. A better approach is to incentivize online payments. Do be accessible to all quality tenants who appreciate the accommodations you provide and will pay their rent on time.

Many online payment tools are available specifically for rent collection. Do your research and select the service that is best for both you and your tenants. Some accept phone payments, checks, and have ways cash tenants can process their payments at a nearby merchant or grocery store.

Eliminate the hassle

Collecting rent can be a huge pain. It is also understandable that you do not want people to know that you always have a lot of cash on your person on the same day each month.

Online rental payments systems automatically assess late fees and will only accept full payment; no option for "I have some now and will pay the rest next week."

Being set up to collect rent online is one of the best ways you can manage your finances and eliminate much of the hassle associated with collecting rent.

How to Write a Tenant Welcome Letter

A tenant welcome letter is a must have for all landlords and property managers. Your letter sets the tone for communication between residents and management.

Neuroscientists Mikhail Rabinovich and Christian Bick have concluded that we need to process information seven times before it is committed to memory. Use brain research and make sure the tenant welcome letter is hand delivered, snail mailed and emailed more than once to each new resident. Here is the template:

***

Dear [resident's first and last name],

Welcome to [your building's name]! We extend a warm greeting from our team and hope you will be happy in your new home. Included in this letter is all of the important information you need to know for a smooth transition.

Your new mailing address is:

[Your resident's new address: Street, Unit Number, City, State, Zip code]

Property Management Contact Information

- Phone number:
- Email address:
- Address:
- Our physical operational hours are Monday-Friday from 9AM-5PM
- Reach our conversational assistant via Chatbot at our website
- Should there be an emergency, please call 911 immediately. Notify us as soon as possible after calling 911

Rent

- Rent is due on the 1st of each month
- Rent can be paid with a check or through www.[your website address].com
- Please make your payment payable to: [your company name]
- You can mail your check, but it must be received on or before the 1st of the month for the rent to be on time.
- Late fees of $____.00 per day begin at 9AM on the 2nd day of each month

Maintenance Requests

- Put all maintenance requests in writing through [your email address] or via your tenant web portal at www.[your website address].com/portal
- We will respond to your request within three business days. Most repairs will made within 24 hours.

Important Phone Numbers

- Garage/recycling company:
- Gas/oil company:
- Water company:
- Cable service:
- Electric company:
- Internet provider:
- Phone company:
- Emergency: Police and fire

- Post Office:

Lease Renewal Rewards Program

- If you would like to renew your lease in one year, we offer financial incentives or your choice of special gifts
- If you refer your friend and your friend leases an apartment with us, we'll reward you with a gift card or a free property upgrade
- Please stop by or contact our leasing office for details!

Apartment Rules and Regulations

Please review and become familiar with our posted rules and regulations. They are in place to provide a safe and convenient community space for everyone. We appreciate your cooperation.

Thank you for trusting us to provide you with a safe and secure place to call home,

[Your company's name]

***

The tenant welcome letter provides a way to convey vital information in one place, convenient for you and your resident. Contact information for local pharmacies, supermarkets, hospitals and schools are helpful information for residents as well.

Resource alert: You'll find a tenant welcome letter template in our resource document at: theresabradleybanta.com/book_resources.

How to Create a Tenant Welcome Package Your New Residents Will Love

Who has moved recently? Do you remember how exhausting the experience was? When your residents move in, they are physically wrung out and their brains are in overdrive. A tenant welcome package from you will do wonders for their day. Who knows, they might even post your act of kindness on social media.

Welcome letter

Again, your welcome letter sets the tone of your relationship with your tenants so let's do a quick review. The welcome letter should include key elements such as:

- How and where to pay rent
- Contact information for the property manager and leasing agents
- Property rules and regulations
- Important phone numbers
- Your system for handling maintenance requests

It's always a good idea to include a positive comment about good working relationships. You'll also want to include information on your rewards and incentive programs. Gifts for timely rent payments or rewards for new tenant referrals equal good news to your new residents.

The essentials

Who remembers to pack soap? That's right, no one. Include the bathroom requirements that everyone needs. Murphy's Law says that these items are found at the bottom of the very last box to unpack.

- Soap
- Toilet paper
- Toothbrush
- Toothpaste
- Shower Curtain Liner

These are the basics people need in a hurry so help them out by including them in your tenant welcome package. Buy these items in sample sizes or purchase them in bulk to economize.

Include the kids

Moving can be a difficult event for children so make sure they are included. A new stuffed animal gives the child someone to hug. Depending on the age, it is easy to find an inexpensive toy or game for a child at the dollar store. Consider a gift certificate at the local ice cream parlor or bakery for a treat.

Yes, paper maps are nearly obsolete, but consider including a map of the apartment building indicating common areas, mailboxes, laundry facilities, fire exits and other important areas. Make it a fun map for kids, hiding treasure notes along the way. There could be a prize waiting for the children at the front desk after they reach all of the "destinations" on the map. The parents will appreciate any effort you make on their child's behalf.

Promote yourself

This is an excellent opportunity to use social media to promote your apartment complex. In your tenant welcome package include all of your social media information on a colorful, large card.

Put all of your social media addresses and sites on one card for easy reference. Encourage residents to celebrate their moving-in day with a post. Depending on your social media, this post could be a photograph or an introduction.

Make sure there is a page on your website devoted to orientating brand new residents. Include FAQs, a map of the building, the basics of the local town, staff introductions and important numbers to know. What would you want or need to know if you just moved in from out of state? Get creative.

What everyone wants

Your new residents would appreciate finding a few bottles of water chilling in the refrigerator on moving day. Water is essential, but what is the best gift for any person who has been moving their furniture all day? They want a quick, easy meal. Include a gift certificate or discount to a local restaurant nearby.

You might get a local eatery to donate a special deal for brand new residents. It is the perfect way to get new customers in their door and you look like a hero. Get that cape ready!

Write it off

The welcome package you give new residents is considered a Business Gift Tax Deduction but, like all tax laws, there is fine print to consider. Nolo.com says, "If you give someone a gift for business purposes, your business expense deduction is limited to $25 per person per year. Any amount over the $25 limit is not deductible. If this amount seems awfully low, that's because it was established in 1954!"

How to Take Over a Property with Tenants

One of the things I love about investing in residential real estate is the opportunity to meet and work with a variety of people. This includes my tenants. But what if you inherent tenants? What if you have tenants that have not met your personal screening criteria and are virtual strangers?

When you first take over a property with tenants already in residence it's difficult to know which tenants to keep. And bear in mind, all of your tenants have rights under their current leases. You can't just waltz in and evict some tenants and raise the rents on others.

These tips will help you get started on the right foot. . .

Get copies of tenant leases before your close on the deal

It's likely that each resident will have a signed lease but make note that not all leases will be current.

Your due diligence during the purchase phase (before you close) should include a request for copies of all leases and rental applications. Also request copies of:

- The most recent financial statements and credit information and reports, if any, on any tenant and of any guarantors of any leases or rents
- Any executed letters of intent with prospective tenants, including lease concessions or special deals
- Leasing status reports from the leasing broker, including pending rental applications
- Leases for all subsidized tenants and documents relating to any inspections by government agencies

Pro tip: It's also a good idea to request copies of historical rent delinquency reports.

What if there are no tenant leases?

When no leases are available, request that the seller's tenants sign estoppel certificates confirming the following lease information:

- Lease start and termination date
- All modifications or amendments that have been made to lease

- Current rental rate and terms of payment
- Amount of advance rentals paid and rent concessions given, if any
- Deposit paid to seller
- Any existing defaults

An estoppel certificate will prevent a tenant from later challenging the facts of their tenancy. And if each tenant already has a lease? It's your right to request that each tenant sign an estoppel certificate.

After you close, meet every tenant in your property

When you first take over a property either you or your property manager should take the time to meet and greet the leaseholder for every rental unit in your property. Don't be tempted to hold an open house or barbeque; it's important that you visit each resident in his or her place of residence.

Visits can be arranged by scheduling a short apartment unit inspection. Make note of needed repairs during your walk-through. Take good notes about your first impressions of the resident and the overall condition of their rental unit.

Tenant information document

It's always a good idea to have each tenant complete a tenant information document that includes:

- Tenant contact information (include emergency contact)
- Spouse or co-tenant contact information
- Description of pets and deposit paid, if any

- Auto make, model and license number
- Driver's license number and social security number
- Place of work and employer contact information
- Income from employment and all other sources of income
- Rent payment made upon signing of lease
- Last month's rent paid in advance, if any
- Confirmation that rent is current
- Amount of rental deposit, if any (include all refundable deposits)
- Copy of current lease
- Verification of ownership of all furnishings (drapes, appliances, etc.)

Even if you've already received copies of the tenant's rental application, it's a good idea to have each tenant complete an updated tenant information document. You can rightly tell them it is for their benefit too. It allows you as the new owner to honor their legal rights.

Welcome letter

This is a good opportunity for you or your property management company to start knocking on doors. Rather than post or mail each welcome letter why not hand deliver it along with your welcome package?

This is your opportunity to put your tenant's mind at ease. They've been wondering about you since the day you closed on the deal. They will be naturally fearful about your intentions and they are definitely wondering what kind of landlord you'll be.

This is the time to let your tenants know you will be scheduling a walk-through in the next couple of weeks. Inform them that you'll be reviewing rental leases for current status and lease renewal anniversaries.

Maintenance: fix or replace one item (to start)

During your scheduled walk through don't ask your new tenant what's wrong with their rental unit. You might end up with a list that includes the mundane to a laundry list covering the tenant's wish list. If your tenant presents a long fix-it list, and you do not immediately make repairs, you could end up looking like the landlord who ignores requests and refuses to fix things promptly.

Instead, ask your tenant, "What is the one thing you would like us to address immediately?" Then address it. It's a win-win for all. Now you're the new landlord who is responsive to tenant's requests.

When you set the right expectations, you've allowed your maintenance team the time they need to do their job.

Offer services and amenities

You might be surprised at how many owners overlook additional sources of income.

Can you charge for amenities such as parking, storage, recycling or community areas? Can you install vending machines in your common areas? Your new tenants will be thrilled to know you'll be introducing new services and amenities.

Introduce rewards programs such as new resident referral bonuses or gift certificates for each tenant who pays rent on time for the next 12 months. Be creative.

Don't forget

It's your job to know and comply with local and state landlord-tenant laws. If you don't have time to brush up on the rules that govern residential real estate be sure you've retained an attorney who specializes in landlord-tenant law.

Make a great first impression

When you take over a property with tenants you will encounter challenges. You will automatically inherit both the 'good tenants' and the 'bad tenants.' When you begin your relationship with your tenants by presenting a positive, proactive attitude you might just turn those 'bad tenants' into good ones. Who knows what the previous management was like?

How to Write a Change of Ownership Letter

When landlords purchase or sell a property, they have many things on their mind and a long list of items that must be completed prior to and shortly after the closing.

One item that should be a top priority for any new property owner is ensuring the previous owner sends notice to all tenants notifying them that the property has changed hands.

It is best to coordinate sending this letter along with a change of ownership letter from the new owner to inform tenants of the new landlord's address, contact information, and rent payment details.

Laws may vary by state

Most of the landlord-tenant laws for commercial and residential property are state statutory and common law. A number of states mandate that the tenants receive written notice within ten days of the change of ownership. New owners are still bound by the old leases signed under the previous owners, including many special provisions or discounts to individual tenants.

Most states require that landlords disclose to tenants in writing the person or persons authorized to receive payments, manage the property, and be contacted in the event of any problems or emergencies.

Be sure you know the laws that apply to any property you own or plan to purchase to ensure you include all required information in your change of ownership letter.

It is always best to have a paper trail

If there is some uncertainty about the agreement tenants have with the previous landlord, be sure to ask for clarification and copies of the written agreements.

Be clear, cordial and assertive with all of your written correspondence. Before sending your letter, read it aloud and think of how you would feel if you were the recipient of such a letter. It is best not to make references to the previous property owners. If there were problems between the old landlord and tenants, it is not your place to judge or take sides.

Send the same letter to all tenants. Keep a copy of the change of ownership letter and record when it was sent.

For your protection and a positive relationship with tenants

Uncertainty, confusion, and misunderstandings all lead to discomfort, fear, and mistrust. These are the roots of legal disputes between tenants and landlords. You want tenants to be comfortable and feel good about what is going on with your property.

Remember that this is your business, but it is their home. A change of ownership letter will help maintain positive communications and provide a convenient way for them to engage with you or the people you have managing your property.

Here are templates for your takeover letter and tenant information document:

***

Dear [resident's first and last name],

You most likely know already that your building has recently changed hands. Because we believe in the importance of a strong tenant-manager relationship we wanted to take this opportunity to introduce ourselves. Naturally you feel some apprehension but rest assured that we take pride in and strive as a team to take care of our residents.

539

Here's what you can expect in the future.

Lease and rent payments:

Your current lease and payment terms remain in full force. You can continue to mail your rent payments to the address below. Please make checks payable to: _____.

If you currently use an automatic draft to pay your rent, please contact your financial institution and request to transfer payments to the financial institution account named below.

For those residents who are on a month-to-month lease, we have attached our rental agreement. We'll follow-up with you shortly to discuss completing a new agreement.

Your resident portal:

We are excited to inform you that you can now easily make rent and other payments via your resident portal at [web address]. Most of the residents in the communities we manage find this to be the easiest and most convenient way to make timely rent payments.

You'll also find news of upcoming community events, tenant incentive programs, links to joining the community via social media, and instructions on contacting our offices among many other valuable resources via your new resident portal. Just follow the new resident steps at: [web address].

If you have questions on billing, or questions on how to use the website or the online payment feature please contact (management company contact).

Property management contact info: (Contact name and number.)

Website address: (Management company website url.)

Resident portal (url): (Management company tenant portal url.)

Address: (Management company full name and address: Street, Unit Number, City, State, Zip code.)

Phone: (Management company phone number. Also provide instructions for communication via text messaging if used with residents.)

Email: (Management company email address and contact name.)

Financial institution: (Account information and instructions for sending rent payments via electronic means.)

Maintenance issues: (Contact for property maintenance requests.)

Your updated information:

Thank you for trusting us to provide you with a safe and secure place to call home. We will do anything within reason to make living here enjoyable for you and your community. But naturally, we need your cooperation. Please take a moment to update your information and to introduce yourself by completing the attached tenant information document. You can mail or email the completed form to the addresses above. You can also complete the tenant information document online at this ink: [web address].

We look forward to providing you with a clean, safe, attractive residence and to providing you with exceptional management and maintenance services.

Very truly yours,

[Your Company's Name]

***

Tenant Information Document:

Date: _____

Resident name: _____

Resident contact information (include emergency contact):

_____

Spouse or co-resident contact information:

_____

Emergency contact:

_____

Description of pets and deposit paid, if any:

_____

Auto make, model and license number:

_____

Driver's license number and social security number:

_____

Place of work and employer contact information:

_____

Income from employment and all other sources of income:

_____

Do you have a written lease agreement? _____

What is your lease start date? _____

What is your lease termination date? _____

Have any modifications or amendments been made to your lease? (please be as specific as possible):

_____

What is your current rental rate? $ _____

Is all (or a portion of) your rental payment subsidized (Y/N)? _____

If yes, please provide details here:

_____

When is your rent due? _____

Are you in default of any payments? _____

Have any advance rental amounts been paid? _____

What is amount paid for your security deposit? $_____

List any of the furnishings owned by you personally (such as carpet, rugs, appliances, blinds, drapes, fixtures, etc.):

_____

_____

We will be scheduling a walk-through in the next couple of weeks. Is there one thing you would like us to address immediately?

_____

Thank you for taking the time to introduce yourself and to update your resident information. We anticipate a long relationship with your community and look forward to working with you!

***

The takeover letter, along with a tenant information document, provides a way to convey and collect vital information in one place. It also sets the tone for a professional relationship.

Resource alert: You'll find both documents in our resource file at: theresabradleybanta.com/book_resources.

The Law and the Landlord-Tenant Relationship

As a landlord, your relationship with the tenant officially begins when they either sign a lease or enter the property. Even if the tenant never occupies the premises or pays rent, as long as they have signed a lease, there is still a landlord-tenant relationship in the eyes of the law. With this relationship comes certain rights and responsibilities, so it is important that both parties fully understand what is expected from them.

By law, if either party is wronged as a result of the rental agreement being broken by the other party, they could be entitled to compensation. Here are just a few things that are expected from the landlord and tenant to keep the relationship on solid footing and stay within the law.

Landlord responsibilities

One of the laws that is applicable to landlords in most states is having to make sure that a rental property is fit for habitation before the tenants first move in. The landlord must also keep the property in a habitable condition through repairs and maintenance after the tenants have moved in. This not only means that the property is structurally sound, but also that it has adequate water, electricity and heating.

In addition, the landlord must provide tenants with a way to dispose of garbage in order to keep the property clean. Anything promised by the landlord in the lease must be supplied to the tenant.

Tenant responsibilities

Tenants must pay their rent in compliance with the terms agreed upon in their rental agreement. They must also abide by the rules of the agreement in terms of behavior and keep the property clean. Any damages to the property because of willfulness or negligence by the tenant or people they permitted on the premises must be repaired.

Tenants are also not allowed to threaten, obstruct, coerce, harass or interfere with the landlord. If there are any serious problems requiring services or repairs to the property, the tenant must inform the landlord immediately.

Staying on the right side of the law

As a landlord, it can be overwhelming to keep track of everything that is required but doing so is the only way to avoid lengthy–and often costly–legal ramifications. Being well-versed in what you can and cannot do by law, along with what the legal rights of tenants are, will help to keep the landlord-tenant relationship operating smoothly.

Laws can differ depending on what state you are in, so be sure to familiarize yourself with what is expected of you as a landlord. I strongly recommend that you consult with a landlord-tenant attorney. Have your attorney review all of your tenant practices and documentation with you.

How to Deal with Problem Tenants

Tenants will rarely adore you—even when you're the best, most responsive and communicative landlord on planet earth. Don't take this personally. Keep doing what you're doing—be responsive to requests and communicate well.

Start with an understanding of human behavior

People often behave funny when they are:

- Embarrassed
- Fearful
- Uncertain

These emotions on the part of your tenant can put a target on your back—even though you are not the cause of the problem.

Your tenants might experience unexpected hardships for a number of reasons:

- Change in financial situation
- Divorce
- Job relocation

When people are afraid or embarrassed, they don't always take a good look in the mirror. It's easier—and sometimes a relief—to identify someone else, or an external factor, as the source of their problem.

Don't take it personally

When you stop and think about it, you'll realize a problem tenant is not really mad at you. They're mad at their circumstances. You're simply asking them to do what they agreed to do—pay rent, pay it on time and treat your property with respect.

Your job is to enforce your agreements and to ask non-complying residents to move on.

What do you do?

Start with an enforceable residential lease agreement. Be sure to review your lease agreement with your landlord-tenant attorney to make sure it complies with local and state landlord-tenant laws.

Thoroughly review the lease with your tenant at the time of signing. Most tenants seem to be in a hurry to sign their lease—without review. Don't let your tenant rush through the lease signing process. Sit down with your prospective tenant and go through the lease agreement line by line. Be certain they understand the terms and have them initial the important provisions.

At a later date you'll always be able to say, "Of course, you remember we went over this when you signed the lease." Problem tenants love to say, "Well I didn't know that. You never told me the rules." Let's just nip that in the bud.

Problem tenants? Serve a notice to quit

So, here we are. Your tenant has stopped paying rent. Or they've just given you 30-days-notice and told you to, "Keep the security deposit for the last month's rental payment." Now what?

The minute your tenant breaks any agreement in your lease, it's your job to take action. Don't assume anything. Don't make up stories about what you think is going on. Get on the phone and contact your resident to find out what's happening. Let them do the talking. Chances are pretty good they already know they're breaking the 'rules.' Why rub their nose in it? Remain calm, professional and courteous at all times.

The only question you should ask is, "How and when are you going to get this straightened out?" If you know your tenant well, and you believe their promise to remedy the situation, put their promise and your agreement to it in writing.

If not, it's time to post a Notice to Quit (a.k.a. Demand for Compliance or Right to Possession Notice). You might be surprised at how quickly a resident complies with the lease agreement when faced with a notice to comply or move. After serving proper notice in accordance with your local legal requirements you're in a position to initiate legal proceedings.

Get everything in writing

Don't make verbal agreements, period. They are quick and easy but as they say on TV, "They won't hold up in court." Get all of the following documented or in writing.

- Tenant application
- Lease agreement
- Lease addendum(s) such as pet agreements and crime free agreements
- Property walk-through checklist
- Reference checks
- Employment and income verification
- Credit and criminal reports

Keep a written record each time you have contact with a resident. I always communicate via e-mail so I have written record of all correspondence and 'conversations.'

If a dispute should end up in court, you may need additional information about your tenant—especially if you're awarded damages and you want to collect. Where does your tenant work? Where do they bank? Who are their relatives and friends? This information is almost impossible to track down after your tenant has moved.

It's impossible to serve legal documents on a tenant if you don't know how to find them.

What to do with a Tenant's Abandoned Personal Property

Your tenant is gone, and you inspect the unit to find that some valuable personal items were left behind. Although the tenants in question lived in your unit, you do not immediately own abandoned personal property they've failed to take with them, so here's how to handle this situation in a way that doesn't expose you to liability.

Determine trash versus treasure

Generally speaking, garbage left behind by tenants like empty soda cans and food can be immediately disposed of. The personal property you have an obligation to handle properly includes items that have value, such as TV sets, wardrobes and pieces of furniture. Get rid of the garbage and keep the items that have value together and safe until you take the next step in the process.

Document the property

Take photos of the entire unit and all of the abandoned property before moving those items anywhere. The idea is to get a snapshot of each item as you found it to show exactly what condition it was in. This way, if the tenant does come back to get the property later, he or she can't claim that you damaged anything on purpose or accidentally while moving it.

Store the property in a safe and secure location

Naturally, you might need to move the property out of the unit right away so new tenants can move in or the unit can be prepared for viewing. Make a log of each item and carefully move all of them to a safe, dry and secure location, as outlined by Pine Tree Legal Assistance. If an item is damaged, you could be held responsible, so be careful when it comes to moving and storage.

Check local and state laws

Your state and local landlord-tenant laws actually set out what you have to do with a tenant's abandoned personal property. While the rules and process vary by state, this usually involves sending the tenant a formal notice in writing that they must come and claim their property before you get rid of it. You have to give the tenant the specified number of days set out by those laws to get their property before you do anything with it, such as sell, donate or trash it. Consult with your attorney on this matter.

Above all, make sure you follow all regulations to the letter when it comes to a tenant's abandoned property. Careful documentation and diligence now can save you a lot of trouble later!

How Renters' Insurance Saves Everyone Money

According to the U.S. Census Bureau, renter-occupied units made up 30.7 percent of the total housing units in the first quarter of 2020. Of those renting their home, only 40 percent carry renters' insurance, according to the latest data available from the Insurance Information Institute (iii.org). By comparison, 95 percent of homeowners have a homeowners' insurance policy.

The Insurance Information Institute poll does indicate a gradual increase in the percentage of tenants carrying renters' insurance over recent years, but a majority of tenants do not seem to understand the importance of having this particular type of insurance.

Why so few tenants have renters' insurance

The main reason is that they are not required to carry a renters' insurance policy. Many homeowners still have a mortgage on their primary residence, and the lender requires they maintain homeowners' insurance.

To attract new tenants and compete with other apartment complexes, many landlords try to keep the initial costs of moving into one of their properties as low as possible. Even though renters' insurance is easily affordable, few people make it part of their budget.

Another reason many renters skip this important coverage is that they assume the landlord has all needed insurance. These tenants do not realize that the typical landlord and owner's policy does not cover possessions of the tenants, only the structures and other buildings.

In most cases, landlords are not responsible for providing accommodations to tenants should their unit become uninhabitable due to a fire or storm. Many renters just don't understand the importance of protecting themselves with adequate coverage.

Help empower your tenants

The National Association of Insurance Commissioners says renters' insurance can help protect tenants financially if someone is injured in their home or files a lawsuit; helps cover the costs of living elsewhere if a covered loss leaves their residence uninhabitable; and provides personal property protection for about $15 to $30 per month.

Other things you can do

Requiring all tenants to have renters' insurance can lower the premiums for your owner's policy. This reduces the need for any across-the-board rent increases.

You can further lower premiums for yourself and your tenants with smoke detectors, sufficient exterior lighting, and a security system for the property. Requiring all tenants to have coverage translates into a safer and more economical residence for everyone on the property.

Disaster can strike any time. Help your tenants be prepared with proper coverage.

Chapter Twenty:
Tenant Retention

The purpose of a business is to create a customer who creates customers. – Shiv Singh

~

The Most Common Costs of Replacing a Tenant

When it comes to tenant replacement, time is money. The moment a tenant returns the keys, costs will accumulate. The sooner you take action and the quicker you get things done, the lower your turnover costs will be. Following are the most common costs and some tips on how to reduce them.

Vacancy loss

Every day that a unit is vacant you will not receive rent, which can turn into a substantial loss. Always take a tiered approach in your lease expiration dates to ensure that everybody does not move out at the end of the same month. To reduce costs caused by vacancies prepare for the tenant's move-out ahead of time and start generating leads before the apartment is empty.

Maintenance

Maintenance costs can be quite high, especially if the previous tenants caused damage. You will be paying for the materials and the labor. To keep maintenance costs low with a move-out, carry out regular inspections of all your units throughout the year and fix small problems promptly.

Replacement costs

Some appliances may be so old or worn out that they need to be replaced. You might also need to replace the carpet, doors or windows. An early inspection before the tenant moves out will allow you more time to find the best deals and to get replacements done quickly.

Cleaning

Most tenants won't leave a rental unit clean enough to show. After maintenance, a proper clean-up will also be necessary, so be sure to factor in the costs of a professional cleaning crew.

Leasing agent rate/commission

Your leasing agent will either charge you an hourly rate or a percentage of the rental income. If you have a low overall tenant turnover, it might be cheaper for you to pay the hourly rate instead of a monthly fee.

Marketing/advertising costs

Have a comprehensive marketing plan ready to generate leads as early as possible. Focus on advertising expiring units before they become vacant. Use the internet and social media to your advantage as a free advertising medium.

Legal fees and administrative charges

Legal fees should be part of your tenant replacement budget. Sometimes you will have to evict tenants, or legal disputes might arise with a move out. Consider working with an attorney who can offer you a flat rate for landlord services. To keep the legal costs low, it is imperative to find tenants who won't give you problems.

Because replacing a tenant is a costly exercise, your focus must be on tenant retention. Keeping those good tenants in your property will equal stable cash flow.

Tenant Retention Strategies You Can Use Today

Your number one goal in tenant retention is to provide your residents with an attractive, safe, comfortable place to live. A place they want to call home. This is increasingly important in today's new construction market where you are competing with brand new properties that offer the latest in style trends and amenities.

So how do you compete if you own an older property? You compete by implementing and practicing solid multifamily tenant retention strategies.

557

Your goal is to reduce the high cost of resident turnover. And in the process, you'll receive some nice side benefits for your property.

Throughout this chapter we'll talk about how to keep your good tenants around and even turn them into your brand ambassadors.

The best curb appeal in town

There's a reason curb appeal is at the top of the list.

Experienced property operators know that first impressions play a key role in attracting new residents. And outdoor property enhancements go a long way in encouraging your existing residents to stick around.

If you were listing your home for sale you would do everything in your power to make the home attractive and inviting. You'd want a prospective buyer to be able to easily picture himself or herself living at your property. The same concept applies to attracting new tenants.

Pay as much attention to outdoor living space as you to do the property interior. Shared outdoor spaces are a great selling point.

Keep the building clean

Community rooms, halls, entryways and laundry facilities can get dirty fast. How often do you visit your property? If you spring a surprise visit on your manager and residents, you might be shocked to see how the property looks.

Some common areas need to be cleaned more often than others. Make sure your cleaning crew stays on top of it—especially the areas where your tenants spend time and money like the laundry room, vending areas and community spaces.

Stay up on property refreshes

In a highly competitive market, it's critical to show your residents that their "home" is getting some love. Simple property refreshes such as new paint, landscaping, and updated common areas and units will go a long way in helping you outperform your competition.

Consider re-staging model units with the latest trendy colors and comfort accessories like pillows and area rugs. Allow residents to personalize their rental unit. For example, paint a wall in a color of your residents choosing.

Offer enhanced security

You can install telephone operated tenant entry systems without breaking your budget. Residents want to know they live in a secure building. This is also a big marketing point.

Install automatic lighting around the property exterior especially in parking areas and areas that are hidden from the main street—or off the beaten path. Make sure your residents are (and feel) safe.

Offer in-community marketing

Do you have residents who are entrepreneurs? Why not create a (free) monthly flyer for resident marketing and advertising? This is a great duty for your on-site manager.

Host apartment community events

Hosting tenant appreciation events like an ice cream social or a community barbecue will help create a feeling of community at your property. Ask your residents to invite their friends and family.

Other events can include wine tastings, pizza parties or a simple "meet and greet your neighbors" gathering.

Encourage resident referrals

Reward your current residents when they tell their friends and family about the great place they live—especially when those referrals become new residents. Give your residents small cash rewards or gift cards for every referral.

Your tenants will be happy to get the word out about a property they love to live in—especially when offered a reward.

Give rewards and bonuses

Reward a resident who consistently pays rent on time by giving them a gift that will enhance your property while also showing your appreciation.

Things like water faucet filtration systems, ceiling fans, and new lighting make great gifts.

Give more expensive gifts like a new bathroom vanity or higher-end counter tops to your excellent long-term residents. This type of gift will enhance your property and make your resident happy.

If you decide to offer this type of unit upgrade, make sure you are on top of what the current market is looking for. Don't let your resident tell you what they want. For example, if wood floors are in high demand in your local market offer to remove the carpet and replace the flooring in one room of the apartment unit.

Welcome new residents

How would you feel if you were moving into a new apartment and the property manager personally greeted you when you arrived, rather than asking you to pick up your key at a leasing office?

Your new residents might not expect or demand five-star communication, hospitality, and customer service—but you should. This level of quality is hard to deliver if your residents never see you. Follow a new resident calendar that includes a:

- Move-in day welcome
- Three-day follow-up for resident orientation and unit walk through.
- Thirty-day resident satisfaction survey with questions such as, "How can we make your living experience better?"

I love to give "welcome home" packages to new residents—and it doesn't cost a lot. You can enlist local merchants for some of the goodies like discount coupons, 2-for-1 deals and free samples. Include area maps, a list of local attractions, shopping and mass transit information.

Provide responsive on-site management

Hire a charming, accessible and affable on-site manager. Your residents will thank you!

Talk to your current residents

Ask your current residents what they love about your property and community. They may love things about the property that you've overlooked like big windows, extra-large living space or closets. This is great information to include in your marketing.

Offer beneficial technology

Technology offers a central strategy in tenant retention and attracting new residents. An interactive website, which includes the following, will become a core foundation of your tenant retention strategies. Leading property management companies, become industry leaders by offering these perks and online services:

- Neighborhood and social directories that include restaurants, local entertainment, shopping, salons, grocery and liquor stores, cultural attractions, and other services such as dog walking, banks and car washes.

- Participating merchants resident discount cards
- Unit floor plans
- Fully interactive online tenant portals for tenant applications, lease signing, rent payments, and maintenance requests
- Professional photo gallery
- Area maps
- Suggestion box (online contact form)
- Web specials such as discounted signing fees
- Tour schedules
- Automated "contact us" forms
- Links to community social media sites

Ask yourself, "is it time for our website and marketing material to get a makeover?" If you haven't addressed this in the past 12-months, the answer is probably, "yes." You want to be on the cutting edge of design and technology.

Offer ancillary services and amenities

How about offering new services and amenities at your property?

- 24-hour fitness center
- Courtyard with new patio furniture and fire pit
- 24-hour business center
- Resident lounge with WiFi
- Gourmet coffee bar
- Storage
- Access-controlled building systems
- Rooftop deck and views

- Services such as pet walking

Do some local research. What are your competitors offering to entice new residents? It doesn't take a lot of cash out of your pocket to offer inexpensive amenities like recycling or complimentary WiFi. And always use these upgrades in your marketing!

Advanced tenant retention strategies

Your tenant retention strategies can also include:

- Tenant information booklets with important information; community and building rules; instructions for unit care; and life safety information.
- Automated tracking systems for tenant communications and maintenance requests.
- Regular contractor reviews: Are your residents receiving quality service from your third-party service providers and more importantly, from your own property maintenance team?
- Established pre-leasing and lease renewal systems.
- Resident satisfaction surveys
- Resident exit interviews (this should become a standard practice)

By doing these small things for your residents you will be setting your community up for best in class. Word will get around that you know how to keep happy residents!

Ten Apartment Amenities That Create Strong Communities

As a multifamily investor, you want to offer apartment amenities that will appeal to potential renters. You also want to encourage your current residents to stick around and to tell their friends about the great place they call home. The following amenities are guaranteed to build strong, healthy communities.

Amenity #1: Your residents

The community you create is more important than any other asset when you're adding value to your apartment complex. Pay attention to your renters. Who do you invite into your community? What makes them unique?

Have you created a community filled with parents with children? Offering a playground can help bring them together. Do you have older residents in your complex? They, and their visiting family members and grandkids, will appreciate outdoor space to share. Look for ways to bring your residents together. By increasing that sense of community, you experience a number of advantages:

- Residents help take care of one another and the property
- People are more reluctant to move because of the relationships they've built
- Your community becomes a place where people want to move

Amenity #2: Natural spaces

Whether you're in the middle of a big city or tucked on the suburbs in rolling countryside, everyone needs a chance to get away once in a while. Add a natural space within your apartment complex: a place where your residents can enjoy nature and relax. Offer greenery, keep up with the flowers and plants, or invite your residents to participate in a community garden.

Amenity #3: Valet recycling

Not only is valet recycling a great way to show just how green your community is, it's the perfect way to add a little extra income. Even better, it can help you avoid expensive recycling contamination fees. Valet recycling also streamlines the entire recycling process, which means you'll feel a little better about your green efforts.

Amenity #4: Short-term rentals

Do you have apartments that are sitting empty on a regular basis? Do your tenants often need to travel for work or only visit your complex during specific seasons? Short-term rentals can provide increased income for you, as the owner, and for your residents. Consider offering this option as part of your lease.

As discussed in Chapter Twenty-Two: Technology, short-term rental management platforms like Pillow.com and ApartmentJet.com emerged early in the game and offered online solutions for multifamily property owners. Both have since folded operations but there are others who are rumored to be designing products to accommodate short-term rentals.

Amenity #5: Guest suites

In addition to short-term rentals, you may find that there are a number of advantages to offering guest suites within your complex, especially if you have high vacancy rates. Not only is this a great way to bring in additional income, it can offer benefits to residents who regularly have long-term visitors but would like for them to have their own space.

Guest suites may help you generate income from apartments that would otherwise sit empty.

Amenity #6: Fitness centers

With an increased interest in fitness across America, many apartment-dwellers are very interested in fitness centers in their buildings. They can save on gym fees when you offer better rates than their local gym, and you can charge a small gym fee for use of the center. Fitness centers also increase convenience for your residents, which can make them very appealing to your target demographic.

Amenity #7: Complimentary memberships

Check out your local area. Are there museums, health clubs, or spas that might be willing to offer a discount if you purchase memberships for your residents? You can also simply pass those discounts on to your residents.

Amenity #8: Walking trails

Fitness centers aren't the only way your residents like to get in shape! Consider putting in walking trails, which will allow people to walk or run straight from the apartment. Look for a layout that will prevent unnecessary road crossings. A good track can help encourage fitness and encourage runners to consider your multifamily dwelling when they're ready to choose a place to rent.

Amenity #9: Green roofs and walls

Have you taken the time to go green throughout your apartment complex? It's not about redecorating. Rather, consider how going green can help increase the appeal to your building.

You may, for example, want to make sure that your walls help hold energy inside (with the added bonus that energy-efficient walls often add a layer of sound dampening insulation–a definite draw for apartment-dwellers). Look at your roof: can you add a rooftop garden? Put in solar panels? With these simple strategies, you can go a little greener and decrease costs both for you and for apartment residents.

Amenity #10: Gathering places for all your residents

It's not just about a playground for the kids—though if your target market includes families, that's certainly something you'll want to consider. Take a look at bark parks, community tree houses, and outdoor grilling areas.

By creating a communal gathering space, you can enhance the sense of community throughout your dwelling and make it more appealing to many families.

Pro tip: Not every amenity will contribute to the bottom line. Some simply appeal to your renters; others may briefly interest them but become outdated overnight. Amenities that will stand the test of time are those that help raise your rental rates and improve quality of life for your renters. Be willing to give up an amenity that isn't working for your investment.

Easy Customer Service Makeover Tips

We all know it costs less to retain current tenants than it does to attract new ones. Showing your residents that you appreciate their loyalty is an essential part of your real estate investment business.

Word-of-mouth marketing is required for long-term success. It is the most credible and persuasive forms of advertising. You do not get recommendations from current residents by simply meeting their expectations; you must go beyond the norm to provide tenant experiences that will inspire them to talk about you.

Increase communication

Communication builds relationships, and relationships with your residents develop into trust. That relationship of trust increases the level of commitment they have toward you.

You want to establish regular opportunities for dialogue between building management and tenants. Use these times to provide useful information and highlight what you're doing for them. Thanks to these frequent friendly communications initiated by you, on the rare occasions that your tenants do have a concern, they will be more at ease contacting someone familiar and it will feel less like of a complaint for them.

Be proactive about quality assurance

With modern technology handling more customer service tasks these days, people dread having to make maintenance requests and are already feeling frustrated before they even contact building management. While some of the major corporations can get by with unhappy customers, you cannot afford to ignore complaints.

Be proactive by conducting more frequent inspections of both the interior and exterior. This anticipatory service strategy eliminates many problems before they occur.

Train your staff properly

Regardless of their position, interpersonal skills are important for every member of your staff. Each contractor and employee represent your company.

Have you ever had an interaction with a store employee who was obviously just going through motions? Those small experiences leave a lasting impression and can affect a tenant's decision to renew their lease or look elsewhere. Reiterate to your staff that resident retention is vital to their income.

Little things matter

The key to happiness in life is appreciating the small things.

Finding enjoyment in the seemingly mundane aspects of our daily lives can enhance our mental well-being beyond measure. The same is true of small creative gestures that add up to many pleasant moments for your tenants. It can be something like an occasional continental breakfast in a common area, something special on their birthdays, or you personally handing out free coffee as they head out to begin their day.

The key to resident retention is that you are constantly thinking of how you can enhance the experience of living in one of your properties.

Technology Strategies That Will Keep You Competitive

Technology is available to make practically every aspect of your life easier and more efficient.

You can monitor your daily calories burned or the amount of sleep you get, set reminders for social events, and communicate with friends located across the country – all from your smartphone. A lot of people reading this might be thinking this isn't exactly news, but the truth is that for multifamily investors and their residents, there is a lot of new technology.

You can remain competitive by being informed and staying ahead of the curve.

Resident technology that keeps you competitive

Your online strategy: Ten years ago, social media looked like a good area for multifamily investors to focus their marketing efforts. However, the recent NMHC/Kingsley Apartment Resident Preferences Survey found that only 13 percent of respondents chose social media as their preferred method of communicating with property managers. However, almost 70 percent said they check apartment ratings and reviews sites when researching properties. Fifty-four percent said these sites influenced their decision, and fifty-two percent said a bad review prevented them from even visiting a community. Monitor how your properties compare to others on these sites.

Online bill pay and other services: Many millennials want to sign leases electronically, make rent payments online, and be able to report maintenance issues 24/7. To attract busy people under the age of 35, you must accept online payments. Digital records are also easier for you to search, access, and manage. Adding these amenities for your residents also saves you money and helps you operate efficiently.

Smart home technology: While it is of little value to many older residents, tech-savvy millennials appreciate the benefits of smart thermostats, smart lamps, and outlets with USB ports. Smart technology features are not yet a must-have, but they do help you stand out from the competition.

Internet access: It is becoming a necessity these days for every home to have access to broadband internet. To help Americans of every income level achieve their fullest potential, the Obama administration introduced the ConnectHome initiative (connecthome.hud.gov). Children with internet access do better in school, and families need a strong connection for everyone's devices.

Consider installing routers throughout your buildings and providing WiFi in your common areas. A good internet connection alone is not enough to attract tenants but having a bad internet connection or no internet access will cause them to move out.

When you use technology to empower your tenants and enhance their lives, you also enable yourself to focus on other business areas and better manage your real estate investments. Resident technologies are covered in detail throughout Chapter Twenty-Two: Technology.

The Best Strategies for Handling Online Property Reviews

Have you read a bad review for a restaurant and then decided to go somewhere else? I read reviews for products before I purchase and for professional services before I make an appointment.

Face it, reviews carry weight and they are everywhere. Your tenants are typing out reviews right now about their personal experiences. Is your property at the top of their list? This could be a good thing or a bad thing.

A big step

Moving into a building, merging into a new community and creating a home is a giant step. You can bet that potential residents are doing their homework and searching online property reviews before they take one physical step into your building.

This is why branding is a critical issue these days. Instead of letting the reviews languish unaddressed, you need to step up and control the focus of the conversation. Show the world your professional side.

Locate your online property reviews

First, find out where the online property reviews have been posted. You can find consumer reviews written just about everywhere but start with the hubs and then keep looking. Always go through and then past the first page of Google.

- ApartmentRatings.com
- ApartmentReviews.net
- Zillow.com
- Apartments.com
- BedBugRegistry.com
- Yelp.com
- Google.com
- Facebook.com and Facebook.com/marketplace
- CraigsList.org

Pro tip: Periodically, conduct an online search of your physical property address and also your property name. For example, do a search for both "123 North Main Street" and "Main Street Apartments." You might be surprised by what pops up!

Compose your response before you post!

When responding to reviews remember that what you write will be on the internet permanently. Your written words will be irrecoverable, glowing in computer screens day and night. If you react and lash out at a negative reviewer no one is ever taking your comments down.

The truth is there is too much entertainment value in a verbal fight. You know that. If you are upset, then take some time to level your head. Think through your response before you tap the post button.

You are responsible for your words

Equally important to remember is the legal aspect of this equation. Your words from an email, text or any online responses can be used in court. Conduct yourself professionally. Get legal questions answered if you are in doubt.

It's important to not disclose anything about a tenant, or the community. Always avoid posting anything private or personal about the reviewer.

What is the formula for a successful online review response?

The first rule in responding to any review is that you are the professional so act like one. Keep your tone businesslike, cool and on point. Keep these pointers in mind.

- Appreciate the feedback—negative and positive
- Stay calm and professional

- Own up to your mistakes
- Don't get personal
- Address specific issues in the review
- Mention action steps taken to address issues and improve customer experiences
- Invite reviewer to write to management directly and resolve issues

You should respond to online property reviews on the site where they are written.

Online property reviews can be free advertising

These days online property reviews mean lost or gained business, money in your pocket. Think of the reviews as free market research. You can discover exactly where your business is flourishing and where your business is lacking.

By reading reviews and learning directly from your market and you will know exactly what potential tenants want. Just as important, you will know exactly how to improve your business and garner more positive reviews!

Use Social Media to Retain Residents

Social media significantly affects how people live their lives, buy products, interact with companies, and find their homes. Some landlords even venture into the legal mine field of using social media to screen potential tenants. While this may give these landlords insight into how these possible tenants really live and view their current landlord, it also comes with some potential problems.

Social media is a double-edged sword

Social media is powerful. We have all heard the horror stories associated with people providing too much information about themselves online. Any parent should monitor and limit how much access their young children have to the internet and social media.

As a landlord, your biggest risk of using social media is probably not the information others may see about you. Being inconsistent in how you utilize it to screen tenants and communicate with current occupants is the problem. If you use social media as part of the screening process for one tenant, you absolutely must use it to screen all of them.

Using social media to retain renters

According to the Pew Research Center (pewresearch.org), 68 percent of U.S. adults get news through social media. It is estimated that more than half of online adults use multiple social media sites regularly.

Focus on making your social media account a community where people can get local news and exchange ideas on managing their household. Initiate some worthwhile conversations and consider offering your social media fans deals and gifts that they can't find anywhere else.

Social media and millennials

Regardless of where your rental properties are located, millennials are an important part of your business. Engaging with them through social media is not required, but it strengthens your connection with them and gives you an advantage over those landlords who do not make the effort to engage

577

these young renters in conversation. That really is what social media is all about.

Millennials want to have a conversation. They are more open with their thoughts and feelings than previous generations, and they want to feel they have influence on what is happening around them. When you use social media to provide them a place to do that, you will find it is easier to fill vacancies and retain current tenants.

The Hottest Trends in Free Tenant Events

Tenant events are a tried-and-true way to help build a sense of community and market vacancies in your apartment complex. These informal get-togethers allow your residents to form bonds and interact with each other while exposing new people to what your property has to offer. They are often part of successful luxury developments,

If you've never held a tenant event before or just aren't sure what to plan, you can try your own variation of one of today's popular themes. Count on a tenant event to bring some life into your residential community.

Whatever resident event you decide to hold, make sure you market it at least six weeks in advance. Giving your residents enough notice will help ensure everyone has enough time to plan for your next big soiree!

Demos: Educate and entertain

Demonstrations are definitely in, and they're also a cost-effective way to almost guarantee interaction between your event attendees. People enjoy learning new things and the satisfaction that comes with creating something, making demos a great way to boost event attendance.

Art, photography classes, cooking—there's a wide variety of instructional event types to choose from. If you're having a hard time deciding what demo to offer, ask your residents for input.

Tap into local resources to find your teacher. You can hire a chef from a popular area restaurant for a cooking lesson, for example, or speak to an area studio for a photography instructor.

Cook-offs: Competition and good food

Competitive cooking shows are popular for a good reason: they combine the natural spirit of competition with delicious food. Hold a cooking challenge event and ask residents to cook or bake their very best example of a particular dish, such as chili, cake or a pie. At the event, have impartial judges pick the winner, and let everyone sample all the dishes entered in the contest. Be sure to award prizes and feature the top dishes in your development's newsletter!

Sports: Camaraderie and fun

As the seasons change, so do the sports on TV. From hockey to baseball and football, many people enjoy and bond over sporting events, but they don't always want to go to the local bar or stadium to do so.

Make a major sporting event or big game with the hometown team an event for your community. Have everyone meet in your property's clubhouse or common area to watch the game, enjoy snacks and socialize.

This has become a popular way to connect residents because it's cost-effective and gives attendees an instant common ground.

Revenue Generating Community Events

Owning an apartment building is, in many ways, like being a community leader. You set the tone for the entire apartment building or complex in your management policies, and how you handle apartment community events.

Many apartment landlords feel that events are an optional expense. But done correctly, community events can become a source of revenue for upkeep and renovations.

By hosting apartment community events in a revenue-positive way, you can bring your community together, offer a warm family environment, and fund future improvement.

Should you host community events?

There are several reasons why apartment owners or managers choose to host community events. Not only do residents love a good holiday party, but these events can also be turned into revenue-generating opportunities.

People in a celebrating mood often don't hesitate to put down a few dollars to multiply their enjoyment. Host a movie and sell popcorn or host a summer fair and sell face painting. These methods are a time-honored tradition of community events.

Determine what your community will enjoy paying for. Party games, raffle tickets, fun holiday contests, DIY catering stations; anything they can get excited about and might reasonably cost a little to play or enjoy. You can also hold revenue-generating events like community bake sales or garage sales and take a fair percentage of the profits as "the venue" in the usual event equation.

Not only will you be building revenue to improve the building and host future events, but the apartment community events you host will bring residents together and make the community more fun to live in. Here are some ideas to get started.

Holiday parties

Everyone knows an apartment that hosts holiday parties makes a warmer community environment. Turn your pool, grounds, or office lobby into a party location for the residents to gather and celebrate a few favorite annual apartment community events.

Halloween parties are always a hit, especially for local parents of small children. A celebration of the holidays is also often a draw when everyone is in a celebrating mood. Easter egg hunts are sometimes a smart addition for the right resident population. Most residents enjoy a big 4th of July BBQ.

These parties can be turned toward revenue by including contests, raffles, and ticketed sub-events that residents will happily join in.

Prize raffles

Prize raffles at your apartment community events are a great way to turn any party into a revenue source. The trick is to balance the price of the prize with the number of tickets you're likely to sell.

The more involved your community becomes in building events, the more revenue you raise. Consider novelty prizes that are fun to win but not high cost, like giant stuffed giraffe or even apartment-prizes like a bonus parking spot for a year.

Raffles are, of course, not your only option. Contests, face painting, photo booths, fortune telling, and other ticket-worthy activities can also be turned into a fun source of party revenue.

Community classes

You can also start hosting monthly or weekly classes for your community. Consider things that local gyms or community centers offer. You can host yoga classes, cooking classes, arts & crafts, car repair… anything your community is interested in.

Set out a schedule and sign-up sheets then invite your residents to participate in close-to-home shared classes for a fee. Or invite them to book your lobby or grounds for their own self-hosted community classes.

Community garage sales

Living in an apartment can make it difficult to hold a garage sale at practical intervals. A great way to change this is to hold an annual garage sale for the entire community.

Pick a warm weekend and invite everyone to use the apartment parking lot or grounds to list all their spare items for sale to each other and drivers. Then take a percentage of the profits as a venue tax while providing refreshments and music to create an annual community market.

Interest & activity groups

Your residents might also be interested in forming activity groups like book clubs or childcare networks. If you act as the host and provide a meeting venue, you can also charge a small dues fee for each resident who joins the club.

Interest and activity groups can be a great way for your community to come together in smaller recurring events based on their natural affinities.

Neighborhood decorations

Some apartment communities get enthusiastic about seasonal decorations, from door wreaths to coordinated Halloween lights. If you coordinate a decoration theme that everyone can get behind, then revenue and holiday cheer can be built by selling decoration kits to tenants. The trick, of course, is to buy decor in bulk for a discount.

Then put together convenient package kits so busy residents can join the community decor plan without having to shop for matching pieces on their own.

Building revenue for community upkeep and future apartment community events is surprisingly easy with an engaged resident population. Get your apartment tenants involved in seasonal events, holiday parties, and shared activities. You'll see a stronger community and revenue-generating opportunities both on the rise.

Eight Tenant Gift Ideas That Will Boost Your Bottom Line

During times of high vacancy, nothing can be worse than lowering your monthly rental prices. And it's no fun having to resort to monetary enticements in order to keep existing tenants or try and draw in new renters.

The following tenant gift ideas will boost your bottom line, fill units, create resident loyalty, and reduce turnover. These gifts will also increase the value of your property.

Show your tenants that you want them to call your property home. Offer your tenant a gift for signing a new lease, as a reward for 12 months of on-time rent payments, or even as an incentive for referring a new renter who signs a lease. The goal is to offer creative gifts that add value to your property.

1. Give your tenants the gift of clean carpets

Offering annual carpet cleaning for a specified period of time is a great resident incentive for renewing tenants with allergies, pets, and children. This can extend the life of your carpets and help the tenants feel a sense of continual upkeep and maintenance. Contact multiple carpet cleaning services in your area, they should offer a corporate or volume discount.

2. Gift your renters a garden shopping spree

Gardening gift cards provide an enticing incentive in the spring for both new and renewing tenants. Teaming up with a local garden center or nursery could also get you discounts on gift cards, landscaping services, and gardening products. Add value to your property while saving money on your upkeep costs.

3. Upgrade your residents' locks

For both new and existing tenants who are tech-savvy and concerned with security, an upgrade to a smart keyless lock is an exciting tenant gift and an inexpensive way to add value to your property. Consumer Reports' (consumerreports.org) June 2019 top pick is the August Smart Lock Pro + Connect Adapter.

The smart lock replaces the interior part of your existing deadbolt and offers multiple features like auto-lock and unlock, and electronic key creation for guests and handymen. The Connect Adapter lets your tenant remotely control the lock and use it with Amazon Alexa, Apple Siri, and Google Assistant's voice control.

4. Give your renters a luxurious everyday spa experience

One thing most renters have in common is that they are looking for luxury accommodations without the luxury price tag. One smart way to achieve this is with rainfall showerheads. Offering this gift to new and existing tenants is a wonderful way to add value to your property while creating a loyal tenant.

5. Upgrade your tenants' wall outlets

With mostly every electronic device utilizing USB charging these days, outlets are a hot commodity in every household. Offer to upgrade both new and existing tenants' electrical outlets to 3.6 AMP Dual USB Charger and 15 Amp Receptacles and you are practically guaranteed a happy renter and a happier property value. Save even more by replacing these yourself.

6. Make your residents smart with this thermostat-wise tenant gift

Make a current tenant very happy by upgrading to a smart thermostat. Consumer Reports recommends the Honeywell Lyric T5 as it gives many smart features without breaking the bank. Save even more by installing it yourself. Just be sure to check that it is compatible with your existing system and wiring. Most smart thermostat manufacturers will offer compatibility checklists or tools on their websites to check out before your purchase.

7. Give your renters the gift of sight when they're not home

In the age of delivery, your renters not only want to see when their packages get dropped off, but they want to make sure no one is taking them. Nest Hello Video Doorbell, also recommended by Consumer Reports, offers new and existing renters an extra sense of security while offering you a boost to your property value.

These doorbells will send a notification to a linked smartphone when they detect motion or when the doorbell is pressed and then save a clip of the video footage. The Hello Video Doorbell has high-quality video capabilities and does not require batteries as it is hardwired. If there is no doorbell wiring, there are battery operated brands.

8. Add extra storage space

For apartment dwellers, storage space is something that they are always at constant odds with. Find an area such as a basement, outbuilding, or storage room and convert it into separated storage closets dedicated to each apartment. Offering this additional storage space to your tenants upon move-in is not only a huge added value to your renter but a value-added to your property as well.

Offering tenant gifts to your existing residents and new renters is a great way to build loyalty to keep tenants longer and fill vacant apartments without lowering prices. In a survey of renters conducted by Software Advice (softwareadvice.com), "half of males and 41% of females aged 26 to 35 say they would be more likely to stay at a rental property if offered an incentive when the lease is nearly up." Be smart with your incentives: give a tenant gift that will add value to your property while making your tenants happy.

Retain Residents with a Tenant Exit Interview and Survey

Losing a tenant, especially a good one, is always an unpleasant experience, but you can still use the situation to your advantage. Tenants who leave have very specific reasons for doing so and discovering these reasons can be very enlightening.

By making use of tenant exit interviews and surveys, you can pinpoint what it is that causes tenants to move out, which enables you to address these issues.

In many cases, the reasons for tenants leaving are completely preventable and by discovering the underlying cause, you will be better prepared to prevent it from happening again in the future. Although it might be too late to prevent a tenant from moving out, you will still be able to gain valuable insights from them.

What to ask during a tenant exit interview

The most obvious thing to ask during a tenant exit interview is why exactly the tenant has decided to move. This will let you know whether it is something that you could have prevented or if there is another reason for their departure.

It is also important to ask them what they thought about the rental cost of the property. If you are losing tenants and they are all complaining about the high rental cost, you might be charging more than the market can bear.

Inquire about the maintenance routine of the property and whether they feel it was adequate. You should also discuss safety with tenants who are leaving. If they ever felt unsafe on the property, there might be a need for additional security measures. Find out if the concerns and requests of the tenants were addressed in a proper and timely manner by management.

Golden opportunity

When conducting a tenant exit interview or tenant exit survey with tenants who are leaving, you can expect them to be brutally honest, especially if they were very unhappy about something. Don't take their criticism personally or turn a deaf ear to it but take note of what you can do differently in the future.

Tenants often hold back on criticism while still renting because they don't want to offend anyone, but those who are leaving will have no such reservations.

Some of the things tenants will complain about can be changed, while others might be factors that are out of your control. The important thing is to get good feedback and then use this information to improve your rental property so you can prevent other good tenants from leaving.

Communication is key

How much are you communicating with your exiting residents? A resident exit survey and interview can be a wealth of information. Residents who are moving out can provide you with honest feedback about their experiences living in your property. That feedback can give you insight into why tenants are leaving, what they liked about your multifamily property, and how you can improve on the experience for your remaining tenants.

The goal of the exit survey is to increase resident loyalty in your current and future residents as well. Building loyalty creates a stronger multifamily community for your tenants and a more stable investment portfolio for you.

Why resident loyalty matters

There are benefits to resident loyalty, for both you and the residents themselves. The most obvious benefit of having loyal, long-term tenants is that you aren't incurring costs for unit turns or spending money marketing your property to new tenants. That can decrease your marketing budget and increase your spending on community improvements.

Loyal tenants care more about the property they are living in, too. That helps decrease operational and maintenance costs. Tenants who enjoy living there are more likely to pay at the high end of the fair market value for the property, too.

Loyalty isn't only good for your bottom line, though. Long-term tenants are happier ones. Loyal tenants can help create a thriving community within your property. They get to know their neighbors and recommend the property to their friends. They are more likely to watch out for each other and for your property.

How a resident exit survey helps build loyalty

So how does an exit survey help you create that kind of loyalty? With feedback that provides you with actionable data.

The goal of the resident exit survey is to get honest feedback from exiting residents. The feedback should include information on what your community is doing well and areas where it can improve. Then you can turn that feedback into a strategy for improving your community and increasing your resident loyalty.

The more feedback you have, the better you'll understand what residents really think about your community and why they choose to leave it. Let's look at a few examples:

- Residents say they are leaving because they are moving closer to work. You've now learned that your property might not appeal to young professionals who need to be closer to the city center. But you might be the perfect place for families seeking a quiet neighborhood. Now you can create a smarter marketing strategy to bring in more long-term residents.
- Residents are moving out because they say the monthly rent is too high. You might need to lower your rental rates to something that's more competitive on the market. Or offer creative move-in specials to attract new residents. Or you might want to add some extra amenities that justify the rental rates and help residents feel they are getting good value for their money.

- Residents note that your maintenance service is top-notch and something they appreciated a lot. Sometimes knowing what to keep is as important as knowing what needs to go.

What questions to include in your survey

What you ask and how you ask it are equally vital to the exit survey process. You'll want to keep the survey short and easy to answer to encourage participation. The more feedback you get, the more useful the survey becomes to you. You'll want to cover a variety of topics, focusing your questions on five key areas:

Leasing
- How did the exiting tenant find the leasing process?
- Did they feel the lease was clearly explained to them during the signing process?

Property
- Was the tenant satisfied with their property?
- Was it clean when they moved in?
- Did they feel the property was a good value for their money?

Amenities
- Was it easy to find parking for their property?
- What amenities did they use the most?
- What amenities did they wish the property had?

Staff
- Were property staff attentive to resident needs?
- Did they find it easy to contact staff?

- Were issues dealt with in a timely manner?

Maintenance
- Was it easy to contact the maintenance staff when needed?
- Were maintenance issues dealt with quickly?

Resources to help create your survey

It's easy to build a simple survey online. An online survey is often easier for residents to fill out (and there are no pieces of paper to misplace!). Survey Monkey (surveymonkey.com) is a great service that allows you to build a customized survey and send it out through an emailed link. They offer templates and examples for formatting your own survey.

If you want to take your surveys to the next level, consider partnering with a professional surveying company such as Ellis (epmsonline.com). They provide touch point surveys to apartment communities. They gather the data, analyze the results to provide you with comprehensive feedback. This can help you improve your move-in and move-out process, identify issues with maintenance requests, and much more. Following is a sample tenant exit survey:

Please rate your experience during the leasing process.

☐ 1   ☐ 2   ☐ 3   ☐ 4   ☐ 5

Disappointing   Exceptional

Did you feel the lease was clearly explained to you during the signing process?

☐ 1   ☐ 2   ☐ 3   ☐ 4   ☐ 5

Disappointing   Exceptional

Was the property...

Satisfactory?   ☐ Yes | ☐ No

Clean when you moved in?   ☐ Yes | ☐ No

A good value for your money?   ☐ Yes | ☐ No

Was it easy to find parking?

☐ 1   ☐ 2   ☐ 3   ☐ 4   ☐ 5

Difficult   Very easy

Were property staff attentive to your needs?

☐ 1   ☐ 2   ☐ 3   ☐ 4   ☐ 5

Disappointing   Exceptional

Did you find it easy to contact staff?

☐ 1   ☐ 2   ☐ 3   ☐ 4   ☐ 5

Difficult   Very easy

Was everything handled in a timely manner?

☐ 1   ☐ 2   ☐ 3   ☐ 4   ☐ 5

Disappointing   Exceptional

Was it easy to contact the maintenance staff when needed?

☐ 1   ☐ 2   ☐ 3   ☐ 4   ☐ 5

Difficult   Very easy

Were maintenance issues dealt with quickly?

☐ 1   ☐ 2   ☐ 3   ☐ 4   ☐ 5

Disappointing   Exceptional

Which of the following amenities did you use the most?

☐ Fitness center   ☐ Coin laundry

☐ Covered parking   ☐ Swimming pool

☐ Storage units   ☐ Coworking space

☐ Recycling program   ☐ Bike storage

☐ Vending machines   ☐ Barbecue

Which of the following amenities would you have used if offered?

☐ In-unit washer/dryer   ☐ Pet services

☐ Smart home technology   ☐ Resident events

☐ Package delivery   ☐ Keyless entry

Please share any additional comments or suggestions:

_____

_____

_____

_____

Thank you for your participation!

Resource alert: This sample tenant questionnaire is also available at: theresabradleybanta.com/book_resources.

Chapter Twenty-One:
Life Safety

Be where the world is going.
– Beth Comstock

~

Life Safety Tips for Apartment Managers & Building Owners

Most people do not go about their daily lives thinking about the many possible threats to their safety. However, as a landlord and property owner, you must be diligent about protecting the safety of all residents and visitors to your premises.

The importance of keeping your property safe

If a tenant gets injured on one of your properties, there is a very high probability that you will be sued. Of course, you have an owner's insurance policy to provide some financial protection, but you also have the responsibility to ensure the premises are safe, secure, and equipped with safe emergency egress.

You can prevent a lot of problems by knowing all building and safety codes for the local area of your properties, scheduling routine life safety inspections, and being sure you perform some safety inspections yourself.

Keep your residents safe

Life safety is one of the most important elements of managing your apartment building. You want to be sure that you take every step necessary to protect the people who will live in your building–not only to keep your building up to code, but to protect your tenants as much as possible.

During your due diligence period before you buy the complex and after that, when you're managing your building, make sure you aren't missing key safety elements–and keep in mind that you may need to add or implement systems to get the building in compliance and up to code.

Plan ahead

When you're considering buying an apartment building, it's critical that you do your due diligence on compliance and code standards. Sometimes, getting the building up to code can be costly–and "I didn't know" won't help you with the legal fines if there's an inspection or an accident.

New statutory provisions often require changes to existing buildings such as the installation of:

- automatic fire sprinkler systems or fire alarm systems,
- energy compliant conservation systems like Denver's Green Roof initiative (denvergov.org),

- or even properly illuminated exit signs.

These will vary widely by city and state. Plan ahead for any modifications that will need to be made to the building before you buy it, and make sure you keep an eye on any code changes over the years so that you can keep your building as safe as possible.

Safe emergency egress

Exit routes and corridors occasionally become cluttered by housekeeping equipment or other materials. Be sure that no carts or other equipment remain in corridors unless someone is actively using them. You may have remodeling, painting, or other contractor projects that lasts for weeks. The area should be roped off from residents and other persons not involved in the project.

If it is an emergency exit route, it must remain open or you must provide a clearly identifiable alternate route. Be sure all emergency exits are maintained and free of any obstructions.

Consider adding the latest safety features

If you're purchasing a high-end property, you may want to go above and beyond for your residents. Consider, for example, items like stovetop firestop (stovetopfirestop.com), or the latest advances in smoke detectors and carbon monoxide detectors, energy saving lighting for exits, smart doorbells and locks, and other technology that will offer clear advantages to your residents. You'll find even more tech ideas in Chapter Twenty-Two: Technology.

Many residents choose their complex based on the safety features it offers. Make sure you know what yours can bring to the table–and remember that going above and beyond can help you offer more to your residents.

Check fire pits and barbecues

Take a look around the property. Does it include fire pits and barbecues that can be used by the residents? While residents can bring in their own items, leaving them responsible for maintaining them, if you offer these additions to your community, keeping up with them falls on you.

Make sure that fire pits and barbecues are properly stored each year, especially when the cold winter months approach. Create safety standards for using them and how they must be cleaned afterwards. Institute regular cleaning and, if needed, maintenance to ensure that these items remain up and running the way they're supposed to.

Examine storage

Are chemicals and flammable liquids stored property? From stored paint to pest control chemicals, they must be stored properly in order to ensure resident safety. Make sure that you check local codes to ensure that you know how these items are supposed to be stored and that you aren't accidentally creating a hazard for your residents.

Also, dispose of old or unused chemicals regularly so that they aren't sitting around your property, causing a problem.

Inspect fire safety equipment

Fire safety equipment, from smoke alarms to sprinkler systems, must be properly installed in order to do anyone any good. Don't take possession of a building without examining its fire safety system! If needed, have an inspector come in just to check it out. You may discover that this simple step helps save you a lot of time and effort in the future.

Look for identifying information

You know the neighborhood and how your units are labeled, but others might not. Check that your property address is clearly visible from all entrances so that if there's an emergency, first responders can quickly find your property.

Look at your rental units, too. They should all have clearly displayed numbers or identifiers. Imagine it from the perspective of a first responder——and keep in mind that the longer it takes to locate a specific unit within your property, the harder it is to get residents the help they need in an emergency.

Check your exits

When you enter a new building, you're often instructed to check the nearest exits. As a property owner, you need to check all of the exists. Does every renter have the ability to quickly and safely exit the property in an emergency? If there's a fire, how will they get out?

Exits should always be clear and unblocked—and if they are blocked by tenants, you need a policy that will swiftly correct the problem. You should also check your exit lighting to ensure that residents can see clearly if they must exit fast in an emergency scenario.

Exit doors

All doors used as a means of egress that are typically closed, like stairway doors or common entrances, should be self-closing. These doors should never be propped open with a wedge. Fire doors are vital pieces of safety equipment. They slow the spread of smoke and reduce the likelihood of injury and death if fire occurs. The National Fire Protection Association (nfpa.org) provides additional information to improve your preparedness for emergency situations.

Exit lighting

Exits should be well-illuminated at all times. Check all exit locations weekly to catch any burned-out bulbs or non-functioning devices.

You should routinely verify that auxiliary lights operate with back-up power. If you do use an emergency supply system (EPSS), it should also be inspected and tested weekly. All periodic testing and inspections of your emergency lighting should be documented and initialed by the person conducting the inspection.

Design your safety policies

Take a look at the apartment complex's existing safety policies. Does it include things like policies and procedures for emergencies? Who is responsible for dealing with first responders? Who should contact you in the event of an emergency? What kinds of emergencies require your presence?

You may also want to design a plan that includes fire drills to help encourage residents, especially those with small children, to learn how to exit the building safely in an emergency.

It can be helpful to hire a life safety consultant for an assessment of your property. Such specialists are aware of all codes and state requirements and can provide an objective view of seemingly innocuous problems that are inexpensive to correct.

Bed Bug Infestations are Your Responsibility

As a landlord, you have many responsibilities, liabilities, and risks. Even if something is not your fault, it may still be your responsibility to correct the situation. A bed bug infestation is one of those things.

Bed bug infestations are becoming more common these days. These tiny bloodsuckers are showing up in movie theaters, hotels, schools, nursing homes, government buildings and even high-end apartment buildings. From these locations, the bed bugs hitch a ride to the apartments, condominiums and homes of unsuspecting people—and perhaps even to one of your rental properties.

Information about bed bugs

Many people think that bed bugs only infest dirty and cluttered homes. That is 100 percent false. Bed bugs do not discriminate against anyone based on age, race, income, or degree of housekeeping. According to the National Pest Management Association (npmapestworld.org), bed bugs can be found in all 50 states.

Infestations frequently occur in urban apartments because a highly mobile population of people live in close proximity to one another. These are ideal circumstances for bed bugs to breed and spread.

Misconceptions breed fear

Although bed bug infestations have been making more headlines recently, many people are not well informed about these tiny pests. According to the Centers for Disease Control and Prevention (cdc.gov), bed bugs are not known to spread any disease, but they may increase the risk of a secondary skin infection due to scratching. Some people may have no physical reaction to a bed bug bite. Other people may experience an allergic reaction from multiple bites that requires medical attention.

Bed bugs know they need to hide to survive. They have a slim, flat body that is perfectly suited to fit in small spaces and the creases of clothing. The bugs can go months without feeding and are typically active at night. They like to stay within eight feet of where people sleep, but they may travel up to 100 feet in a night.

Landlord responsibilities for bed bugs

The National Conference of State Legislatures (ncsl.org) provides a list of state bed bug laws. You should also be proactive about educating your tenants about bed bugs and how they spread. Most people will modify their behavior to reduce the risk of having an infestation.

Respond promptly to any questions or reported occurrences of bed bug infestations in one of your properties. Some states, like Florida, explicitly require that landlords pay to exterminate pests like bed bugs. You may not be able to prevent an infestation, but you can be prepared in advance to respond correctly.

Basic Emergency Procedures for Your Apartment Complex

No one wants to consider a potential disaster, but natural disasters do happen. You can give your residents the best possible chance of dealing with a disaster by planning ahead of time. The best way to prevent panic is education.

Have an emergency plan

Identify your goals and objectives for your emergency plan. The Federal Emergency Management Agency (fema.gov), your insurance agent, local fire department and local police department can help you put together your plan.

Create and distribute your building's emergency plan in paper and digital forms. The plan should address what to do in case of snowstorm, blackout, flood, fire, hurricane, tornado, earthquake and any other unforeseen emergency. It should be on your website tenant portal for easy access at all times.

Before an emergency occurs, your tenants should be prepared. If your residents need to remain in the building during the emergency event they'll need:

- Information on shutdowns of major building systems
- Locations of emergency exits in the building
- Location of the nearest shelters
- Phone numbers of emergency responders—medics, firefighters and police
- Evacuation routes and emergency kits (see below)
- Sources of vital information: National Weather Service (weather.gov), FEMA (fema.gov), Red Cross (redcross.org), USA.gov and Centers for Disease Control and Prevention (cdc.gov)

Share FEMA's PrepareAthon playbook materials with family members and tenants (ready.gov/prepareathon).

Prepare yourself

If an emergency occurs, you will also need a solid plan of action for yourself and/or other responsible parties. A few starting questions to consider:

- Who is the first point of contact? For tenants? For emergency personnel and first responders?
- Who is shutting off water, gas, and electricity?
- What are building procedures in case of power failure?

Know what tasks need to be performed and who is responsible for completing them. Designate back-up people. Have your residents and staff's contact information in several different places. You will want to do a roll call if anything happens.

- Maintain and update the list of your residents. Have one contact person or check-in phone number for everyone. Emergency responders might ask you to provide a list of residents and staff to make sure everyone is immediately accounted for.
- Keep your keys and codes organized and accurately labeled. Medics might need access to locked doors to save someone's life.
- Have a special emergency plan for those with disabilities and the elderly. Notify emergency responders of the residents in your building who might require extra assistance ahead of time.

Everyone should have an emergency kit prepared ahead of time. Basic recommended items include:

- Non-perishable food items—a 3-day supply
- Drinking water—a 3-day supply
- A flashlight
- A battery-operated radio
- Prescription glasses if needed
- Extra medications and/or medical supplies—a 3-day supply
- Two-way radios
- A manual can opener
- First aid supplies
- An airtight container for important documents
- A multi-purpose tool
- Sanitation and personal hygiene items—a 3-day supply
- A cellphone with charger
- Family contact information
- A map of the area
- Extra keys

- Emergency blankets
- Extra cash
- If needed—baby supplies and/or pet supplies

Hopefully you will never need to use your emergency plan but plan ahead!

Multifamily Disaster Management and Resilience Planning

If you think you are hearing more about extreme weather these days, you aren't wrong. Scientific American (scientificamerican.com) reported in 2018 that weather around the world is likely to continue to become more extreme.

Record-breaking temperatures and massive storm systems are moving through regions around the world more frequently. It's something that multifamily property owners need to pay attention to. Extreme weather can have a catastrophic effect on your investment portfolio, and you should be prepared with a disaster management plan.

How to prepare your multifamily buildings for a disaster

You can mitigate the potential damage by taking steps to make your properties more resilient to the effects of a storm. Here are actionable tips for multifamily disaster planning that you can implement today:

Know the hazards and assess the risk

The first step to prepare your multifamily communities is to know what you need to prepare for and what to include in your disaster management planning. You'll want to know what disasters are possible and the likelihood of them happening.

If you live in the same region as your multifamily property, then you'll have a good idea of the risks based on your own life experience. If you don't live nearby, though, it may take some research. For example, a multifamily property on the coast of Florida may be at very high risk for hurricane damage. A property in Kansas, though, is more likely to worry about the effects of a tornado. But both of them could be in a flood plain.

So, when you are assessing the risk, consider both regional factors as well as factors that could affect your particular neighborhood.

Mitigate the risk and build resiliency

Once you know the risk, you can start to take steps to mitigate it. When you reduce the risk of damage, you increase your property's resiliency. Resiliency is the property's (and community's) ability to bounce back from disaster and get back to "life as normal." The more resilient your property is, the less disaster will cost you and the safer your residents will be.

How you mitigate the risk will depend on what hazards you are likely to face. Enterprise Green Communities (enterprisecommunity.org) has a terrific manual for property owners called "Strategies for Multifamily Building Resilience." In it, the authors lay out different options for disaster protection, disaster management planning, risk adaptation, system backup, and community support. It's a must-read and good resource for property owners.

Balance ROI with the costs of mitigation

One of the most important steps a successful multifamily investor will do when mitigating risk is to make sure they are balancing the costs with the potential return on investment (ROI). You could spend a large fortune on creating a disaster-proof property. But you may end up spending too much on a disaster that never happens and devastate your investment portfolio in the process.

Smart investors will weigh the cost of mitigation against the return on their investment. For instance, if your building is prone to flooding, putting in a sump pump may be a relatively inexpensive step towards protecting it from water damage. But installing resilient elevators may not be cost-effective in a low-rise dwelling.

It's also worth checking out if there are any government incentive programs that help reduce the costs of risk mitigation. You can speak to your insurance agent or do some online research to discover what disaster management incentives are offered in your area.

Create a disaster management plan

Another important step is to make sure you and your staff know what to do, when to do it, and how to get it done in a disaster. This will involve creating and writing disaster management plans. These manuals should include information such as:

- How to shut up systems such as gas and water
- What companies to call for repairs

- Information on contacting insurance companies
- How to access tenant contact information
- How to communicate information to tenants about disaster relief efforts
- Plans for securing the property after a disaster

Visit the National Multifamily Housing Council (nmhc.org) for more information about creating a comprehensive disaster plan for your community.

Plan how to cope with disaster-related costs

Finally, know how you'll manage the costs associated with a disaster. They will tally up quickly. Your insurance should help cover a lot of the costs but take time to review your policies and ensure you have the right coverage.

Don't forget that if the disaster ends up displacing your tenants, they won't owe you rent. That can have a big impact on your immediate cash flow. Know how you'll cover the costs and ensure funds are set aside for emergencies.

Make sure your residents prepare, too

One of the best things a property owner can do is to ensure residents prepare for disaster, too. Resident preparation can go a long way towards increasing a building's resiliency. Encourage residents to take steps such as:

- Preparing an emergency kit
- Checking their renter's insurance coverage

- Following you on social media for emergency updates

Help your residents prepare for extreme weather by passing these tips along. Partner with them in protecting your building.

Resilience in the Face of a Pandemic

If you'll recall, resiliency is your ability to bounce back from disaster. But what about pandemics? COVID-19, the worst global pandemic in 100 years, created many challenging issues for the multifamily community.

During the pandemic landlords were asked to halt evictions, avoid rent increases, create payment plans for tenants, identify helpful resources for residents in need of assistance and develop a response plan for limiting staff and resident exposure to the virus.

It fell to property operators to develop a response plan to limit spread and keep employees and tenants safe. You can take steps to mitigate losses by making your properties more resilient to the effects of a pandemic. Here are some ideas you can implement today.

Identifying helpful resources for residents

During the COVID-19 pandemic tenants who struggled to pay rent, or even put food on the table, found support through the following and other resources:

- COVID-19 Emergency Rent Relief Assistance Program through the federal Coronavirus Aid, Relief and Economic Security Act (CARES Act)
- Salvation Army
- Volunteers of America
- Healthcare facilities
- Religious services
- Local human services departments offering assistance for rent and food

Even in times of no pandemic it's a good idea for landlords to create a list of local services that offer support to tenants. Include a list in your tenant welcome package.

Rent vacation?

During the COVID-19 pandemic there was an underlying fear that under a rent mortarium non-paying residents who could not now be evicted, would take a "rent vacation." The CARES Act and substantial unemployment benefits greatly reduced the number of non-payers. Even so, landlords sued over eviction moratoriums arguing that the bans were unconstitutional.

Landlords can limit rent defaults and tenant turnover with the adoption of some form of a grace and forgiveness policy. For instance, you can offer creative strategies for collecting rent through payment plans and rent deferral programs. Leading property management company Yardi (yardi.com) offers software that allows landlords and property managers to manage and track rent deferral payment plans and recoveries. Landlords can also consider:

- Waiving or limiting late fees
- Accepting partial payments
- Discounting rent for advance payment of multiple months
- Reducing rent by a nominal amount

Pro tip: If your grace and forgiveness policy is limited to those tenants economically impacted by the crisis, you will have to develop written qualifying criteria. This is a policy decision a landlord must discuss with an attorney.

Social distancing the name of the game

Local ordinance and the guidelines set forth by the feds and CDC (cdc.gov) offer recommendations for shared or congregate housing. This guidance is designed to help landlords develop protocols for:

- Sanitizing high touch areas
- Completion of emergency maintenance requests
- Usage limitations on elevator, pool, and other shared spaces
- Signage and notices for residents

The CDC also offers guidelines for cleaning and disinfecting shared spaces even offering lists of approved cleaning supplies and hand sanitizers.

Help for landlords

Some of the best coverage, legal updates and strategies for dealing with residents during a pandemic can be found at:

- Multi-Housing News (multihousingnews.com)
- National Multifamily Housing Council (nmhc.org)
- The National Apartment Association (naa.hq)

Pro tip: Your local landlord/tenant law firm should be your first stop when planning for dealing with resident issues and potential issues. You'll need their assistance in dealing with delinquencies and evictions during a rent moratorium and while a crisis unfolds.

Resiliency through design

The good news is that often competitive advantages arise out of upheaval or turmoil. A shift in desired apartment amenities is one possible result of a pandemic. Smart apartment operators can rise to the occasion and create resiliency by implementing creative strategies.

Healthy homes: Provide outdoor and open spaces, fresh circulating air, and oversized windows that give natural light. Balconies, porches, yards, and terraces will also appeal to residents as will entryways that act as a buffer from the outdoors to the indoors. Consider offering hand sanitizers at points of entry.

Work from home: Quiet environments, doors for more privacy, access to technology and strong internet connections will be appealing to tenants. The ability for residents to change personal space based on needs will also be an attractive amenity. For instance, responsive space can be used for schooling at home during the day and converted to another use such as a workout room or family space in the evening.

Resiliency through technology

Social distancing: Shutter your leasing office and offer your prospects a virtual tour experience through interactive 3D interior tours; guided video tours; virtual walkthroughs using VR headsets; and street level imagery via Google Street View. Touchless technology for lighting, appliances, temperature controls and package delivery also contribute to a safer environment.

Marketing: Enhance your marketing efforts by embedding 3D virtual tours on your website or tenant portal, incorporating sharable links in your social media postings, and by including links on your emails and text messages.

Internet listing service Apartments.com is using Matterport 3D (matterport.com) across its listing platform for all 3D virtual tours. And there are some DIY solutions as well. 3D tours can be created by using panoramic photography and stitching images together through apps like Google's Carboard Camera. RICOH Tours (ricohtours.com) gives you the ability to create 3D immersive tours using your mobile phone and their special camera.

Communication is key

Property managers who meet resident expectations in terms of communication, training, maintenance and sanitization have an edge amid uncertain times. Landlords who take a humanitarian approach to dealing with a crisis, whether a pandemic or natural weather disaster, will develop a reputation for leadership and understanding that will place them at the top of their profession.

Flood Safety Tips for Your Apartment Building and Residents

Storm surges, floodplain locations, flash floods, and snowpack runoff are just a few of the ways flooding can happen. You can't stop Mother Nature. Take proactive measures for your multifamily property and prepare your residents with the following flood safety tips.

Flood your residents with the right information

The best way to avoid mistakes is to plan ahead.

Hold an informative meeting on flood safety with your team and community. Organize an informational package in paper and digital form for your residents. Spell out in specific details what to do and where to go if a flooding emergency takes place. Share:

- Pre-disaster plans
- Storm procedures
- Disaster relief information
- Evacuation routes
- Shelter locations
- Emergency response numbers
- Information on shutdowns of major building systems
- Recommended items in an emergency kit
- Flood safety steps you can take before a flood

Listen to the NOAA weather radio as well as local news for updated weather news. Monitor updates. Share and follow the flood safety directions provided by local officials.

615

The Red Cross has a free Android and iTunes app with pre-loaded instructions for flooding which will work even when cell towers are down. Keep all of your multifamily residents informed on weather conditions. Notify emergency responders of any disabled residents in your building in advance.

How can you prepare your multifamily building today to avoid flood damage?

FEMA recommends the following steps to protect your property from flood damage.

- **Waterproof:** Seal basements and areas susceptible to flooding.
- **Sump pump:** Check that your sump pump is in good working condition. Install a battery-operated model in case of power failure.
- **Debris:** Remove debris and clean your downspouts and gutters.
- **Elevate:** All electrical panels, switches, utilities, appliances should be elevated.
- **Anchor:** Fuel tanks should be anchored.
- **Shut off valves:** Locate the shut off valves for water, electricity and gas. Call your utility company with any questions.

Invest in flood insurance for your multifamily property

Take photographs and videos of your multifamily property now and file copies with your insurance company. Over document your building and anything that might need to be replaced. (Read: everything)

Be aware that most insurance companies do not cover floods in their regular policy. Landlords need separate flood insurance coverage. In the U.S. the National Flood Insurance Program (NFIP) is the only flood insurer.

Advise residents about personal property and flood insurance

Renter's insurance will cover the possessions of your tenants for a wide variety of unplanned events but not floods. Flood insurance would be an additional policy but a wise purchase.

Your responsibilities after a flood as a landlord

As a landlord you are responsible for the building and apartment repairs that are needed after flooding. The housing you rent must be livable and meet all local housing, health and safety laws. If the floods render your building unlivable you may have to provide alternative housing while your multifamily building is being repaired.

Make sure your lease agreement has specific wording that covers conditions if the rental property is partially or completely destroyed. Always check with a landlord attorney to make sure your lease is compliant with state laws on the subject.

Create an emergency call list

Time is of the essence when it comes to water damage. As soon as the flooding has stopped, assess the water damage to your apartment building. Document all damage with photographs and take corrective action.

Have the name and numbers of at least two reliable contractors for every possible repair on hand now so you aren't scrambling when an emergency occurs.

Let's hope you never have to deal with flooding in your property but now you know the flood safety steps to take if it does happen!

Chapter Twenty-Two:
Technology

We are stuck with technology when what we really want is just stuff that works. – Douglas Adams

~

Smart Tech for Multifamily Properties: The Pros and Cons

Smart home technology is growing in popularity in the multifamily property industry. Many property owners are installing devices in both individual rental units and common areas. And smart tech can be a smart move. Offering this kind of technology in your property can increase your fair market rental value, attract higher-paying tenants, and make your property stand out on the market.

But it's not without its drawbacks. You need to weigh the pros and cons of offering smart home technology before you start investing in it.

What smart tech is right for multifamily properties?

Smart technology shouldn't be a gimmick. It should provide a valuable service to you and your residents. That service might be a convenient amenity, energy savings, or increased security. Here are some of the most popular smart home tech items in multifamily properties:

- **Smart locks and digital doorman.** Rekey properties without incurring an additional cost and create a system that acts as a digital doorman for deliveries and guests.
- **Smart home lighting.** Turn lights on and off from a smartphone, reducing energy costs and providing an extra layer of security for vacant properties.
- **Automatic temperature controls.** Stop paying to heat empty properties with smart thermostats, controlled by a smartphone from anywhere with an internet connection.
- **Automated water sensors.** Sensors alert you to the presence of water when there shouldn't be, helping you put a stop to potential water damage issues.
- **Building-wide WiFi.** Offer building wide WiFi for free or a nominal charge as a rental perk.

Is smart tech right for your property?

Smart tech won't be the right choice for every property in your portfolio. But if you have a Class A property, then you can't compete on the market without it. Renters at this level expect it. Class B properties should have the tech if the current market is demanding it. Otherwise, you won't need to consider it for at least a few more years until the prices drop or the tech becomes obsolete.

Smart home tech can be a great addition for Class C properties, but you'll need to choose the items carefully. Make sure current rental rates will support the investment and look for less expensive options. Chapter Twenty-Three: Pro Tips for Success, includes a detailed description of Class, A, B and C properties.

Make sure you protect yourself & your residents

The biggest negative when it comes to smart tech in your multifamily property is the risk it creates for you and your renters. You'll need to put safeguards in place to mitigate that risk. Because this technology is all connected to your internet service, you'll need protection from cyber-attacks. That includes encryption for sensitive data as well as anti-virus and anti-malware software.

You may want to partner with an experienced IT company who can help you keep your smart tech up to date with the latest protection. Leslie Carhart, a cybersecurity professional, offers advice for property managers considering smart home tech. At a minimum, she says, property managers need to prevent resident access to controls and have networks professionally secured.

Remember that you'll need to teach renters how to responsibly use the new technology. Then put community rules and guidelines in place. This will ensure that everyone knows the rules and understands what will happen if they don't use the technology properly.

Consider putting tenant's devices to work

You can spend a small fortune installing smart technology in your multifamily property. But you don't have to. One of the ways to cut costs is by putting your residents' own devices to work. Most systems will connect through their smartphone, so you won't need to provide a separate hub for operation.

Many residents likely already have an Amazon Echo (amazon.com/echo) or Google Nest device (google.com) that can control smart home technology. If they don't, think about using these devices as a renewal incentive or rental concession. They are inexpensive, will operate all the smart home technology, and can be a big perk for renters.

Put resident's digital assistant to work

Amazon has sold more than one hundred million Alexa digital assistants. Think that's impressive? Google's digital assistant is available on more than one billion devices around the world. As a property owner, are you putting those digital devices to use? Many property managers are embracing the popularity of these devices by using them to connect with their residents. Programs can help residents make maintenance requests and send voice memos to management.

Some property managers are making digital assistants an amenity in itself. Encouraging smart home tech not only appeals to tech-savvy renters, but it can also help reduce operating costs. When residents can turn down the heat and turn off lights no matter where they are in the world, it's a win-win for everyone.

Questions to ask before you invest

Ready to take the smart tech plunge for your multifamily property? Here are a few questions to answer before you start shopping.

- **How will installing the technology help my property?** It could make it more competitive on the market or attract a new demographic of renters. Smart home tech also offers asset protection for owners and operational perks for property managers. For instance, automated water sensors such as LeakSmart (leaksmart.com) help protect your investment property against the threat of water damage.

- **How much could we save on energy costs?** An in-depth analysis of what you are currently spending on common areas will determine what the tech could help you save. Remember that your renters could end up saving, too, making your property a more attractive one.

- **Will there be a return on the smart tech investment?** If you purchase the devices, will it help you increase the fair market rental value of your property? Or are you unlikely to see much increase? Don't invest in it if it won't pay you back in the long run.

- **Can I actually afford to buy the technology?** Don't buy the technology if it's going to create cash flow issues for you. Carefully price out everything you are going to need and look at your annual budget.

- **How could it complicate my job as a property owner?** You'll be responsible for the maintenance and upkeep of the technology, especially in common areas and possibly in your individual units as well. Ask your property manager if they have the resources necessary to help out with this task.

Once you've answered these questions, you should have a clearer idea about what technology is right for your property and where to start investing.

What's New in Smart Apartment Technology?

Some of the new renters entering the market are becoming apartment dwellers for the first time. The Urban Institute's Housing Finance Policy Center (urban.org) reports that there are about 19 million renters who were homeowners at some time in the previous 16 years. Many of these folks have a foreclosure or some other negative mark on their credit that prevents them from qualifying for another home loan.

There are also millennials who have never owned a home and have no credit. What seems like bad news for the housing market can be good news for apartment owners and landlords. Many are now trying to hold onto their renters by providing the smart home luxuries that were previously only targeted at homeowners.

IOTAS

Leading the way in smart apartment technology is startup IOTAS (iotashome.com). Their goal is to provide tenants with an apartment that learns from their usage habits and lifestyle to save on energy costs, enhance their daily lives, and help them be more efficient overall. For example, at bedtime, the system ensures that all doors are locked, lights are off, and the temperature is set to the occupant's sleep preference. Renters can program the IOTAS system themselves, or it has the ability to learn the preferences of renters based on their daily routine.

For the landlords and property owners, they hope to keep renters loyal, optimize rental income, and provide a wealth of useful information about tenant populations.

Targeting millennials

Just as they are dominating the housing market, this group of newly forming households is the largest segment of new renters. According to Bailey Brand Consulting (baileygp.com), about 75 percent of millennials believe technology enhances their lives. For apartment owners to remain competitive, they must embrace smart apartment technology for their units and have it available to an ever-increasing segment of their renters. If you think the current generation of renters is tech-savvy, just think about how the next wave of new renters will be a few years from now.

Investing in the latest technological advancements in rentals is likely to reap rewards for many years to come.

Multifamily Tech Ideas You'll Love

Technology can be a powerful tool when it comes to managing your multifamily properties. It can help you save time, connect with your residents, and market your properties to an increasingly digital audience. Here are some of the best multifamily tech tools and ideas you should consider giving a try in your properties.

Take your property tours online

Even the best leasing agent can only handle a handful of resident tours each day. If you put the right technology to use, though, your capacity for tours is practically limitless. Many multifamily property owners are opting for online and self-guided tours.

The self-guided tour allows potential residents to browse apartments and the communal facilities on their own, sometimes guided with a smartphone app. For example, Tour24 (tour24now.com) serves as an extension to leasing teams by letting prospective renters to do self-guided tours. When you aren't relying on your agent to show potential renters around, you free them up to focus on delivering top customer service to those most interested in the property.

Virtual tours incorporate YouTube videos, 3D tours of the property, and even augmented reality to showcase the space. Property management software designer AppFolio (appfolio.com) offers some great tips for making your virtual tours the best they can be. Visit their site and be sure to take a look at their terrific property management tips blog while there.

Go digital with your doorman

Between package deliveries, dog walkers, and food drop-offs, how many non-residents are coming to the front door of your building each day? It can be an almost endless flow of people for some buildings. Without a doorman, how are you balancing safety concerns with meeting the needs of your residents? Some property owners are embracing multifamily tech with smart doorbell systems and creating virtual doormen.

This new multifamily tech integrates into the building's existing infrastructure without any new wiring. Touch screens by the front door allow visitors to contact the apartment they need. If no one is home, no problem. The screen can connect the visitor to the apartment resident through their smartphone. It's all the benefits of a doorman with a more personalized digital approach.

Vendors like brivo (brivo.com) and Mobile Doorman (mobiledoorman.com) have created cloud-based access control systems and apps that allow residents to interact with your property from their mobile devices.

Using smartphones to create a community hub

There is a good chance most of your residents have a smartphone within reaching distance right now, so put them to use. There are apps on the market right now that are turning resident's smartphones into digital community hubs for your building. Residents pay their rent and make service requests through the app, as well as get push notifications in emergencies. It's one of the most cost-effective ways to connect with your residents.

Want to get your building started with a smart community hub? Check out Resident 360 (resident360.com). This app does it all.

Safely embrace the sharing economy

Short-term rentals can be a great way to bring a new income stream to your multifamily property. Managing those short-term rentals can be a headache, though. Technology to the rescue! They made an app for that.

There are now short-term rental management apps that will help you set availability as well as track who is currently in your property. It's a much easier way to manage the process, work with your long-term residents, and retain the financial benefits.

Prior to the COVID-19 pandemic you could take advantage of short-term rental operators like Pillow.com where building owners could split revenue with residents listing their space when they are out of town. ApartmentJet.com was another such operator designed specifically for multifamily property owners and managers dealing with the occasional short-term rental. Both platforms were acquired, pre-pandemic, by Expedia (Expedia.com) whose goal was to offer flex living space. It too, decided to wind down this program during the pandemic but rest assured new concepts will emerge.

Stay on top of multifamily tech trends

Learning about the latest real estate tech trends can help you stay at the forefront of this competitive industry. Not only can technology help reduce your operating expenses, but it's something that more and more of your residents are going to demand.

What's the Best Multifamily Property Management Software for You?

Software for multifamily property management is a great tool for your arsenal. With management software, you can automate parts of your current processes and procedures, saving a ton of time and decreasing the chance of costly mistakes. In short, a property management program can make you more efficient and streamline your daily and overall operations, making tenants happier and your job easier.

While the right multifamily property management software can be a time-saving dream, the wrong kind can become the stuff of nightmares. Before you buy, identify the "right" program for you by looking at the specifics of your situation.

What do you need to automate?

The whole point of using software is to do your job better and faster, so there's no point in wasting time on a program that is filled with features you'll never use.

Make a list of what you need to automate and what you don't. If you're spending hours annually on property inspections, for example, you'll want a program that lets you enter the inspection data, create and save reports and issue automatic reminders. However, if you carry out inspections infrequently or have another company handle them, software that is packed with inspection tools probably won't do much for you.

Do you have special considerations?

Some property management software and apps have special features that are situation specific. One example is ET Water, included on Multifamily Executive's "Hot Property Management Apps" list. This app uses local data to create a custom watering schedule for your landscaping that communicates via WiFi. It's a great app if you have expensive plants, a dry climate or other greenery concerns, but if your landscaping is minimal or you have a company handle your lawn and grassy areas, it's not of much value to your properties.

What's your comfort level?

A program with all the bells and whistles can seem like a great idea and it may very well be, but you want to be realistic about your tech habits. If a program that's loaded with features is likely to frustrate you or won't be something you'll stick with, look for a more user-friendly program, even if that means sacrificing some features or tools you are interested in. Once you get into the habit of using property management software, you can try going with a more comprehensive program.

Some of the most popular multifamily property management software platforms are:

- AppFolio (appfolio.com)
- ResMan (myresman.com)
- Yardi (yardi.com)
- Buildium (buildium.com)
- RealPage (realpage.com)

Always check the reviews and compare costs of the property management programs and apps you're considering before you buy and try free demos if they're available. Putting a little time and research will help you find the right program for your business at the right price.

Lease Units Like A Pro with Today's Technology

Whether you're an experienced property owner or you've just invested in your first multifamily dwelling, knowing how to lease units is imperative. It's time to step into the 21st century! Today's tenants aren't looking for slow, outdated methods. Instead, make sure that you have the right technology to make leasing a snap for your multifamily dwelling.

Make yourself available

Managing an apartment complex or other multifamily property isn't a 9-5 proposition. In order to lease units like a pro you need to be available to answer questions, schedule tours, and make contact with potential tenants. Tenants often look for new apartments when they aren't at work, rather than during traditional office hours. They might check things out on their commute, or they might sit down for a few minutes at lunchtime.

Whether you answer the phones yourself or use an alternative, potential tenants need to be able to reach you. Try using a call center or conversational assistant to ensure that there's always someone on call. LeaseHawk (leasehawk.com) offers a new AI-powered leasing assistant called ACE AI (Answers Calls Every time). It answers your callers' questions after hours or when your staff is unavailable.

Make contact convenient through texting

Many people today simply don't have time to talk on the phone, nor do they want to wait until it's convenient to, say, step out of the office and make a phone call. Others find phone conversations anxiety-provoking, especially if they struggle to hear you over ambient noise.

Make sure you're willing to text, especially the small details! This simple step can reduce anxiety and make it easier for potential tenants to connect with you at any time, no matter where they are.

Put together a fantastic website

In the digital age, being able to find your listing is critical. You can't afford to just market your apartment complex by throwing an ad in the paper. This is not an effective way to lease units. Instead, put together a fantastic, responsive website, including all the right elements:

- **A responsive, mobile-friendly design:** Remember, you never know when people are going to look for vacancies in your apartment complex, and the majority of internet traffic is now mobile. If your website isn't mobile responsive, you'll be missing out on both potential renters and search engine ranking.
- **Automated pricing:** People are looking for all the information in one place–and that includes what it's going to cost them to rent your apartment. Without pricing information, they will turn to another option.
- **Key information:** What are potential renters looking for when they visit your website? Include all the right information so that they can clearly see everything they want to know about your apartment:

  - **Apartment and community amenities.** What's nearby? Do you offer a swimming pool? Green space? A gym? Make sure you talk up all the important details of your complex.

632

- o **Tons of photos and floor plans.** Let potential renters get a good idea of what they're considering when they look at your multifamily dwelling.
- o **Neighborhood, community, and local merchant information.** Where do your residents do their grocery shopping? What activities do they enjoy? Is there a park nearby? Talk up the community so that renters can see what they're getting into no matter where they are when they check out that information.
- o **Online and self-guided property tours.** Let prospective renters walk through the apartments as though they're there.
- o **Full disclosure information.** Provide access to rent, fees, deposits, utilities, and anything else your tenants might need to know. This may save you a lot of time down the road, since it will prevent renters from needing to ask questions and increase the odds that you'll get renters who are genuinely interested in your vacant unit.

Lead generation through Google and internet listing services (ILS) is vitally important. You need to be able to find potential renters who are ready to choose your property—a great website will help you get there. With a poor website, on the other hand, you may struggle to get noticed, and that in turn can decrease your chances of successfully leasing units.

Beyond the lead: Making those conversions

Once you've caught your leads through a great website and marketing strategy, make sure you're taking the right steps to convert them to renters with the following:

- **Property and individual unit amenities:** Depending on your price range and your market, you need to offer amenities that will help your complex stand out. Don't just be another face in the crowd; instead, look for ways to offer bonuses to your renters, whether that means a laundry complex, a swimming pool, or a community space where members of your community can come together.
- **Curb appeal:** What does the apartment complex look like when people first walk up? Is it genuinely appealing to potential renters? Visual appeal matters, especially as potential renters are forming their first impressions.
- **A team that's trained to listen:** Your team needs to know what renters want, how to give it to them, and how to offer a fantastic customer service experience.
- **Great online reviews:** Managing your reviews is a critical point in the leasing and lead generation process. Bad reviews can kill your leads! Ask current and past tenants, especially happy ones, for reviews. Issue regular surveys to get a better idea of what tenants like and dislike. This simple step can go a long way toward helping you lease units, keep your tenants happy and your reviews good.

Resident surveys and online reviews are covered in detail in Chapter Twenty: Resident Retention.

Mobile-first: What Your Property Manager Needs to Know

Welcome to the mobile-first age. You already know that high web traffic is crucial for your brand's visibility. Sites that attract the most visitors typically appear at the top of search results after a query is entered on

Google. However, you may not be aware of how the world's leading search engine is perceiving your website.

Current tenants should be able to reach you easily and (perhaps more importantly) potential tenants should see you first.

Previously, Google ranked sites in terms of traditional desktop hits and SEO strength. This made the amount of traffic drawn via mobile devices such as iPhones and Droids a bit less important. That is no longer the case. Google now places a higher priority on the traffic generated by mobile platforms when determining a site's placement in search results.

Responsive web pages

Responsive web pages are sites that serve all devices via identical sets of URLs. Translation: the same site is accessible to your tenants whether they are on their desktop, tablet, or phone. The information and display are automatically formatted to match what is appropriate for the device that they happen to be using. The experience won't be clumsy via a phone *or* tablet.

The mobile-first strategy was adopted for a reason. Opting to use devices such as smartphones to browse the internet is becoming the go-to for the average web surfer. Less people are choosing to use a laptop or desktop to view a webpage. Thus, a site's presentation on a mobile platform has become much more important.

Make sure that your website is set as a "responsive" or "dynamic serving" site. This way, visitors can easily browse your homepage from all devices.

If you're not properly preparing your web presence, those who do manage to find you on the net will have an awkward experience. Your website will look awkward and unprofessionally arranged.

Mobile-first makeover

Gearing up for the next chapter of the digital age is about more than just aesthetics. A smart strategy for composing a site that will be well-received across all platforms is focusing on content that will be easily digestible on the smaller device.

It's easier to project upwards than it is to squeeze later. Content that looked great on your desktop may not show as well on the smaller screens. Check the content on your desktop site. Would it look cluttered even on a responsive site via a tablet or phone? If so, consider a more concise rewrite.

Pro tip: Stay ahead of the digital game and make sure your web presence is ready for the mobile-first era. Your bottom line will likely thank you sooner rather than later.

Provide Exceptional Customer Service via Your Tenant Portal

Modern renters expect to take care of business online. A tenant portal allows your valuable residents to conduct business with you online and in a single place.

Give your renters what they're looking for

Well-designed multifamily property management software makes life easy for you and residents. This software is a viable option to designing and managing your own property management website. Whichever option you choose, keep in mind prospective renters seek online features that make renting a breeze.

When choosing your online options start with a few essential items your tenants will need.

For prospective residents

Start at the beginning. You have a potential new resident. What would they want to see to make a decision about living at your community? Your website is their introduction to your world. When prospective residents visit you online, they want to see

- Standard floor plans
- Photos and videos of available units
- Your proximity to town amenities
- Your property amenities
- A FAQ page—with links to your social media sites
- Upcoming community events and news
- Tenant incentive programs

Of course, they'll want to fill out an application! And when a prospect can complete and submit a rental application on the spot, you minimize your risk of losing them to the competition.

For your brand-new resident

Let's assume everything checks out, the money clears and you give your prospective resident the green light. A well-organized tenant portal allows residents to

- Exchange shared documents
- Complete and sign lease agreements
- Make security deposit and rent payments
- Enroll in tenant incentive programs
- Download a PDF copy of your tenant handbook
- Sign off on video and/or photos of individual unit inspections

Help your new resident settle in

Another important part of your tenant portal is your new resident orientation page. This page is for tenants about to move-in or those freshly moved-in. Information is valuable, so approach this page as if you just moved into town. Introduce your new resident to your community. Make them feel at home with the following:

- Tenant welcome letter—PDF version
- Staff introductions
- Map of the building with emergency exits indicated
- Important local numbers: hospitals, schools, pharmacies and emergency services
- Basics of the local town: map of area, public transportation, playgrounds and shopping options

- How-to tutorials on submitting maintenance requests and paying rent online
- Links and invitations to join your social media
- Instructions on contacting customer service

Pro tip: A tenant portal allows you to provide outstanding customer service securely and safely and will make life easier for you and your residents.

Paperless: Why it's Necessary and How You Can Achieve It

Converting your property management company to a paperless operation is both simple and necessary. Adopting an enhanced digital platform:

- boosts your bottom line
- reduces clutter
- maximizes your exposure
- lends a hand to the environment as well.

Whether you're a full-service property management firm or just getting your feet wet in the multifamily world, here are steps that you can take to streamline your operations, bolster your earnings, and stay on pace with the competition.

Electronic bill pay

The phrase "you have to spend money to make money," doesn't always have to be taken so literally.

Long term, perpetual investment in paper billing and other mailers to your tenants is costing you both time and money. A web-based paperless approach to billing cuts down on man-hours. It also removes the overhead spent on paper invoices and improves the likelihood of receiving payment on time.

Tenants can now pay their rents via the online tenant portal at any time day or night, when it's most convenient for them. This means:

- No more trips to the post office
- No more buying stamps
- In a matter of minutes rent can be paid instantaneously after receiving the invoice via their email.

Maintaining maintenance

Paying their bill isn't the only task that your tenants should be able to complete online. Whether you own/manage one property or 100, maintenance and repairs are a large part of your responsibility.

Allowing tenants to issue a paperless maintenance request via an app or on your website allows you to deploy the necessary resources to fix the problem. Your tenants don't have to wait on hold, hunt down a superintendent, or reach you directly. Everybody wins.

Web presence

As previously stated, a website is no longer a nifty feature or an alternative way to contact a business. Your web presence is your lifeblood.

The previous recommendations ensure that your current tenants can easily access you and pay their bills. New tenants (and investors) need to find you on the web. Commanding high web traffic is crucial for your brand's visibility.

Pro tip: Prioritizing a digital presence over a paper one is crucial for businesses of all sizes. Make sure that your web presence is primed for a digital world and that your tenants have clear paths to fulfill their duties.

Must-Have Apps for Landlords

There is no doubt that certain apps can help save time and effort in the long run. The process of finding the right apps for landlords can consume large amounts of time. How much time have you spent browsing through the app store, reading descriptions and scanning reviews? It can be a time warping experience. Let's make it simple.

Being a landlord can keep you busy, but the right technology will simplify your complicated life. The following technologies are landlord tools that will help you flourish and expand your business.

Landlordy

If you download only one new app from this list, then Landlordy (landlordy.com) is the one to get. Landlordy organizes your single or multifamily rentals all in one place. Enter your rental unit data, send rent invoices, receipts and/or copies of documents to your residents or yourself.

There is a screen with all relevant tenant information, including tenant phone and email, photos, lease details, fees and notes. Pretty solid, right? That's just the tip of the iceberg. After you enter the data, Landlordy sends you reminders for regular checks and maintenances for essential appliances like gas furnaces, smoke and CO detectors. Yes, all of those little details in one place. You can add information on appliances, attach user manuals, notes, error codes and photos to access them easily. Landlordy has tutorials and a useful blog on their website.

Dropbox

Dropbox (dropbox.com) has become essential in today's world of sharing and managing files. Dropbox backs up and uses file synchronization between mobile devices and Windows, Mac or Linux computers. It helps you keep your most important files safe—online or offline. Many other apps, including Landlordy work with Dropbox to keep documents, videos or photos organized. This is how business is done. No one wants to spend time with their file cabinet.

Scanbot

Scanbot (scanbot.io) is another one of the top apps that works seamlessly with Dropbox. Scanbot is, literally, a document scanner in your phone or tablet. That's amazing in itself, right? Just hold your mobile device over a document and Scanbot will automatically detect it, take the scan and even make corrections. Choose PDF or JPEG file formats for your new scans, and they will be automatically uploaded to your Dropbox account. You can scan all kinds of media: contracts, receipts, business cards, whiteboards, flip charts notes, newspaper articles, as well as barcodes and QR codes. Your mobile office just got easier.

PDF Expert 5

PDF files are part of everyday life. Hands down, it is one of most universal formats to send a document to another person. Almost any computing device can view them, and they will almost always display as needed with formatting and layout intact across all manner of platforms and devices. PDF Expert 5 (apple.com) is for anyone who reads, annotates or edits PDF documents on iPad or iPhone. It allows you to markup documents with highlights and handwriting, insert text, sign and even merge other PDFs. Here is another app that uses Dropbox integration.

Inventory Pro

The Inventory Pro app (inventory-pro.co.uk) is simple and straightforward. It provides an easy way to record the condition of a property before and after tenants. The app includes text descriptions, photographs and video options for each room. You can itemize everything and assign a star rating system to document the current condition of each item.

Inventory Pro includes a PDF document generator for your reports so you can share the information with tenants, real estate agents and property managers. In the UK the Inventory PDF Report can act as a legally binding document. In the US documenting your properties before and after tenants just makes sense to prevent legal hassles.

roOomy

We all know that a staged home will sell faster than an empty one, right? Here is the app for the gap between tenants. roOomy (rooomy.com) is a futuristic app for virtually staging any apartment or house "through the power of 3D, Augmented and Virtual Reality."

All you have to do is take a photo of the room that you would like to stage. Second, measure the room. At that point the magic happens. roOmy turns the room into a 3D space where you can now add furniture and decor.

If you are getting ready to lease an apartment or home, you can delete existing furniture in the photos and replace them virtually with updated pieces. This will create a fresh, updated look in listing photos. You can save and share your room designs with your social media networks to attract tenants.

This is becoming one of our favorite landlord tools. You really have to see the before and after photographs for yourself to understand the power of this technology. Besides landlords, this app would be great for sellers or renovators.

Happy Inspector

This is a similar app to Inventory Pro, but one difference is that Happy Inspector (happyco.com) has 100% offline functionality. There is no cellular data or WiFi needed to make your property inspections. After going through an inspection with a tenant you can record an electronic signature. Add your own branding to reports to stay professional and store the inspection results online.

This app provides reminders on inspection dates. It also makes inspections easy by allowing for a simple tap to rate the condition of every part of the unit. Photographs can be taken directly from the app and saved in the inspection form to document any damage.

LandlordStation

LandlordStation (landlordstation.com) serves several basic, useful purposes. Let me say off the bat that LandlordStation doesn't have an app yet, but the website converts to mobile devices beautifully.

They provide tenant screening, renters insurance, online rent payment and secure document signing services. These online services will keep your residents happy and will keep you competitive in the housing market. Equally important, going online and eliminating paperwork will make your life easier.

The tenant screening LandlordStation provides is comprehensive. The basic check can be expanded to include criminal and eviction records. You can include phone verifications of rental and employment history and references of potential tenants. Sounds like an easy button for landlords!

Need a Package Delivery System at Your Multifamily Rental Property?

One of the biggest concerns that urban dwellers and residents of multifamily units have is whether their packages will arrive in a timely manner… or at all. In fact, with rise of e-commerce most apartment residents view a package delivery system as a must-have amenity.

Up to 30% of Americans have been victims of "porch piracy," and countless more have had to jump through hoop after hoop to recover costs from lost, delayed, or damaged shipments. Still others have decided to completely forgo online orders to their apartment, and instead deal with the inconvenience of using their office, or a family member's residence, as their "ship-to" address.

In contrast, multifamily housing communities that offer a streamlined package delivery system help prevent many of these issues and add to their residents' happiness and peace of mind. With such factors in mind, what are some package delivery system solutions currently on the market that could work for your multifamily unit(s)? Here are three possibilities to consider, along with their pros and cons:

Incorporating package delivery into regular staff duties

Some communities have had to dedicate staff members, or at least portions of their staff members' work shifts, solely to the purpose of delivering packages to residential units. For instance, during times of package room "spillover" one property developer and manager has had to task community staff members with unit deliveries in shifts of 8 hours at a time.

Software developers have come up with some ways to save time and boost efficiency for property managers that opt to go this route. For instance, MRI Real Estate Software (mrisoftware.com) has developed an app for smartphone and tablets that scans packages, verifies delivery to the correct unit, and then notifies the resident of the shipment's successful arrival.

- **Pros:** This solution avoids the need for ever increasing storage space and ensures maximum convenience and safety for residents' packages. Some communities cover basic costs by charging a small convenience fee to their residents who benefit from this service or increasing rent.

- **Cons:** There may be some costs around software purchase, installation, and training. However, the biggest drawback is payroll costs: either you'll need to hire more staff, or your current staff will have to juggle yet another task in their busy schedule.

Installing smart lockers/individual unit lock boxes

Another option that has gained some traction in the last few years is the installation of "smart lockers" or lock boxes for each individual unit in a community. The delivery person would have access to the lock box's code and could put the resident's package in this secure location. Then, when the resident comes home from work later that day, he or she will be able to enter the code and retrieve the package with maximum convenience. This is similar to the Amazon Key service (amazon.com/key), except more geared towards apartment living instead of houses with a garage.

While many property managers and residents view this as an ideal package delivery system, the costs of installing individual lock boxes could be significant (or even exorbitant). For instance, even without space considerations, a basic BoxLock (getboxlock.com) package costs upwards of $200 for an individual apartment; if you are managing 50 units, installing a product at every residence would run well over $10,000 in costs!

- **Pros:** This is a highly secure package delivery system, and your staff members don't have to get heavily involved in the actual delivery process.

- **Cons:** Purchase and installation could be extremely costly.

Using a centralized depot

Many communities dedicate a room, or a specific space to package storage. Usually packages are placed in a secured locker for later pickup by residents; or in certain gated communities where the depot is near or adjacent to the guardhouse. Hub by Amazon (amazon.com/hub) and Luxer One (luxerone.com) are both examples of a centralized solution.

One potential advantage of employing a centralized package depot lies in the fact that steadily increasing pressure from the USPS is being put on Congress to mandate a move to such centralized locations for all apartment communities. However, such a move could be full of potential problems (design/construction costs, available space, increased staffing, etc.) for currently existing communities.

Additionally, space issues, combined with negligent or forgetful residents, could lead to package "spillover," which would in turn lead to a number of other issues, such as a reduction in the level of package security.

- **Pros:** This is generally a high-security solution, it does not require increased payroll costs, and one day it may even be mandated by law.
- **Cons:** Centralized depots often come with space, security, and clutter issues.

There are several methods of providing a secure and streamlined package delivery system to the residents in your multifamily units.

Chapter Twenty-Three:
Pro Tips for Success

*Business, more than any other occupation, is a continual
dealing with the future; it is a continual calculation, an
instinctive exercise in foresight. – Henry R. Luce*

~

Stay on Top of Apartment Trends

As an investor, an owner-operator, or a developer in multifamily real
estate, what are you doing to calculate for the future? With uncertainty in
politics, the economy, and more, it's easy to throw up your hands and leave
the predictions on apartment trends to Miss Cleo. Sorry to say, that's not
going to cut it in this industry. With the right tools and knowledge at your
disposal, you'll be ready to anticipate problems before they show up.

Knowledge is power (and profit)

In this industry, you basically need to know everything, preferably in
advance, if you want to maximize your profits. While that may be a

bit of an exaggeration, there are several ways you can stay as in the know as possible.

Keep tabs on the competition

To keep a competitive edge, it's important to know what your major competitors and industry leaders are up to. Pay attention to social media accounts of your top competitors to see what marketing techniques they are employing and what demographics they might be targeting. Take note of what amenities they are—and are not—hyping at the moment. A little Facebook stalking can go a long way in this industry.

Research the hottest—and coldest—markets

Staying on top of nationwide apartment trends and predictions can make a huge difference in your profitability. The last thing you want is to invest in a new property just as the market has peaked. When the only way is down, your profits follow suit.

Before you make any decisions about where to invest, you must get a clear picture of the area's potential. That means taking into account factors like local job growth, average rental rate increases, population growth, and vacancy rates. Research nationwide economic trends as well as local market trends for the best picture of overall market health.

Pinpoint the trendiest amenities

You can have a great marketing campaign and a property in the hottest apartment market in the country, but if you aren't offering what renters want, you'll miss out. Multifamily Executive (multifamilyexecutive.com) is one of the best places online to track apartment trends. From food trucks to pet spas to an indoor half-pipe skate park, you'll have plenty of ideas about what attracts the newest generation of renters.

"Problems" you may have missed

Be proactive, not reactive. When you stay on top of industry news, you can often get the jump on the ever-evolving array of problems that can crop up for property owners.

Investors just a few short years ago had no idea their buildings may soon be overrun with mountains of Amazon boxes and multitudes of short-term subletters. It's hard to tell what the next big issue may be but keeping up with apartment trends can help you spot a problem before it becomes insurmountable. Here are just a few major issues you could be dealing with now or in the very near future:

Amazon avalanche

A property owner with a highly hands-off approach might be caught off guard by the (seemingly) sudden avalanche of Amazon packages being dumped on properties each day. Someone with a finger on the pulse of trends, however, will know that package deliveries have dramatically increased in recent years, causing many apartment leasing offices to be overwhelmed and overrun with packages.

The Airbnb dilemma

As a property owner who plays by the rules, it might be shocking to learn that some tenants try to sublet *your* apartments via Airbnb or other short-term rental sites. Alas, it's a real problem that can be difficult to track and control.

Staying in the know can allow you to see how other owners have tackled the issue. Airbnb is trying to work with the real estate industry for a mutually beneficial relationship.

What about rent control?

Rent control is a hot topic in many major cities where the cost of living is high, or where it's anticipated to rise. It's a policy issue that many politicians and local officials latch on to for a variety of reasons. You can bet that when housing becomes an issue rent control becomes a hot topic of politicians.

The National Multifamily Housing Council (nmhc.org) provides well researched information about the true cost of rent control to a local economy. When the issue pops up in local politics, it will be important to have your facts ready to present in the media or to local officials.

Top resources to stay up on apartment trends

Here is a quick list of reputable sources for information you need.

- HousingFinance.com
- HousingWire.com
- MultifamilyExecutive (multifamilyexecutive.com)
- Kiplinger's annual real estate report (kiplinger.com)
- National Multifamily Housing Council (nmhc.org)

- National Apartment Association (www.naahq.org)

Study Your Rental Market and Outperform Your Competition

As an owner of rental property, you are competing with other local rental properties for residents. This is your opportunity to shine! When you know what the rental market offers and what your target demographic wants you will outperform your competition. Here's how to do it.

Who wants to live at your property?

The answers will influence your

- Marketing decisions
- Target demographics
- Renovations, upgrades and amenities decisions
- Exit strategies

Working adults with children will want a neighborhood with good schools, parks, grocery shopping, public transportation and low crime.

Young single adults are influenced by trendy attractions, social activities and major employment centers. American households are changing and it's your job to stay current on housing trends.

Is your rental competition snoozing?

There's nothing worse than getting caught taking a nap when everyone else is hitting balls out of the park.

Don't let complacency get a foothold. If every rental property around you offers stainless steel appliances and granite counter tops, and you expect to command the same rents without offering like amenities, you're definitely in dreamland.

On the other hand, when you know what the other owners are up to (or not up to) you'll know how to attract the best residents around; get the highest rents; and make a killing when you sell your property.

- What does the local rental market want?
- Does the local rental community give it to them?

Pro tip: Set up some local property tours as a prospective renter. Look at properties from the eye of your target demographic. When you understand the desires of your target renter your life as a real estate investor becomes much easier.

Do your residents boast about how much rent they pay?

In some markets the rental rate is the only thing that matters. Some residents want to pay the least amount of rent possible. In other markets residents are willing to pay a premium in exchange for great amenities. A high rental amount can even become a bragging right.

What's important to your target demographic? Free rent, paid utilities and low security deposits? Or high-end upgrades and amenities like a building wide WiFi network? If your market is only interested in the lowest rent possible exchange some 'freebies' for higher rent.

For example, you can:

- Offer free parking if your lot is not full.
- Let your resident paint one wall the color of their choice.
- Replace the lighting fixture or counter space in the bathroom.
- Install a water faucet filter.
- Replace shades on overhead lights.
- Install new blinds.
- Double the kitchen counter and storage space with a rolling island.
- Install wood laminate design flooring in the main living room.

None of these 'upgrades' will break your bank and residents will be happy to pay a little more.

Amenities – the key to bragging rights

Families will want an in-unit washer and dryer above all other amenities. If your units are short on space install stacking washer/dryers. If residents in neighboring rental properties are walking to the local laundry you've just outsmarted your competition.

Another option is to complete a higher-end renovation on your community laundry room by adding new paint; trendy floor tile; upgraded energy-smart appliances; comfortable seating; and entertainment like TV and audio.

Young adults may want the bare minimum in their personal unit while insisting on great social common areas. Why not convert existing common areas to new uses? For example, turn an unused storage area into bicycle parking or a recycling area—or both. Install small stackable washers and dryers in each unit and convert your laundry to a wireless café and resident lounge. Re-deck the pool or add an outdoor kitchen with barbecue. Update the common areas with fresh color schemes.

Don't get stuck with the wrong unit type and size

You must know what the market wants! If local market demand is for two- and three-bedroom units and you buy a property with all studio apartments you will struggle with leasing from day one. Or, you might own a property with 100% occupancy in two-bedroom units while one-bedroom units sit empty for months and months.

Understand the value of community

Families will want a family-oriented community. They don't want to live in a singles rental. They want a nice, safe, secure, clean living environment. Spend some of your renovation budget refreshing the interior of the property and upgrading the landscaping.

Seniors may prefer to live with other seniors in a quiet, clean property with easy access to entryways and parking. A pet friendly residence may be a priority.

The social scene will appeal to young adults.

It's imperative that you study the neighborhood and determine the nature of the overall local community before you buy your property.

Take a little drive

Here are some ideas for evaluating a neighborhood before you buy. These tips are also a great way to measure how your property fits in the mix if you already own a rental property. As you drive around ask yourself the following questions.

- Who lives in the area?
- What is the reputation of the neighborhood?
- Why would people enjoy living there?
- Does the neighborhood consist of families or mostly young adults?
- Are people loitering at street corners?
- Are there plenty of runners, walkers and bike riders?
- Is the neighborhood deteriorating or showing signs of positive change and improvements?
- What types of cars do the locals drive? At what time of day are they parked at home?
- Does it look as though crime might be an issue? Are windows and doors barred?
- How nice is the landscaping?
- Is the area clean or full of trash?
- Do you see signs of pride of ownership?

In addition to driving around you'll find the answers to these and other questions by visiting with local residents and shop owners. Local property managers are also a terrific source of information.

What about bugs?

I saw a new apartment building come on the market the other day. The listing agents didn't include the asking price, so I hopped on Google and did an address search. The top Google search result read "Bed Bug Report for 1234 Cherry St." and linked to the site bedbugregistry.com. This is not what I expected to find. Although the owners may have satisfactorily resolved the issue it is always a good idea to check the property and the neighborhood for pest complaints.

Research supply and demand

Contact apartment rental leasing agents and property management companies directly to gather information on local rental demand and supply. Search Craigslist.com and Zillow.com on your specific market. Is it a renter's market where supply and vacancies are high? Or will you be able to complete some nice, simple refreshes on your property and command higher rents because supply is low?

Leasing agents, commercial property brokers and property management companies are also a perfect source for getting information about market rents, rental concessions, vacancies and listing volume.

Build a Multifamily Portfolio: Key Metrics for Success

Investing is more than just handing over the cash and becoming a property owner who earns passive income. It involves logic and cost-analysis. You have to determine whether or not an investment will yield the profits you want.

Quality of asset

When considering a multifamily property, you want to determine its quality which is based on a classification. Classifications grade a property based on a combination of geographical and physical characteristics, which help determine the level of risk or the possible amount of return associated with acquiring the property.

- **Class A:** The highest quality buildings in their market and area. They're usually built within the past 10 years, have the newest and latest amenities, and high-income earning tenants. Class A properties command the highest rent and the highest price per square foot. They're typically found in central business districts (CBDs) or sometimes in Class B areas. Class A properties are typically professionally managed and have little to no deferred maintenance issues.

- **Class B:** One step down from Class A properties and are generally older. They tend to have lower-income tenants and lower rents than Class A buildings and are not always professionally managed. These older properties may have some deferred maintenance issues but are mostly well-maintained. Class B properties are often seen as "value-add" properties that can be upgraded to Class B+ or sometimes Class A with renovations, updated amenities and improvements.

- **Class C:** Typically, more than 30 years old and located in economically depressed locations. Class C properties are generally in need of renovation and have dated amenities. They are usually located in low- to middle-income areas and rents are below those of Class B properties.

- **Class D:** Well over 30 years old and located in fringe markets. Class D properties are usually in need of extensive renovation and offer no amenity packages to residents. They are usually tenanted with a more transient demographic and can be operationally challenging without the proper management know-how and experience.

As you decide on the right multifamily property to invest in, consider the one that has the lowest level of risk and the highest amount of return, which are typically Class A, B and C properties. Building classification will also be a determining factor in your ability to obtain financing for the property.

Market conditions

The multifamily real estate market is constantly changing. So if you're looking to invest, you need to know what the current market conditions are to determine if it will be profitable for you. You have to consider things like supply vs. demand, demographics, position in real estate cycle, population, and employment growth. These factors play a huge role in the success of your multifamily investment venture.

Current and future property repair costs and maintenance expenses

Not all properties are made equal. Some are in great condition, while others may need extensive repair and maintenance. While acquiring a property in poor condition may seem like it's better for your pockets, understand that repair and maintenance costs add up.

You may find some hidden gems on the market that may need sprucing up and bring in great income, but it's important to do a cost-analysis first to see if the property you're considering will be worth the investment in the long run.

Multifamily portfolio diversification

Diversification is crucial to your real estate investing portfolio. It involves investing in different types of assets and in different geographic locations. This minimizes your portfolio's overall risk because it lessens the impact you'd see from a single asset loss. This is especially helpful if your deals outperform or underperform based off your original projections. Here are some examples of a diversified portfolio:

- **Single assets in multiple locations:** You might choose to invest in apartment buildings in Denver, Atlanta, and Portland.
- **Multiple assets in a single location:** You own a fourplex, several single-family properties, and a small apartment building in a single market or its suburbs.

Value-add opportunities

Value-add properties are great real estate investments because they can give you higher returns after increasing income with physical upgrades, better management, and added services and amenities. These features can lead to forced appreciation of the property, meaning it increases in value.

An infusion of capital into value-add properties can attract new tenants, help retain existing tenants, and generate higher rents, which can do wonders for your cashflow.

Multifamily portfolio sensitivity (risk) analysis

When performing a sensitivity analysis on a multifamily portfolio, you're trying to figure out how different factors might affect each property's returns and how a change in each factor would affect profits. Essentially, sensitivity risk analyses help you figure out the worst-case scenario for investing in a particular property and for weeding out non-performing properties.

A sensitivity analysis helps you answer questions like:

- What's the lowest rent you can charge, and still return a profit?
- At what vacancy rate will you start losing money?
- What happens if interest rates go up or down?
- What if demand for my asset or market goes up or down?

Compare property metrics

Once you've performed analyses on the properties you're thinking about investing in, it's time to sit down and compare the potential risks against the potential returns.

What properties are the least risky? Which ones are the riskiest? Are they risks you're willing to take? Are you almost certain you'll get a return? That your assets will appreciate in value? These are questions you want to ask yourself as you decide which investment property will be the most profitable.

Review and compare each of the following metrics for every property in your multifamily portfolio and for those you're thinking about acquiring:

- **Cash on Cash Return (COCR):** Ratio of annual before-tax cash flow to total cash invested.
- **Return on Investment (ROI):** Gain or loss relative to amount invested.
- **Net Operating Income (NOI):** Total revenue from rents and any additional income sources after all operating expenses such as insurance, property taxes, and maintenance costs have been deducted.
- **Capitalization Rate (cap):** Assumed, unleveraged rate of return (cash) before mortgage payments and income taxes.
- **Debt Service Coverage Ratio (DSCR):** Measurement of the cash flow that is available to pay the property's current debt obligations.
- **Operating Expense Ratio (OER):** Property expenses as percentage of gross operating income.

If these metrics intimidate you, don't worry. They intimidated me when I first started too. That's why I offer consulting and mentoring services for multifamily real estate investors who want to get their feet wet but are afraid that the water's too cold. Or who want to go bigger, faster.

You can also hop back to Chapter Nine: Deal Analysis for quick refresh on the topic.

Scale Your Multifamily Portfolio with a SWOT Analysis

There is a difference between owning a building and owning a business. If you've invested in multifamily properties and want to develop a thriving business, you need to think strategically about your income-producing assets. This becomes even more important when you are looking to scale your portfolio.

If you've acquired a new property, are looking to buy more, or haven't ever had a critical assessment of your current properties, you need to consider taking your portfolio through a SWOT analysis.

What is a SWOT analysis?

SWOT is an acronym for Strengths, Weaknesses, Opportunities, and Threats. You'll hear it used a lot in a business setting, especially in the areas of project management and investing. The SWOT analysis is a strategy-building tool that involves critically thinking about those four areas and determining what they are for your business. Or in this case, for your multifamily property portfolio.

Mind Tools (mindtools.com) writes, "What makes SWOT particularly powerful is that, with a little thought, it can help you uncover opportunities that you are well-placed to exploit. And by understanding the weaknesses of your business, you can manage and eliminate threats that would otherwise catch you unawares."

In other words, it's an excellent way to develop a plan to scale your portfolio in the most beneficial ways possible. Let's look at some of the areas to explore during a SWOT analysis of your property portfolio.

Strengths

When examining the strengths, you'll want to think about what's working with your current investments. Are you in an up-and-coming neighborhood? Is your building in great shape? Do you have a good reputation within the community?

Knowing what your strengths are can help you capitalize on them for future growth.

Questions to ask yourself:

- What does your property do better than any other in the area?
- Do you see opportunities to add value to your property or to the community?
- Can you find readily available and cost-effective resources?

Weaknesses

No portfolio is perfect. So where are the weaknesses in yours? Maybe you don't have a great management team in place. Or you aren't organized when it comes to record keeping. Or the neighborhood you are currently in is declining along with rental prices. Perhaps you are struggling with structural issues.

It's important to be objective about your weaknesses. After all, you can't fix them if you don't acknowledge they are there in the first place.

Question to ask yourself:

- What is the biggest problem you face on a daily basis concerning your properties?
- Are there gaps in leadership or motivational problems?
- Is your property poised for resilience?

Opportunities

Once you know your strengths and weaknesses, it's a lot easier to determine where there are opportunities for growth. That might include implementing new marketing strategies or making improvements to your properties. It may be finding areas where you can reduce expenses and increase revenue. It could even be knowing what industries are growing in your area and likely to bring in more potential renters.

The goal is to find ways to use your strengths to mitigate your weaknesses.

Questions to ask yourself:

- What trends are happening in your area that could benefit your current or future properties?
- Can you positively shift the presentation and perception of your property?
- Can you improve energy efficiency and implement other green strategies?

Threats

So what's stopping you from growing? These are the threats that you need to identify and overcome to maximize your portfolio's potential. There may be regulatory changes that could threaten your investments. Or higher risks associated with new financing. Maybe a saturated rental market is holding you back.

Knowing what the threats are will help you make plans and avoid potential damage.

Questions to ask yourself:

- What is standing in the way of you growing your property portfolio?
- Can you meet the demands of shifting consumer tastes and changing social patterns and lifestyles?

How SWOT can help you scale

Once you've identified the strengths, weaknesses, opportunities, and threats within your multifamily property portfolio, you'll have the information that you need to plan how to scale your business.

The key to a good SWOT analysis, though, is that it is impartial. It's hard to be impartial about something you've worked so hard to build, so try to step back and take the emotions out of the process. Some people find it much easier to have a mentor go through their SWOT analysis with them. Not only will they be able to offer impartial advice, but they may also be able to see your portfolio from angles you hadn't considered before.

667

The SWOT analysis can give you a blueprint about how to move forward with your investments. You will be able to identify investment opportunities that can build a stronger portfolio. You'll also know what areas of your business need help and be able to invest your time and energy in building them up.

A good SWOT analysis should help you focus your efforts and know what you need to do in the future to maximize your growth potential.

Pro tip: It takes a lot of time and hard work to start investing in multifamily properties. Collaboration with a mentor can help you take your portfolio and business to the next level.

Conclusion

The truth is you will never have real confidence in your ability to successfully acquire and operate multifamily real estate until you get out there and start taking action. Let's face it, you weren't a pro at riding a bike on your first try either. Everyone is shaky at first. To ride a bike, you had to get a feel for the balance and that's true for any new skill.

The resources and tips in this book are designed to keep you on track and profitable. If you enjoyed reading it, please share your thoughts by posting an online review over an Amazon. And while there you might want to check out my book *Invest In Apartment Buildings: Profit Without the Pitfalls*.

Thanks for taking the time to read this. I'd welcome an opportunity to work with you.

Glossary

1031 Exchange: The Internal Revenue Code §1031 defers tax on capital gains. Within the 1031 exchange, you can reinvest your proceeds from your investment real estate sale into the purchase of another property. This eliminates or limits the tax you'd normally have to pay on those proceeds on your taxes that year.

50% Rule: The 50% rule is a very quick and very rough estimate of a rental property's potential profitability. It's used to determine what percentage of rental property income is used to pay expenses—excluding debt service (mortgage payments). Investors typically use the rule to green-light prospective property acquisitions.

Amenities: Amenities are those building features that improve the quality of life for your residents. Not only are they useful for your residents they can help property owners raise rental rates. Some common amenities are fitness centers; recycling programs; pet services; coworking spaces; package delivery systems; pools and other community gathering places.

Ancillary income: Property income that is not considered rent. It can be achieved by adding new amenities, services and fees. Services and fees such as pet fees or concierge services and strategic implementation of today's smart apartment technology can all increase property revenue.

Annual Property Operating Data (APOD): Document that lists a property's gross income, vacancy and credit loss, operating expenses, net operating income (NOI), debt service and cash flow.

Appreciation: The increase of a property's value over time.

Asset Class: Building classification to determine quality of asset. Classifications grade a property based on a combination of geographical and physical characteristics, which help determine the level of risk or the possible amount of return associated with acquiring the property.

> **Class A:** The highest quality buildings in their market and area. They're usually built within the past 10 years; have the newest and latest amenities, and high-income earning tenants; and command the highest rent and the highest price per square foot. They're typically found in central business districts (CBDs) or sometimes in Class B areas. Class A properties are typically professionally managed and have little to no deferred maintenance issues.

> **Class B:** One step down from Class A properties and generally older. They tend to have lower-income tenants and lower rents than Class A buildings and are not always professionally managed. These older properties may have some deferred maintenance issues but are mostly well-maintained. Class B properties are often seen as "value-add" properties that can be upgraded to Class B+ or sometimes Class A with renovations, updated amenities and improvements.

> **Class C:** Typically, more than 30 years old and located in economically depressed locations. Class C properties are generally in need of renovation and have dated amenities. They are usually located in low- to middle-income areas and rents are below those of Class B properties.

Class D: Well over 30 years old and located in fringe markets. Class D properties are usually in need of extensive renovation and offer no amenity packages to residents. They are usually tenanted with a more transient demographic and can be operationally challenging without the proper management know-how and experience.

Asset Management: Asset management covers the development, operation, maintenance, administration and realization of value of investment assets. The goal is to maximize value and investment returns.

Assumptions: Assumptions are used in pro forma budgeting to predict property economics and performance. Property assumptions can cover the future of vacancy rates; property expenses; market rents and other income; market conditions such as cap rates and financing rates; and sales prices. They can also be referred to as drivers.

Boomer: Refers to persons born after World War II generally between 1946-64. They are one of the largest generations renting apartments and pioneered the rise in technology.

Brand: Your brand is what distinguishes you from your competitors and clearly conveys your core values and company characteristics. Businesses of all sizes have a reputation and identity. Your building's appearance, reputation, community, and external marketing are all a part of your brand.

Breakeven Ratio: Aka Breakeven Occupancy. Gives you the percentage occupancy your building must maintain annually in order to break even after all expenses and debt have been paid. The formula for calculating

Breakeven Ratio is: Effective Gross Income / Operating Expenses + Debt Service = Breakeven Ratio.

Budget: Projections for income and expenses over a specified amount of time such as the next 12-months. A budget includes things like operating income; operating expenses; capital improvements; cash reserves; and other operating costs such as debt service (mortgage payment). A property budget can assist owners in predicting cash needs and profitability for the future.

Building Systems: The critical systems of your building and property such as boilers and HVAC systems; roofs; landscaping; life safety features; electric and plumbing systems; parking; windows and insulation; and stairs, elevators and balconies.

CATP: Acronym for cash flow; appreciation; tax benefits; and principal paydown.

Cap rate (capitalization rate): Your assumed, unleveraged rate of return (cash) before mortgage payments and income taxes.

Cap Ex: Capital expenses are large expenses that contribute to the long-term value of the property. Capital expense reserves are needed to cover major costs such as roof replacement, HVAC upgrades, and parking lot resurfacing.

Capital: Sum of money or other asset which is invested for a particular purpose such as investing in real estate or buying or starting a business.

Capital Improvement: Capital improvements are any major property improvements that add significant value to your property, such as updating your electrical or plumbing systems or replacing your roof.

Cash Flow: Net Operating Income (NOI) less Debt Service. In other words, rents and other income minus expenses, debt service and cash reserves. The formula for calculating cash flow is: NOI – Debt Service = Annual Cash Flow

Cash on Cash Return (COCR): Ratio of annual before-tax cash flow to total cash invested. Calculated as the percentage return you receive in cash only similar to the rate of interest earned on an investment. The formula for calculating COCR is: Annual Cash Flow / Initial Investment = Cash on Cash Return.

Common Area(s): Common areas of your multifamily dwelling are the areas that are used by everyone, rather than belonging to a specific unit. These might include the pool or clubhouse but can also include hallways and stairwells exterior to the units.

Curb Appeal: Outdoor property enhancements that increase the value of your property and create positive first impressions. Curb appeal can include things like new exterior paint, modern signage, landscaping and planters. Curb appeal plays a key role in attracting new residents.

Debt Partner: If you're a debt partner, you're loaning money and getting the agreed-upon interest rate in return until the debt is repaid. Unlike an equity partner, you do not have an ownership interest in the real estate, although you may end up with the real estate if the borrower defaults and the real estate was used as collateral for the loan you made.

Debt Service: All mortgage payments. Usually this is just principal and interest and does not include taxes and insurance.

Debt Service Coverage Ratio (DSCR): Measurement of the cash flow that is available to pay the property's current debt obligations. The formula for calculating DSCR is: NOI / Annual Debt Service = DSCR

Depreciation: IRS allowance for tax deductions based on the loss in property value over time and also on improvements to the property.

Due Diligence: The inspection of existing property documents such as operating statements (financials), tenant leases, title, contracts and agreements. It also includes a physical inspection of the property. Helps determine property value, future cash needs and potential for profitability.

Effective Rental Income: Potential rental income less vacancy and credit losses. See: Vacancy and Credit Loss.

Effective Gross Income: Aka Gross Operating Income, Total Annual Income, Total Income Collected and Total Income. This figure includes all property income from rent, laundry, utility reimbursement, vending, parking, storage and other fees.

Equity Partner: As an equity partner, you get a percentage of asset ownership. This means you may have a voice in some decisions, as set out by your agreement with the other parties involved and get part of the cash flow on a regular basis.

Estoppel Certificate: When no tenant leases are available, a buyer can request that the seller's tenants sign estoppel certificates confirming such items as: lease start and termination date; rental rate and terms of payment; deposit balance; and amendments made to the lease agreement. An estoppel certificate will prevent a tenant from later challenging the facts of their tenancy.

Equity: The market value of your property less the amount of debt service (mortgage payment) or liens owed.

Exit Strategy: Strategies for removing yourself from an investment. Exit strategies can include an outright sale of the property, a refinance, a repurposing of its use, or even an indefinite hold. Each choice may have a different impact on overall investment returns.

Fair Housing Laws: The Fair Housing Act of 1968 and the later amendments cover several protected classes and categories of people. For example, it is against the Fair Housing Laws to discriminate against potential tenants due to their race, gender, family status and age.

Forced Appreciation: Increasing a property's value through strategic improvements to management and operations and through upgrades and renovation.

Gross Rent Multiplier (GRM): The GRM is a rough screening tool used to determine if a property is in line with similar properties. The ratio is determined by taking the purchase price divided by the annual gross rents of an investment property. The formula for calculating GRM is: Purchase Price / Annual Gross Rents = GRM.

Hard Money Loan: Short-term loans secured by real property and with typically higher interest rates and fees than those of conventional loans.

They are usually not dependent on creditworthiness and often come with quicker approval.

Historical Financials: A properties historical operating data, balance sheets and statements of income, for a specified period—typically for the immediately preceding 12-months. Also known as trailing financials or T12's.

House Hacking: House hacking is a trendy term for a small multi-unit investment property (1-4 units) where the investor lives in one of the building units and rents the remaining units to tenants.

ILS: Aka Internet Listing Service. Online search database for listing residential real estate rental units and properties for sale or rent.

Inspection Notice: Your findings from your inspection of the property are provided to the seller in an Inspection Notice. It becomes part of the buy and sell contract.

Landlord-Tenant: Local, state and federal rules that govern residential rental real estate. As long as you have signed a lease, there is a landlord-tenant relationship in the eyes of the law.

Lease Agreement: A real property rental agreement that outlines the duties, roles and responsibilities of a landlord (property owner) and tenant (property resident).

Loss to Lease: Also known as loss to market. Loss to lease is the difference between your gross potential market rent and your actual rent. It is only a loss to your potential income so it's not deductible as a loss.

Millennial: Refers to persons born between 1981-96.

Net Operating Income (NOI): Total revenue from rents and any additional income sources after all operating expenses such as insurance, property taxes, and maintenance costs have been deducted. The formula for calculating NOI is: Annual Income – Annual Operating Expenses = NOI (debt service is not included).

Occupancy Rate: The percentage of occupied rental units to total available rental units at a particular time.

On-Site Property Manager: Aka Resident Manager. The party responsible for the day-to-day operations of a property. Duties include marketing and leasing rental units; community relations; general property maintenance; and make ready inspections. The on-site manager typically lives on the premises and is compensated via a combination of salary, free rent or rent credits, fees and bonuses.

Open House: In residential rental real estate an open house is a scheduled period of time where prospective renters can tour or view a property.

Operating Expenses: Aka Total Annual Expenses and Total Expenses. These expenses can include management fees, taxes, insurance, repairs and maintenance, utilities, advertising fees, leasing fees, unit make ready costs, accounting and legal fees, landscaping, common area cleaning, trash removal and pest control. Operating expenses do not include debt service.

Operating Expense Ratio (OER): The percentage of property income that is used to pay expenses *excluding* debt service. The formula for calculating the OER is: Operating Expenses / Effective Gross Income = Expense Ratio.

677

Passive Real Estate Investment: An investment where the investor plays no active role in the process of investing beyond their financial contribution.

Personal Guarantee: When you sign a personal guarantee on a loan, it means you are putting up your own home, bank accounts, and other assets to cover the loan, even if the loan is made to your LLC or other business structure.

Pocket Listing: A term for a property with a signed listing agreement that is not entered into the Multiple Listing Service (MLS).

Potential Gross Income: Aka Potential Rental Income and Annual Gross Rents. This refers to the property's potential total rental income at full occupancy.

Premise History: A detailed account provided by the local police department that lists all police reports and service calls for a particular property.

Pro Forma Budget: Financial analysis that projects income and expenses over a specified future time period and is based on known facts and assumptions. The budget is designed to anticipate results from certain actions.

Property Manager: The party responsible for the day-to-day operations of a property. Duties can include marketing and leasing rental units; income and expense accounting; accounts payable; rent collection; evictions and legal issues; banking; community relations; general property maintenance and renovation; pre-leasing and make ready inspections; and hiring or contracting service providers such as trash removal, snow removal, landscaping and laundry.

Property Financials: Documents such as cash flow statements, balance sheets, profit and loss statements, general ledgers, monthly accounts receivable (A/R) and collection and delinquency reports.

Qualified Opportunity Zones (QOZ): Created by the 2017 Tax Cuts and Job Act, the program started as a way to encourage investments within economically depressed areas. The government, in turn, gives investors a deferment and reduction on capital gains taxes. The longer the investment stays in place, the bigger the tax break.

REO: Acronym for Real Estate Owned. Refers to real estate owned by a corporation such as a bank or asset management company because it was taken back by a lender through the process of foreclosure.

RUBS: Acronym for Ratio Utility Billing System. Also sometimes referred to as Resident Utility Bill-back System. RUBS is a method used to establish a tenant's utility costs. It's typically calculated on square footage; number of bedrooms or residents; usage measured by sub metering or other systemized means; or a combination of any of these factors.

Real Estate: Property encompassing land and buildings or other improvements plus water, mineral deposits, crops and natural resources.

Real Estate Investment Portfolio: A collection of real property assets held and managed by an individual or group of investors.

Rent Roll: The rent roll is a spreadsheet that lists the rental status and details of each individual unit in an apartment building. The data can include unit descriptions; monthly rental rate and fees; lease start and end dates and tenant delinquencies.

Rent Study/Survey: In addition to telling you the current rental rates for a specific area, a rent comparability study can give you occupancy rates, identify which features are attracting tenants, and indicate where the rental rates for the area are heading in the foreseeable future.

Renovation: Changes and improvements to a physical property.

Replacement Reserve: Aka Capital Reserves. Funds earmarked, or held in trust, for the replacement of major building systems like roofing, HVAC, plumbing, sidewalks and asphalt, and windows—building components with a shorter life cycle than the property itself.

Reposition: Changes and improvements to a property's management; operations; reputation and brand; tenant base; capital structure; and physical appearance. The goal is to add value to the property.

Return on Investment (ROI): Gain or loss relative to amount invested.

Revenue: Property income derived from various sources including rent, subsidized rent, pet rent, utility reimbursement (RUBS), laundry services, and security deposit forfeiture. It also includes fees for pets, late payments, parking, storage rental, and rental applications.

SWOT Analysis: Acronym for Strengths, Weaknesses, Opportunities, and Threats. The SWOT analysis is a strategy-building tool that involves critically thinking about those four areas and determining what they are for your business and helps you exploit opportunities and eliminate threats.

Seller Credit for Repairs: A credit at closing which is used to pay for property repairs.

Short-Term Rental Property: Aka STR or Vacation Rental. A furnished home, apartment or condominium that is rented for a specified, short period of time.

Submarket: Defined areas within a primary market such as a neighborhood or suburb.

T12: Twelve-month trailing property financials.

Unit Turn: Aka Make-Ready. The act of making a vacant residential unit rent ready through refreshes such as new paint, carpet, minor repairs and general cleaning.

Value Add Strategy: Strategies to add value to an underperforming asset by addressing deferred maintenance, increasing net operating income (NOI) and putting top-notch management in place. For example, you might increase property income with the addition of new ancillary amenities or through the implementation of new operations policies. See: Reposition.

Vacancy Rate: The percentage of all available rental units that are unoccupied during a specific period of time.

Vacancy and Credit Loss: Estimated loss of rental revenue due to non-payment of rent and vacancies.

Welcome Letter: A letter which welcomes a new resident to a property and conveys vital information that covers instructions for making rent payments and submitting maintenance requests; property rules and regulations; and management and emergency contact information.

Welcome Package: A gift package for new residents.

Works Cited

NMHC. Quick Facts: Resident Demographics. National Multifamily Housing Council. Retrieved July 6, 2020 from https://www.nmhc.org/research-insight/quick-facts-figures/quick-facts-resident-demographics.

New York City Department of Consumer Affairs. (2018, December). How neighborhoods help New Yorkers get ahead. https://www1.nyc.gov. https://www1.nyc.gov/assets/dca/downloads/pdf/partners/Report-HowNeighborhoodsHelpNYersGetAhead.pdf.

Mueller, G. Middle Initial. (Updated annually). Real estate market cycle report. University of Denver Daniels College of Business. https://daniels.du.edu/burns-school.

Riquier, A. (2018, November 26). A tax break to hasten gentrification? Housing market's Opportunity Zones may miss their target. MarketWatch. https://www.marketwatch.com/story/a-tax-break-to-hasten-gentrification-housing-markets-opportunity-zones-may-miss-their-target-2018-11-23.

Ackerman, J. M., Nocera, C. C., Bargh, J. A. (2010, June 25). Incidental Haptic Sensations Influence Social Judgments and Decisions. Science. https://science.sciencemag.org/content/328/5986/1712.

Frederick, R. (2008, October 24). Science Magazine Podcast. https://science.sciencemag.org/content/suppl/2008/10/23/322.5901.608b.DC1/SciencePodcast_081024.pdf.

Crusco, A. H., Wetzel, C. G. (1984, December 1). The Midas Touch: The Effects of Interpersonal Touch on Restaurant Tipping. Sage Journals. https://journals.sagepub.com/doi/abs/10.1177/0146167284104003.

C-SPAN (2011, Nov. 4). Changing American Households. census.gov. https://www.census.gov/newsroom/pdf/cah_slides.pdf

Eventbrite. Millennials Fueling the Experience Economy. Retrieved November 1, 2017 from www.eventbrite.com. http://eventbrite-s3.s3.amazonaws.com/marketing/Millennials_Research/Gen_PR_Final.pdf

Stackla. Bridging the Gap: Consumer & Marketing Perspectives on Content in the Digital Age. https://stackla.com/resources/reports/bridging-the-gap-consumer-marketing-perspectives-on-content-in-the-digital-age.

Ankeny. J. (2010, April 13). Building a Brand on a Budget. Entrepreneur. https://www.entrepreneur.com/article/205992.

Nielsen, J. (2006, October 8). The 90-9-1 Rule for Participation Inequality in Social Media and Online Communities. Nielsen Norman Group. https://www.nngroup.com/articles/participation-inequality.

Perrin, A., Anderson, M. (2019, April 10). Share of U.S. adults using social media, including Facebook, is mostly unchanged since 2018. Pew Research Center. https://www.pewresearch.org/fact-tank/2019/04/10/share-of-u-s-adults-using-social-media-including-facebook-is-mostly-unchanged-since-2018.

Mann, J. (2013, February 1). Come Live With Me In Brooklyn (Song A Day #1492). YouTube. https://www.youtube.com/watch?v=VZJqUyS5tvc.

WSU Insider. (2012, November 26). WSU researchers tie simple scent to increased retail sales. Washington State University. https://news.wsu.edu/2012/11/26/wsu-researchers-tie-simple-scent-to-increased-retail-sales.

Energy Star. ENERGY STAR for existing multifamily housing. Retrieved July 6, 2020 from https://www.energystar.gov/buildings/owners_and_managers/existing-buildings/find_resources_your_property_type/energy_star_multifamily_housing.

National Association of REALTORS®. (2019). 2019 Profile of Home Buyers and Sellers. https://www.nar.realtor/sites/default/files/documents/2019-profile-of-home-buyers-and-sellers-highlights-11-07-2019.pdf.

Gilmer, M. The Psychology of Arrival. LandscapingNetwork. Retrieved April 21, 2017 from https://www.landscapingnetwork.com/front-yard-landscaping/home-entry.html.

Friedman, J., Taylor, C., Fournier, A., Fowler, E., Brinker, C. (2016, December). Multifamily Energy Efficiency Retrofits: Barriers and Opportunities for Deep Energy Savings. https://neep.org/sites/default/files/resources/REEO_MF_Report.pdf.

American Veterinary Medical Association. (2017-2018). U.S. pet ownership statistics. AVMA.org. https://www.avma.org/resources-tools/reports-statistics/us-pet-ownership-statistics.

The Humane Society of the United States. Why you should spay/neuter your pet. Humane society.org. Retrieved July 6, 2020 from https://www.humanesociety.org/resources/why-you-should-spayneuter-your-pet.

Termite Treatment and Control. Distribution of Termites in USA. Retrieved July 22, 2019 from https://www.termitestreatment.com/distribution-of-termites-in-usa.

Schenkman, L. (2009, November 23). In the Brain, Seven Is A Magic Number. Inside Science. https://www.insidescience.org/news/brain-seven-magic-number.

Fishman, S. Are Gifts to Business Clients Deductible? Nolo. Retrieved May 4, 2017 from https://www.nolo.com/legal-encyclopedia/are-gifts-business-clients-deductible.html.

U.S. Census Bureau. (2020, April 28). Quarterly residential vacancies and homeownership, first quarter 2020. https://www.census.gov/housing/hvs/files/currenthvspress.pdf.

Insurance Information Institute. Facts + Statistics: Renters insurance. Retrieved April 12, 2016 from https://www.iii.org/fact-statistic/facts-statistics-renters-insurance.

For rent: protecting your belongings with renters insurance. National Association of Insurance Commissioners. Retrieved April 12, 2016 from https://www.naic.org/documents/protecting_your_belongings_with_renters_insurance.htm.

National Multifamily Housing Council. NMHC/ Kingsley Apartment Resident Preferences Report. NMHC,org. Retrieved March 4, 2016 from https://www.nmhc.org/residents.

Shearer, E., Matsa, K. E. (2018, September 10). News Use Across Social Media Platforms 2018. Pew Research Center. https://www.journalism.org/2018/09/10/news-use-across-social-media-platforms-2018.

Wroclawski, D. (2019, June 16). 6 Smart-Home Upgrades to Help Sell Your House. Consumer Reports. https://www.consumerreports.org/smart-home/smart-home-tech-upgrades-to-help-sell-your-house.

Short, T. (2016, April 26). Survey Reveals Tenant Incentives That Really Work. Software Advice. https://www.softwareadvice.com/resources/survey-reveals-4-tenant-incentives-that-really-work.

Bed Bug Facts & Statistics. PestWorld.org. Retrieved June 17, 2016 from https://www.pestworld.org/all-things-bed-bugs/bed-bug-facts-statistics.

Bed Bugs FAQs. Centers for Disease Control and Prevention. Retrieved June 17, 2016 from https://www.cdc.gov/parasites/bedbugs/faqs.html.

Farquhar, D. State Bed Bug Policy. National Conference of State Legislatures. Retrieved June 17, 2016 from https://www.ncsl.org/portals/1/documents/environ/envhealth/bed_bug_pp_11-16.pdf.

The 2019 Florida Statutes. Landlord's obligation to maintain premises. http://www.leg.state.fl.us/Statutes/index.cfm?App_mode=Display_Statute&Search_String=&URL=0000-0099/0083/Sections/0083.51.html.

Harvey, C. (2018, February 15). Extreme Weather Will Occur More Frequently Worldwide. Scientific American. https://www.scientificamerican.com/article/extreme-weather-will-occur-more-frequently-worldwide.

Enterprise Green Communities. (2016, June). Strategies for Multifamily Building Resilience. EnterpriseCommunity.org. http://www.cplusga.com/wp-content/uploads/2016/06/enterprise-manual.pdf.

National Multifamily Housing Council. (2014, November). Emergency Preparedness Guidance for Apartment Firms. https://www.nmhc.org/uploadedFiles/Articles/Analysis_and_Guidance/Emergency%20Preparedness%202014-11.pdf

Hacks4pancakes. (2019, January 28). Security Things to Consider When Your Apartment Goes 'Smart'. tisiphone.net. https://tisiphone.net/2019/01/28/security-things-to-consider-when-your-apartment-goes-smart.

Urban Institute. Housing Finance Policy Center. Retrieved April 29, 2016 from https://www.urban.org/policy-centers/housing-finance-policy-center.

Bailey Brand Consulting. Meet the Millennials: The Consumers to Change it All. Retrieved April 29, 2016 from https://assets.baileygp.com/email/bailey/millennials/Bailey_Brand_Consulting_Meet_The_Millennials.pdf.

Matney, L. (2019, January 4). More than 100 million Alexa devices have been sold. TechCrunch. https://techcrunch.com/2019/01/04/more-than-100-million-alexa-devices-have-been-sold.

Gebhart, A., Nieva, R (2019, January 7). Google Assistant expands to a billion devices and 80 countries. CNET. https://www.cnet.com/news/google-assistant-expands-to-a-billion-devices-and-80-countries.

McNulty, L. (2014, September 12). Five Hot Property Management Apps. Multifamily Executive. https://www.multifamilyexecutive.com/design-development/products/five-hot-property-management-apps_o.

Weise, E. (2018, December 13). Were your Amazon packages stolen? Porch pirates run rampant this holiday season. USA TODAY. https://www.usatoday.com/story/tech/2018/12/14/porch-pirates-package-theft-climb-more-americans-shop-online/2218910002/.

Mail and Package Delivery Policy. National Multifamily Housing Council. Retrieved October 28, 2019 from https://www.nmhc.org/advocacy/issue-fact-sheet/mail-and-package-delivery-policy-fact-sheet.

Hempel, J. (2018, July 3). Airbnb's Newest Weapon Against Regulation: The Real Estate Industry. Wired. https://www.wired.com/story/airbnbs-newest-weapon-against-regulation-the-real-estate-industry.

The High Cost of Rent Control. National Multifamily Housing Council. Retrieved October 28, 2019 from https://www.nmhc.org/news/articles/the-high-cost-of-rent-control.

SWOT Analysis How to Develop a Strategy For Success. MindTools. Retrieved March 4, 2019 from https://www.mindtools.com/pages/article/newTMC_05.ht

Websites Mentioned

airbnb.com

amazon.com/echo

amazon.com/hub

amazon.com/key

apartments.com

apartmentjet.com

apartmentratings.com

apartmentreviews.net

appfolio.com

apple.com

axiometrics.com

bedbugregistry.com

berkadiarea.com

boutiqueapartments.com

brivo.com

buildium.com

ccim.com/cire-magazine

cdc.gov

census.gov

cfra.org

city-data.com

connecthome.hud.gov

consumerreports.org

corelogic.com

craigslist.org

denverbcycle.com

denvergov.org

doee.dc.gov

dropbox.com

dsireusa.org

duro-last.com

energystar.gov

epa.gov

epmsonline.com

eventbrite.com

facebook.com/marketplace

fanniemae.com

fema.gov

findaccim.com

getboxlock.com

google.com

google.com/alerts

greenbuttondata.org

happyco.com

hotpads.com

housingfinance.com

housingwire.com

hud.gov

inventory-pro.co.uk

iotashome.com

irr.com

kiplinger.com

landlordstation.com

landlordy.com

leaksmart.com

leasehawk.com

loopnet.com

luxerone.com

marcusmillichap.com

matterport.com

mf.freddiemac.com

mobiledoorman.com

mrisoftware.com

multifamilyexecutive.com

multi-housingnews.com

myresman.com

naahq.org

ncsl.org

nfpa.org

nmhc.org

nngroup.com

npmapestworld.org

pewresearch.org

pillow.com

ready.gov/prepareathon

realpage.com

realtor.com

realtor.org

redcross.org

rent.com

resident360.com

ricohtours.com

rooomy.com

sahfnet.org

scanbot.io

seia.org

stackla.com

stovetopfirestop.com

surveymonkey.com

theresabradleybanta.com

theresabradleybanta.com/book_resources

tour24now.com

trashbutler.com)

uli.org

urban.org

urbaneapts.com

us.jll.com

usgbc.org

weather.gov

yardi.com

yelp.com

zillow.com

Index

Made in the USA
Monee, IL
06 June 2021